POLICING

Third Edition

John L. Worrall
Professor of Criminology
University of Texas at Dallas

Frank Schmalleger
Distinguished Professor Emeritus
University of North Carolina at Pembroke

 Pearson

330 Hudson Street, NY, NY 10013

Vice President, Portfolio Management: Andrew Gilfillan
Portfolio Manager: Gary Bauer
Editorial Assistant: Lynda Cramer
Senior Vice President, Marketing: David Gesell
Field Marketing Manager: Thomas Hayward
Product Marketing Manager: Kaylee Carlson
Senior Marketing Coordinator: Les Roberts
Director, Digital Studio and Content Production: Brian Hyland
Managing Producer: Cynthia Zonneveld
Content Producer: Holly Shufeldt
Manager, Rights Management: Johanna Burke
Manufacturing Buyer: Deidra Smith, Higher Ed, LSC Communications
Creative Digital Lead: Mary Siener
Managing Producer, Digital Studio: Autumn Benson
Content Producer, Digital Studio: Maura Barclay
Full-Service Management and Composition: iEnergizer Aptara®, Ltd.
Full-Service Project Managers: Alexis Ferraro at iD8-TripleSSS Media Development
   and Megha Bhardwaj iEnergizer Aptara®, Ltd.
Project Management Support: Susan Hannahs, SPi Global
Cover Design: Melissa Welch, Studio Montage
Cover Art: 123RF ©Scott Betts
Printer/Bindery: LSC Communications
Cover Printer: LSC Communications
Text Font: Times LT Pro 10/12

Library of Congress Cataloging-in-Publication Data

Names: Worrall, John L., author. | Schmalleger, Frank, author.
Title: Policing / John L. Worrall, Frank Schmalleger.
Description: Third edition. | Boston : Pearson, [2018] | Includes index.
Identifiers: LCCN 2016039884 | ISBN 9780134441924 (alk. paper) |
   ISBN 0134441923 (alk. paper)
Subjects: LCSH: Police—United States. | Law enforcement—United States. |
   Criminal justice, Administration of—United States.
Classification: LCC HV8139 .W67 2018 | DDC 363.2/30973—dc23 LC record available at
   https://lccn.loc.gov/2016039884

5

ISBN 10:   0-13-444192-3
ISBN 13: 978-0-13-444192-4
SVE ISBN 10:   0-13-445360-3
ISBN 13: 978-0-13-445360-6

Dedication

For Margie Malan. Thanks for your constant love and support.

J. L. W.

For law enforcement officers everywhere. Thanks for all that you do and for the risks that you take so the rest of us don't have to.

F. S.

Brief Contents

Contents

PART 2 A Career in Policing

PART 3   On the Job

PART 4   Legal Issues

Preface

Introducing the Justice Series

When best-selling authors and instructional designers come together, focused on one goal—improving student performance across the CJ curriculum—you come away with a groundbreaking new series of print and digital content: the *Justice Series*.

Several years ago, we embarked on a journey to create affordable texts that engage students without sacrificing academic rigor. We tested this new format with Fagin's *CJ 2010* and Schmalleger's *Criminology* and received overwhelming support from students and instructors.

The Justice Series expands this format and philosophy to more core CJ and criminology courses, providing affordable, engaging instructor and student resources across the curriculum. As you flip through the pages, you'll notice this book doesn't rely on distracting, overly used photos to add visual appeal. Every piece of art serves a purpose—to help students learn. Our authors and instructional designers worked tirelessly to build engaging info-graphics, flow-charts, and other visuals that flow with the body of the text, provide context and engagement, and promote recall and understanding.

We organized our content around key learning objectives for each chapter and tied everything together in a new objective-driven end-of-chapter layout. Not only is the content engaging to the student, but it's easy to follow and focuses the student on the key learning objectives.

Although brief, affordable, and visually engaging, the Justice Series is no quick, cheap way to appeal to the lowest common denominator. It's a series of texts and support tools that are instructionally sound and student approved.

New to This Edition

This, the third edition of *Policing*, was extensively revised and updated with the latest research, statistics, and court cases available. Several changes have been made throughout the book, including coverage of the President's Task Force on 21st Century Policing. Case studies at the end of each chapter have also been updated, and highlight the latest issues facing police administrators. Key chapter-by-chapter revisions include:

Chapter 1. The President's Task Force on 21st Century Policing is discussed. The end-of-chapter case now discusses building a better police department.

Chapter 2. The end-of-chapter case now discusses New York City's controversial stop-and-frisk initiative.

Chapter 3. Joe Arpaio, the controversial Maricopa County, Arizona, Sheriff is once again featured in the end-of-chapter case, with the latest updates. Data and research through this chapter are also updated.

Chapter 4. The chapter now begins with a discussion of drug decriminalization and police hiring.

Chapter 5. The chapter now begins with discussion of the dangers and unpredictability of police work. It ends with a case study of police subculture and officer stress.

Chapter 6. The relationship between de-policing and rising crime is explored.

Chapter 7. A discussion of predictive policing begins the chapter, and it concludes with an exploration of the police use of drones.

Chapter 8. This chapter now continues discussion of the 2015 President's Task Force on 21st Century Policing.

Chapter 9. Several new technological additions to the law enforcement tool chest are covered, including predictive analytics, automated license plate recognition, the use of body-worn cameras, and social media.

Chapter 10. The chapter begins with discussion of the 2014 U.S. Supreme Court case of *Riley* v. *California*, which dealt with the question of whether a police officer's warrantless search of an arrestee's cell phone violates the Fourth Amendment.

Chapter 11. The chapter begins with discussion of the 2015 U.S. Supreme Court case of *Mullenix* v. *Luna*, in which the Court tussled with the thorny issue of determining whether the doctrine of qualified immunity applied to a police officer's use of deadly force when a lower court had ruled that it did not. A new section on "sentinel event reviews" is included toward the end of the chapter.

Chapter 12. The new end-of-chapter case highlights the possibility of receiving a probationary sentence for manslaughter.

Chapter 13. The chapter begins with discussion of the 2016 Washington, D.C.-based Police Executive Research Forum's report entitled, *Use of Force: Taking Policing to a Higher Standard*. The section on use-of-force policy has been updated to reflect the most recent changes to law enforcement practice. The section on "applications of force" has been updated to include the most recent data, as has the section on patterns of deadly force.

Additional Highlights to the Authors' Approach

- A solid historical foundation is laid—with attention to the origins of modern policing, the nature of American law enforcement, and organizational issues—while staying connected to current events and issues.

- An evidence-based perspective takes center stage with "Think About It" boxes that appear in each chapter and in the book's comprehensive coverage of the latest in policing research.

- Theories of policing are introduced throughout, but a practical emphasis is maintained with chapters and sections on "Becoming a Cop" and "A Career in Policing."

- The text incorporates newsworthy and hot topics in policing with informative chapter-opening vignettes and compelling end-of-chapter case studies.

- Legal issues in policing, including liability and criminal procedure, and challenges, including deviance and the use

of force, receive thorough treatment in four dedicated chapters.

- A concise, conversational writing style keeps student interest and facilitates comprehension.

Groundbreaking Instructor and Student Support

Just as the format of the Justice Series breaks new ground in publishing, so does the instructor support that accompanies the series.

▶ Instructor Supplements

Instructor's Manual with Test Bank

Includes content outlines for classroom discussion, teaching suggestions, and answers to selected end-of-chapter questions from the text. This also contains a Word document version of the test bank.

TestGen

This computerized test generation system gives you maximum flexibility in creating and administering tests on paper, electronically, or online. It provides state-of-the-art features for viewing and editing test bank questions, dragging a selected question into a test you are creating, and printing sleek, formatted tests in a variety of layouts. Select test items from test banks included with TestGen for quick test creation, or write your own questions from scratch. TestGen's random generator provides the option to display different text or calculated number values each time questions are used.

PowerPoint Presentations

Our presentations offer clear, straightforward. Photos, illustrations, charts, and tables from the book are included in the presentations when applicable.

To access supplementary materials online, instructors need to request an instructor access code. Go to **www.pearsonhighered.com/irc**, where you can register for an instructor access code. Within 48 hours after registering, you

will receive a confirming email, including an instructor access code. Once you have received your code, go to the site and log on for full instructions on downloading the materials you wish to use.

Alternate Versions

eBooks

This text is also available in multiple eBook formats. These are an exciting new choice for students looking to save money. As an alternative to purchasing the printed textbook, students can purchase an electronic version of the same content. With an eTextbook, students can search the text, make notes online, print out reading assignments that incorporate lecture notes, and bookmark important passages for later review. For more information, visit your favorite online eBook reseller or visit **www.mypearsonstore.com**.

REVEL™ is Pearson's newest way of delivering our respected content. Fully digital and highly engaging, REVEL replaces the textbook and gives students everything they need for the course. Seamlessly blending text narrative, media, and assessment, REVEL enables students to read, practice, and study in one continuous experience—for less than the cost of a traditional textbook. Learn more at **pearsonhighered.com/revel**.

▶ REVEL for Policing, 3e by Worrall and Schmalleger

Designed for the way today's Criminal Justice students read, think and learn

REVEL offers an immersive learning experience that engages students deeply, while giving them the flexibility to learn their way. Media interactives and assessments integrated directly within the narrative enable students to delve into key concepts and reflect on their learning without breaking stride.

REVEL seamlessly combines the full content of Pearson's best-selling criminal justice titles with multimedia learning tools. You assign the topics your students cover. Author Explanatory Videos, application exercises, and short quizzes engage students and enhance their understanding of core topics as they progress through the content.

Author Explanatory Videos

Point/CounterPoint Videos

Instead of simply reading about criminal justice topics, REVEL empowers students to think critically about important concepts by completing application exercises, watching Point/CounterPoint videos, and participating in shared writing (discussion board) assignments.

Track time-on-task throughout the course

The Performance Dashboard allows you to see how much time the class or individual students have spent reading a section or doing an assignment, as well as points earned per assignment. This data helps correlate study time with performance and provides a window into where students may be having difficulty with the material.

NEW! Ever-growing Accessibility

Learning Management System Integration

REVEL offers a full integration to the Blackboard Learning Management System (LMS). Access assignments, rosters and resources, and synchronize REVEL grades with the LMS gradebook. New direct, single sign-on provides access to all the immersive REVEL content that fosters student engagement.

The REVEL App

The REVEL App further empowers students to access their course materials wherever and whenever they want. With the REVEL App, students can access REVEL directly from their iPhone or Android device and receive push notifications on assignments all while not being tethered to an Internet connection. Work done on the REVEL app syncs up to the browser version, ensuring that no one misses a beat.

Visit **www.pearsonhighered.com/revel/**

▶ Acknowledgments

The authors would like to thank their colleagues inside and outside of academia, including (but not limited to) Robert Taylor, University of Texas, Dallas, and Larry Gaines, California State University, San Bernardino. Thank you to the following reviewers for their insightful suggestions: James Cunningham, State Fair Community College; Brandon Kooi, Aurora University; John Reinholz, Bryant and Stratton College. Thanks also go to our families whose love and continued support inspire us to write.

John L. Worrall is professor of criminology at the University of Texas at Dallas (UTD). A Seattle native, both his M.A. (criminal justice) and Ph.D. (political science) are from Washington State University, where he graduated in 1999. From 1999 to 2006, he was a member of the criminal justice faculty at California State University, San Bernardino. He joined UTD in the fall of 2006.

Dr. Worrall has published articles and book chapters on topics ranging from legal issues in policing to crime measurement. He is also the author or coauthor of numerous textbooks, including *Introduction to Criminal Justice* (with Larry J. Siegel, 16th ed., Cengage, 2018) and *Criminal Procedure: From First Contact to Appeal* (5th ed., Pearson, 2015). He is also editor of the journal *Police Quarterly*.

Frank Schmalleger, PhD, holds degrees from the University of Notre Dame and The Ohio State University, having earned both a master's (1970) and a doctorate (1974) in sociology with a special emphasis in criminology from The Ohio State University. From 1976 to 1994, he taught criminal justice courses at the University of North Carolina at Pembroke. For the last 16 of those years, he chaired the university's Department of Sociology, Social Work, and Criminal Justice. In 1991, he was awarded the title Distinguished Professor, and the university named him professor emeritus in 2001.

Dr. Schmalleger is the author of numerous articles and many books, including the widely used *Criminal Justice Today* (Prentice Hall, 2017), *Criminology Today* (Prentice Hall, 2018), *Criminal Law Today* (Prentice Hall, 2016), and *The Definitive Guide to Criminal Justice and Criminology on the World Wide Web* (Prentice Hall, 2009).

He is also founding editor of the journal *Criminal Justice Studies*. He has served as editor for the Prentice Hall series Criminal Justice in the Twenty-First Century and as imprint adviser for Greenwood Publishing Group's criminal justice reference series.

1

Origins and Evolution of American Policing

1 Outline the origins of policing.

2 Summarize the various eras of policing.

3 Outline the emergence of state and federal law enforcement agencies.

Angel Zayas/Pacific Press/Alamy Stock Photo

INTRO THE PRESIDENT'S TASK FORCE ON 21ST-CENTURY POLICING

In 2015, the President's Task Force on 21st-Century Policing released its final report, providing a number of recommendations intended to improve American police practices.[1] The task force was formed by President Obama to address issues that had been raised by events in Ferguson, Missouri; Baltimore, Maryland; Charleston, South Carolina; and New York City, in which unarmed black men died at the hands of police officers—often for seemingly minor offenses.

In their report, task force members recognized that "the trust between law enforcement agencies and the people they protect and serve is essential in a democracy. It is key to the stability of our communities, the integrity of our criminal justice system, and the safe and effective delivery of policing services."

One of the major findings of the task force was that building trust and nurturing legitimacy on both sides of the police/citizen divide is "the foundational principle underlying the nature of relations between law enforcement agencies and the communities they serve."

As the task force authors knew, more people are likely to obey the law when they believe that those who are enforcing it have authority that is perceived as legitimate by those subject to the authority. In other words, the

David Grossman/Alamy Stock Photo

public confers legitimacy only on those who it believes are acting in procedurally just ways.

The task force also found that law enforcement agencies cannot build community trust if they are seen as external forces coming in from outside to impose control on the community—like an occupying army. Hence, the task force recommended that law enforcement culture should embrace a guardian—rather than a warrior—mindset to build trust and legitimacy both within agencies and between the police and the public.

▶ The Origins of Policing

For students of policing, an appreciation of history is essential in order to understand the contemporary structure of law enforcement in the United States today. As a result of historical circumstances, the American system of policing is nearly unique in the world. Most countries today rely on one or only a few agencies for law enforcement. In the United States, however, there are thousands of law enforcement agencies with hundreds of thousands of employees. No other country has a policing system that looks quite like ours.

LEARNING OUTCOMES 1 — Outline the origins of policing.

The study of policing history is important for another reason: For better or for worse, history often repeats itself. History repeats itself for worse when policy makers make decisions in a vacuum, without regard for those who have faced the same problems before. In other words, the failure to appreciate what was once tried without success leads to a costly repetition of past mistakes. Some critics of recent changes in American policing, such as the shift toward community policing, for example, argue that what we are now doing signals a return to days of old, which may not be desirable.

Alternatively, a technique or program that looks totally innovative and desirable today may have been purposefully avoided in the past. An example, which we will later cover more thoroughly, is federal–local law enforcement partnerships, which some see as especially important in the fight against terrorism. Critics of such efforts suggest that we are inching toward a national police force, a notion that, to the minds of many, is antithetical to our nation's system of government.

History can repeat itself for the better when we revisit the successful strategies of the past. The decentralization that served policing early on in our nation's history, for example, is now part and parcel of recent reforms in policing around the country.

From Private to Public Policing

One of the earliest known methods of policing, called *kin policing*, involved families, clans, and tribes enforcing informal rules and customs. Each member of the group was given authority to enforce the established rules, and individuals who deviated from community norms were often dealt with harshly.[2] This method of policing changed during the rise of the Greek citystates and the Roman Empire, and law enforcement evolved from what was essentially a private affair to a public one.

Greece and Rome began to use appointed magistrates to enforce the law. These unpaid individuals were largely responsible for law enforcement until about the third century BCE in Rome and the sixth century BCE in Greece. The first *paid* law enforcement official was the *praefectus urbi*, a position created in Rome about 27 BCE.[3] By 6 CE, Rome had a large force of these individuals who patrolled the streets day and night. Once the Roman Empire fell, though, law enforcement became the responsibility of the individual monarchies throughout Europe.

Kings used military forces for law enforcement, but they also relied on so-called night watches, or groups of citizens who roamed the streets looking for signs of trouble. Members of the night watch were given the authority to investigate crimes and to make arrests. The night watch system eventually evolved into the **frankpledge system**, which became more formalized around the twelfth century when kings appointed individuals known as chief-pledges to ensure that the system worked.[4] In the frankpledge system, ten households were grouped into a **tithing**, and each adult male member of the tithing was held responsible for the conduct of the others. Ten tithings were known as a hundred, or **parish**, and a group of several parishes eventually came to be called a **shire**. Shires resembled modern-day counties in terms of their size. The term **sheriff** comes from the Old English word **shire-reeve**, which means "the keeper of the shire." The shire-reeve was granted authority by the Norman kings to levy fines against criminals and also to levy fines against the parishes for failing to capture criminals.

In England, the Second Statute of Westminster (1285)[5] required that each parish appoint two constables.[6] Their duties were to inspect the arms of the parish and to assist the sheriff with law enforcement. Men over the age of 15 formed the *posse comitatus*, which assisted with the pursuit and capture of dangerous criminals. Magistrates, who eventually came to be known as *justices of the peace*, began to be appointed by the king or the sheriff around the thirteenth century. They had primary responsibility for adjudicating crimes, not unlike modern-day judges. In England, from which we derive many of our traditions, this was the predominant model of law enforcement until the nineteenth century.

What set early approaches to policing apart from modern policing practices is that most of the officials charged with enforcing laws were volunteers. If paid, they were not salaried as police officers are today. Sheriffs, for example, were allowed to appropriate a portion of the money collected in the king's name.[7] Even though these developments signaled a shift from private to public policing, much of the job of enforcing the law remained largely private; there simply were not enough public officials to do the job. As the years passed, though, policing took ever-greater steps in the direction of becoming a governmental function.

One of the most significant steps toward fully public policing occurred in 1735, when two London parishes were given authority to pay their **watchmen** out of tax collections.[8] Then, toward the middle of the eighteenth century, John and **Henry Fielding**, two Bow Street magistrates, started to pay men to serve as constables and patrol the streets at night.[9] These **Bow Street Runners**, or **thief takers**, patrolled the city on foot and the surrounding areas on horseback. They also performed investigations, and for that reason, they have been described as the first known detective unit.[10]

In 1800, the Thames River Police were paid by public moneys.[11] Private police forces did not disappear, however. Outside London in more rural areas, much law enforcement was still the responsibility of churches, communities, parishes, magistrates, and a variety of other individuals. Moving beyond England, other countries also started to form public police agencies. France, Prussia (Germany), Russia, China, and India all made the gradual shift from private to public law enforcement.[12] As police officers came to be paid with public funds, the shift away from private policing became more apparent.

The Influence of the English Model

To a large extent, policing in London became the model for policing in America. Historians have called attention to various forces behind the emergence of American policing, several of which we will consider shortly, but what early American policing looked like stemmed a great deal from the English approach.

In 1822, British home secretary **Sir Robert Peel** criticized the state of policing in London. Some years later, he was responsible for passage of the "Act for Improving the Police in and Near the Metropolis," otherwise known as the **Metropolitan Police Act**. Adopted by Parliament in 1829, this legislation created the world's first large-scale organized police force in the city of London.[13] As others have noted, the Metropolitan Police Act "introduced a centralized and unified system of police in England" and constituted a revolution in traditional methods of law enforcement.[14] The legislation heralded the end of the old, fragmented, and ineffectual system of parish constables and represented the dawn of a whole new era of policing.[15]

Two men, Charles Rowan and Richard Mayne, were appointed to oversee development of the force. They adopted a military organizational model. This was resisted to a large degree by British citizens out of fear that the line between policing and the military would be too thin, and that police might behave like an occupying army. Rowan and Mayne, however, went to great lengths to ensure that their officers behaved properly, and the police force eventually gained widespread acceptance.

Sir Robert Peel's contribution lies not just in the creation of the first organized police force, however. He was among the first to envision a broader role for officers than just crime fighting. Peel emphasized the *prevention* of crime. He also felt that uniforms were necessary because they would make officers stand out in a crowd and thus discourage crime.[16] Beyond that, Peel identified a series of principles that he said ought to characterize any police force (Figure 1–1).

Policing Comes to America

The first North American colonists settled along the eastern seaboard. They hailed from a number of countries, including Spain, France, Holland, Sweden, and of course England. The first of these settlements, Jamestown, was established in 1607 in what is now Virginia. The colony at Plymouth, Massachusetts, followed, set up by the Pilgrims in 1620. Swedish and Dutch citizens settled around what is today New York City.

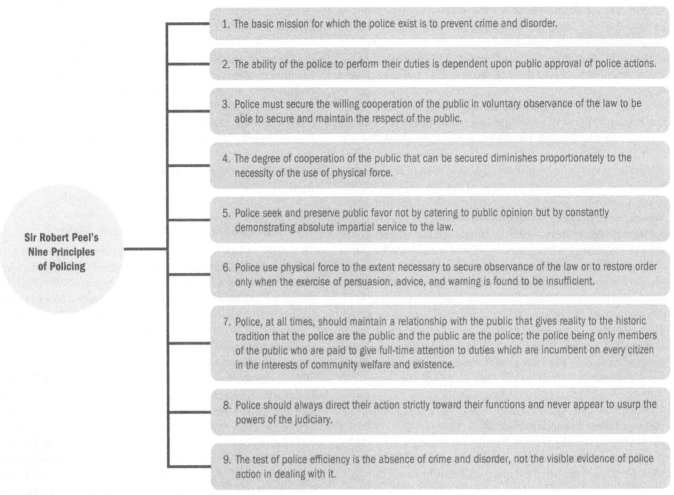

FIGURE 1–1 **Sir Robert Peel's Nine Principles of Policing.**
Source: From "The Metropolitan Police Act of 1829: An analysis of certain events influencing the passage and character of the Metropolitan Police Act in England," *Journal of Criminal Law, Criminology, and Police Science,* vol. 55, no. 1 (March 1964), pp. 141–54.

The Spanish claimed land in what is now the southern United States and in the Caribbean. All of these people had visions of expanding their settlements, but given their distance from the European mainland, doing so was difficult. Expansion was particularly difficult for the English and French because Spain's presence was significant.

Early on, churches in America were heavily involved in crime control, though without a formal criminal justice system. People who strayed from acceptable forms of conduct were often shunned by their congregations. According to one historian, church congregations functioned as the "police and courts of first resort."[17] Moreover, when corporal punishments were used, they were often carried out in public. The use of stocks, floggings in the public square, and even public hangings were common methods of dealing with wayward individuals. Public punishments, often witnessed by hundreds of people, made clear to everyone the consequences of inappropriate behavior.

As more colonists moved to the New World, however, they "brought the law in their baggage."[18] That is, they brought knowledge of English criminal codes, law enforcement agencies, and methods of punishment, and they adapted them to serve the needs of their new communities.

Chaos in the Cities

As America came of age, more immigrants arrived and settled in urban areas. Cities became increasingly crowded, dangerous, and dirty. For example, from 1850 to about 1880, New York City's population grew until almost a million people were crowded into the two-square-mile center of the city. The city's East Side housed nearly 300,000 people who lacked toilet facilities, heat, fire protection, and other essentials. Unemployment levels were high, and sickness abounded. Cholera outbreaks were common, killing thousands of people at a time.

By the mid-1800s, crime had become common throughout many American cities. People stole and looted to survive. Organized gangs formed, fought for territory, and contributed to the violence and mayhem within the city. By one account, by 1850, New York City had become America's most terrifying city.[19] Other large cities like Boston, Chicago, and Philadelphia hardly fared better.

Early efforts to control crime fell on the shoulders of appointed constables and citizen volunteers. The constables patrolled during the daytime; citizens patrolled at night. But as the cities grew and became more dangerous, this system could not keep pace with crime.[20] In 1844, the first metropolitan police department was formed in the New York City area. It initially patrolled only during the daylight hours, leaving the preexisting night watch to patrol the city during darkness. The early New York City force was modeled after London's Metropolitan Police and consisted of only 16 officers appointed by the mayor.[21] The force was reorganized and expanded to 800 officers in 1845 under Mayor William Havemeyer, who divided the city into three police districts. This period also saw the elimination of the old night watch system and the construction of station houses and local courts.[22] Twelve years later, in 1857, the police in Manhattan, Brooklyn, Staten Island, Westchester County, and the Bronx were consolidated into one department under a governor-appointed board of commissioners, becoming what we think of today as the New York City Police Department (NYPD).[23] Prior to the consolidation, 18 separate police forces patrolled within the area that comprises present-day New York City.[24] Some of them were better equipped and organized than others. Lacking, however, was a centralized police mandate, good communications, and coordinated efforts.[25]

On the one hand, the combined force of 1857, which initially consisted of 6,396 members, was welcomed by people who were distressed about problems of social disorganization and crime within the city. On the other hand, there was concern that the new police force might become a standing army (recall that our nation was founded, in part, out of frustration with overreaching, centralized government).[26] Other large cities quickly followed the New York example, establishing their own police forces. They did so in response to surges in violence, conflict, multiple riots, and citizen fears that America's experiment in self-governance might not survive.

London's police, as we have already seen, served as something of a model for policing in many American cities. Reformers in America were impressed with what London's **bobbies** did to prevent, and not just respond to, crime.[27] London's police stressed highly visible patrols intended to discourage crime. But the police forces of New York and other large cities differed from their English counterparts in at least two important ways. First, unlike police in London, America's first police officers were heavily involved in politics.[28] Most police officers at the time answered to political leaders or ward bosses in the areas they served. Officers' very jobs were dependent on remaining in the good favor of whatever political figure was in charge at the time. Second, in stark contrast to their counterparts in London, American police officers were more willing to use force.[29] These two unique features of American policing contributed in no small part to policing as it is known today.

The Move West

As American pioneers moved westward, they did not leave the problems of the cities behind. In fact, the frontier mentality of fending for oneself and providing one's own self-protection fueled plenty of violence. Guns, knives, and fists were commonly used to resolve disputes in newly settled areas. Sheriffs and their marshals were appointed by town leaders to provide what little law enforcement was available on the frontier. These officials' authority, though, was not always welcomed or respected. Theirs was a lonely and dangerous job, and they repeatedly became the targets of outlaws. Making matters even more difficult, prominent outlaws of the day, including Billy the Kid and Jesse James, were apparently idolized as much if not more than the sheriffs and marshals themselves. Law enforcement was, at best, unreliable; at worst, it was nonexistent. Indeed, some of the new "lawmen" worked both sides of the law, depending on which side offered them the best opportunities and rewards. Consequently, frontier communities often formed their own posses and vigilante citizen groups to confront any person or group intent on disrupting social stability.[30]

Even these efforts eventually failed, despite support from the community. Not unlike what happened in the big cities, once populations in the West grew, something more was needed. It was inevitable that the kinds of agencies formed along the eastern seaboard would be replicated in cities throughout the West. An example was Stephen Austin's corps of fighters, a group of tough men he enlisted to protect the settlers he was bringing into the Tejas, Mexico, area. This corps of rangers eventually aided in the Texas revolution against Mexico, providing scout services for the U.S. Army during the Mexican–American War. They came to be known as the **Texas Rangers**, and their efforts ushered in a period of enhanced border patrol in Arizona and New Mexico as well as the formation of state police forces throughout the Southwest.[31]

Organized police forces in early America were born of necessity. A single law enforcement official rapidly became inadequate as populations surged. Densely populated cities could not realistically be patrolled with one or even a few officers. But unlike the evolution of policing in other nations, Americans rejected centralized power and shunned any national police force. Law enforcement became a local effort that reflected local priorities and issues. That is why today we see thousands of distinct police agencies at various levels of government all across the United States. Even if there had been a desire during this period for a centralized police agency, it is doubtful it could have succeeded given the size of the territory for which it would have been responsible. Early police agencies could not have survived without some connection to the communities they patrolled.

This decentralized policing model (which is discussed in more detail in Chapter 3) has been hailed as representing the American ideal, but there was a downside. As police agencies proliferated across America, they varied widely in terms of quality and professional commitment. Some may argue that policing today is not as highly regarded an occupation as it could be, but in the late nineteenth century, policing was generally viewed as routine, unglamorous work. Officers were held in low regard and, because the pay was poor, cities had difficulty recruiting qualified candidates. So desperate were some cities to hire police officers that, as one historian observed, "illiteracy, poor health, chronic drunkenness, or a criminal record were no barriers to a job as a police officer."[32] Pressure for agencies to grow, combined with close relationships between the police and politicians and others in positions of influence, resulted in poor-quality police work. What's worse is that a commitment to crime control and community service was secondary. Nonetheless, this period of politics and ineptitude has been described as the first significant era of policing in America.

Policing the Slaves

Unique circumstances existed in the American South during this early period. There, **slave patrols** represented a crude form of policing. Slave patrols were created in the eighteenth century to apprehend runaway slaves and to ensure that slaves did not rise up against their owners. The slave patrols were largely a private activity carried out by citizen volunteers, leading to a serious lack of control of the slave patrols' actions. When they apprehended runaway slaves, they often meted out "justice" on the spot, frequently using violence.

Due process of law was a distant concern. Slave patrols could (and did) arbitrarily enter private residences for the purpose of rounding up those who fled from bondage. The patrols were largely an outgrowth of fear on the part of wealthy white landowners that slaves were a dangerous group in need of careful scrutiny and control. With the end of the Civil War came the dissolution of the slave patrols. They did, however, provide the impetus for the Ku Klux Klan, whose mission of terrorizing black families and black communities was not entirely different from that of the slave patrols.

▶ Policing Eras

As we have just seen, from the colonial period to the late nineteenth century, organized police forces of various kinds emerged across America. Like early policing on the other side of the Atlantic, law enforcement began as a private affair and eventually became public. Once police agencies were an established presence, they grew in number and influence. They also evolved in response to the demands and pressures of the time. Most researchers agree that these changes occurred in three distinct eras: the **political era**, the **reform era**, and the **community era**.[33] See Figure 1–2 for a summary.

LEARNING OUTCOMES 2 · Summarize the various eras of policing.

The Political Era

In 1895, "the realities of patrol work mocked Robert Peel's dream of a continuous visible presence . . . police patrol barely existed at all."[34] Corruption was widespread, and some cities assigned unmanageable beats to their officers. In 1880, for example, Chicago officers patrolled more than three miles of streets—on foot. Large portions of other major metropolitan areas were not patrolled at all. Residential districts were all but ignored in most cities.[35] In addition, communication systems were inadequate, making it next to impossible for sergeants and other command officials to call officers to crime scenes.

Regulating Criminals

Historians generally agree that police officers of the political era did more to regulate criminal activity than to control it:

Think About It...

An Introduction to Evidence-Based Policing Evidence-based policing is a hot topic in contemporary law enforcement. Its goal is to use research to guide practice and evaluate practitioners. There is little consensus about what is effective in policing. Many practitioners have an almost unshakable faith in the ability of police officers to prevent crime by simply driving around and keeping a watchful eye on the community. But evidence-based policing isn't about opinions; it's about the facts, about what the data and rigorous research show. How does evidence-based policing differ from the way in which policing was performed in times past? In what ways does it improve policing? Might it in some ways distract from the police mission?

Rob Byron/Shutterstock

TIMELINE

Historical Eras in American Policing

1840s–1930s

Political Era Close ties between the police and political officials

Police were organized in paramilitary style, focused on serving the politically powerful

Politicians appointed/hired the police

Came about because of a need for social order and security in a dynamic and rapidly changing society

Source: World History Archive/ SuperStock

1930s–1970s

Reform Era Police gained pride in their profession

Law enforcement focused on "traditional" crime-fighting and the capture of criminals

Crackdown on organized crime

Progressive policing policy led by August Vollmer and O. W. Wilson

Came about because citizens called for reform and the removal of politics from policing

Source: SuperStock

FIGURE 1–2 **Historical Eras in Modern Policing.**

"Officers established relationships with professional criminals, especially pickpockets, tolerating certain kinds of crime in return for information or stolen goods."[36] They were also heavily involved in providing essential services for those in need. The recently discovered diary of a Boston police officer from 1895 reveals that one of the most common services officers provided was shelter for the homeless.[37] In Cincinnati, for instance, the police station was "a place of last resort for the desperately poor."[38] Police stations came to be dirty, disease-ridden places as a result of this practice, so the sheltering of the homeless came to a halt near the end of the nineteenth century.

Many police officers, along with the politicians and ward bosses they served, were corrupt. By one account, jobs in some early police departments were sold as investment opportunities.[39] Corruption flourished at all levels of government as a result of restrictions on various "vices." Laws limiting drinking, gambling, and sex provided ample opportunity for the criminal element to provide much-desired products and services. Such illegal activities could only thrive, of course, with support from local law enforcement. The payoffs to officers who provided protection for criminals were significant. Detective Thomas Byrnes, head of the New York City Detective Bureau from 1880 to 1895 and widely said to have been corrupt, acquired a fortune of more than $350,000 by the late 1880s (that's about $5 million today).[40] Byrnes was forced to resign by Theodore Roosevelt in 1895 when Roosevelt became head of the New York City Police Commission.

Patronage Problems

To get elected, political candidates at the turn of the twentieth century made promises to the voters, especially promises of employment. Once a candidate was elected, jobs of various sorts, including police jobs, were used to reward the politician's supporters. Newly hired police officers adopted a number of measures to ensure that their "bosses" remained in power. There are many accounts of police officers, assigned to maintain order at polling stations, who pressured voters to support particular candidates.

An example of political patronage run amok was **Tammany Hall** in New York City, the name given to the Democratic Party "machine" that played a significant role in the city's politics from the late nineteenth to the early twentieth centuries. The most notorious Tammany leader was **William M. "Boss" Tweed**. Tweed's control over the political machine was so complete that he was eventually elected to the New York Senate. By most accounts, he and his cronies were corrupt and heavily involved in a wide range of criminal activities. His career eventually ended in a storm of corruption controversy, and he was ultimately sent to prison. During his heyday, though, he relied heavily on police officers to keep him in office and in control of the ward.

The Reform Era

Frustrations over the likes of Boss Tweed ushered in an era of profound reform. In early 1892, Reverend Charles Parkhurst described New York City's mayor and his aides as "a lying, perjuring, rum-soaked, and libidinous lot of polluted harpies."[41] He also claimed that the police existed for no reason other than "to protect and foster crime and make capital out of it." Using his church as his forum, Parkhurst began a crusade to bring reform to the political system in New York City. He and a number of other like-minded individuals were largely responsible for the appointment of Theodore Roosevelt as commissioner of the New York City Police Department.

Once Roosevelt took charge, he forced corrupt officers to resign and launched a series of unannounced nighttime inspections of the police department. He even took to the streets and approached officers in civilian attire. He initiated disciplinary action against officers who were asleep or away from their posts. Roosevelt resigned in 1897, claiming that the NYPD had been reformed; the reality was that little had actually changed.[42] Nonetheless, Roosevelt's efforts were quickly duplicated in a number of other cities that were experiencing similar problems. Reform efforts failed in these places, too. According to historian Sam Walker, "the reformers never came to grips with the basic problems of police administration."[43] They claimed that corrupt officers lacked moral character but ignored some of the deeper issues, such as how the department's rank structure (or absence of one) contributed to the problems that reformers lamented. Reform efforts floundered for several years until police reformer August Vollmer changed their focus.

1970s–2001

Community Era Police departments work to identify and serve the needs of their communities

Envisions a partnership between the police and the community

Police focus on quality-of-life offenses

Broken windows model of policing

Came about because of a realization that effective community partnerships can help prevent and solve crimes

Source: UpperCut Images/ Superstock

2001–Today

The New Era Came about because of the terrorist attacks of September 11, 2001, and ongoing threats to the safety and security of Americans with this copy: Evidence-based policing became the gold standard for assessing the effectiveness and cost-benefits of law enforcement programs.

Source: Alliance Images/ Alamy Stock Photo

August Vollmer's Legacy

August Vollmer—the first police chief of Berkeley, California, and perhaps the foremost presence in America's police reform movement—argued that policing should be regarded as a public service, as a profession focused on improving society. During his address to the International Association of Chiefs of Police in 1919, Vollmer argued that the police had "far greater obligations than the mere apprehending and prosecution of lawbreakers." The police, he claimed, should go "up stream a little further" by trying to prevent crime by working with families, schools, and other influential institutions. He called for organizational reforms in police agencies, elevated standards of recruitment and retention, and the adoption of modern management techniques, such as those used in the business sector and military.[44]

There was something of a contradiction in Vollmer's message, however. On the one hand, he called for the expansion of the police role to include crime prevention. On the other, he called for increased crime-fighting efforts. It was crime fighting that won out in the end, leading to "a centralized, authoritarian bureaucracy focusing on crime control."[45]

Vollmer did more than call for reforms. As chief of the Berkeley Police Department during the early twentieth century, he transformed his department in the following ways:

- Increased the size of the force, from 3 officers to 27
- Put officers on bicycle and motorcycle patrol
- First to adopt fingerprinting technology to aid in criminal investigations and collaborated with University of California in making other advances
- First police leader of note to hire officers with college degrees
- Created the Berkeley Police School in 1908

In short, Vollmer's reforms were consistent with a reform mentality intended to move policing toward professional stature. He took his ideas beyond Berkeley by evaluating numerous police agencies around the country, including the scandal-ridden Los Angeles Police Department.[46] In 1921, Vollmer was elected president of the International Association of Chiefs of Police (IACP), a position he used to spread his ideas about police reform.

The Crime Commissions

As one of the authors of the 1929 **Illinois Crime Survey** (a series of influential reports on homicide, juvenile justice, and justice operations in Chicago), Vollmer criticized "the corrupt political influence exercised by administrative officials and corrupt politicians."[47] He was also the lead police consultant to the 1931 National Commission on Law Observance and Enforcement, popularly known as the **Wickersham Commission** after its head, George W. Wickersham. The commission was appointed by President Herbert Hoover in 1929 to investigate the real operations and problems of the criminal justice system. Again, Vollmer called attention to corruption, excessive political influence and meddling in criminal justice, poor leadership and management, ineffective recruitment practices, poor-quality training programs, and other issues.

The work of the Wickersham Commission and others not mentioned here, coupled with Vollmer's reformist vision, led to some consensus that a professional model of policing would greatly benefit America. It was hoped that policing would become a civil service profession divorced from politics. Reformers had faith in centralization, crime fighting, scientific investigations, and, above all, police work that followed the letter of the law.

Interestingly, one of the most significant developments that fueled this change was the Great Depression. With less money to spend, many cities had to cut back on services, which included the closing of some police precincts. This brought police officers under the control of a central police station, consistent with the managerial model Vollmer had envisioned. Some have called this the *professional era*, others the *legalistic era*, and still others the *reform era*. Regardless of what it was called, what occurred was a dramatic change in the way policing was practiced in the United States. It did not happen quickly, though. The process played out over decades, leading up to the 1960s and the third of America's key policing eras: the community era.

The Community Era

The community era is, by most accounts, the era of contemporary law enforcement. It stresses service and almost a customer-friendly element to police work. Routine and traditional police functions such as patrol, investigations, and the like remain, but many police agencies have changed their mission statements to reflect a new way of thinking epitomized by O. W. Wilson.

O. W. Wilson and the Limitations of Professionalism

August Vollmer's protégé, **Orlando Winfield (O. W.) Wilson**, served as chief of the Wichita, Kansas, Police Department between 1928 and 1939. As chief, he clamped down on corruption and brutality, firing 20% of the officers on the force. His department's mission statement, the "Square Deal Code," eventually became the template for the code of ethics of the International Association of Chiefs of Police.[48] His reforms, many of which were quite radical, were not necessarily welcomed with open arms, even by some people outside the police department. For example, his efforts to aggressively enforce vice laws met with so much resistance that he resigned in 1939.

Despite Wilson's resignation, he went on to gain national prominence. His 1938 textbook, *Municipal Police Administration*, became a leading work (its eighth edition was published in 1979). A year later, he became a professor of police administration at his mentor's old stomping grounds, the University of California, Berkeley. He remained there until 1960, during which time he started the nation's first doctoral program in criminology and wrote another successful policing text, *Police Administration*.[49] He went on to write other influential works, including a manual on how to allocate police patrols according to calls for service.[50] More importantly, he called for a shift from foot patrol (the dominant mode of patrol at the time) to automobile patrol. On top of that, he called for one- rather than two-officer patrols to maximize police resources.

Although O. W. Wilson was certainly a progressive reformer, he may have done more to usher in the community era than many realize. In 1960, during the twilight of his career, Wilson was appointed by Chicago Mayor Richard Daley to reform the city's police department in the wake of a scandal. Wilson used many of the same tools as he did in Wichita, Kansas, including reorganization of the department, widespread firings, improved personnel standards, and improved communications. Despite his best efforts, however, civil rights leaders continued to criticize the department, citing police brutality and discrimination in police employment. Wilson was defensive about the discrimination allegations because he had taken significant steps to diversify the predominantly white police department.

These problems led to a great deal of resentment of police in the African-American community, vestiges of which remain today in various cities. Wilson retired in 1968, marking the end of a notable career. What he did not, or could not, fix became abundantly clear in 1969, when some Chicago police officers appeared to run amok on national television, brutally beating protestors outside the Democratic Party's national convention. Wilson was clearly a Progressive Era reformer, but his actions (or, as some would say, failure to act) in Chicago started the push for something else.

Toward Customer Service

It is perhaps a simplification to say that the community era is characterized by customer service, but at its core, this new era of policing is about connecting the community and the police in a way that was not accomplished during the reform era. Following the public outcry in the wake of the Chicago fiasco and other publicized instances of strained police–public relations, it was no mystery why a new era emerged. Research began to reveal that the police could not reduce crime by their own efforts alone, another reason the dawn of the third era was at hand.

The sentiments of the community era were expressed in a prescient article authored by University of Alaska Professor John Angell at the beginning of the 1970s.[51] Angell argued that traditional police management practices were culture bound, that they were inconsistent with the humanistic democratic values of the United States, that they demanded that employees demonstrate "immature" personality traits, and that they couldn't cope with environmental pressures. In his view, a more community-centered model would (1) improve community relations, which suffered under the bureaucratic, military model of law enforcement; (2) improve officer morale by allowing them a measure of flexibility in the performance of their duties; and (3) improve interagency coordination.

Some aspects of the community era look remarkably similar to policing near the turn of the twentieth century, but without the corruption, patronage, and other problems that characterized the political era. Community era reformers have sought authorization from community members and extensive citizen support; a broad mandate that stresses the provision of services; a decentralized, responsive organizational structure; and close relations with citizens. A strong tie to citizens would be achieved through foot patrol, problem solving, the preservation of quality of life, and a host of other tactics—all of which were designed to ensure citizen satisfaction and all of which look remarkably similar to practices that were in place before the birth of the reform era.

Since, by most accounts, we are in the midst of the community era, much more needs to be said about it. Accordingly, we will devote a full chapter to this topic. In Chapter 8, we will look in depth at why the community era came to pass, what it looks like today, and what its prospects are for the future.

- -

A New Era?

Few people would deny that the September 11, 2001, terrorist attacks on the United States changed the world. The attacks led to one of the most dramatic reorganizations of the U.S. government, including the formation of the cabinet-level Department of Homeland Security. They also led to untold number of changes in America's police agencies. When, for instance, the nation's terrorist alert level is elevated, it is the local law enforcement agencies that take on most of the responsibility for increased vigilance.

Following 9/11, local police agencies entered into uncharted territory with multiagency partnerships, terrorist response training, and the like. Whether community policing era initiatives can survive the more militaristic style of law enforcement that followed September 11 remains to be seen. A new era of policing, however, began during the first decade of the twenty-first century. It is characterized not only by coordination among police agencies in the fight against terrorism but also by an emphasis on evidence-based policing. Evidence-based policing, which is formally defined in Chapter 9, can be seen as "the use of the best available research on the outcomes of police work to implement guidelines and evaluate agencies, units and officers."[52] Evidence-based policing has become increasingly important in an age of financial restrictions and budgetary shortfalls—where money for public agencies and services is spread more thinly than before. Identifying policing programs that work and that are cost effective is one hallmark of the new era of policing that has emerged following the 9/11 terrorist attacks.

Think About It…

Citizen Contact Patrol One approach to improving civilian attitudes toward the police—and thereby reducing crime— consists of door-to-

Huntstock, Inc/Alamy Stock Photo

door visits by police officers. Consistent with the ideals of the community era, this citizen contact patrol has police officers knock on people's doors, introduce themselves, give out information, and otherwise try to make policing more personal in nature. This technique has been used by police to do everything from obtaining information about who is carrying guns on the street to providing citizens with tips about reducing burglaries.

Should police officers be encouraged to go door-to-door? Is there any possible downside to citizen contact patrol? If so, what is it?

▶ *Beyond Local Law Enforcement*

Most of our discussion of police history thus far has focused on local law enforcement: municipal police and sheriff's depart-

ments. There is also an interesting history behind state and federal law enforcement, but the story is much shorter. With the exception of the U.S. Marshals Service, which was founded in the late eighteenth century, the history of state and federal law enforcement goes back only to the nineteenth century.

The Emergence of State Agencies

When Texas declared its independence from Mexico in 1836, the Texas Rangers were already an established law enforcement agency. As discussed earlier, they did not begin as a state-level organization. Their initial focus was defending the community, but they adopted policing responsibilities after Texas independence was declared. The early Rangers often took the law into their own hands and were not as concerned with equal treatment and due process as police are today. In 1935, Texas created the Department of Public Safety (DPS), which remains in existence to this day. The Texas Rangers are part of the Texas DPS, as are the troopers of the Texas State Patrol. Once the Rangers came under the supervision of the DPS, conduct problems, excessive force, and the like were reined in.

The other states eventually formed their own state-level police agencies, but they often took unique forms. The Pennsylvania State Police, for example, was founded in 1905 in response to the difficulty local police were having resolving state-specific issues. For example, the western Pennsylvania mining region attracted scores of immigrant workers and experienced ethnic violence and labor disputes. A major coal strike in 1902 prompted President Theodore Roosevelt to appoint a commission to look into the problems of maintaining order in the mining region. This led to the establishment of the state police. Unlike the Texas Rangers and other state agencies, the Pennsylvania State Police consisted largely of men with National Guard and army experience. The Pennsylvania State Police also had their share of problems in the beginning, just like the Rangers, but they gradually assumed greater law enforcement responsibilities and adopted professional standards.

As automobiles became more common and highways were built, state police agencies shifted much of their focus toward the enforcement of traffic laws. What we see today, then, is a mixture of state agencies, some with general law enforcement responsibilities, and others with a traffic enforcement focus. Today, nearly every state has at least one state-level police agency. We will look at them in more detail when we discuss the organization of law enforcement in America in Chapter 3.

The First Federal Agencies

U.S. Marshals

In 1789, President George Washington appointed the first 13 U.S. Marshals in accordance with the Judiciary Act. Until the Secret Service was established in 1865, the U.S. Marshals focused their efforts on apprehending counterfeiters. Between 1790 and 1870, the marshals were also required to take the national census every ten years, a responsibility that was eventually transferred to the Bureau of the Census. During the nineteenth century, the marshals did everything from arrest fugitive slaves to confiscate property used to support the Confederacy.

More than anything, though, in the latter part of the nineteenth century, the marshals and their deputies were responsible for maintaining law and order in the Old West. On October 26, 1881, in Tombstone, Arizona, Marshal Virgil Earp and his deputies (brothers Wyatt and Morgan Earp and John H. "Doc" Holliday) gunned down Frank and Tom McLaury and Billy Clanton in a vacant lot just down the street from the O.K. Corral. Movies like *Tombstone* and *Wyatt Earp* have recounted this series of events. Since the nineteenth century, the U.S. Marshals Service has taken on a range of duties quite distinct from those of days past. We will look at both the history and the modern duties of the U.S. Marshals in Chapter 3.

Postal Inspectors and Secret Service

Another early federal law enforcement effort involved U.S. postal inspectors, whose job was to target crimes committed via the mail. In 1865, the Secret Service was established with the mission to suppress counterfeiting. That responsibility remains today, along with a number of others, including the protection of the president.

The FBI

The Bureau of Investigation, now known as the *Federal Bureau of Investigation (FBI)*, was formed in 1908. The agency began with 8 Secret Service agents, 14 newly hired investigators, and 12 accountants; their task was to investigate antitrust land fraud and similar matters. The agency grew rapidly and became the primary investigative agency for federal crimes. It ascended to a position of high visibility during the 1920s, when J. Edgar Hoover was appointed to lead the agency. Under Hoover's charge from 1924 to 1972, the FBI apprehended a number of dangerous offenders and engaged in numerous high-profile investigations, perhaps most notably the kidnapping of ace flyer Charles Lindbergh's baby.

Hoover was a controversial director. He routinely fired agents who displeased him, and it is alleged that he blackmailed political leaders and illegally disrupted the activities of the Black Panther Party; Martin Luther King, Jr.'s Southern Christian Leadership Conference; the Ku Klux Klan; and other groups. Today, FBI directors cannot serve more than a ten-year term due to concerns that they may become too powerful. To his credit, though, Hoover did a great deal to usher in the professional policing era through his insistence on a crime-fighting role for FBI agents. The FBI is discussed in greater detail in Chapter 3.

Building a Better Police Department

What would the ideal American police department look like if we were to start over entirely and build it from scratch? That's the question that was asked by the prestigious Bloomberg news service a year ago. The article noted that there are over 18,500 police departments in the United States, but most have fewer than ten officers. Complicating things, there are few nationally mandated standards relating to police work, and the application of rigorous scientific methods to police techniques is often lacking. While much lip service is given to "scientific policing," or "evidence-based policing," in which established best practices are valued, the Bloomberg authors say that "if the medical profession used research the way police use research, we'd still be using leeches."

One of the article's recommendations is to hire older officers instead of 21-year-olds right out of the police academy. Young people are often still developing emotionally and intellectually, and shouldn't have "the coercive power of carrying a gun," says the article.

LJ Mil/Alamy Stock Photo

Higher education is suggested as another way of developing the ideal police department. While many American police departments require that new hires have only a high school diploma, a number of Scandinavian nations require a college degree in criminal justice. Education encourages critical thinking, and can help officers make better decisions.

Source: From Building a Better Police Department by Drake Bennett, Published by Bloomberg © 2014.

The article discussed here raises several interesting questions:

1. Should age requirements for police officers be increased? If so, what should be the starting age?
2. Should educational requirements for police officers be raised? If so, what should they be?
3. Can police departments make better use of scientific evidence? If so, how?

Outline the origins of policing.

Policing in the Western world began as a private affair and became a public, or governmental, responsibility. Policing in America looks as it does today largely because it was inherited from the English, beginning with the frankpledge system, the watchman system, and Henry Fielding's Bow Street Runners.

1. What were the major milestones in the historical development of policing in the Western world?

2. What is the significance of due process of law for American policing?

frankpledge system The ultimate outgrowth of the night watch system of social control, dating to the twelfth century, in which ten households were grouped into a tithing, and each adult male member of the tithing was held responsible for the conduct of the others.

tithing Under the frankpledge system, a group of ten households.

parish Under the frankpledge system, a group of ten tithings. Also referred to as a *hundred*.

shire Under the frankpledge system, a collection of several parishes.

sheriff The modern-day term for the Old English *shire-reeve*. In the United States today, the senior law enforcement official in a county.

shire-reeve The Old English term for *sheriff*. Literally, "the keeper of the shire."

watchman An early officer on foot patrol who, during the hours of darkness, watched for fires and criminal activities. Upon detecting such events, the watchman's role was to sound the "hue and cry" to evoke a defensive response from the citizenry. This style of policing dates back to the early to mid-eighteenth century in England.

Henry Fielding (1707-1754) An English magistrate who founded what some have called London's first police force, the Bow Street Runners.

Bow Street Runners An early English police unit formed under the leadership of Henry Fielding, magistrate of the Bow Street region of London. Also referred to as *thief takers*.

thief taker An alternative name for Henry Fielding's Bow Street Runners.

Sir Robert Peel (1788-1850) A former British home secretary whose criticisms of the state of policing in London led to the passage of the Metropolitan Police Act and the establishment of the world's first large-scale organized police force in that city in 1829.

Metropolitan Police Act The legislation adopted by the British Parliament in 1829 that established the world's first large-scale organized police force in London.

bobby The popular British name given to a member of Sir Robert Peel's Metropolitan Police Force.

Texas Rangers A militia originally formed by Stephen F. Austin in 1823 to protect the territory of Texas against Native American raids, criminals, and intruders. Today, the Rangers serve as part of the Texas Department of Public Safety.

slave patrol A crude form of private policing, often carried out by citizen volunteers. Slave patrols were created in the eighteenth century to apprehend runaway slaves and to ensure that slaves did not rise up against their owners.

due process of law A right guaranteed by the Fifth, Sixth, and Fourteenth Amendments and generally understood, in legal contexts, to mean the due course of legal proceedings according to the rules and forms established for the protection of individual rights. In criminal proceedings, due process of law is generally understood to include the following basic elements: a law creating and defining the offense, an impartial tribunal having jurisdictional authority over the case, accusation in proper form, notice and opportunity to defend, trial according to established procedure, and discharge from all restraints or obligations unless convicted.

Summarize the various eras of policing.

American policing has evolved through three distinct eras: the political, reform, and community eras. We may be on the cusp of a fourth policing era, which some are calling the homeland security era.

1. Identify and describe the major eras of policing discussed in this chapter. Are the eras distinct or overlapping? Explain.

2. What were the findings of the National Commission on Law Observance and Enforcement? What significance did those findings have for American policing?

political era The period of American policing during the late nineteenth and early twentieth centuries during which police forces served more to regulate crime pursuant to the wishes of corrupt politicians (who used patronage to give police jobs to handpicked loyalists) than to control crime in the interests of the public good.

reform era The period of American policing during the early to mid-twentieth century, during which efforts were made to professionalize police forces and to eliminate the influence of corrupt politicians.

community era By most accounts, the contemporary era of U.S. law enforcement, which stresses service and an almost customer-friendly approach to police work.

Tammany Hall The corrupt Democratic Party political "machine" that operated in New York City in the late nineteenth and early twentieth centuries and that used patronage to control city operations.

William M. "Boss" Tweed (1823-1878) A corrupt American politician who became notorious as the powerful leader of New York City's Tammany Hall.

August Vollmer (1876-1955) An early and especially effective advocate of police reform whose collaboration with the University of California established the study of criminal justice as an academic discipline.

Illinois Crime Survey A series of influential reports, published in 1929, on homicide, juvenile justice, and justice operations in Chicago that criticized the corrupt political influence on the justice system.

Wickersham Commission A commission appointed by President Herbert Hoover in 1929 to investigate the operations and problems of the criminal justice system. Formally known as the National Commission on Law Observance and Enforcement.

Orlando Winfield "O. W." Wilson (1900-1972) A Progressive Era reformer, professor of police administration, and protégé of August Vollmer whose writings and teachings continue to influence contemporary U.S. law enforcement.

LEARNING OUTCOMES 3

Outline the emergence of state and federal law enforcement agencies.

State and federal law enforcement agencies have their own, unique histories. With the exception of the U.S. Marshals Service, which was founded in the late eighteenth century, the history of state and federal law enforcement goes back only to the nineteenth century. Among the earliest organized state police agencies were the Texas Rangers and the Pennsylvania State Police.

1. Illustrate the development of state and federal law enforcement agencies in the United States.

2. How did the development of those agencies parallel the development of local police forces?

3. How did it differ from the pattern of development seen in local agencies?

References

1 The President's Task Force on 21st Century Policing, *Final Report* (Washington, DC: The White House, May 2015).

2 B. L. Berg, *Law enforcement: An introduction to police in society* (Boston: Allyn and Bacon, 1992), pp. 15–16.

3 W. Kunkel, *An introduction to Roman legal and constitutional history*, 2nd ed. (Oxford: Clarendon Press, 1973).

4 W. J. Bopp and D. D. Schultz, *A short history of American law enforcement* (Springfield, IL: Charles C. Thomas, 1972), pp. 9–10.

5 There are three "historical" Statutes of Westminster, dated 1275, 1285, and 1290 (known as "First," "Second," and "Third"), relating to the government of the Kingdom of England. There is also a 1931 Statute of Westminster, relating to the British Empire and its dominions.

6 W. L. M. Lee, *A history of police in England* (repr., Montclair, NJ: Patterson Smith, 1971).

7 D. H. Bayley, *Patterns of policing: A comparative international analysis* (New Brunswick, NJ: Rutgers University Press, 1985), p. 29.

8 J. J. Tobias, "Police and public in the United Kingdom," *Journal of Contemporary History* (January–April 1972), pp. 201–19.

9 G. Armitage, *The history of the Bow Street Runners, 1729–1829* (London: Wishart, n.d.), p. 123.

10 A. C. Germann, F. D. Day, and R. R. Gallati, *Introduction to law enforcement and criminal justice* (Springfield, IL: Charles C. Thomas, 1978).

11 S. Spitzer and A. T. Scull, "Social control in historical perspective: From private to public responses to crime," in *Correction and punishment*, ed. D. F. Greenberg, pp. 265–86 (Beverly Hills, CA: Sage, 1977).

12 Bayley, *Patterns of policing*, pp. 31–32.

13 Germann, Day, and Gallati, *Introduction to law enforcement and criminal justice*.

14 J. L. Lyman, "The Metropolitan Police Act of 1829: An analysis of certain events influencing the passage and character of the Metropolitan Police Act in England," *Journal of Criminal Law, Criminology, and Police Science*, vol. 55, no. 1 (March 1964), p. 141.

15 Roy Ingleton, "The early days of policing in Kent" (Part 6), Kent Police Museum, www.kent-police-museum.co.uk/core_pages/pasttimes_early_days_pt6.shtml (accessed July 4, 2008).

16 L. Radzinowicz, *A history of English criminal law and its administration since 1750* (New York: Macmillan, 1957), p. 177.

17 E. L. Ayers, *Vengeance and justice: Crime and punishment in the nineteenth century American South* (New York: Oxford University Press, 1984), p. 181.

18 B. Chapin, *Criminal justice in colonial America, 1606–1660* (Athens: University of Georgia Press, 1983), p. 146.

19 F. Browning and J. Gerassi, *The American way of crime* (New York: G. P. Putnam's Sons, 1980).

20 L. H. Randolph, *Biographical sketches of distinguished officers of the army and navy* (New York: Henry E. Huntington, 1905), pp. 82–88.

21 R. B. Fosdick, *American police systems* (New York: The Century Co., 1920), p. 62.

22 G. L. Lankevich, *American metropolis: A history of New York City* (New York: New York University Press, 1998), pp. 84–85.

23 Fosdick, *American police systems*, p. 82.

24 Others date the NYPD's official beginning as January 1, 1898—the day that the five boroughs of Manhattan, the Bronx, Brooklyn, Queens, and Staten Island joined together under a charter as the City of Greater New York. What should be clear, however, is that what was essentially a citywide police force operated in the area prior to the 1898 charter.

25 Some of the information in this paragraph comes from Bernard Whalen, "The birth of the NYPD," www.nycop.com/Aug_00/The_Birth_of_the_NYPD/body_the_birth_of_the_nypd.html (accessed July 5, 2008).

The department was further expanded in 1995, when the city's housing and transit police were merged into the NYPD.

26 B. Vila and C. Morris, eds., *The role of police in American society: A documentary history* (Westport, CT: Greenwood Press, 1999), p. 25.

27 W. Miller, *Cops and bobbies* (Chicago: University of Chicago Press, 1977), p. 2.

28 Vila and Morris, eds., *The role of police in American society.*

29 Ibid.

30 R. Brown, *Strain of violence* (New York: Oxford University Press, 1975).

31 B. Smith, *Police systems in the United States* (New York: Harper and Brothers, 1949).

32 Illinois Association for Criminal Justice, *Illinois crime survey* (1929; repr., Montclair, NJ: Patterson Smith, 1968), p. 359.

33 G. L. Kelling and M. H. Moore, "The evolving strategy of policing," in *Perspectives on policing*, vol. 4 (Washington, DC: National Institute of Justice, 1988).

34 Walker, *Popular justice*, p. 57.

35 J. C. Schneider, *Detroit and the problem of order, 1830–1880* (Lincoln: University of Nebraska Press, 1980), pp. 26–27, 121.

36 Walker, *Popular justice*, p. 59.

37 A. von Hoffman, "An officer of the neighborhood: A Boston patrolman on the beat in 1895," *Journal of Social History*, vol. 26, no. 2 (Winter 1992), pp. 309–30.

38 E. H. Monkkonen, *Police in urban America, 1860–1920* (Cambridge: Cambridge University Press, 1981), pp. 87, 89.

39 Walker, *Popular justice*, p. 62.

40 "Thomas F. Byrnes," in *Wikipedia, The free encyclopedia*, revised May 18, 2008, http://en.wikipedia.org/w/index.php?title=Thomas_F._Byrnes&oldid=213279082 (accessed December 4, 2015).

41 C. H. Parkhurst, *Our fight with Tammany* (1895; repr., New York: Arno Press, 1970), p. 5.

42 H. P. Jeffers, *Commissioner Roosevelt: The story of Theodore Roosevelt and the New York City Police, 1895–1897* (New York: Wiley, 1994).

43 Walker, *Popular justice*, p. 65.

44 A. Vollmer, "Predelinquency," in *Proceedings, 1919*, ed. International Association of Chiefs of Police, pp. 77–80 (New York: Arno Press, 1971).

45 Walker, *Popular justice*, p. 131.

46 Illinois Association for Criminal Justice, *Illinois crime survey* (1929; repr., Montclair, NJ: Patterson Smith, 1968), p. 359.

47 For more on Vollmer's legacy, see J. Liss and S. Schlossman, "The contours of crime prevention in August Vollmer's Berkeley," in *Research in law, deviance, and social control*, vol. 6 (Greenwich, CT: JAI Press, 1984); A. Vollmer and A. Schneider, "The school for police as planned at Berkeley," *Journal of Criminal Law and Criminology*, vol. 7 (1917), pp. 877–98; G. E. Carte and E. H. Carte, *Police reform in the United States: The era of August Vollmer* (Berkeley: University of California Press, 1975).

48 Walker, *Popular justice*, p. 172.

49 O. W. Wilson and R. C. McLaren, *Police administration*, 4th ed. (New York: McGraw-Hill, 1977).

50 O. W. Wilson, *The distribution of police patrol forces* (Chicago: Public Administration Service, 1941).

51 J. E. Angell, "Toward an alternative to the classic police organizational arrangements: A democratic model," *Criminology*, vol. 9 (1971), pp.185–206.

52 L.awrence W. Sherman, *Evidence-based policing* (Washington, DC: Police Foundation, 1998), p. 2, www.policefoundation.org/pdf/Sherman.pdf.

2

Policing in the American Context

Kenneth Graff/Shutterstock

A TURNAROUND IN POLICING

A few years ago, the city of Camden, New Jersey, was forced to make drastic cuts in staffing levels at the city's police department—including layoffs of more than 160 of the city's 360 sworn officers. About the same time, smaller cuts were made in other New Jersey municipalities, resulting in a loss of 167 of Camden's 1,265 officers, layoffs of 82 of Jersey City's 829 officers, and a loss of 60 officers out of Atlantic City's 365-member force.[1]

Camden, which had to make the staffing cuts due to significant budgetary problems, asked county law enforcement officers to take on more duties at crime scenes, and the Camden County Prosecutor's office provided homicide investigators who also partnered with the police to investigate all shootings. Camden's poor fiscal status stemmed from a $26.5 million budget shortfall that developed even after a 25% citywide spending cut was implemented in 2010.[2]

Today, things have turned around. The old City of Camden police department has been replaced with a county-wide police force called the Camden County Police. A new community-oriented policing strategy has supplanted a previous hostile attitude that built barriers between the police and the community. Officers have been moved from desk jobs and squad cars onto walking beats and

A Camden, New Jersey, police car on patrol. How have financial problems impacted policing in America?

interaction with the public has greatly increased. The new chief says the shift was intended to overcome years of mistrust. Average response time for calls for service is now 4.4 minutes, down from more than 60 minutes before the changes. By 2016, the number of open-air drug markets had been cut nearly in half, and murder rates—which have been among the highest in the country—were falling.[3]

► Policing in American Government

LEARNING OUTCOMES 1 Explain how the U.S. government's features of democracy and federalism impact policing.

The United States is a representative democracy and the world's oldest functional federation (a union consisting of several more or less self-governing states). These unique arrangements have affected the structure and organization of government agencies at all levels, including the police.

Policing in a Democracy

Democracy is usually defined as government by the people. It vests supreme authority in the citizenry, usually through free elections and the representatives the citizens choose to elect. Other features of a democracy include equality of rights, privileges, and opportunities; open government; and due process protections against unreasonable arrest and prosecution. To many, democracy also means that people should be free from excessive government influence in their lives. See Figure 2–1 for an overview of the elements of democracy.

Nearly everyone values the full exercise of democratic principles, yet others express serious concern when those principles are threatened. Consider the recent outcries over electronic eavesdropping of domestic phone conversations by federal investigators as part of antiterrorism intelligence gathering. Some people feel that such eavesdropping is necessary to maintain security.

Others, though, fear that it threatens core democratic values and is unreasonably intrusive.

In an effort to balance these opposing views, a police force in a democratic nation should be one that "is subject to the rule of law embodying values respectful of human dignity, rather than the wishes of a powerful leader or party; can intervene in the life of citizens only under limited and carefully controlled circumstances; and is publicly accountable."[4] In other words, most of us would likely agree that the police should be able to enforce the law, but they shouldn't go "too far" and run roughshod over people's rights.

1. Sovereignty of the people
2. Government based upon consent of the governed
3. Majority rule
4. Minority rights
5. Guarantee of basic human rights
6. Free and fair elections
7. Equality before the law
8. Due process of law
9. Constitutional limits on government
10. Social, economic, and political pluralism
11. Values of tolerance, pragmatism, cooperation, and compromise

FIGURE 2–1 The Pillars of Democracy.

Consequences of Democracy for Police

Robert Kennedy once pointed out that "every society gets the kind of criminal it deserves." Kennedy also said, "What is equally true is that every community gets the kind of law enforcement it insists on."[5]

There are many ways to interpret Kennedy's observations, but one is especially relevant here. With its concern over people's rights and privacy, democracy ensures that a certain amount of crime is inevitable. In other words, some of the crime problems our country has might be due to the very nature of our government. Consider those who manufacture methamphetamine in clandestine laboratories. If they know that the police can arbitrarily enter the facility at any time, they might choose an alternative pursuit. On the other hand, if they know that there are steps the police must take before they can enforce the law, they might be willing to take a chance. Figure 2–2 provides an overview of how democracy influences policing.

Policing and Federalism

One of democracy's most distinguishing features is policy making by majority rule, either directly by the people, as in a direct democracy, or through elected representatives, as in a representative democracy. The very term *democracy* comes from the Greek words *demos*, meaning "people," and *kratos*, meaning "rule." In other words, *democracy* means "ruled by the people." One can even go further and call ours an advanced or liberal democracy because of its concern with the rule of law, the separation of powers, and, most important, people's liberties. But democracy alone does not fully describe our system of government. The government structure in the United States is also characterized by **federalism**. Policing in a federalist nation is quite distinct from policing in nonfederalist nations (see Figure 2–3 for a comparison between federalist and other systems of government).

Federalism, often confused with democracy, is another feature of American government that has served to shape the policing apparatus in the United States. Federalism is a political doctrine wherein power is divided (often constitutionally)

Features of a Democracy

- Equality of rights, privileges, and opportunities
- Open government
- Due process protections against unreasonable arrest and prosecution

Consequences of a Democracy for Police

- Concern for people's rights and privacy means that a certain amount of crime is inevitable.
- The Bill of Rights ensures that the government cannot go too far without answering to the people.
- The Fourth Amendment to the Constitution mandates that the police meet specific legal requirements before they can enter private residences, make arrests, and seize evidence.

FIGURE 2–2 Policing and Democracy.

between a central governing body (e.g., the federal government) and various constituent units (the states).

Federalism helps facilitate democracy because it promotes participation in all levels of government. If one had ambitions to enter political office, one would likely start

Unified
- Central authority makes all laws and holds all power.

Confederation
- There is no strong central government.
- Constituent units make laws and hold power.

Federalist
- Laws are made by the central governing authority as well as by the constituent units. The federal government makes laws for the entire nation, but federalism also gives the states power to make their own laws.
- In the United States, we have both the federal Constitution and individual state constitutions, consistent with the idea of shared power. The federal government and each state also have their own legal codes.

FIGURE 2–3 Types of Government.

with the goal of becoming a county supervisor, a city councilperson, or an elected state official. With experience, a political veteran might then rise to ranks of U.S. senator or representative.

A perusal of the U.S. Constitution suggests a system of **dual federalism**, in which the only powers vested in the federal government are those explicitly listed in the Constitution; the rest are left to the states. This suggested arrangement is the textbook definition of federalism. In reality, though, ours is more a system of cooperative federalism, meaning that some of the lines between federal and state power are blurred or at least have fluctuated over time. For example, Article I, Section 8, of the U.S. Constitution gives the federal government the power to regulate interstate commerce, but this authority has been interpreted so broadly that the federal government can effectively control much of what happens at the state level. To this day, we see plenty of federal influence over even local criminal justice policies.

Consequences of Federalism for Policing

Inherent in federalism is the concept of different levels of government. Consequently, American federalism effectively defines various levels of law enforcement. Our two-tiered governmental structure (states and the federal government) inherently divides law enforcement within those levels. Further, federalism can affect relationships between the agencies at the various levels of government. For example, if the federal government grants money to local government, it can exercise a measure of control. Applying this to policing, the Office of Community Oriented Policing Services in the U.S. Justice Department gives various grants to local law enforcement agencies throughout the states, but typically with strings attached. One such string is that the money must be used to support community policing activities.

Federalism also adds to the dynamics of law enforcement because it creates relationships (and perhaps tensions) between levels of government (Figure 2–4). For example, "turf wars" sometimes occur between federal and state or local law enforcement agencies. In movies and television programs, such jurisdictional conflicts are often portrayed as some small-town police chief or sheriff laying claim to a particular criminal case before the "feds" get involved. Turf wars do indeed exist, but interagency (and interlevel) cooperation is now the word of the day, especially in the "war on terror." If it weren't for federalism, though, there would be neither tension nor cooperation across levels of government because different levels wouldn't exist in the first place.

▶ The Police Organizational Environment

Every organization operates within an environment that consists of not just the organization's physical surroundings but also human dimensions. In a democracy where the power of the people is emphasized, this is all the more apparent. Couple this with the highly visible nature of police organizations, and it

Features of a Federalist Government

- Division of power lies between a central governing body and various constituent bodies.
- Dual federalism: Any powers not explicitly vested to the federal government are left to the states.
- Cooperative federalism: Lines between federal and state power are blurred or have fluctuated over time.

Consequences of Federalism for Police

- Law enforcement is divided between federal and state levels.
- Tensions may result between federal and state agencies.
- Cooperation between various agencies is important.

FIGURE 2-4 Policing and Federalism.

becomes clear that the police in the United States function within one of the most complex organizational environments imaginable. First, they serve and interact with citizens. Second, they are government organizations and, as such, regularly interact with other government entities, such as city councils and county boards of supervisors. Third, the media in the United States keep a close eye on the police, perhaps because we as citizens are intrigued by what the police do (or don't do). Finally, police organizations interact with their peer agencies at various levels of government. See Figure 2–5 for a summary.

 LEARNING OUTCOMES 2 Discuss the influence of various environmental factors on policing.

The Community

By far, the most significant environmental factor in law enforcement is the community. In sheer magnitude, the number of citizens dwarfs all other factors that influence the police. Not every citizen carries quite the same level of influence as, say, an evening newscaster, but given that there is roughly one sworn law

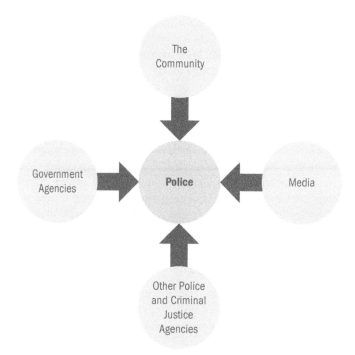

FIGURE 2-5 The Police Environment.

enforcement officer for every 400 to 500 citizens in the United States, the voice of the citizenry must be reckoned with. Through the democratic process, citizens also influence the elected officials who speak for them. The president, members of Congress, county boards of supervisors, city mayors, and city councils—all of whom exert a measure of control over law enforcement activities—come to their posts with a mandate from their constituents.

Law enforcement officials have a vested interest in maintaining positive relationships with the communities they serve. The service element of the famous police mantra "protect and serve" all but requires a measure of concern for what community members think. But the protection function also requires citizen support. Much crime takes place behind closed doors, and police cannot always detect it without input from concerned citizens. A lack of citizen support can also influence law enforcement organizations through the political process. For example, public dissatisfaction with a local police department could prompt the mayor to seek a replacement for the chief.

Fortunately, the police rarely fight an uphill battle for public support. Studies reveal that the vast majority of citizens view police favorably.[6] One study revealed that about two-thirds of Americans felt their local police agencies and sheriff's departments were effective, friendly, and fair.[7] What about the other third? Some people regard authority figures with suspicion.[8] Moreover, a significant percentage of that one-third comprises minorities, and many minorities not only do not support police but also view them with contempt.[9] Such perceptions are often an outgrowth of strained racial relations in some of America's high-crime, poor inner-city neighborhoods. Even that two-third majority is not unwavering in its support; various factors can affect whether police will be viewed favorably.

The importance of citizen support for the police is reflected in a vast literature. Scores of researchers have modeled support for the police in an effort to identify who is supportive and who is not. A common thread running throughout most of the studies is a focus on four categories of factors thought to be associated with support for police: race, age, gender, and prior contact with the police. Some researchers have also looked beyond these to other factors, such as education, location, and other demographic and economic considerations. Who cares? Knowing who is least supportive of police can give law enforcement administrators the information needed to target those groups for efforts intended to improve the police image.

A problem measuring support for the police is that support is a multidimensional concept. In other words, what do we mean by support? Are the police effective? Are they friendly? One researcher has identified five dimensions of support for the police.[10] Three of them address "efficacy," or effectiveness. They include the ability of police to protect citizens, solve known crimes, and prevent crime. The other two dimensions deal with "image," particularly the perceived friendliness and fairness of the police. Why does this matter? It appears, for example, that race affects perceptions of the ability of police to solve crime but not to protect citizens or prevent crime. We will not go into more detail on these dimensions but rather present the "big picture" concerning support for the police.

Race and Support

Race is perhaps the most powerful predictor of support or lack of support for the police.[11] In general, Caucasians view the police far more favorably than non-Caucasians.[12] A Texas study revealed, for example, that Hispanics often express dissatisfaction with local law enforcement. Minority perceptions of police also differ depending on what types of functions police engage in. Use of force incidents tend to be regarded with less support than, say, attendance at neighborhood meetings.[13] Moreover, race often works in conjunction with other factors to shape public opinions of the police. A minority resident from a poor, high-crime neighborhood who has had undesirable contact with police in the past will tend to maintain negative attitudes. In contrast, someone from a wealthy neighborhood where crime is not much of a concern will, in general, be more supportive.

Age and Support

Like the relationship between race and support for the police, the relationship between age and support is not particularly surprising; young people tend to be much less supportive of police than the elderly.[14] The authors of one study found, for example, "a direct, almost linear relationship between age" and support for the police.[15] This means that as age went up, support for police went up in almost perfect parallel fashion. Why, then, are young people not supportive of police? For one thing, they value their freedom and like to buck authority from time to time. Another explanation is that young people commit more crimes than the elderly and therefore find themselves in unwelcome contact with authorities more often.[16] The same line of reasoning applies to young drivers; they receive more speeding tickets than the elderly and therefore find themselves on the receiving end of unwelcome contact with police. Yet another explanation is that young people are also the victims of more crime than the elderly. Some excessively victimized youth may harbor sentiments that the police cannot effectively make a dent in the crime problem.

Men versus Women

The relationship between gender and support for the police is much less clear. One team of researchers argued, for example, that men and women view the police similarly.[17] In another study, the researchers found that women hold a more "idealized" image of the police and are therefore more supportive of them.[18] Further substantiating that finding, a later study revealed that younger males were less supportive of police than women.[19] By no means is there consensus in the literature, however. Depending on who exactly is surveyed (different samples of men and women), the literature reveals contradictory findings.[20] It stands to reason, then, that at least in terms of gender, police agencies need to appeal to both men and women.

Prior Contact

Prior contacts with the police can clearly influence support levels. Generally, involuntary contacts, such as following a stop for speeding, are not linked with support for the police.[21] In fact, the more involuntary contacts a person tends to have with officers, the less supportive of them he or she will be.[22] On that note, people who live in neighborhoods where most police contacts are involuntary (e.g., officers always responding to 911 calls) are less inclined to support the police than people in less crime-prone neighborhoods.[23] Importantly, though, it is not the sheer number of involuntary contacts that affect one's attitude toward police. If the experiences are regarded as favorable—if, for example, motorists feel they were treated fairly and with respect by officers—then they maintain relatively high levels of support for police.[24] Returning to the broader subject of this chapter, it behooves police officers to know what kind of neighborhoods they serve, what their problems are, and what types of calls officers have gone on in the past. This knowledge can arm them with the information to reach out to historically unsupportive elements.

Other Factors Affecting Public Perceptions

Like gender, education's effect on police support is unclear.[25] On the one hand, less educated individuals might fail to appreciate the difficulties associated with police work and, as a result, hold them in lower regard. On the other hand, a highly educated person may be critical of police, perhaps through detailed knowledge of legal concerns, policy requirements, and the like. A study on this subject by one of this text's authors revealed no link at all between education levels and support for the police.[26]

Income levels and education go hand in hand—at least to a point. This has prompted some researchers to look at the links between income levels and support for police. One study suggests, not surprisingly, that the wealthy are, on balance, more supportive of the police than are the poor.[27]

Still other factors appear to predict support or lack of support for the police. People who perceive an excess of disorder in their neighborhoods tend to be less supportive of police.[28] Likewise, there is evidence that individuals who "dislike the characteristics of their neighborhoods" do not hold the police in high regard.[29]

Others have found that people's attitudes about the world in general and their political beliefs are predictive of support; those with conservative leanings tend to be more supportive of police.[30]

Next, whether one lives in a rural or urban area can affect support.[31] Whether one has been a crime victim is important, too. In particular, victims whose experience was perceived as unpleasant hold the police in low regard.[32] When victims and other concerned citizens are empowered, however, their support levels improve.[33] For example, people who take charge of a problem in their neighborhood, such as by implementing block watch (perhaps in conjunction with the local police department), tend to be supportive of police. Finally, on the subject of police involvement, one study revealed that certain police residency requirements (e.g., those that require officers to live in the cities they serve) may affect support for the police.[34]

Sheriffs and the Electorate

Most of the research we just discussed dealt with people's impressions of municipal police agencies. A few researchers have looked at citizens' support for sheriff's deputies,[35] but what about sheriffs themselves? There is not much research on the subject of elected sheriffs, but this much is true: Sheriffs are elected and, so, need to be more concerned than most police administrators with citizen support, especially *voter* support. The sheriff, as well as a would-be sheriff who is hoping to be elected by the citizens of a given county, owes much of his or her livelihood to the voting public.

The literature discussed in the previous section provides a valuable service to practitioners. It tells them, scientifically, who is least supportive of the police. To the extent, support is necessary to get the job done, then, the findings of those studies constitute useful information. A rash of crime in one area *could* be solved with sufficient support from neighborhood residents, such as for intelligence-gathering purposes. Sheriffs, though, are concerned about citizen support not only from a crime control standpoint but also for purposes of getting reelected.

While sheriffs are elected, they are not all-powerful public officials. They, like police chiefs, generally have to answer to county boards of supervisors (the county equivalents of city councils—see below) or their equivalent entities. One of the core functions of a county board of supervisors is setting the annual budget for all county agencies—including the sheriff. Moreover, board members are usually elected to their posts (often as nonpartisans) from various districts within a county. The result is that the sheriff answers directly not only to the voters but also to county supervisors, who themselves are elected.

Government Officials

Law enforcement agencies are government entities, but a host of non–law enforcement government officials—at the federal, state, and local levels—exercise significant control and influence over them:

- The president appoints the heads of federal law enforcement agencies.

- Governors set state policy and prioritize spending for certain projects.

- Courts issue decisions that affect the activities of officers on the street.
- Legislatures make funding decisions.
- Mayors hire and fire police chiefs.

The list goes on, but the point is that one of the key environmental influences on law enforcement in America is government. In the sections that follow, we look at executive, legislative, and judicial influence. Although there are far more sources of influence than we can possibly cover here, there are a few standouts. For the executive, they are city councils, mayors, police commissions, and other appointing authorities. For the legislative, the roles of the U.S. Congress and the state legislatures in shaping America's law enforcement apparatus are most important. Finally, courts at all levels of government have a dramatic influence on policing (Figure 2–6).

Executive Influence

There are basically two forms of city government in the United States, the **council-manager form** and the **mayor-council form** (see Figure 2–7). The difference between the mayor-council and council-manager forms is the presence or absence of a city manager. City managers are supposed to be apolitical, but mayors are not. Both systems of municipal government have interesting implications for law enforcement.

City Councils. City councils do plenty to exercise control over municipal police agencies. For example, they enact policies that agencies underneath them must implement. Likewise, they can control the purse strings, deciding how much money is allocated to city agencies. They also get involved in dismissals in the event that a police chief fails to perform important functions. In some cities, councils do this directly. Other cities give the city manager authority to make personnel decisions for all city agencies. Still other council-manager cities give the city manager authority to make decisions with the council's approval. It obviously benefits the chief to know who makes key decisions under any system of municipal government.

The council-manager form of city government gives the impression that politics are removed from the process. Presumably, with several officials instead of one partisan mayor, it would be somewhat difficult to make drastic personnel decisions

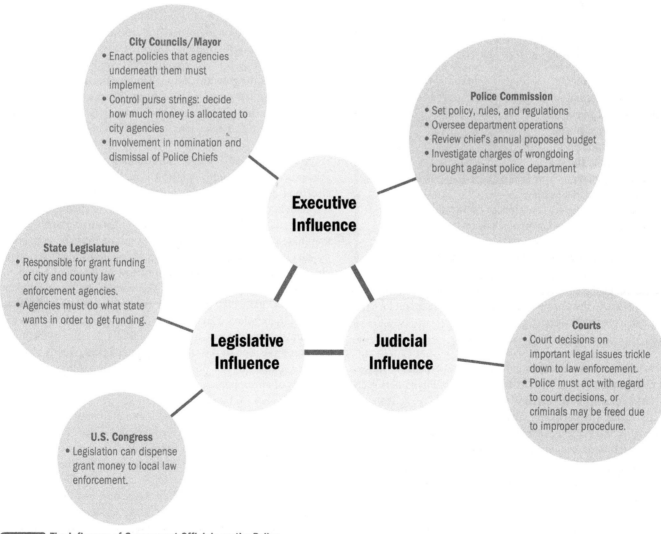

FIGURE 2–6 The Influence of Government Officials on the Police.

City Councils/Mayor
- Enact policies that agencies underneath them must implement
- Control purse strings: decide how much money is allocated to city agencies
- Involvement in nomination and dismissal of Police Chiefs

Police Commission
- Set policy, rules, and regulations
- Oversee department operations
- Review chief's annual proposed budget
- Investigate charges of wrongdoing brought against police department

State Legislature
- Responsible for grant funding of city and county law enforcement agencies.
- Agencies must do what state wants in order to get funding.

Executive Influence

U.S. Congress
- Legislation can dispense grant money to local law enforcement.

Legislative Influence

Judicial Influence

Courts
- Court decisions on important legal issues trickle down to law enforcement.
- Police must act with regard to court decisions, or criminals may be freed due to improper procedure.

Council-Manager Form

- This form is most common in cities of more than 12,000 people.

- An elected city council usually consists of 5 to 12 people.

- The city council makes all policy decisions for the city.

- The power of the mayor is significantly limited:
  - Performs ceremonial duties
  - Serves as the voice, and often the leader, of the council
  - Vote of the mayor carries no more weight than that of other council members

- A city manager presides over the city's day-to-day operations and implements policy enacted by city council.

Mayor-Council Form

- This form may be strong-mayor or weak-mayor.

- *Strong-mayor variation:* Mayor has almost limitless authority over city operations, including hiring and dismissal of key officials.

- *Weak-mayor variation:* Mayor serves largely at the behest of the city council.

- The weak-mayor variation is more common in small towns.

- In both variations, the mayor is responsible for city operations; there is no city manager.

FIGURE 2–7 Forms of City Government.

Think About It...

Police Newsletters
Some police agencies publish both printed and electronic newsletters that are distributed throughout the community. Unfortunately, research shows that such community newsletters rarely reduce crime rates. Other forms of public education, particularly education about domestic violence, appear to be ineffective as well. However, studies show that these newsletters may have a positive effect in reinforcing citizens' participation in community safety. Should the police be responsible for disseminating newsletters to the community? Are newsletters sufficient to bolster community support?

concerning the police department. That does not mean, however, that city councils sit on the sidelines while problems persist in law enforcement. Just recently, the council of Troy, Texas, a city about halfway between Dallas and Austin, fired not just the police chief but the entire department.[36] The city council cited poor performance and insubordination as key reasons for its decision. While replacements were being sought, the city was forced to rely on the local sheriff's department for law enforcement services.

Mayors. As mentioned, large cities tend to favor the council-manager system of government. At the beginning of 2006, the city of San Diego changed from a city manager to a strong-mayor form of government. (See the city's organizational chart in Figure 2–8.) The change was approved by the city's voters. According to the city, "Under the new system the Mayor is the City's chief executive officer, similar to the governor or the president. The Council is the legislative body, providing checks and balances to the Mayor's new authority."[37]

Mayors generally wield more authority in council-mayor systems. Today, though, it is fairly rare for a mayor to exercise total authority over the hiring and firing of a city's first responders. This is true for San Diego, too, despite its move to a strong-mayor system. The city's new rules allow the mayor to nominate the police chief, but the nominee must be approved by the city council. Likewise, the mayor can dismiss the police chief, but such action is subject to review by the city council.

Not every police chief can take comfort in knowing that mayors are generally prohibited from dismissing them on a whim. Often, when a new mayor is elected, perhaps from an opposing political party, he or she makes a number of changes in the composition of the city's top management. Newly elected mayors sometimes fire police chiefs to "shake things up." City councils often support such reorganizations when a new administration comes on board.

Police chiefs can sometimes make city mayors look bad. That is one of the alleged reasons why New York City's police commissioner, William J. Bratton, was forced out of his position by Mayor Rudolph W. Giuliani in 1996 (he returned, though, after a stint as police chief in Los Angeles). Bratton had appeared on the cover of *Time* magazine, and the accompanying article gave Bratton, rather than Giuliani, full credit for New York's precipitous drop in crime during the mid-1990s. There had also been rumors that the two men did not get along.

FIGURE 2-8 **City of San Diego Organization Chart.**
Source: Courtesy of the City of San Diego Police Department.

Police Commissions. Some large cities, regardless of their form of government, also maintain a **police commission**, which generally acts like a corporate board of directors, setting policy and overseeing the department's operations. The Los Angeles Police Commission, for example, consists of five civilian volunteers. The commissioners are generally not just "average" citizens. They tend to be prominent attorneys and/or successful businesspeople. The composition of a police commission can change, however, and tends to when a new mayor is elected.

The Los Angeles Police Commission is perhaps best known for its decision in 2002 to deny then-embattled Police Chief Bernard Park's bid for a second five-year term. Parks asked the Los Angeles City Council to overturn the commission's decision, but it refused.[38] Hiring and firing decisions, though, are not usually the foremost responsibility of police commissions. Honolulu's police commission, while involved in such decisions, spends the bulk of its time reviewing department rules and regulations, reviewing the chief's annual proposed budget, and investigating charges of wrongdoing brought against the city's police department by members of the public and other police officers. It is critical for a police chief in a city with a police commission to understand the political process and the interplay among council, commission, and mayor.

Other Appointing Authorities. Moving from the local to the federal level, there are other appointing authorities besides mayors, city managers, city councils, and police commissions who exercise control over top law enforcement officials. The heads of federal law enforcement agencies are appointed by the president and approved by the Senate. Interestingly, it is also generally much easier for a top federal law enforcement executive to be fired than it is for a local police chief. The president can simply urge a cabinet-level agency head to fire the head of a particular unit. That's what happened in 2004, when the Interior Department fired National Park Police Chief Teresa Chambers. She allegedly spoke about "taboo" topics with reporters from the *Washington Post* and acted with a lack of discretion in various areas: "improper budget communications, making public remarks regarding security on federal property, improper disclosure of budget deliberations, improper lobbying, failure to carry out a supervisor's instructions, and failure to follow the chain of command."[39]

Justice Department law enforcement agencies have also seen their share of administrative "replacements." Some readers may recall then-U.S. Attorney General Janet Reno's decision to fire FBI Director William Sessions in 1993 and replace him with Louis Freeh (who himself is no longer director). The point is that every law enforcement executive, whether federal or local, cannot get too comfortable in his or her position.

The tenure of the typical law enforcement administrator is generally pretty short. Although there are legitimate reasons for local police chiefs and their federal equivalents to leave their posts, such departures are often the result of political pressure or a firing decision. Fortunately, there are at least some checks and balances in place, but law enforcement executives are not unlike professional football coaches in that their jobs are tenuous, their futures are uncertain, and job security is a far cry from that of the lower-ranking street-level police officer. The successful law enforcement administrator *must* play politics.

Legislative Influence

Executive officials, such as mayors, are clearly important parts of the police environment. So are state legislatures and the U.S. Congress. While these bodies do not directly set local law enforcement agencies' budgets, they can exert influence in a number of key respects. Consider President Clinton's **Violent Crime Control and Law Enforcement Act of 1994**. It is the legislation that ushered in what is now known as the Office of Community Oriented Policing Services (the COPS Office) in the U.S. Justice Department. The COPS Office has dispensed billions of dollars in grant money to local law enforcement agencies to improve their community policing capabilities and hire 100,000 new officers. While the Violent Crime Control Act was one of Clinton's pet projects, it would not have succeeded were it not for Congress's decision to send the bill to the White House for that all-important signature.

Moving down from the federal level, nearly every state maintains an office that is responsible for grant funding of city and county law enforcement agencies. In California, the organization is called the Office of Emergency Services. It has no direct effect on local law enforcement, but it does have an indirect effect. It gives out competitive grants to local agencies provided that they implement a program or add to an existing program that is consistent with the funding program's mission. In other words, to get the grant, the agency must do what the state desires. Some grants reflect gubernatorial priorities, others reflect the legislature's desires, and still others reflect a measure of consensus over what is important to both governors and legislatures. One point is clear, however: Governors can do next to nothing in the name of crime control and prevention without the approval of the state legislature. For this reason, local law enforcement agencies need to be in tune with what is regarded as important in the state capital, especially if they want more money.

Judicial Influence

Judicial influence over local law enforcement also cannot be ignored. So influential is the judiciary, in fact, that we devote the better part of Chapters 10 and 11 to it. The U.S. Supreme Court decides important legal issues that trickle down to law enforcement at all levels of government, and state supreme courts often resolve issues that never make it to the U.S. Supreme Court. Lower appellate courts at both the state and the federal level, coupled with state supreme courts and the U.S. Supreme Court, decide criminal appeals that often bear on whether police employed proper procedures. If police officers act without regard to what the courts decide, they will be responsible for the embarrassing release of known criminals. Considering the importance of public opinion, as we have already seen in this chapter, legal mistakes that result in criminals going free are to be avoided at all costs.

The Media

The media, which include both print and television news sources, can be both the best friend and the worst enemy of every police organization. On the one hand, the media can provide favorable coverage of successful investigations, aid in the capture of fugitives, and encourage concerned citizens to call in crime tips.

Unfortunately, the media often get it wrong. This has prompted several large law enforcement agencies to hire media liaisons, some of whom are sworn officers. They assist in the preparation of press releases that present the agency's side of the story and do not give the press an opportunity to misconstrue the facts.

Media Portrayals of the Police

Most of us are familiar with how the media portray police. News reporters, who adhere to the "if it bleeds, it leads" philosophy, often make it look as though the police do nothing more than apprehend violent criminals. Television shows like *COPS* and *Dallas SWAT*, among others, highlight the most action-packed side of an occupation that is often anything but thrilling. As one researcher put it,

> these programs convey images of crime, criminals, law enforcement officials, and the criminal justice system which are incomplete, distorted, and inaccurate. . . . Viewers are led to believe policing is an action-packed profession, criminals frequently resist capture, crime is predominately violent, crime is the work of minorities, and the police regularly succeed in their endeavors to combat illicit activity.[40]

Additionally, the media have been criticized for increasing people's fear of crime, intensifying racist sentiments, and generally providing people with an incomplete picture of what police work is really like.[41]

Not all press coverage is inadequate. Freedom of the press, for better or for worse, is one of the key principles on which this country was founded. Even reality programs like *COPS* often get it right. Researchers have observed, for example, that "public display . . . plays an important function for citizen understanding of the criminal justice system."[42] Moreover, "police officers received overwhelmingly positive publicity, media networks corral a healthy bottom line, and interested viewers benefit from a few minutes of action and

Media Portrayals of the Police

Media coverage can be inaccurate and incomplete, but can also be beneficial to police.

Inaccuracies
- Glorify the investigation aspect of policing
- Give the impression that scores of officers are routinely hurt and killed on the job[i]
- Portray an arrest rate that is far in excess of official arrest rates[ii]
- Portray the triumph of justice when, in reality, justice is not always served[iii]
- Give an impression that many criminal apprehensions are resolved with the suspect's death
- Increase people's fear of crimes
- Intensify racist sentiments

Benefits
- Help citizens understand the judicial system
- Provide positive publicity for police
- Can encourage public to provide information to police

Police Portrayals of Police Work

Police can provide information to counter inaccurate or unfavorable media portrayals.

Impression Management
- Presents information in a way that creates a favorable image of police
- Requires **dramaturgical discipline** to present an appropriate balance of facts and favorable publicity for police

The Public Information Officer
- Some police departments have a **public information officer** who provides all police information to the news media.
- A public information officer does not guarantee a good public image for the department.
- Training and encouraging all officers to provide information to the media may be a more effective strategy for improving the media image of a police department.

[i] J. Livingston, "Crime and the media: Myths and reality," *USA Today Magazine* 122 (May 1994): 40–42.
[ii] J. R. Dominick, "Crime and law enforcement on prime-time television," *Public Opinion Quarterly* 37 (1973): 241-50; and Oliver, "Portrayals of crime, race, and aggression in 'reality-based' police shows."
[iii] D. Zillman and J. Wakshlag, "Fear of victimization and the appeal of crime drama," in *Selective exposure to communication,* ed. D. Zillman and J. Bryant, pp. 141-56 (Hillsdale, NJ: Lawrence Erlbaum, 1985).

FIGURE 2–9 The Police and the Media.

close-to-first-hand observation of police work."[43] Generally, though, there are several limitations associated with media coverage of police work in particular and crime in general.

How the media (whether via the evening news or reality police programming) portray law enforcement officials has important implications for how the police do their job. Citizen support is likely affected by media coverage. Even influential politicians can't be immune from the distorted images of police work presented on television and in newspapers. Media coverage of police work can lead to unrealistic expectations and misguided opinions about controversial incidents. See Figure 2–9 for more on media portrayals of police in relation to police portrayals of police work.

Impression Management

Smart police administrators do not let the media shape their image. Instead, they engage in what is known as **impression management**. As a police chief told the International Conference on Police–Media Relations,

> The future sees law enforcement becoming more and more transparent. We are sharing more and more information. We have to do this. We have to wake up and smell the roses. You have to really build media relations, formulate a plan, and provide other police with information on how to be prepared to deal with the media.[44]

According to one researcher, impression management best serves the public interest by reporting actual facts rather than by putting a "spin" on the information that police agencies

release.[45] At the same time, though, the police are most definitely "performers" in the media relations game. They generally strive to maintain a professional image. Thus, there is a balance to be achieved between putting too much spin on reporting and simply reporting the essential facts in a given case. This has been called **dramaturgical discipline**. The term *dramaturgy* refers to dramatic composition. In short, the police have to "posture and perform."[46] As one officer notes,

> We can use drama to inform the public and still be accurate. . . . And if . . . cops [don't like] this, they had better go back to a time when TV didn't exist; like it or not, we live in a media/video/showbiz world. We can either understand and work with it or live in a bubble.[47]

The police, like the media, have an interest in the portrayal of a certain form of drama. For example, while the media often report the darkest side of crime, the police routinely publicize their successful apprehensions and investigations. This is dramaturgy. Too much of it, though, is regarded unfavorably by the public—and by the press. The "discipline" side of dramaturgical discipline is about finding the appropriate mix of facts and favorable police publicity.

The Public Information Officer: An Asset?

In one of the most impressive media relations studies to date, Lovell surveyed and spent time at a number of city police departments in an effort to uncover the most successful practices those agencies engaged in to maintain a favorable public image.[48] He surveyed not citizens but rather police chiefs and those in their departments who were charged with reporting to the media. Even so, the study yielded a veritable knowledge gold mine. One important finding is that crime has little bearing on media image; that is, police departments whose jurisdictions include the most crime-prone cities are not regarded unfavorably by the press simply because crime rates are high.

Lovell also sought to determine whether having a dedicated **public information officer** was preferable over other approaches. A public information officer is the municipal police department's equivalent of the White House's press secretary. He or she is the key point of contact through which the media must go to gather information. The public information officer also crafts press releases, holds news conferences, and otherwise serves as a department liaison to the press. Relatively few agencies have public information officers, however, relying instead on either departmental policies on how officers are supposed to interact with the media or training on how to handle media inquiries. Interestingly, Lovell found that departments with comprehensive media policies or public information officers were *not* more likely to report a favorable media image than departments that allowed the press to speak with officers at all levels of the agency:

> It is not so much the presence of a media police [or a public information] officer but the content of the strategy within that contributes to effective impression management. One such strategy that emerged as significantly and positively associated with a favorable police image is best summarized as department "openness." Those departments that both authorized and encouraged its officers to communicate with news reporters were more likely to assess the quality of their department's image as favorable.[49]

Lovell also found that although media training (i.e., teaching officers how to interact with the media) had a positive effect on a department's image, the effect was modest. Above all else, Lovell found that police administrators need to adopt a "media strategy" rather than a "media policy." In other words, one more entry in the typical police policy manual is not enough. Policy manuals tend to spell out what police officers *cannot* do. Lovell feels that while media policies are essential, such policies should also encourage officers to engage in proactive communications with the media when appropriate to seek out the press if the circumstances merit it.

Other Law Enforcement Agencies

Every law enforcement agency—and in fact every organization or group—communicates with others like it and with the entities that represent its employees. The chief, for example, might pick up the phone and call his or her counterpart in the next city over. Agencies also communicate with one another across radio frequencies. These varieties of communication are staples in modern law enforcement. Another key means by which police agencies communicate with one another and learn what their colleagues are up to is through participation in professional associations.

Professional Associations

Every profession has at least one association for its members. Academics join associations that are unique to their fields and participate in those associations' annual meetings. Medical doctors join huge professional groups like the American Medical Association. Lawyers, whether prosecutors, defense attorneys, or others, have their respective associations. Schoolteachers join associations. Even occupations that are not necessarily regarded as professions have their own associations. Law enforcement personnel are no different. There are far too many police associations to list and describe here, but four are quite prominent and well known.

The **International Association of Chiefs of Police (IACP)** is the best-known law enforcement association. The organization's title suggests that membership is limited to police chiefs, but the IACP uses the term *chief* somewhat loosely. Officers with executive authority are allowed to join as so-called active members. Associate memberships are available to anyone with sufficient background in law enforcement practice or study, including academics and trainers. The association also extends honorary and distinguished service memberships to other people, including a number of non–law enforcement personnel. All told, the IACP boasts a membership of more than 20,000 people in 89 countries across the globe.

IACP was founded in 1893. Its constitution describes the association's mission as follows:

> As a leadership organization the Mission of the International Association of Chiefs of Police is to advance professional police services; promote enhanced administrative, technical, and operational police practices; foster cooperation and the exchange of information and experience among police leaders and police organizations of recognized professional and technical standing throughout the world; champion the recruitment and training of qualified persons in the police profession; and encourage all police personnel worldwide to achieve and maintain the highest standards of ethics, integrity, community interaction, and professional conduct.[50]

IACP facilitates interagency communication through several means. One is an annual meeting that convenes in a different city each year. At the meeting, there are panels, presentations, and training sessions. The meetings, which are generally organized around two subjects—law enforcement technology and education, provide members ample opportunity to network with one another in both formal and informal settings. IACP also conducts various training programs throughout the year. The association's Research Center conducts a wide variety of police-related studies and disseminates the results, usually by posting them online. IACP also publishes *The Police Chief*, a print and online magazine that is widely read by law enforcement administrators throughout the United States. All in all, IACP provides a valuable interagency communication function for police administrators.

Though far smaller than the IACP, the **National Black Police Association** was formed in 1972 as a parent association for local and regional black police associations.[51] According to the association, it "is a nationwide organization of African American Police Associations dedicated to the promotion of justice, fairness, and effectiveness in law enforcement." Basically, the National Black Police Association has succeeded in creating a network of minority police officers throughout the United States. Though the association's title suggests otherwise, membership is not restricted to African-American police officers, although they do make up the bulk of the membership. Unlike IACP, the National Black Police Association does not hold an annual meeting for all members, but its regional affiliates hold their own meetings. There are five such regions.

The **International Union of Police Associations (IUPA)** represents rank-and-file police officers and their unions from across the country. The IUPA describes itself as follows:

> The International Union of Police Associations is the only AFL-CIO union chartered exclusively for law enforcement and law enforcement support personnel. The AFL-CIO affiliation places I.U.P.A. in a position of strength within the labor movement. While I.U.P.A.'s officers, active and retired law enforcement officers, fight to improve the lives of their brothers and sisters in law enforcement, I.U.P.A. works to improve legislation that protects and affects public safety officers, as well as representing the needs of law enforcement officers and support personnel, whether that be for better equipment, more staff or a fair wage.[52]

The IUPA is more a lobbying organization than a professional association. It holds meetings but not on par with, for example, IACP. One of the marks of a lobbying organization is the use of us-versus-them language in its correspondence. For example, the National Rifle Association regularly battles those who would threaten Second Amendment rights, and the American Civil Liberties Union challenges people who threaten civil liberties. The IUPA, not surprisingly, tends to not speak highly of police administrators, who are regarded as the "bad guys" in nearly every union contract negotiation.

In addition to its lobbying efforts, the IUPA facilitates communication among police officers and among the unions that represent them. Some agencies have their own unions, and police officers in other agencies join regional and state unions. The IUPA is the body that represents *all* their interests in the nation's capital.

The largest police association in the world is the **International Police Association (IPA)**, though it is less known to most Americans than the IACP. The IPA boasts a membership of almost 376,000 people with national sections in 62 countries around the globe. The IPA's core functions are, in its words, to promote "global and cultural friendship among peace officers."[53] Beyond that, the IPA describes its other concerns:

> It is committed to the principles set out in the *Universal Declaration of Human Rights* as adopted by the United Nations in 1948 and recognizes that any form of torture is absolutely inconsistent with these principles. Its aims include the development of cultural relations amongst its members, a broadening of their general knowledge and an exchange of professional experience.

In addition, it seeks to foster mutual help in the social sphere and to contribute, within the limits of its possibilities, to the peaceful co-existence of different peoples and to the preservation of world peace.[54]

The IPA's national sections (those consisting of one country's members) hold annual meetings. The main annual meeting, known as the *IPA World Congress*, provides an opportunity for law enforcement professionals from around the world to meet one another, share information, and learn of operational "best practices" that have proved successful in other agencies. The IPA's role is especially important in the wake of September 11. International cooperation is the word of the day, and the IPA serves to promote such cooperation.

▶ Police as a Piece of the Criminal Justice Puzzle

Police work does not stop with an arrest. Police officers have duties to perform throughout the criminal justice process, even well after trial. Also, police officers do not work in a criminal justice vacuum. Their relationships with prosecutors and corrections officials are important, now more than ever.

The Criminal Justice Process

Police officers are involved in many different stages of the criminal justice process. They are often called on, for instance, to testify at trial. Figure 2–10 provides an overview of the criminal justice process and identifies stages where police officers may be called on to act or assist.

LEARNING OUTCOMES 3 — Summarize the police role in the criminal justice process.

Think About It...

Police-Corrections Partnerships A possible "dark side" to police-corrections partnerships is known as *mission distortion*. Mission distortion refers to situations where the definition of one's professional mission becomes blurred. For instance, actively working with the police makes it convenient for some community corrections officers to gravitate toward a greater emphasis on law enforcement priorities at the expense of their responsibilities to provide services to their clients. Moreover, police–probation partnerships threaten to increase the likelihood of community corrections officers serving as stalking horses for police officers. Should police officers team up with probation officers to conduct enhanced supervision of probationers? Can police-corrections partnerships lead to mission distortion?

A.Ramey/PhotoEdit

Police in the Pretrial Phase

Once a suspect has been arrested, he or she is searched. This is done for the protection of the officer as well as to discover any contraband in the suspect's possession. The suspect is then transported to the police station and booked. **Booking** is the process of fingerprinting, processing, and photographing the suspect, after which he or she is typically placed in a holding cell. The suspect may also be required to submit to a Breathalyzer or other test or be required to participate in a lineup.

After booking, the police present their case to the prosecutor (usually by filing a report of some sort or by contacting the prosecutor). If the prosecutor believes the evidence is persuasive enough, he or she will bring charges against the suspect, subject to certain restrictions specified in the Constitution and clarified by the Supreme Court. Once charges are brought, the suspect is then referred to as a *defendant*. If the charges are minor, the police may release the defendant rather than detaining him or her, in which case the defendant will be required to appear at court at some later date.

Through their investigations, police effectively "build" criminal cases for prosecutors. Without this assistance, prosecutors would be going into trial blind. When the process breaks down, particularly when the police forward weak cases to the prosecutor, a conviction is difficult to secure.

Some jurisdictions rely on a grand jury rather than allowing prosecutors to determine whether charges are appropriate. When a grand jury is used, it often works closely with the prosecutor, who presents the information that the grand jury needs to make its decision. Police officers often testify before grand juries in order to help make the case against a possible criminal defendant. The police role in grand jury investigations can be an important one because the suspects who are being investigated—and possibly indicted—do not enjoy the right to be present at the hearing or to offer evidence in their own defense.

Police at Trial

Once the pretrial process has concluded and the charges stand, a trial may or may not take place. If the defendant pleads guilty, then a trial is not necessary. However, if the defendant pleads *not guilty*, the case is set for trial. At trial, the prosecutor bears the burden of proving that the defendant is guilty beyond a reasonable doubt. This often entails calling on one or more investigative or arresting police officers to provide testimony. Police officers need to be prepared to be put under oath and provide testimony, usually for the prosecution, depending on the nature of the charges.

Police after Trial

Generally, police officers have little to no role during the sentencing hearing or appellate phase. They do, however, continue to work the same streets to which convicted criminals are eventually released. Clearly, many police officers thrive on putting away bad guys, but there is little excitement in arresting the same person over and over. It is therefore advantageous for police officers to work with officials whose responsibility involves the supervision of convicted criminals. Not only does such cooperation promote successful reintegration of offenders into society, but it can also assist the law enforcement function. Police officers who team with probation officers, for instance, can creatively circumvent the Fourth Amendment and search probationers with relative ease. Collaborative methods like this are taken up in the next two sections.

FIGURE 2–10 The Police in the Criminal Justice System.

Relationships with Prosecutors

Police officers work closely with prosecutors (Figure 2–11). They may have almost no direct contact with prosecutors, save, perhaps, for testifying against a defendant in a criminal trial, but prosecutors depend on police officers to bring them cases. Were it not for police officers, few prosecutors would be employed. It is generally not their responsibility to go find suspected criminals and press charges. The police take the first step. Likewise, the police depend on prosecutors. Prosecutors present the government's case against criminal defendants. When they fail in this regard, criminals are released back into society and become police officers' problem all over again. It is in the interest of both officials to work together, whether one-on-one or otherwise.

Throughout most of this country's recent history, prosecutors have been reactive; that is, they have waited until police officers brought them cases to prosecute. To a large extent, this model persists today; many prosecutors thrive on taking serious offenders to court and sending them to prison for long

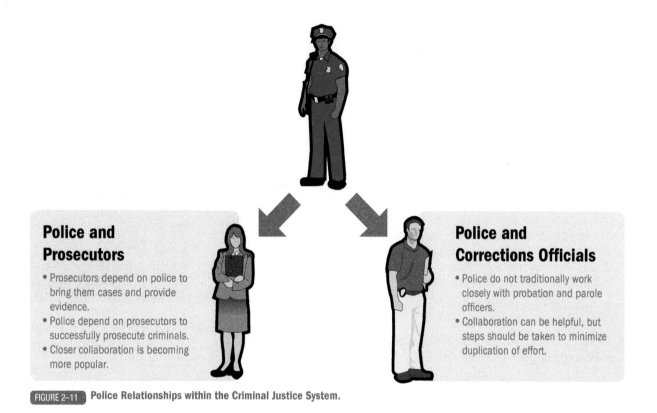

Police and Prosecutors

- Prosecutors depend on police to bring them cases and provide evidence.
- Police depend on prosecutors to successfully prosecute criminals.
- Closer collaboration is becoming more popular.

Police and Corrections Officials

- Police do not traditionally work closely with probation and parole officers.
- Collaboration can be helpful, but steps should be taken to minimize duplication of effort.

FIGURE 2–11 **Police Relationships within the Criminal Justice System.**

periods of time. These prosecutors rely on the police for the preparation of key aspects of the cases, such as documenting a confession. This traditional prosecutorial role has been described as follows:

> The traditional . . . prosecutor likes to think of himself as the consummate carnivore: a learned lawyer, a compelling oral advocate, a relentless pursuer of the truth who fights crime by putting "bad guys" in jail. His allies in this fight are the . . . investigative agencies. Those agencies identify trends in criminal behavior and "bring" the prosecutor the significant cases.[55]

It would be inaccurate to say that prosecutors are totally dependent on police officers for the preparation of their cases. Many prosecutors' offices have commissioned peace officers who serve as investigators. California is one state that follows this model. There is also much to be said about knowing the law and crafting an argument. Prosecutors cannot rely on police officers in this regard. Being lawyers, they know the law better than the typical police officer. A skilled prosecutor will take the evidence that the police present and use it creatively to mount an argument before a judge or jury.

The traditional prosecutors, then, act more or less reactively. They are not concerned with preventing crime, reaching out to other agencies, and collaborating with their law enforcement colleagues. Recently, though, prosecution has changed. Collaboration, especially with police, is gaining momentum. Prosecutors are becoming more receptive to partnering and collaboration with various entities inside and outside the criminal

justice system. Police–prosecution partnerships are becoming quite popular.

Relationships with Corrections Officials

It is perhaps easier to conceive of close working relationships between police and prosecutors than between police and corrections officials. This may be because, in terms of the criminal justice process, police and prosecutors work more closely together in time than police and corrections officials. In other words, a case moves directly from the police department to the prosecutor's office but not from the police to, say, a parole officer. With few exceptions, corrections officials usually enter the picture after the criminal trial and sentencing stages.

When we talk about "corrections officials" in this chapter, we are not referring to jail or prison personnel. Rather, our concern is with relationships between police officers and both probation officers and parole officers. Police officers have learned that such relationships can be quite helpful.

Parole officers do much of the same work as police; for efficiency's sake alone, it just makes sense to collaborate. While parole officers supervise individuals who were recently released from prison, they cannot supervise their clients perfectly, partly because of the high caseloads some parole officers oversee. Consequently, police officers often encounter parolees. When parole officers and police officers work together, however, duplication of effort should be minimized. Also, some police departments are actively involving themselves in the reentry process, especially in the days right after the parolee is released from prison.

Judicial Control over Police Practice

On August 12, 2013, a federal district court judge found the City of New York liable for a pattern of unconstitutional stop-and-frisk activities by the New York Police Department (NYPD). The judge decided in part that

> the City adopted a policy of indirect racial profiling by targeting racially defined groups for stops based on local crime suspect data. This has resulted in the disproportionate and discriminatory stopping of blacks and Hispanics in violation of the Equal Protection Clause. Both statistical and anecdotal evidence showed that minorities are indeed treated differently than whites.

The following facts were uncontested in the case (i.e., both New York and the plaintiffs agreed to them):

- Between January 2004 and June 2012, the police department conducted over 4.4 million *Terry* stops.

- The number of stops per year rose sharply from 314,000 in 2004 to a high of 686,000 in 2011.

- Fifty-two percent of all stops were followed by a protective frisk for weapons. A weapon was found after 1.5% of these frisks. In other words, in 98.5% of the 2.3 million frisks, no weapon was found.

- Eight percent of all stops led to a search into the stopped person's clothing, ostensibly based on the officer feeling an object during the frisk that he suspected to be a weapon or immediately perceived to be contraband other than a weapon. In 9% of these searches, the felt object was in fact a weapon. Ninety-one percent of the time, it was not. In 14% of these searches, the felt object was in fact contraband. Eighty-six percent of the time, it was not.

- Six percent of all stops resulted in an arrest, and 6% resulted in a summons. The remaining 88% of the 4.4 million stops resulted in no further law enforcement action.

- In 52% of the 4.4 million stops, the person stopped was black; in 31%, the person was Hispanic; and in 10%, the person was white.

- In 2010, New York City's resident population was roughly 23% black, 29% Hispanic, and 33% white.

- In 23% of the stops of blacks and 24% of the stops of Hispanics, the officer recorded using force. The number for whites was 17%.

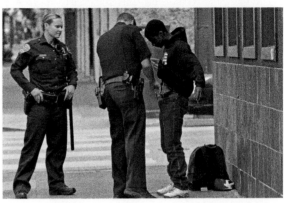

Rafael Ben-Ari/Alamy Stock Photo

- Weapons were seized in 1.0% of the stops of blacks, 1.1% of the stops of Hispanics, and 1.4% of the stops of whites.

- Contraband other than weapons was seized in 1.8% of the stops of blacks, 1.7% of the stops of Hispanics, and 2.3% of the stops of whites.

- Between 2004 and 2009, the percentage of stops where the officer failed to state a specific suspected crime rose from 1% to 36%.[56]

In late 2015, in an effort to lower the risk of civil liability, and to reduce citizen complaints over police stops, the NYPD began providing "Stop slips" to anyone stopped but not arrested.[57] Similar in appearance to parking "tickets," the slips read: "When a police officer reasonably suspects that a person has committed, is committing or is about to commit a felony, or a Penal Law misdemeanor, the officer is authorized . . . to stop, question and possibly frisk that person for a weapon." The slip also contains a checklist that the officer must complete before it is issued. The seven checklist choices are (1) concealing or possessing a weapon, (2) engaging in a drug transaction, (3) proximity to the scene of a crime, (4) matches a specific suspect description, (5) acting as a lookout, (6) casing victim or location, and (7) other. The other category, while broad, requires the officer to specify the reason for the stop in writing. The officer's name, rank, and shield number are then written on the slip, along with the name of the officer's supervisor.

An NYPD internal order, issued to officers when the slips were distributed, makes clear that two factors that police were previously able to cite—furtive movements by a suspect, or simply being in a high crime area—are not sufficient cause for a stop. That order also says that people can't be stopped "because they are members of a racial or ethnic group that appears more frequently in local crime suspect data."

NYPD street stops have dramatically decreased in number since the lawsuit began, and totaled less than 50,000 in 2015.

This case raises several interesting questions, among them are the following:

1. Do you agree with the judge's decision? Why or why not?
2. Are the statistics described above sufficient to support the judge's decision?
3. What limits, if any, should be placed on judicial control over policing?
4. What role did the public play in this case?
5. How prevalent is racial profiling in American policing? What can be done?

Explain how the U.S. government's features of democracy and federalism impact policing.

Democracy and federalism have contributed to the unique nature of policing in America. Democracy is the institutionalization of freedom. Among democracy's implications for policing is the need to balance due process against crime control. Federalism divides government power and decision-making capabilities between levels of government, and this has led to the creation of federal, state, and local law enforcement agencies in the United States.

1. What are the distinguishing features of policing in a democracy?

2. How has our system of federalism affected policing in the United States?

democracy A form of government that vests supreme authority in the people, usually through their freely elected representatives.

federalism A political doctrine holding that power is divided (often constitutionally) between a central governing body (e.g., the federal government) and various constituent units (the states).

dual federalism An interpretation of the U.S. Constitution that suggests a system in which the only powers vested in the federal government are those explicitly listed in the document, with the remaining powers being left to the states.

Discuss the influence of various environmental factors on policing.

The environment of policing includes citizens, government officials, the media, and other law enforcement agencies. Citizen support for police is affected by factors like race, age, sex, and prior contact. Government influence over policing occurs through executive, legislative, and judicial channels. The media can both help and hurt law enforcement agencies, but skilled police administrators engage in impression management to ensure a favorable public image. Two methods of promoting interagency communication are participating in professional associations and keeping abreast of research.

1. What is the policing environment?

2. Which aspect of the policing environment do you believe is most important?

council-manager form The most common form of city government in cities of more than 12,000 people. It consists of an elected city council (usually between 5 and 12 people) responsible for all policy decisions for the city. Mayors under this form of municipal government generally perform ceremonial duties and serve as the voice—and often the leader—of the city council.

mayor-council form A form of municipal government that can be categorized in two ways. The strong-mayor variation gives the mayor almost limitless authority over city operations, including the hiring and dismissal of key officials. In the weak-mayor variation, which is more common in small towns, the mayor serves largely at the behest of the city council.

police commission An agency maintained in some large cities that acts like a corporate board of directors, setting policy and overseeing the police department's operations.

Violent Crime Control and Law Enforcement Act of 1994 The U.S. legislation that established the Office of Community Oriented Policing Services (the COPS Office) in the U.S. Justice Department.

impression management A media relations concept that involves controlling the presentation of information to achieve a desired public perception.

dramaturgical discipline Achieving a balance between merely reporting facts and putting a "spin" on those facts to create a desired impression.

public information officer A police department's spokesperson. The media must go through the public information officer to gather information about the department.

International Association of Chiefs of Police (IACP) Founded in 1893, the best-known association for law enforcement professionals.

National Black Police Association The parent association, founded in 1972, for local and regional associations of African-American police professionals.

International Union of Police Associations (IUPA) An international police association, founded in 1954 and chartered by the AFL-CIO, that represents all rank-and-file officers and functions more as a lobbying group than as a professional association.

International Police Association (IPA) Founded in 1950, the largest police professional association in the world.

Summarize the police role in the criminal justice process.

The police are central participants in the overall criminal justice system. They participate in the criminal justice process during the pretrial, trial, and post-trial stages, and they interact regularly with prosecutors and corrections officials.

1. What is the role of the police in the criminal justice system during trial?

2. What role do the police play in the corrections process?

booking The process of fingerprinting, processing, and photographing a suspect, after which he or she is typically placed in a holding cell. The suspect may also be required to submit to testing (such as for alcohol) or be required to participate in a lineup.

References

1 "Large cuts in staff for Camden, Newark police could threaten anti-crime progress," NJ.com, December 5, 2010, www.nj.com/news/index.ssf/2010/12/large_cuts_in_staff_for_camden.html (accessed December 6, 2013).

2 George Berkin, "Camden police layoffs and economics," NJ.com, January 21, 2011, http://blog.nj.com/njv_george_berkin/2011/01/camden_police_layoffs_and_econ.html (accessed December 6, 2013).

3 Kate Zernike, "Camden turns around with new police force," The New York Times, August 31, 2014, http://www.nytimes.com/2014/09/01/nyregion/camden-turns-around-with-new-police-force.html?_r=1 (accessed January 30, 2016).

4 G. T. Marx, "Police and democracy," http://web.mit.edu/gtmarx/www/dempol.html (accessed December 7, 2015).

5 Robert F. Kennedy quotations from MemorableQuotations.com, www.memorablequotations.com/rfk.htm (accessed December 7, 2015).

6 See, e.g., S. K. Ivkovich, "Shades of blue: A cross-national study of public support for the police," paper presented at the annual meeting of the American Society of Criminology, Toronto, June 20, 2008; S. G. Brandl, J. Frank, J. Wooldredge, and R. C. Watkins, "On the measurement of public support for the police: A research note," Policing: An International Journal of Police Strategies & Management, vol. 20, no. 3 (1997), pp. 473–80; and E. Erez, "Self-defined desert and citizen's assessment of the police," Journal of Criminal Law and Criminology, vol. 75 (1984), pp. 1276–99.

7 J. L. Worrall, "Public perceptions of police efficacy and image: The fuzziness of support for the police," American Journal of Criminal Justice, vol. 24 (1999), pp. 47–66.

8 D. Bayley, Forces of order: Police behavior in Japan and the United States (Berkeley: University of California Press, 1976); S. M. Lipset and W. Schneider, The confidence gap: Business, labor, and government in the public mind (New York: Free Press, 1983).

9 S. Albrect and M. Green, "Attitudes toward the police and the larger attitude complex: Implications for police–community relations," Criminology, vol. 15 (1977), pp. 67–87; T. Jefferson and M. A. Walker, "Ethnic minorities in the criminal justice system," Criminal Law Review, vol. 28 (1993), pp. 83–95; R. B. Parks, "Linking objective and subjective measures of performance," Public Administration Review, vol. 44 (1984), pp. 118–27.

10 Worrall, "Public perceptions of police efficacy and image."

11 F. Furstenberg and C. Wellford, "Calling the police: The evaluation of police service," Law and Society Review, vol. 7 (1973), pp. 393–406; I. Hadar and J. Snortum, "The eye of the beholder: Differential perceptions of police by the police and the public," Criminal Justice and Behavior, vol. 2 (1975), pp. 37–54.

12 D. Smith and R. Hawkins, "Victimization, types of citizen–police contacts, and attitudes toward the police," Law and Society Review, vol. 8 (1973), pp. 135–52.

13 R. Scaglion and R. Condon, "The structure of black and white attitudes toward the police," Human Organization, vol. 39 (1980), pp. 280–83.

14 D. Walker, R. Richardson, O. Williams, T. Denyer, and S. McGaughey, "Contact and support: An empirical assessment of public attitudes toward the police and the courts," North Carolina Law Review, vol. 51 (1972), pp. 43–79.

15 R. G. Zevitz and R. J. Rettammel, "Elderly attitudes about police service," American Journal of Police, vol. 9 (1990), pp. 25–39.

16 D. Sagi and C. Wellford, "Age composition and patterns of change in criminal statistics," Journal of Criminal Law, Criminology, and Police Science, vol. 59 (1968), pp. 29–35.

17 Hadar and Snortum, "The eye of the beholder."

18 J. Preiss and H. Ehrlich, *An examination of role theory: The case of state police* (Lincoln: University of Nebraska Press, 1958).

19 J. Q. Wilson, *Thinking about crime* (New York: Vintage, 1985).

20 T. Winfree and C. Griffiths, "Adolescent attitudes toward law enforcement," in *Juvenile delinquency: Little brother grows up*, ed. T. Ferdinand, pp. 79–99 (Beverly Hills, CA: Sage, 1977); M. E. Correia, M. D. Reisig, and N. P. Lovrich, "Public perceptions of state police: An analysis of individual-level and contextual variables," *Journal of Criminal Justice*, vol. 24 (1996), pp. 17–28.

21 C. Vedder and O. Keller, "The police and middle class conflicts," *Police*, vol. 9 (1965), pp. 6–8.

22 C. Wirths, "The development of attitudes toward law enforcement," *Police*, vol. 3 (1958), pp. 50–52; T. Bercal, "Calls for police assistance: Consumer demands for governmental service," *American Behavioral Scientist*, vol. 13 (1970), pp. 681–91.

23 D. Bordua and L. Tifft, "Citizen interviews, organizational feedback, and police–community relations decisions," *Law and Society Review*, vol. 6 (1971), pp. 155–82; A. Schwartz and S. Clarren, *The Cincinnati team policing experiment: A technical report* (Washington, DC: U.S. Government Printing Office, 1978).

24 M. E. Correia, M. D. Reisig, and N. P. Lovrich, "Public perceptions of state police: An analysis of individual-level and contextual variables," *Journal of Criminal Justice*, vol. 24 (1996), pp. 17–28.

25 M. E. Correia, M. D. Reisig, and N. P. Lovrich, "Public perceptions of state police: An analysis of individual-level and contextual variables," *Journal of Criminal Justice*, vol. 24 (1996), pp. 17–28; L. Cao, J. Frank, and F. Cullen, "Race, community context, and confidence in the police," *American Journal of Police*, vol. 15 (1996), pp. 3–22.

26 J. L. Worrall, "Public perceptions of police efficacy and image."

27 O. Marenin, "Supporting the local police: The differential group basis of varieties of support," *Police Studies*, vol. 6 (1983), pp. 50–56.

28 L. Cao, J. Frank, and F. Cullen, "Race, community context, and confidence in the police," *American Journal of Police*, vol. 15 (1996), pp. 3–22; D. Lewis and G. Salem, *Fear of crime: Incivility and the production of a social problem* (New Brunswick, NJ: Transaction Books, 1986).

29 P. Jesilow, J. Meyer, and N. Namazzi, "Public attitudes toward the police," *American Journal of Police*, vol. 2 (1995), pp. 67–88.

30 Albrect and Green, "Attitudes toward the police and the larger attitude complex"; R. Chackerian, "Police professionalism and citizen evaluations: A preliminary look," *Public Administration Review*, vol. 34 (1974), pp. 141–48; K. S. Larsen, "Authoritarianism and attitudes toward the police," *Psychological Reports*, vol. 3 (1968), pp. 349–50; E. Zamble and P. Annesley, "Some determinants of public attitudes toward the police," *Journal of*

Police Science and Administration, vol. 15 (1987), pp. 285–90.

31 See, e.g., H. Jacob, "Black and white perceptions of justice in the city," *Law and Society Review*, vol. 5 (1971), pp. 69–89; A. Mirande, "Fear of crime and fear of the police in a Chicano community," *Sociology and Social Research*, vol. 64 (1980), pp. 528–41.

32 I. Hadar and J. Snortum, "The eye of the beholder"; J. Garofalo, *The police and public opinion: An analysis of victimization and attitude data from 13 American cities* (Washington, DC: U.S. Government Printing Office, 1977).

33 Jesilow et al., "Public attitudes toward the police"; Q. C. Thurman and M. Reisig, "Community-oriented research in an era of community-oriented policing," *American Behavioral Scientist*, vol. 39 (1996), pp. 570–86.

34 D. W. Murphy and J. L. Worrall, "Residency requirements and public perceptions of the police in large municipalities," *Policing: An International Journal of Police Strategies and Management*, vol. 22 (1998), pp. 327–42.

35 R. Weisheit, E. Wells, and D. Falcone, *Crime and policing in rural and small-town America: An overview of the issues* (Washington, DC: U.S. Department of Justice, 1995); D. Falcone and L. Wells, "The county sheriff as a distinctive policing modality," *American Journal of Police*, vol. 14 (1995), pp. 123–49.

36 Associated Press, "Town to police: 'You're fired,'" October 23, 2006, www.cbsnews.com/stories/2006/10/23/national/main2114983.shtml (accessed December 6, 2013).

37 City of San Diego, http://www.sandiego.gov/city-manager/ (accessed December 7, 2015).

38 James Sterngold, "Police chief rebuffed in Los Angeles," *New York Times*, April 18, 2002, www.nytimes.com/2002/04/18/us/police-chief-rebuffed-in-los-angeles.html (accessed December 6, 2013).

39 GovernmentExecutive.com, "Park police chief fired," July 9, 2004, www.govexec.com/dailyfed/0704/070904a1.htm (accessed December 7, 2015).

40 J. L. Worrall, "Constitutional issues in reality-based police television programs: Media ride-alongs," *American Journal of Criminal Justice*, vol. 25 (2000), pp. 41–64. See also P. G. Kooistra, J. S. Mahoney, and S. D. Westervelt, "The world of crime according to 'COPS,'" in *Entertaining crime: Television reality programs*, ed. M. Fishman and G. Cavender, pp. 141–58 (New York: Aldine De Gruyter, 1998); M. B. Oliver, "Portrayals of crime, race, and aggression in 'reality-based' police shows: A content analysis," *Journal of Broadcasting and Electronic Media*, vol. 38 (1994), pp. 179–92.

41 J. M. Carlson, "Crime show viewing by preadults: The impact on attitudes toward civil liberties," *Communication Research*, vol. 10 (1983), pp. 529–52; J. M. Carlson, *Prime time law enforcement: Crime show viewing and attitudes toward the criminal justice system* (New York:

Praeger, 1985); R. M. Entman, "Modern racism and the images of blacks in local television news," *Critical Studies in Mass Communication*, vol. 7 (1990), pp. 332–45; R. M. Entman, "Blacks in the news: Television, modern racism and cultural change," *Journalism Quarterly*, vol. 60 (1992), pp. 341–61; G. Gerbner and L. Gross, "Living with television: The violence profile," *Journal of Communication*, vol. 26 (1976), pp. 173–99; R. P. Hawkins and S. Pingree, "Uniform messages and habitual viewing: Unnecessary assumptions in social reality effects," *Human Communication Research*, vol. 7 (1981), pp. 291–301.

42 R. Costello and F. Biafora, "Just the facts ma'am: The supreme court says 'no' to media ride-alongs," *Journal of Criminal Justice and Popular Culture*, vol. 7 (1999), pp. 15–25, quote on p. 15.

43 J. L. Worrall, "Constitutional issues in reality-based police television programs," 42–43.

44 J. S. Lovell, *Media power and information control* (Washington, DC: National Institute of Justice, 2002), p. 179.

45 Ibid.

46 Ibid.

47 Ibid.

48 Ibid.

49 Ibid., pp. 188–89.

50 International Association of Chiefs of Police, *Constitution* (Alexandria, VA: International Association of Chiefs of Police, 2006). Reprinted by permission.

51 The National Black Police Association website, www.blackpolice.org (accessed December 7, 2015).

52 International Union of Police Associations Mission Statement, www.iupa.org. Reprinted by permission.

53 International Police Association, www.ipa-usa.org/ (accessed December 7, 2015).

54 From "Aims of the IPA?" www.ipa-iac.org/content. php?pageId=20. Reprinted by permission of the International Police Association.

55 E. Glazer, "Thinking strategically: How federal prosecutors can reduce violent crime," *Fordham Urban Law Journal*, vol. 26 (1999), pp. 573–606.

56 *Floyd* v.*City of New York*, 08 Civ. 1034 (SAS), decided August 12, 2013.

57 Rocco Parascandola, "NYPD officially debuts stop-and-frisk 'receipts' and new rules for cops," *New York Daily News*, September 28, 2015, http://www.nydailynews. com/new-york/nyc-crime/nypd-debuts-stop-and-frisk-receipts-new-rules-cops-article-1.2374455 (accessed March 25, 2016).

3

Law Enforcement Agencies and Their Organization

1 Describe the different law enforcement agencies in America.

2 Describe how law enforcement organizations differ from other types of organizations.

3 Summarize the trends and issues associated with private policing.

Jonathan Larsen/Diadem Images/Alamy Stock Photo

THE EFFECT OF POLICE ON CRIME

In a recent study that used statistical analysis to determine the correlation between police staffing levels and crime rates in medium-size to large U.S. cities, Aaron Chalfin and Justin McCrary found that an average of $1.60 is saved for every dollar spent on police work.[1] The savings come from reduced victimization costs, but the study also showed that policing has a greater impact on violent crime rates than on property crime rates. Chalfin and McCrary, whose focus is the economics of crime, studied 220 metropolitan areas throughout the country and determined that while policing is generally cost effective, some cities are better at using police resources than others. One of the most effective small cities in the study was Gary, Indiana, where every dollar spent on policing resulted in a $14 benefit in crime reduction. In contrast, only 20 cents in benefits accrued in Sunnyvale, California, for every policing dollar spent. The conclusion reached by Chalfin and McCrary is that U.S. cities are underpoliced and that an increase in an offender's chances of being caught decreases crime.

Law enforcement officers from a variety of agencies join together at a memorial service for a fellow officer. How many different levels of law enforcement agencies can you identify?

While Chalfin and McCrary focused only on local police, there are many different levels and types of law enforcement organizations in the United States. This chapter identifies and explores each of these levels.

► Agencies of Law Enforcement

The federal government has a number of its own enforcement agencies, as does each state government. Additionally, county- and municipal-level agencies can be all across the country, including specialized agencies that don't necessarily fit neatly into any government category.

How Many Are There?

Counting the number of law enforcement agencies in America is not unlike counting the number of citizens. The decennial census of people living in the United States always falls short on some level because the number of residents does not remain constant. Some people die; others are born. Not surprisingly, police agencies follow similar patterns. New agencies are created when newly incorporated cities need their own police force. Merging municipalities and shrinking towns can lead to the combination or elimination of police departments. This makes counting cops a difficult task at best.

Some researchers have identified as few as 15,000 agencies, others as many as 40,000. What's the actual number? One of the more rigorous studies in this area relied on various sources of data and came up with a very defensible estimate of a little more than 20,000 federal, state, and local agencies.[2] The study's authors also estimated that these agencies employ some 680,000 sworn personnel.[3] That means there is roughly one sworn law enforcement officer for every 500 people in the United States.[4]

Federal Agencies

There are many federal law enforcement agencies, especially if we define them as any agency charged with the enforcement of federal laws. Most arms of the federal government have at least some enforcement component. The Internal Revenue Service, for example, has its own criminal enforcement division. Likewise, the U.S. Fish and Wildlife Service's Office of Law Enforcement ensures that relevant statutes are upheld. Even the various branches of the military have their own law enforcement arms. A comprehensive list of federal law enforcement agencies is provided in Figure 3–1. These enforcement agencies don't exactly come to mind, however, when we think about federal law enforcement. Instead, it is the familiar agencies like the Federal Bureau of Investigation (FBI) and the Drug Enforcement Administration (DEA) that come to mind. A focus on these well-known agencies shortens the list considerably.

LEARNING OUTCOMES 1 Describe the different law enforcement agencies in America.

Before the September 11, 2001, attacks on the United States, it was somewhat difficult to succinctly describe the organization of federal law enforcement. Agencies were housed in a number of different cabinet-level departments, including Justice, Treasury, Agriculture, Energy, and Health and Human Services. After September 11, America witnessed one of the most significant efforts to restructure the federal government in generations.

The **Homeland Security Act of 2002** created what is now known as the Department of Homeland Security (DHS), a cabinet-level department. Homeland Security now houses a number of law enforcement agencies that, prior to September 11, used to be found scattered throughout the federal government. The names of some of these agencies also changed. It has been a few years now since these changes were ushered in, but people are still sometimes confused about the names and parent agencies

Department of Agriculture	Bureau of Prisons

Department of Agriculture

U.S. Forest Service

Department of Commerce

Bureau of Export Enforcement

National Marine Fisheries Administration

Department of Defense

Air Force Office of Special Investigations

Army Criminal Investigation Division

Defense Criminal Investigative Service

Naval Investigative Service

Department of Energy

National Nuclear Safety Administration

Office of Mission Operations

Office of Secure Transportation

Department of Health and Human Services

Food and Drug Administration, Office of
   Criminal Investigations

Department of Homeland Security

Federal Law Enforcement Training Center

Federal Protective Service

Transportation Security Administration

U.S. Coast Guard

U.S. Customs and Border Protection (CBP)—
   includes U.S. Border Patrol

U.S. Immigration and Customs Enforcement (ICE)

U.S. Secret Service

Department of the Interior

Bureau of Indian Affairs

Bureau of Land Management

Fish and Wildlife Service

National Park Service

U.S. Park Police

Department of Justice

Bureau of Alcohol, Tobacco, Firearms
   and Explosives

Bureau of Prisons

Drug Enforcement Administration

Federal Bureau of Investigation

U.S. Marshals Service

Department of Labor

Office of Labor Racketeering

Department of State

Diplomatic Security Service

Department of Transportation

Federal Air Marshals Program

Department of the Treasury

Internal Revenue Service–Criminal Investigation
   Division

Treasury Inspector General for Tax Enforcement

Department of Veterans Affairs

Office of Security and Law Enforcement

U.S. Postal Service

Postal Inspection Service

Other Offices with Enforcement Personnel

Administrative Office of the U.S. Courts

AMTRAK Police

Bureau of Engraving and Printing Police

Environmental Protection Agency–Criminal
   Investigations Division

Federal Reserve Board

Tennessee Valley Authority

U.S. Capitol Police

U.S. Mint

U.S. Supreme Court Police

Washington, DC, Metropolitan Police
   Department

FIGURE 3–1 Federal Law Enforcement Agencies.

of various federal law enforcement agencies. To make sense out of the new organization, we will build our discussion of these agencies around two categories. We will begin with the law enforcement agencies found within Homeland Security and then discuss those found within the U.S. Department of Justice (also see Figure 3–2 for a summary).

Homeland Security Agencies

The DHS now houses the U.S. Secret Service. The Secret Service used to be located within the Department of the Treasury.

The move to DHS became effective on March 1, 2003. DHS also houses what used to be called the U.S. Customs Service. It is now called Customs and Border Protection. Finally, what used to be called the Immigration and Naturalization Service has basically been split into two separate entities, Immigration and Customs Enforcement and Citizenship and Immigration Services. The first of these is of special interest to us here.

The Secret Service. The Secret Service is perhaps best known for its role in protecting the president and other government

Department of Homeland Security		Justice Department	
The Secret Service	• Provide protection for the president and other government officials and their families • Enforce the suppression of counterfeit currency • Investigate organized crime and money laundering schemes	FBI	• Since 9/11, the FBI continues to be heavily involved in investigating terrorism; however, its primary function is enforcing federal laws
U.S. Customs and Border Protection	• Primarily responsible for controlling and protecting America's orders and ports of entry, including international airports and international shipping ports • Foremost concern is to combat terrorism	U.S. Marshals Service	• The agency's main responsibilities are judicial security and fugitive investigation
Immigration and Customs Enforcement	• Concerned primarily with illegal immigration	Bureau of Alcohol, Tobacco, Etc.	• A tax-collection, enforcement, and regulatory arm of the U.S. Department of Justice • Screens the applications and issues firearms licenses and targets illegal firearms trafficking
		Drug Enforcement Administration	• Primarily responsible for enforcing controlled substance laws and regulations

FIGURE 3–2 Responsibilities of Key Federal Law Enforcement Agencies.

officials and their families. Tourists to the White House also see the Secret Service's uniformed officers protecting the president's residence. These individuals are members of the Secret Service's Uniformed Division. The agency was first created, though, to suppress counterfeit currency (Figure 3–3). From its beginnings in 1865, that has been one of the agency's primary functions. That is why, prior to September 11, the Secret Service was housed in the Treasury Department. The Counterfeit Division, however, is only one of several nonprotection divisions within the Secret Service.

For example, the Financial Crimes Division also investigates organized crime and **money laundering**. The Secret Service's Forensic Services Division assists with these and counterfeit currency investigations. As of this writing, the Secret Service employs several thousand agents in more than 125 offices worldwide.

Customs and Border Protection. The establishment of U.S. **Customs and Border Protection (CBP)** after September 11 combined several elements of various federal agencies that had

previously been separate. The entire U.S. Border Patrol was combined with portions of the U.S. Customs Service, U.S. Immigration, and the Animal and Plant Health Inspection Service. Today, the agency consists of more than 60,000 employees whose mission is, simply, to control and protect America's borders and ports of entry, including international airports and international shipping ports. Because CBP is part of DHS, one of its foremost concerns is combating terrorism. The agency claims dual goals, however: fighting terrorism and "facilitating legitimate trade and travel."[5]

The most well-known component of CBP is the Border Patrol. The agents that make up this division number nearly 21,000. Border Patrol agents, combined with every other official in CBP, make it one of the largest uniformed law enforcement agencies in the United States.[6]

Immigration and Customs Enforcement. Closely connected to but independent of CBP is **Immigration and Customs Enforcement (ICE)**. Whereas CBP is more concerned with border protection and customs checks, ICE focuses on investigation and is

FIGURE 3–3 Brief History of the U.S. Secret Service.
Source: From USSS History, U.S Secret Service.

particularly concerned with illegal immigration. There are three main branches of ICE:

- Homeland Security Investigations
- Enforcement and Removal Operations
- Management and Administration

Of these, the first and second are most interesting to us. The Office of Enforcement and Removal Operations enforces immigration laws by ensuring the departure from the United States of "removable aliens." Homeland Security Operations consists of over 10,000 employees, including 6,700 special agents assigned to 200 cities in the United States and 47 countries around the world.[7]

Prior to October 2009, the Federal Protective Service (FPS) was housed within ICE. It is responsible for securing more than 9,000 federal facilities worldwide. Its approximately 900 FPS officers are now part of the National Protection and Programs Directorate, part of DHS.[8]

Justice Department Agencies

With the exception of the Secret Service, the DHS agencies previously discussed are relatively new and unfamiliar. More accurately stated, their names are new and unfamiliar. The agents and staff who do the work have been around for some time—in one position or another. Some of the Justice Department agencies discussed in this section are, in contrast, quite familiar. Even people with no criminal justice education will recognize agencies like the FBI or the U.S. Marshals Service. Because there is much misinformation about these agencies, we will cover them in some detail. We will also discuss the Bureau of Alcohol, Tobacco, Firearms, and Explosives (ATF) and the DEA.

It should be clear why the Homeland Security agencies we have just discussed are housed where they are: Each has a unique opportunity to target terrorists and otherwise break up terrorist plots. Why are the FBI, DEA, ATF, and USMS in the Justice Department? This placement owes much to the 1870 Act to Establish the Justice Department.[9] As a result of this legislation, the Justice Department was tasked with handling the legal business (especially via prosecutions of criminal activity) of the United States and was given full control over all federal law enforcement. Of course, things have changed since 1870, and there are now law enforcement agencies, bureaus, and officials throughout the federal government. Through thick and thin, the agencies we are about to discuss have remained in the Justice Department for decades, and they will likely remain there for the foreseeable future.

Federal Bureau of Investigation. The **Federal Bureau of Investigation (FBI)** remains in the U.S. Department of Justice, but its mission has changed to some extent as a result of September 11. Its mission is now to "protect and defend the United States against terrorist and foreign intelligence threats, to uphold and enforce the criminal laws of the United States, and to provide leadership and criminal justice services to federal, state, municipal, and international agencies and partners."[10] To be sure, the FBI had a role in terrorism investigation before September 11, but that was not one of the agency's foremost concerns. The September 11 attacks moved terrorism to the front of the line. Indeed, the FBI's "Most Wanted" list now includes known terrorists like Ayman Al-Zawahiri, Osama bin Laden's successor.

Although the FBI is now heavily involved in investigating terrorism, its primary function is enforcing federal laws. It is to the federal government what state police agencies are to states, sheriff's departments are to counties, and municipal police agencies are to cities. It is, in short, the investigative arm of the U.S. Department of Justice. Its statutory authority can be found in Title 28, Section 533, of the U.S. Code. A number of other statutes, including the Congressional Assassination, Kidnapping, and Assault Act (Title 18, Section 351, U.S. Code), also name the FBI as the agency charged with enforcement. Moreover, the FBI has jurisdiction to enforce more than 200 categories of federal law that proscribe all sorts of criminal activity.

As of 2013, the FBI employed nearly 36,000 people, including almost 14,000 special agents and 22,000 support staff.[11] The agency's budget for fiscal year 2012 was approximately $8 billion. FBI officials can be found all around the globe. The headquarters are in Washington, DC, housed in the J. Edgar Hoover Building on Pennsylvania Avenue. But there are 56 field offices located in major cities, approximately 400 resident agencies in smaller cities, and more than 60 international offices. The international offices are called *legal attachés* and are housed in U.S. embassies worldwide. The chain of command and various components of the FBI can be seen in the agency's organizational chart (Figure 3–4).

U.S. Marshals Service. The **U.S. Marshals Service (USMS)** is America's oldest law enforcement agency (Figure 3–5). Marshals were key law enforcement officials in the Old West, but at the turn of the twentieth century, their responsibilities started to shift.

TIMELINE

The Development of the U.S. Marshals Service Over Time

1910	1920	1920–1960
Francisco Madero revolts (on U.S. soil) against Mexican President Porfirio Diaz. U.S. Marshals protect the U.S.-Mexico border against Diaz's supporters, who were attempting to harm Madero.	Eighteenth Amendment ratified, making the manufacture, sale, and transportation of intoxicating beverages illegal. U.S. Marshals were the key enforcement agents.	U.S. Marshals started to perform bailiff functions in U.S. courts.

FIGURE 3–5 The Development of the U.S. Marshals Service Over Time.

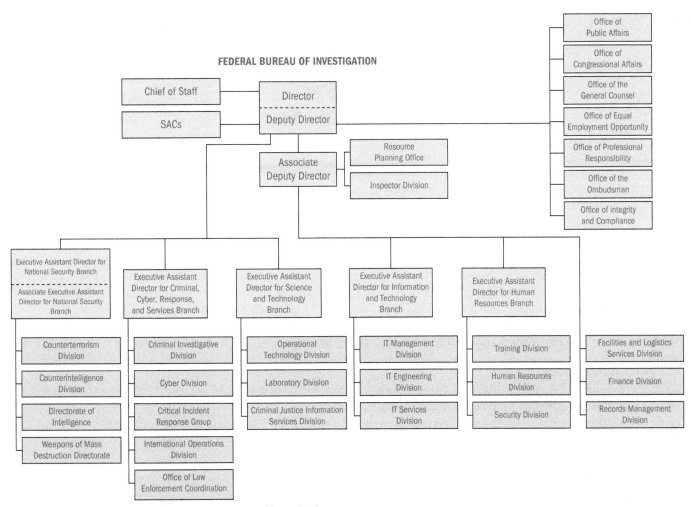

FEDERAL BUREAU OF INVESTIGATION

FIGURE 3–4 **Organizational Chart of the Federal Bureau of Investigation.**
Source: From Organizational Chart, Federal Bureau of Investigation.

Today, there are more than 3,700 deputy marshals throughout the United States. They work for 94 presidentially appointed U.S. marshals (one for each federal district). When staff members are added to the mix, the USMS employs over 5,200 people in more than 200 offices both in the United States and abroad.[12] The agency's main responsibilities are judicial security and fugitive investigation. Marshals protect federal judicial officials, including judges, attorneys, and jurors. The USMS arrests more federal fugitives than all other federal agencies combined. In fiscal year 2016, for instance, marshals arrested more than 33,000 federal fugitives.

Marshals work in task forces alongside local law enforcement agencies to apprehend fugitives. Less familiar are USMS units like the Special Operations Group, which is similar to a local police agency's special weapons and tactics (SWAT) team. As for witness security, the agency has protected, relocated, and given new identities to approximately 8,500 individuals. The USMS has also joined up with customs enforcement and immigration officials to more efficiently deport criminal aliens. Marshals are also responsible for housing more than 50,000 federal detainees. More details about the USMS appear in Figure 3–6.

1971	1979	1980s
Witness Security Program was established and overseen by the U.S. Marshals Service.	U.S. Marshals Service took charge of apprehending federal fugitives.	U.S. Marshals Service assumed responsibility for managing and disposing of assets seized by all federal law enforcement agencies.[11] The federal Asset Forfeiture Program is housed in the U.S. Marshals Service and manages more than $1.2 billion in cash, conveyances, and real property.

U.S. Marshals Service
Justice. Integrity. Service.

U.S. Department of Justice

Fact Sheet

U.S. Marshals Service
2016

- The U.S. Marshals Service is the nation's oldest and most versatile federal law enforcement agency.
- Federal marshals have served the country since 1789, often in unseen but critical ways.
- The Marshals Service occupies a uniquely central position in the federal justice system. It is the enforcement arm of the federal courts, involved in virtually every federal law enforcement initiative.
- Presidentially appointed U.S. marshals direct the activities of 94 districts — one for each federal judicial district.
- Approximately 3,752 deputy U.S. marshals and criminal investigators form the backbone of the agency.
- The duties of the U.S. Marshals Service include protecting the federal judiciary, apprehending federal fugitives, managing and selling seized assets acquired by criminals through illegal activities, housing and transporting federal prisoners and operating the Witness Security Program.
- The agency's headquarters is just across the Potomac River from Washington, D.C.

Judicial Security
- Since 1789, the U.S. Marshals Service has been the enforcement arm of the federal courts and has been responsible for protecting the federal judicial process.
- The agency ensures the safe and secure conduct of judicial proceedings at approximately 440 locations in 94 federal court districts and provides protection for federal judges, other court officials, jurors, the visiting public and prisoners.
- The Threat Management Center provides a national 24/7 response capability to review and respond to threats against the judiciary.
- The Marshals also manage contracted security services inside federal court facilities, which are funded by the judicial branch's court security appropriation. The agency oversees the daily operation and management of security services performed by approximately 5,000 court security officers within the 94 U.S. District Courts and 12 circuits of the U.S. Court of Appeals.

Fugitive Operations
- The U.S. Marshals Service is the federal government's primary agency for fugitive investigations.
- The Marshals have the broadest arrest authority among federal law enforcement agencies.
- The Marshals provide assistance to state and local agencies in locating and apprehending their most violent fugitives.
- The Service arrests 273 fugitives *every day* on average.
- U.S. Marshals task forces combine the efforts of federal, state and local law enforcement agencies to locate and arrest the most dangerous fugitives.
- Task force officers are state and local police officers that receive special deputations with the Marshals. While on a task force, these officers can exercise U.S. Marshals authorities, such as crossing jurisdictional lines.
- U.S. Marshals work with the international law enforcement community to apprehend fugitives abroad as well as to seek foreign fugitives living or residing in the United States.
- The U.S. Marshals "15 Most Wanted" fugitive program draws attention to some of the country's most dangerous and high-profile fugitives. These fugitives tend to be career criminals with histories of violence, and they pose a significant threat to public safety.

Office of Public Affairs
March 11, 2016
www.usmarshals.gov

FIGURE 3-6 **U.S. Marshals Service Responsibilities.**
Source: From Fact Sheet: U.S. Marshals Service, U S Department of Justice.

Asset Forfeiture

▶ The Department of Justice Asset Forfeiture Program is a key component of the federal government's law enforcement efforts to combat major criminal activity by disrupting and dismantling illegal enterprises, depriving criminals of the proceeds of illegal activity, deterring crime and restoring property to victims.

▶ The U.S. Marshals Service plays a critical role in identifying and evaluating assets that represent the proceeds of crime as well as efficiently managing and selling assets seized and forfeited by DOJ.

▶ The Marshals Service manages a wide array of assets, including real estate, commercial businesses, cash, financial instruments, vehicles, jewelry, art, antiques, collectibles, vessels and aircraft.

▶ Proceeds generated from asset sales are used to operate the program, compensate victims and support various law enforcement efforts.

Prisoner Operations

▶ The U.S. Marshals Service is responsible for the custody of federal prisoners beginning at the time of remand and ending when prisoners are acquitted, arrive at a designated Federal Bureau of Prisons facility to serve a sentence or are otherwise ordered released from Marshals custody.

▶ The Marshals Service ensures the safe, humane care of federal prisoners in its custody.

▶ The agency provides housing, medical care and transportation for federal prisoners throughout the U.S. and its territories and brings prisoners to their court-ordered appearances.

▶ All individuals arrested on federal offenses are brought before a U.S. magistrate or U.S. district court judge for their initial court appearances. The court determines if they are to be released on bond or remanded into the custody of the Marshals Service to await trial.

▶ The Marshals Service does not own or operate detention facilities but partners with state and local governments through intergovernmental agreements to house approximately 60 percent of our prisoners. In addition, the agency contracts with private facilities and the Federal Bureau of Prisons for prisoner housing, with both sources housing approximately 20 percent each of Marshals prisoners.

Prisoner Transportation

▶ The U.S. Marshals' Justice Prisoner and Alien Transportation System transports prisoners between judicial districts and correctional institutions in the U.S.

▶ JPATS is one of the largest transporters of prisoners in the world — handling 716 movements per day on average.

▶ JPATS transports prisoners in federal custody between federal judicial districts to hearings, court appearances and detention facilities.

▶ JPATS operates a fleet of aircraft to move prisoners over long distances more economically and with higher security than commercial airlines.

▶ JPATS is the only government-operated, regularly-scheduled passenger airline in the nation.

Witness Security

▶ The U.S. Marshals Service operates the federal Witness Security Program, sometimes referred to as the "Witness Protection Program."

▶ The Witness Security Program provides for the security, safety and health of government witnesses and their authorized family members, whose lives are in danger as a result of their cooperation with the U.S. government.

▶ Witnesses and their families typically get new identities with documentation.

▶ The Witness Security Program has successfully protected an estimated 18,600 participants from intimidation and retribution since the program began in 1971.

Office of Public Affairs
March 11, 2016
www.usmarshals.gov

Bureau of Alcohol, Tobacco, Firearms, and Explosives. Unlike the USMS and the FBI, the **Bureau of Alcohol, Tobacco, Firearms, and Explosives (ATF)** has not been a part of the Justice Department for very long. On January 24, 2003, it was transferred from the Department of the Treasury to Justice, in accordance with the Homeland Security Act. Vestiges of ATF remain in the Treasury Department, however. Specifically, the Treasury Department is still responsible for certain tax and trade functions associated with ATF. The move from the Treasury Department to the Justice Department included a name change for the agency, from simply the Bureau of Alcohol, Tobacco, and Firearms to the Bureau of Alcohol, Tobacco, Firearms, and Explosives. The *ATF* acronym remains in place, however, even though explosives are now one of the agency's key concerns.

ATF is basically a tax-collection, enforcement, and regulatory arm of the U.S. Department of Justice. The Gun Control Act of 1968 required that every manufacturer, importer, and dealer of firearms obtain a Federal Firearms License. ATF screens the applications and issues the licenses. Dealers are required to comply with applicable federal laws and to keep records of all firearms sales, and ATF conducts inspections of gun dealerships to ensure compliance. ATF also targets illegal firearms trafficking.

As for explosives, ATF investigates explosions and cases of arson. It has been particularly involved, for instance, with investigations of arson and bombings at abortion clinics throughout the United States. Finally, the agency regulates distilleries, wineries, breweries, and tobacco manufacturers and retailers. Its National Laboratory Center ensures that the labels on alcoholic beverages do not contain misleading information.

Besides staff, ATF employs both special agents and inspectors. The agents are the criminal investigators and enforcement officials. Inspectors' responsibilities do not include investigation and enforcement per se. Rather, they help people start new businesses, such as firearms dealerships, liquor stores, and the like. Inspectors also visit dealerships and retail establishments to ensure compliance with the law. ATF also employs a number of lawyers, auditors, chemists, and computer experts. The agency is headquartered in Washington, D.C., where the majority of the agency's approximately 5,000 employees work. The remainder staff about 25 field offices located throughout the United States and in a handful of foreign nations.

Drug Enforcement Administration. The **Drug Enforcement Administration (DEA)** is tasked with enforcing controlled substance laws and regulations. The agency brings to justice people and organizations involved in the illegal growing, manufacture, and distribution of controlled substances. To accomplish these tasks, the DEA's primary responsibilities include the following:

- Investigation and preparation for the prosecution of major violators of controlled substance laws operating at interstate and international levels.

- Investigation and preparation for prosecution of criminals and drug gangs who perpetrate violence in our communities and terrorize citizens through fear and intimidation.

- Management of a national drug intelligence program in cooperation with federal, state, local, and foreign officials to collect, analyze, and disseminate strategic and operational drug intelligence information.

- Seizure and forfeiture of assets derived from, traceable to, or intended to be used for illicit drug trafficking.

- Enforcement of the provisions of the Controlled Substances Act as they pertain to the manufacture, distribution, and dispensing of legally produced controlled substances.

- Coordination and cooperation with federal, state, and local law enforcement officials on mutual drug enforcement efforts and enhancement of such efforts through exploitation of potential interstate and international investigations beyond local or limited federal jurisdictions and resources.

- Coordination and cooperation with federal, state, and local agencies and with foreign governments in programs designed to reduce the availability of illicit abuse-type drugs on the U.S. market through nonenforcement methods such as crop eradication, crop substitution, and training of foreign officials.

- Responsibility, under the policy guidance of the secretary of state and U.S. ambassadors, for all programs associated with drug law enforcement counterparts in foreign countries.

- Liaison with the United Nations, Interpol, and other organizations on matters relating to international drug control programs.[13]

The DEA is one of the larger federal law enforcement agencies. It employs over 9,000 people, including over 4,600 special agents. The agency has 221 domestic offices in 21 divisions throughout the United States. It also has 86 offices in 67 foreign countries.[14]

State Agencies

Most state police agencies were initially created for a specific purpose. The Texas Rangers, for example, were established in 1835, even before Texas attained statehood, and functioned largely as a military organization responsible for patrolling the republic's borders. Massachusetts was the second state to create a law enforcement agency. It was developed with the intent of targeting vice crimes. Today, numerous state policing agencies exist. Table 3–1 shows that the number of personnel employed by state law enforcement agencies is significantly less than the number employed in local police departments.

State law enforcement agencies are usually organized according to one of two models. In the first, a **centralized policing model**, the tasks of major criminal investigations are combined with the patrol of state highways. A number of states rely on these centralized agencies, the names of which often include *state police* or *state patrol*. The second model, the **decentralized policing model**, is more like a traditional municipal police agency. Figure 3–7 highlights the key points of the centralized and decentralized state policing models.

TABLE 3-1 | STATE AND LOCAL LAW ENFORCEMENT AGENCIES AND EMPLOYEES IN THE UNITED STATES

Type of Agency	Agencies	Full-Time Employees			Part-Time Employees		
		Total	Sworn	Civilian	Total	Sworn	Civilian
Total	15,388	1,045,360	724,690	320,670	83,499	39,101	44,398
Local police	12,326	604,959	477,317	127,642	57,317	26,745	30,572
Sheriff's office	3,012	351,904	188,952	162,952	25,179	12,356	12,823
Primary state	50	88,497	58,421	30,076	1,003	0	1,003

Source: From *Local Police Departments, 2013: Personnel, Policies, and Practices,* U S Department of Justice.

The Centralized Model

The Pennsylvania Constabulary, known today as the Pennsylvania State Police, was the first modern force to combine the duties of criminal investigations and state highway patrol. It has been described as the first modern state police agency. Michigan, New Jersey, New York, Vermont, and Delaware are a few of the states that patterned their state-level enforcement activities after the centralized Pennsylvania model. Some state agencies give greater emphasis to one or more of the responsibilities than to others. The Washington State Patrol, for example, is well known for its very active presence on state highways, but through its investigative and forensics bureaus, it assists local agencies in solving crimes throughout the state. The California Highway Patrol is also known foremost as a traffic enforcement agency because of its obvious presence on California roads and freeways. A centralized model organizational chart is shown in Figure 3–8.

The Decentralized Model

North Carolina, South Carolina, and Georgia are a few of the many states that employ both a highway patrol and a state bureau of investigation. The names of the respective agencies may vary, however, even though their functions are largely the same. In North Carolina, for example, the two major state-level law enforcement agencies are the North Carolina Highway Patrol and the State Bureau of Investigation. Georgia fields a highway patrol and the Georgia Bureau of Investigation, and South Carolina operates a highway patrol and the South Carolina Law Enforcement Division.

States that use the decentralized model usually have a number of other adjunct state-level law enforcement agencies. North Carolina, for example, has created a State Wildlife Commission with enforcement powers, a Board of Alcohol Beverage Control with additional agents, and a separate Enforcement and Theft Bureau for enforcing certain motor vehicle and theft laws. Other states have merged historically separate agencies into one parent organization. Oregon's State Police is an example. In 1993, the legislature in that state approved a law that merged the Oregon State Fire Marshal's Office, Oregon Emergency Management, the Law Enforcement Data System, and the Oregon Boxing and Wrestling Commission into the State Police.

State Policing Models

Centralized

Decentralized

Key Points

Assist local law enforcement departments in criminal investigations when asked to do so

Operate identification bureaus

Maintain a centralized criminal records repository

Patrol the state's highways

Provide select training for municipal and county officers

Most prevalent in the southern portion and some Midwestern portions of the United States

Draws a clear distinction between traffic enforcement on state highways and other state-level law enforcement functions

FIGURE 3-7 Centralized versus Decentralized State Policing Models.

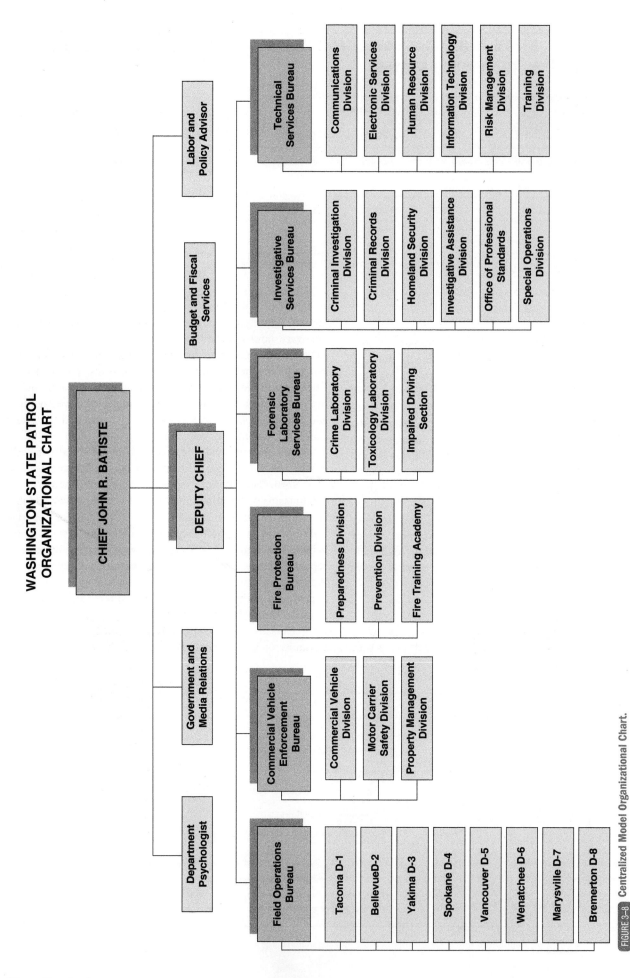

WASHINGTON STATE PATROL ORGANIZATIONAL CHART

CHIEF JOHN R. BATISTE

Department Psychologist

Government and Media Relations

DEPUTY CHIEF

Budget and Fiscal Services

Labor and Policy Advisor

Field Operations Bureau
- Tacoma D-1
- BellevueD-2
- Yakima D-3
- Spokane D-4
- Vancouver D-5
- Wenatchee D-6
- Marysville D-7
- Bremerton D-8

Commercial Vehicle Enforcement Bureau
- Commercial Vehicle Division
- Motor Carrier Safety Division
- Property Management Division

Fire Protection Bureau
- Preparedness Division
- Prevention Division
- Fire Training Academy

Forensic Laboratory Services Bureau
- Crime Laboratory Division
- Toxicology Laboratory Division
- Impaired Driving Section

Investigative Services Bureau
- Criminal Investigation Division
- Criminal Records Division
- Homeland Security Division
- Investigative Assistance Division
- Office of Professional Standards
- Special Operations Division

Technical Services Bureau
- Communications Division
- Electronic Services Division
- Human Resource Division
- Information Technology Division
- Risk Management Division
- Training Division

FIGURE 3–8 Centralized Model Organizational Chart.

Source: From Washington State Patrol Organizational Chart, Washington State Patrol.

Local Agencies

Local police agencies, including city and county agencies, are a third level of law enforcement activity in the United States—the other two being federal and state. The term **local agencies** encompasses a wide variety of organizations. **Municipal police departments** and **sheriff's departments** are most familiar. Other, lesser-known agencies, such as campus police departments and transit police, are also categorized as "local." Even some public schools have a police presence, as do airports, state capitols, medical facilities, state parks, certain prosecutor's offices, and other organizations. The personnel employed in local agencies far outnumber all federal and state law enforcement officials combined.

Some local police departments are highly visible because of their size, huge budgets, innovative programs, and—perhaps above all else—the attention they receive from the press, television producers, and moviemakers. The nation's largest law enforcement agency, the New York City Police Department, for example, has about 45,000 full-time employees, including about 35,000 full-time sworn officers.[15] Likewise, the police departments in Los Angeles, Chicago, Houston, and other large cities employ thousands of sworn officers. These agencies are routinely featured in television shows and "cop" movies, but far greater in number, albeit less visible, are small-town police and county sheriff's departments.

There are approximately 12,326 municipal police departments and 3,012 sheriff's departments in the United States (out of the roughly 20,000 law enforcement agencies in the country).[16] These numbers are only estimates, given the difficulty associated with counting cops, but the point is that there are many of them. Most areas are patrolled and served by officials from one or both of these types of agencies.

Municipal Police

Every incorporated municipality in the country has the authority to create its own police force. Some very small communities hire only one officer to fill the roles of chief, investigator, and night watch—as well as everything in between. The majority of local agencies employ fewer than ten full-time officers, and about 25% (approximately 3,000) employ fewer than five full-time officers.[17]

A few communities contract with private security firms for police services, and still others have no active police force at all, depending instead on local sheriff's departments to deal with law violators. Some cities also contract with county sheriff's departments to provide law enforcement services. Whether a city has a police force or any police presence at all depends on funding as well. Hiring a police officer, putting the person through training, paying benefits, and so on can cost hundreds of thousands of dollars.

City police chiefs are typically appointed by the mayor or selected by the city council. Their departments' jurisdictions are limited by convention to the geographic boundaries of their communities. Municipal police departments are all organized in a fairly similar fashion. Larger agencies have many more personnel and divisions, of course, but they still follow a fairly ordinary bureaucratic structure. Typically, the chief is near the top, followed by deputy chiefs, captains, lieutenants, sergeants, and so forth. The number of ranks varies from one agency to the next. To illustrate, see Figure 3–9. The first presents the

FIGURE 3–9 **Another Example of a Municipal Police Department Organizational Chart.**
Source: From Rockwall Police Department, http://www.rockwallpolice.org/images/OrgChart.jpg (accessed on November 8, 2016).

organizational chart of the Los Angeles Police Department, while the second shows the organization of the McKinney (Texas) Police Department.

Sheriff's Departments

Sheriff's departments are responsible for law enforcement throughout the counties in which they function. Sheriff's deputies mostly patrol the unincorporated areas of the county, or those that lie between municipalities. They do, however, have jurisdiction throughout the county, and in some areas they routinely work alongside municipal police to enforce laws within towns and cities. If a traffic accident occurs within city limits, for example, a sheriff's deputy may appear on the scene first and take control.

Sheriff's departments are also generally responsible for serving court papers, including civil summonses, and for maintaining security within state courtrooms. They run county jails and are responsible for more detainees awaiting trial than any other type of law enforcement department in the country. Sheriff's departments remain strong across most of the country, although in parts of New England, deputies mostly function as court agents with limited law enforcement duties.

Sheriffs are usually elected officials,[18] unlike city police chiefs. This creates a somewhat different set of priorities for them. Police chiefs answer to city officials, but sheriffs answer to voters. If the voters are displeased with a sheriff's performance, come election time they can move a new sheriff into office.

In most jurisdictions, not just anyone can run for the position of sheriff. Ohio, for example, requires not only past law enforcement experience but experience in law enforcement administration as well.[19] The law ensures that all unqualified candidates are screened out in advance of elections.

▶ The Organization of Law Enforcement Agencies

An **organization** can be defined as "a consciously coordinated social entity, with a relatively identifiable boundary, that functions on a relatively continuous basis to achieve a common goal or set of goals."[20] To be "consciously coordinated" means that someone (or perhaps a group of people) is managing the organization. The notion of "social entity" refers to the fact that organizations are groups of people. Finally, "identifiable boundary" refers to an organization's service population. By this definition, police departments are organizations, as are schools, businesses, and nonprofit groups. However, police departments—and nearly all law enforcement agencies in general—differ from other types of organizations in a number of key respects.

How Police Departments Differ from Other Organizations

Police organizations differ from other types of organizations, most obviously because usually only the police have both legitimate arrest power and authority to use force. The National Guard has been activated in various places and from time to

time has been given arrest authority, such as in the wake of Hurricane Katrina. The Posse Comitatus Act prohibits the military from engaging

in domestic law enforcement functions, but if Congress so allows, the act can be circumvented. In any case, the National Guard and the military are still connected with the government, not unlike the typical police agency. Perhaps it is useful, then, to distinguish between government and civilian law enforcement organizations.

The closest parallel civilian organization to the modern law enforcement agency is a private security company. Such companies may look like police departments, but most private security officials are not sanctioned to use force in the course of their duties, nor are they authorized to make arrests in the traditional sense. In either case, they have to rely on sworn law enforcement officials to take over at a certain point.

Police organizations differ from other organizations in more than just arrest powers and use of force:

1. Their status as *public* agencies makes them quite distinct from the realm of private business.[21]

2. Unlike private organizations, they exist within a political environment, as do other public organizations, such as prosecutor's offices and universities.

3. They work in the public eye and must follow all the rules applicable to government agencies.

4. They are not run for profit, as are private security agencies and some private prisons.

5. They are often hamstrung by bureaucratic rules and regulations that can stifle creativity and flexibility.

Like most public agencies, police organizations have limited resources. They often have to pursue grants and other sources of "soft money" (i.e., funding apart from their year-to-year budgets) just to make ends meet. Many private companies have no shortage of cash in the bank, and when they don't have the money they need, they can take out loans. This is not a luxury available to public-sector organizations, although parent governments can borrow typically through the issuance of bonds. Finally, whereas many businesses answer to the shareholders, police organizations have to answer to the public. They may not have to answer *directly* to the public, but as we have already seen, some law enforcement executives (such as sheriffs) do answer to the voters.

Law enforcement organizations also differ from other types of public and private organizations because the people who work in them generally fall into one of two categories: staff and line officials. A distinct "chain of command" is usually established in most law enforcement agencies.

Staff versus Line Duties

Staff (**nonsworn personnel**) assist line officials (**sworn personnel**). In some organizations, there are as many or more staff than line personnel. Secretaries and administrative assistants, human resources personnel, crime analysts, 911 dispatchers, record keepers, and a host of other functional specialists tend to fall into this category. The chief in most large agencies has a secretary or an office manager. This person is usually non-sworn. In very large agencies, the office manager may have additional assistants under his or her command. Likewise, crime analysts are often nonsworn, but the units they work in tend to be headed by sworn officials, such as sergeants. By contrast, sworn personnel consist of all the commissioned peace officers within the organization, from the chief or sheriff all the way down to the frontline officers or deputies. Small rural police agencies are not always organized in this fashion, but the typical agency has at least some mix of staff and sworn personnel. This is not the case in most other public agencies.

Chain of Command

Every organization, public or private, follows a chain of command. Private companies tend to have a chief executive officer, a president, or both at the helm. Schools have principals. Most prosecutor's offices are run by an elected district attorney. In this respect, police agencies, sheriff's departments, and other law enforcement agencies are no different; someone is in charge. Where law enforcement agencies part ways with other organizations, though, is in the **chain of command**.

The functional structure of a command chain incorporates the notion of **span of control**, which refers to the number of subordinates supervised by one person. The bigger the organization and the higher up the ladder a person ascends, the greater that person's span of control.

Command structures differ from one police agency to the next, but they share much in common with the military command structure (see Figure 3–10). This also makes law

enforcement agencies different from most other organizations. While this command structure has its advantages, it is also significantly limited, as we will see shortly.

Traditional and Contemporary Organization

The traditional approach to police organization hails from Sir Robert Peel's recommendation that agencies follow the military model. One of the first principles Peel espoused was that "the police must be stable, efficient, and organized along military lines."[22] As we just saw, Peel's legacy lives on. But because few police organizations follow the military model in every detail, they are often said to be **quasi-military** in structure. The leaders of law enforcement agencies are not called generals, for instance. Also, there tend to be fewer distinct ranks in the typical police organization than in the military. Even so, there is much similarity to the military model in terms of how most police agencies are organized.

Classical Organizational Theory

Peel's advocacy of the military model for policing was echoed by O. W. Wilson and other influential figures in early American policing. But what is the logic for this model of organization? What makes the quasi-military model so desirable? To answer these questions, we need to look beyond policing to the realm of organizational theory—particularly to the legacy of two key individuals, **Frederick W. Taylor** and **Max Weber**.

Taylor studied organizations for the purpose of improving worker productivity. During his time, people often worked to the point of exhaustion. People were assigned tasks they were unfamiliar with or were incapable of performing adequately. In a word, they worked ineffectively. Taylor's contribution was in the area of increasing worker productivity through careful attention to how work was allocated and who performed what functions. Weber, on the other hand, studied the features of successful organizations. Together, Weber and Taylor ushered in an era of scientific management. They believed that scientific principles should be applied to workplaces so that workers could be as productive as possible with the least amount of effort. Perhaps above all else, Taylor stressed the role of managers in ensuring a smooth-running workplace.

Max Weber is widely recognized as one of the first people to study **bureaucracy**. He did not *invent* bureaucracy, nor is he responsible for all the negative connotations the term takes on today. But Weber did identify five principles that he suggested are characteristic of an effective bureaucratic organization.[23] These principles can be applied to law enforcement:

1. *Well-defined hierarchy of authority.* In every traditional police organization, superior–subordinate relationships are based on authority, from the patrol officer up to the chief. Each person at a higher position or rank has more authority than do his or her subordinates.

2. *Specialization.* Every person's job is broken into precise, routine, and well-defined tasks. By dividing tasks among several work groups, the organization becomes more efficient.

Military (Army/Marines/Air Force) | **Police Force**

General — Chief of Police
Lieutenant General — Assistant Chief
Major General — Deputy Chief
Brigadier General — Commander
Colonel
Lieutenant Colonel
Major
Captain — Captain
Lieutenant — Lieutenant

FIGURE 3–10 **Chain of Command: Military versus Civilian Police.**

3. *Formalization.* There must be a well-established system of rules and regulations detailing workers' duties to ensure uniformity and reduce discretion.

4. *Impersonality of management.* Decisions should be made without regard to personalities or individuals. Decision making should be based on the goals and objectives of the agency.

5. *Personnel decisions based on merit.* Positions should be filled and promotions made according to merit—that is, based on the experience and qualifications of the individual. The agency must strive to put the best qualified individuals in each position.

Does this sound like the typical police agency? The answer is most certainly yes. Every agency today has clearly defined levels of authority, specialization, and formalization. Authority is accomplished via the rank structure. Specialization is evident not just in levels of supervision (the vertical dimension) but also within the agency's various divisions (the horizontal dimension). These two features can be seen in the organizational charts presented earlier in this chapter. Concerning formalization, every law enforcement agency has a policy manual that employees must follow. Also, merit-based personnel decisions are standard in modern police agencies.

Contemporary Organizational Theory

The classical model of police organization has its limitations. Critics feel that the classical approach is, in a word, "mechanistic."[24]

Think About It...

Private Security Some researchers have looked at the problems of car theft and burglary in parking garages, especially when there is little monitoring of the vehicles temporarily stored there. These researchers have focused on whether the addition of guards, security attendants, and closed-circuit television reduces these crimes. Studies show that guards and security attendants do deter criminals, but the costs of employing attendants or security guards may raise parking fees. Concerning the deterrent effect of patrol in general, the evidence is mixed. One review found that police presence was significantly associated with reduced crime in only 10 of 36 studies. Will private security become more important as time goes on? Why? What strengths does private security have that ordinary policing does not?

David Stuart/Shutterstock

A contrasting view of organizations is that they are "organic," like living, breathing entities made up of real human beings. The mechanistic view of organizations separates the people element from the command structure. The organic view does the opposite; it allows employees greater input and responsibility in decision making, especially at the lower levels. Applying this thinking to policing, an organic organizational structure would elevate the status of the line officers by giving them some control over the organization's mission, day-to-day operations, and key decisions. Advocates believe that this is a more flexible and adaptive method of organization.[25]

Participatory management is an important concept in police management circles today. It refers to a form of leadership that allows subordinates to participate in decision making and planning, especially with regard to the manner in which their own units are operated. Related to this is the use of **quality circles**, groups of qualified officers from all ranks who work together (often around one table) to solve organizational problems.

Contingency theory recognizes that there are often different types of tasks within a single organization: repetitive and nonrepetitive tasks. The former calls for standardization and control, while the latter calls for flexibility and participatory management. How is this manifested in the typical police agency? On the one hand, consider the traffic enforcement division. Its tasks are repetitive, and it can easily be managed via a traditional organizational model; there is little need for flexibility in writing tickets. On the other hand, a problem-solving unit within the same agency may need to be structured to allow team members to be creative and do what it takes within the limits of the law to effectively target certain crimes. This is the very definition of contingency theory; organizational strategies are contingent on the tasks at hand.

The final approach to organizational style considered in this chapter is the **systems perspective**, which is rooted in biology. This view posits that organizations are living organisms that strive for a state of equilibrium, or balance, and that affect or are affected by their environment.[26] The last element is most telling. Today, it is very clear that police organizations do not operate in a vacuum. They affect their surroundings through officers' actions and inactions. They are also affected by the environment (i.e., the media, public opinion, relationships with other government officials, relationships with private business, and so on). They are, to use some organizational terminology, "open systems." Systems theory differs from the other approaches in its concern with organizational parts—and their relationships to one another—as more than the whole being. The systems view of organizational design takes the same approach—making sure all the pieces of the whole work together to ensure survival.

▶ *Private Policing and Security*

The police are not the only ones in the business of crime control and prevention. Public police (municipal police officers, sheriff's deputies, state troopers, and so on) work alongside scores of private police and security officials.[27] People employed as private police officers or security personnel outnumber public police officers by three to one.[28] The number of companies engaged in providing private police or security services has been estimated at more than 10,000.[29] They employ more than 500,000 personnel, including more than 10,000 store detectives, nearly 100,000 managers and staff, and nearly 400,000 security officers.[30]

The contract security industry (consisting of companies that enter into contracts with businesses to provide security) estimated in 1999 that it employed 719,000 uniformed personnel.[31] Other estimates place the number of people involved in either private policing or security at more than 2 million.[32] Despite their numbers, private police and security professionals have largely escaped the notice of police scholars.[33]

LEARNING OUTCOMES 3 Summarize the trends and issues associated with private policing.

Private Security versus Private Policing

Security guards are highly visible to the public. They work in retail establishments, hotels, gated communities, and sports venues, to name just a few locations. These guards come immediately to mind when we consider private policing, but they represent the proverbial tip of the iceberg. In this regard, it is useful to distinguish between **private security** and **private policing**. According to Elizabeth Joh, a law professor at the University of California, Davis, *private security* refers to the industry that provides "for-profit security products and services, which include three broad categories: the provision of guards, equipment, and investigation or consulting services."[34] Home owners who buy a home security system do so from the private security industry. *Private policing*, on the other hand, refers to "the acquisition and use of these products and services, as well as the application of specialized knowledge in areas like crime control, investigation, and risk management."[35] In other words, private police are supplied by the private security industry.

Our concern here is not with the private security industry per se. Rather, our interest is in private policing's provision of security, crime prevention, and crime-control functions. Whether we call it *security* or *policing* is not particularly important, but for consistency's sake, we will use the term *private policing* from here on out, knowing that private policing owes its livelihood to the private security industry. Private police could be trained personnel supplied by the private security industry or ordinary people—trained in the trade or not—who are not affiliated with any known security company but are hired to provide security services.

Private Policing versus Public Policing

One of the hallmarks of public policing is that it is funded by tax dollars. One distinguishing feature of private policing, on the other hand, is its "client-driven mandate."[36] Client-driven relationships in the world of public policing are usually regarded as unethical. For example, most people regard it as inappropriate for a store owner to offer perks (such as free merchandise or discounts) to a city police officer. An officer who receives such benefits from a citizen may be more inclined to favor that person with additional security or to ignore minor

criminal offenses. Stepping over into the private policing realm, though, few people would object to a store owner who hires a private police officer for additional protection.

Private Policing Methods

Private policing can also be distinguished from public policing by its methods. South African criminologist Clifford Shearing has identified four such methods.[37] First, private police personnel focus largely on loss control and prevention. Retail security guards, for instance, are in the business of making sure their clients' products are not stolen or embezzled. The term *loss prevention* can encompass much more than lost merchandise. Some private police focus on the prevention of accidents and costly mistakes. According to Joh, "The emphasis on loss also means that private police are disengaged from the moral underpinnings of the criminal law; they focus instead on property and asset protection."[38] "Moral underpinnings" refers to the what's right/what's wrong aspect of the laws that public police are charged with enforcing. Whereas public police target situations deemed by constituents and law-making bodies to be problems, private police are not limited by these issues; they do what their clients want without regard to moral issues.

The second main private policing method is prevention: "Private police stress preventive means over detection and apprehension to control crime and disorder."[39] Their concern is not so much with the punishment of wrongdoers. Rather, it is with preventing the disruption of legitimate business activities. It is ironic, in fact, that retailers often place signs throughout their establishments warning that "shoplifters will be prosecuted to the fullest extent of the law." For one thing, retailers have limited say over whether someone will be charged with theft; prosecutors make this decision. In addition, retailers' concern with prosecution is typically incidental to their more immediate concern for making sure the business doesn't lose money.

That is why private police rely on surveillance. Casino owners, for example, go to great pains to keep an eye on things and make sure that dishonest gamblers do not line their pockets at the casino's expense.

Private policing is also distinguished from public policing by its focus on "private justice" rather than public justice. As Joh points out, private security provides a functional alternative to the public police and the criminal justice system.[40] Consider, for example, employee theft from a retail store. What would the store's owner rather do—go to the trouble of prosecuting the employee or simply fire the person? The latter choice would be the easiest. What about the gambler who counts cards in a blackjack game and gets caught? He or she would sooner be banned from the casino than charged with any criminal violation. "In a private justice system," Joh says, "the resolution of problems is left to the control and discretion of private police and their clients, who may see some incidents as unworthy of the lost time and resources necessary to assist in a public prosecution."[41] Indeed, some businesses are willing to absorb a certain amount of loss rather than incurring the costs of pursuing formal criminal charges against a wrongdoer.

The fourth distinguishing feature of private policing is a concern with private rather than public property. Generally, public police do not have the luxury of entering private places without proper cause or an invitation. At the opposite extreme, private police generally don't care what happens in public spaces. Their job is, for the most part, protecting private property. Often they work in quasi-public places, such as privately owned malls that are open to the public, but their loyalties lie with the businesses that employ them, not the general public.

For a summary of the differences between private and public policing, see Figure 3–11.

Controversies in Private Policing

Private security is controversial in a number of respects. First, it is important to note that private security is but one part of a larger privatization movement in criminal justice.[42] Private prisons, for instance, have emerged to provide a presumably

Private	Public
Focus on loss prevention	Focus on right vs. wrong and enforcing public policy
Focus on prevention, not punishment	Focus on detection, apprehension, and punishment
Private justice—punishment up to discretion of business	Public justice—punishment depends on the law
Concerned with protection of private property and clients	Concerned with protection of public property and the general public

FIGURE 3–11 **Private versus Public Policing.**

cost-effective alternative to state-run correctional facilities. Critics charge that privatization turns criminal justice into a for-profit venture, which could translate into detrimental cost-cutting measures. Second, some people have charged that private policing is poised to replace public policing. Nothing could be further from the truth, however. As Sklansky puts it, "Private policing poses no risk of supplanting public law enforcement entirely, at least not in our lifetime, and it is far from clear to what extent the growing numbers of private security employees are actually performing functions previously carried out by public officers."[43]

Perhaps the most significant controversy associated with private policing deals with constitutional concerns. In general, because private police are nongovernmental, they are not bound by the same legal requirements as public police. As Sklansky notes,

> Perhaps the most basic and invariable principle of criminal procedure is that constitutional restrictions on policing—the limitations imposed by the Fourth, Fifth, and Sixth Amendments, the prophylactic rules of evidentiary exclusion constructed to reinforce those limitations, and the analogous rules of state constitutional law—apply only to investigative action attributable to the government.[44]

The U.S. Supreme Court has yet to tackle the issue of private policing head-on. It decided one case in 1964 involving an amusement park security guard who had been "deputized" by the county sheriff,[45] ruling that the security guard was a state official and thus was bound by the same legal constraints as public police officers. Beyond that case, the Supreme Court has had little to say. State courts, however, have been much more vocal, and most of them have refused to treat private police as state actors. For example, private police have been exempted from the Fourth Amendment,[46] the *Miranda* rule,[47] and entrapment restrictions.[48] We will look at these issues from a public policing perspective in Chapter 10.

It would be a mistake to construe these decisions as granting unbridled power to private police. It is true that some private police do have more power than ordinary citizens, and deputizing private police officers gives them—briefly—the same authority as public police. Additionally, many private police officers are off-duty public police officers. Yet most private police do not enjoy the same legal powers as public police: "Many private security guards . . . possess no greater legal capabilities than do ordinary citizens to forcibly detain persons who are suspected of or have in fact committed a crime."[49] In many states, ordinary citizens can arrest people for misdemeanors committed in their presence and for felonies that they have probable cause to believe were committed.[50]

Joe Arpaio, "America's Toughest Sheriff"

Joe Arpaio, the controversial sheriff of Maricopa County, Arizona, bills himself as "the world's toughest sheriff." He is well known for his desert jail's "tent city," where inmates sometimes live outside in 110-degree heat. Arpaio is also famous for the pink underwear that he has required male inmates to wear (and that has been sold to them to raise revenue for the county) and for the chain gangs that he reinstituted. On one occasion, Arpaio even had his inmates march down public streets wearing only their pink underwear.

In 2013, the 9th Circuit Court of Appeals weighed in on the sheriff's pink underwear policy, saying that it appeared to be "punishment without legal justification," and noted that it's fair to infer that the selection of pink as the underwear color was meant to symbolize the loss of prisoners' masculinity.[51]

The pink underwear policy became the basis of a recent civil rights lawsuit. In 2001, Eric Vogel was detained as part of a burglary investigation and subsequently arrested for assaulting an officer. After being booked in the Phoenix Jail, Vogel was placed on a psychiatric hold pursuant to a diagnosis that he was paranoid and psychotic. When he was forced to "dress out," which meant he had to change into a prison uniform and pink underwear, he refused. When he was forcibly changed, he yelled that he was being raped.

Following Vogel's release, he was involved in a minor car accident with his mother. Police were summoned. Fearing a return to the Phoenix Jail, Vogel fled the scene and attempted to walk four or five miles to his home. The next day, he died of cardiac arrhythmia. His family sued Sheriff Arpaio and Maricopa County, claiming, in part, that the pink underwear policy caused Vogel's death. In 2014, the suit was settled when Maricopa County commissioners agreed to pay $240,000 to Vogel's estate.

Finally, in 2015, Arpaio called for expansion of "mall posses,"—a concept that uses legally armed citizens who volunteer to patrol shopping malls during the holiday season. In 2015, Arpaio's local holiday posse mall patrol used 383 volunteer

A. T. Willett/Alamy Stock Photo

posse members and provided a total of 2,244 man hours of patrol. Posse members assisted other law enforcement agencies in 133 incidents, with the most notable being medical assistance calls and shoplifter apprehension.

Sheriff Arpaio represents an "extreme case" in the world of law enforcement executives—a phrase that he applied to himself in a book he coauthored with Len Sherman, *America's Toughest Sheriff: How We Can Win the War against Crime*. Arpaio has been reelected to a sixth term, although in 2016, federal judge G. Murray Snow asked the U.S. Attorney's Office to file criminal contempt charges against the sheriff due to his alleged failure to follow the judge's instructions in a case of racial profiling.[52]

The case featured here raises a number of important questions:

1. Did a due process violation occur in Vogel's case?
2. Are Sheriff Arpaio's policies outrageous?
3. Would an appointed city police chief be allowed to adopt policies similar to Arpaio's?

Describe the different law enforcement agencies in America.

The roughly 20,000 law enforcement agencies in the United States are found at the federal, state, and local levels. Most federal law enforcement agencies are located in the Department of Homeland Security and the Department of Justice. Most state police agencies follow either a centralized or a decentralized model. Local law enforcement agencies consist mostly of municipal police departments and county sheriff's offices. Other agencies operate at the local level, but they are the exception.

1. Identify and describe a number of key federal law enforcement agencies and explain their roles.

2. What two models of state law enforcement can be identified? What are the differences between them?

Homeland Security Act of 2002 U.S. legislation enacted after the terrorist attacks of September 11, 2001, that created the cabinet-level Department of Homeland Security.

money laundering The process by which criminals or criminal organizations seek to disguise the illicit nature of their proceeds by introducing them into the stream of legitimate commerce and finance.

Customs and Border Protection (CBP) The U.S. law enforcement agency, established after the terrorist attacks on September 11, 2001, that combined the entire U.S. Border Patrol with portions of the U.S. Customs Service, U.S. Immigration, and the Animal and Plant Health Inspection Service. CBP was given the mission of controlling and protecting America's borders and ports of entry, including international airports and international shipping ports.

Immigration and Customs Enforcement (ICE) The largest investigative component of the federal Department of Homeland Security. ICE focuses specifically on illegal immigration.

Federal Bureau of Investigation (FBI) The investigative arm of the U.S. Department of Justice.

U.S. Marshals Service (USMS) The oldest American law enforcement agency. Its mission includes judicial security and fugitive investigation and apprehension.

Bureau of Alcohol, Tobacco, Firearms, and Explosives (ATF) A tax-collection, enforcement, and regulatory arm of the U.S. Department of Justice.

Drug Enforcement Administration (DEA) The U.S. law enforcement agency tasked with enforcing controlled-substance laws and regulations.

centralized policing model The less prevalent model of state police organization, in which the tasks of major criminal investigations are combined with the patrol of state highways.

decentralized policing model A model of policing in which central governments exercise relatively few police powers and in which the majority of police services are provided by separate local and regional agencies.

local agency One of the three levels of law enforcement activity in the United States—the other two being state and federal—that encompasses organizations like municipal police departments, sheriff's departments, and other lesser-known agencies (including campus police, transit police, and specialized agencies at public schools, airports, state capitols, medical facilities, state parks, certain prosecutors' offices, and others). Together, the personnel in these local agencies far outnumber all state and federal law enforcement officials combined.

municipal police department One of the types of local law enforcement agencies in the United States. Specifically, the law enforcement agency that serves a municipality.

sheriff's department One of the types of local law enforcement agencies in the United States. Specifically, the law enforcement agency that serves a county or parish.

Describe how law enforcement organizations differ from other types of organizations.

Law enforcement organizations differ from other organizations in several respects, but there are two *key* differences: Law enforcement organizations have line and staff personnel, and most follow a quasi-military command structure. The quasi-military organizational model is not without its faults, which led to the emergence in police agencies of modern organizational theories and designs (e.g., contingency theories).

1. How do police organizations differ from other types of organizations?

2. What does it mean to say that law enforcement organizations follow a quasi-military model?

3. What are the benefits as well as the disadvantages of a quasi-military model of organization for law enforcement agencies?

organization A group in which individuals work together to accomplish specified tasks or goals.

nonsworn personnel Support staff members of a law enforcement agency who are not empowered to make arrests.

sworn personnel Members of a law enforcement agency who are empowered to make arrests.

chain of command The supervisory channel within a law enforcement organization.

span of control The number of subordinates supervised by one person.

quasi-military An organizational structure that follows the military model to some extent, but with subtle differences.

Frederick W. Taylor (1856–1915) A classical organizational theorist who posited that worker productivity could be increased through careful attention to how work was allocated and who performed what functions.

Max Weber (1864–1920) A classical organizational theorist, widely acknowledged as the father of bureaucracy, who identified five principles that he suggested are characteristic of an effective bureaucratic organization.

bureaucracy The administrative structure of a large or complex organization, typically employing task-specialized bureaus or departments.

participatory management A form of leadership that allows subordinates to participate in decision making and planning, especially with regard to the manner in which their own units are operated.

quality circle A group of qualified employees from all ranks who work together, often around one table, to solve organizational problems.

contingency theory A management theory that recognizes that there are often different types of tasks within a single organization, including repetitive tasks that call for standardization and control and nonrepetitive tasks that call for flexibility and participatory management.

systems perspective A view of organizational style, rooted in biology, that posits that organizations are living organisms that strive for a state of equilibrium, or balance, and that affect or are affected by their environment.

LEARNING OUTCOMES 3

Summarize the trends and issues associated with private policing.

Private police officers outnumber sworn public police officers by roughly three to one. Private police are hired to serve a client's interests, and thus their priorities differ from those of public police. The most significant controversy in private policing is whether private police can be regarded as governmental actors for purposes of the law. The integration of private and public policing resources continues to be an ongoing challenge for public safety managers everywhere.

1. What is the relationship between public police departments and private security agencies?

2. How can public police departments and private security agencies benefit one another?

private security The industry that provides for-profit security products and services, which include three broad categories: the provision of guards, equipment, and investigative or consulting services.

private policing The acquisition and use of security products and services, as well as the application of specialized knowledge in areas like crime control, investigation, and risk management, by nonsworn personnel.

References

1 Aaron Chalfin and Justin McCrary, "Are U.S. cities underpoliced? Theory and evidence," National Bureau of Economic Research, Working Paper No. 18815, May 30, 2013.

2 E. R. Maguire et al., "Counting cops: Estimating the number of police departments and police officers in the USA," *Policing: An International Journal of Police Strategies and Management*, vol. 21 (1998), p. 109.

3 Ibid.

4 We divided 314 million (there are approximately this many people in the United States as of this writing) by 680,000 and rounded up.

5 U.S. Customs and Border Protection, *Vision and strategy, 2020*, p. 6, http://www.cbp.gov/sites/default/files/documents/CBP-Vision-Strategy-2020.pdf (accessed December 7, 2015).

6 U.S. Customs and Border Protection, "On a typical date in fiscal year 2014, CBP . . . ," http://www.cbp.gov/newsroom/stats/typical-day-fy2014 (accessed December 7, 2015).

7 See https://www.ice.gov/hsi (accessed December 7, 2015).

8 See www.dhs.gov/about-national-protection-and-programs-directorate (accessed December 7, 2015).

9 16 Stat. 162.

10 Federal Bureau of Investigation, "Quick facts," www.fbi.gov/about-us/quick-facts (accessed December 7, 2015).

11 Ibid.

12 http://www.usmarshals.gov/duties/factsheets/facts.pdf (accessed August 25, 2016).

13 See www.justice.gov/dea/about/mission.shtml (accessed December 7, 2015).

14 See http://www.dea.gov/docs/factsheet.pdf (accessed December 7, 2015).

15 New York City Police Department website, www.nyc.gov/html/nypd/html/faq/faq_police.shtml#1 (accessed December 7, 2015).

16 B. A. Reaves, *Local police departments, 2013: Personnel, policies, and practices* (Washington, DC: Bureau of Justice Statistics, 2015). These are most recent figures available as of this writing (December 7, 2015).

17 Ibid.

18 This is not the case in every state.

19 Ohio Revised Code, Section 3313.616 (2006).

20 S. P. Robbins, *Organization theory: Structure, design, and applications* (Englewood Cliffs, NJ: Prentice Hall, 1990).

21 H. G. Rainey, *Understanding the managing of public organizations* (San Francisco: Jossey-Bass, 1991).

22 A. Germann, F. Day, and R. Gallati, *Introduction to law enforcement and criminal justice* (Springfield, IL: Charles C. Thomas, 1978).

23 M. Weber, "Bureaucracy," in *Organizations*, vol. 1, ed. J. Litterer, pp. 29–31 (New York: Wiley, 1969).

24 T. Burns and G. Stalker, *The management of innovation* (London: Tavistock, 1961).

25 J. Kuykendall and R. Roberg, *Police administration* (Los Angeles: Roxbury, 1997).

26 L. Bertalanffy, "General systems theory: A new approach to the unity of science," *Human Biology*, vol. 23 (1951), pp. 302–61.

27 See, e.g., M. K. Nalla and C. G. Heraux, "Assessing the goals and functions of private police," *Journal of Criminal Justice*, vol. 31 (2003), pp. 237–47.

28 E. Joh, "The paradox of private policing," *Journal of Criminal Law and Criminology*, vol. 95 (2004), pp. 49–131.

29 R. Behar, "Thugs in uniform," *Time*, March 9, 1992, p. 44.

30 W. C. Cunningham and J. J. Strauchs, "Security industry trends: 1993 and beyond," *Security Management*, vol. 36 (1992), pp. 27–30, 32, 34–36.

31 Freedonia Group, *Private security services—Demand and sales forecasts, market share, market size, market leaders* (Cleveland, OH: Freedonia Group, 2015).

32 Cunningham and Strauchs, "Security industry trends," pp. 27–30, 32, 34–36.

33 ASIS International, *The United States security industry: Size and scope, trends, and data* (Alexandria, VA: ASIS International, 2013).

34 Joh, "The paradox of private policing," p. 67.

35 Ibid.

36 Ibid., p. 62.

37 C. D. Shearing and P. Stenning, "Modern private security: Its growth and implications," in *Crime and justice: A review of research*, ed. M. Tonry, pp. 193–246 (Chicago: University of Chicago Press, 1981). See also C. D. Shearing and P. C. Stenning, *Private policing* (Newbury Park, CA: Sage, 1987).

38 Joh, "The paradox of private policing," p. 62.

39 Shearing and Stenning, "Modern private security."

40 Joh, "The paradox of private policing," p. 62.

41 Ibid., p. 63.

42 See, e.g., D. Shichor and M. J. Gilbert, eds., *Privatization in criminal justice: Past, present, and future* (Dayton, OH: Lexis-Nexis, 2001).

43 D. A. Sklansky, "The private police," *UCLA Law* Review, vol. 46 (1999), p. 1166.

44 Ibid., pp. 1230–31.

45 *Griffin* v. *Maryland*, 378 U.S. 130 (1964).

46 See, e.g., *Wade* v. *Byles*, 83 F.3d 902 (7th Cir. 1996); *Gallagher* v. *Neil Young Freedom Concert*, 49 F.3d 1442 (10th Cir. 1995); *United States* v. *Francoeur*, 547 F.2d 891 (5th Cir. 1977); *People* v. *Taylor*, 271 Cal. Rptr. 785 (Ct. App. 1990); *United States* v. *Lima*, 424 A.2d 113 (D.C. 1980) (en banc); *People* v. *Toliver*, 377 N.E.2d 207 (Ill. App. Ct. 1978); *People* v. *Holloway*, 267 N.W.2d 454 (Mich. Ct. App. 1978); *State* v. *Buswell*, 460 N.W.2d 614 (Minn. 1990).

47 See, e.g., *United States* v. *Antonelli*, 434 F.2d 335 (2d Cir. 1970); *City of Grand Rapids* v. *Impens*, 327 N.W.2d 278 (Mich. 1982).

48 See, e.g., *United States* v. *Cruz*, 783 F.2d 1470, 1473 (9th Cir. 1986); *State* v. *Garcia*, 528 So. 2d 76 (Fla. Dist. Ct. App. 1988); *Perez* v. *State*, 517 So. 2d 106 (Fla. Dist. Ct. App. 1987); *People* v. *Gorski*, 494 N.E.2d 246 (Ill. App. Ct. 1986); *State* v. *Farmer*, 510 P.2d 180 (Kan. 1973); *Commonwealth* v. *Lindenmuth*, 554 A.2d 62 (Pa. Super. Ct. 1989).

49 Joh, "The paradox of private policing," p. 64.

50 See, e.g., J. Hall, "Legal and social aspects of arrest without a warrant," *Harvard Law Review*, vol. 49 (1935), p. 566.

51 "Arpaio loses appeal on pink-underwear case," Jacques Billeaud, Associated Press, March 4, 2013.

52 Kimberly Hutcherson, "Judge seeks criminal contempt charges against Sheriff Joe Arpaio," CNN, August 20, 2016, http://www.cnn.com/2016/08/20/us/arpaio-criminal-contempt-charges-referral/index.html (accessed September 1, 2016).

4

Becoming a Cop

1 Outline the hiring process, including testing, interviewing, and various screening procedures.

2 Recount academy and field training elements of police hiring.

3 Summarize the issues faced by female and minority police officers.

4 Summarize the issues police officers confront on the job.

DRUG DECRIMINALIZATION AND POLICE HIRING

Not long ago, a personal history of drug use—including that of marijuana—would automatically disqualify an applicant for a law enforcement position. Now, however, as states (and perhaps the federal government) move to decriminalize possession and use of small amounts of cannabis for private personal recreational use, the traditional hiring practices of police departments are being challenged. One 2015 California survey, for example, found that many police departments in that state have begun to change hiring standards by discounting prior marijuana use.[1] Some departments simply don't ask applicants about marijuana use, and a few will accept applications from potential new hires who admit to having used marijuana in the recent past.

Although many police supervisors have long held that drug use by officers was inconsistent with the role of law enforcers, and some believed that such use might lead to corrupt policing practices including the acceptance of bribes, attitudes have begun a significant shift in keeping with changed laws and public acceptance of practices that had previously been viewed negatively. Even the FBI may be considering hiring agents who have experimented with marijuana. In 2014, for example, FBI director James

A lighted marijuana cigarette. How has growing marijuana decriminalization impacted police hiring practices?

Comey, told reporters that the Bureau's need to hire high-quality cybersecurity experts might mandate such a change.[2] Comey appeared to be referring to the belief that the prior behavior of many such candidates might involve the use of marijuana.

▶ *Hiring and Training*

Becoming a police officer involves much more than just taking an exam, passing a background check, and spending a few weeks in the police academy. For many, policing is a lifelong pursuit. First, of course, candidates need to apply for police work and be hired. In addition to test scores, the applicant's interview performance, character, and medical and drug history all factor into the hiring decision. Hiring is only the first step, however. Academy training comes next, followed by field training. The performance of police officers is measured throughout their careers. Those officers who hope for promotion must demonstrate that, through their job performance, they have the ability and qualifications to take on greater responsibilities.

LEARNING OUTCOMES 1 — Outline the hiring process, including testing, interviewing, and various screening procedures.

Law enforcement is generally regarded as a **civil service** job. Civil service is a system in which employees are hired, retained, advanced, disciplined, and discharged on the basis of merit, or their abilities and qualifications. Civil service is in contrast to the **patronage system** of old. You may recall from Chapter 1 that during the political era, police hiring decisions were based more on an individual's political support for whomever was in charge than on the applicant's individual qualifications.

Civil service was implemented to enhance police professionalism. Many states, local governments, and even the federal government have **civil service commissions** that ensure that employees in civil service positions receive specific protections such as job security and equal pay for equivalent work. Knowing that policing is a civil service job provides an appreciation for the intricacies and nuances of the hiring process; because people who become police officers tend to stay in their positions for a long time, considerable attention must be given to hiring the right people.

The Hiring Decision

Whether a person will be hired as a police officer depends on a number of conditions. Generally, candidates are evaluated on the basis of their test score, interview performance, personal background, performance on a polygraph exam, medical history, and past drug use (Figure 4–1). The problem, as police specialist Ken Peak has observed, is that agencies are often made to feel as though they have to find people who can "walk on water."[3] Early police reformer August Vollmer once said that candidates for the position of police officer should

> have the wisdom of Solomon, the courage of David, the patience of Job and leadership of Moses, the kindness of the Good Samaritan, the diplomacy of Lincoln, the tolerance of the Carpenter of Nazareth, and, finally, an intimate knowledge of every branch of natural, biological, and social sciences.[4]

Suffice it to say, that's a tall order!

Recruitment

Position announcements placed in newspapers, career websites, college campuses, and civil service or municipal government websites.

Testing Requirements

Written examination to gauge intelligence (as well as reading and writing abilities) and physical agility test to determine if the applicant is physically fit to perform the duties of a police officer.

The Interview

About 90% of police departments conduct an oral interview of candidates who successfully met or exceeded the department's predetermined testing requirements.

Background Investigation

Sometimes called a *character investigation*, in which an investigator will peer into all conceivable elements of the applicant's life.

Polygraph Exam

About two-thirds of America's law enforcement agencies rely on polygraph exams as part of the employment screening process to encourage honesty during questioning.

Medical and Drug Screening

Besides detecting past or current drug use, screening also assesses medical fitness to perform the job.

FIGURE 4–1 The Police Hiring Process.

Recruitment

Jobs in policing can be quite competitive, depending on the position and the timing. For positions regarded as prestigious, such as those with the federal government, getting a job can be quite difficult. Timing can be important. One applicant for the Seattle Police Department during the early 1990s took the exam with roughly a thousand other people in a lecture hall at the University of Washington, but the department had a mandate to hire only about a dozen officers.

Fortunately for those looking for police work, such stories are now the exception. In fact, police departments around the country are increasingly having to come to grips with a somewhat shallow hiring pool.[5] Recently, the National Association of Police Organizations put recruitment at the top of a list of problems facing police departments today.[6]

The hiring crisis in law enforcement is not to be taken lightly. The Los Angeles Police Department saw a 50% reduction in applications over the course of three years.[7] The Chicago Police Department had 25,000 applicants in 1993 and only 1,900 in 2000.[8] Why the sudden decline?

There are many reasons for today's lack of qualified applicants. One has been the war in the Middle East, which has drained young men and women from the U.S. civilian workforce. Another explanation has been the relative strength of the economy; police departments have a hard time competing with higher-paying private-sector jobs. An increasing (though relatively small) number of agencies are also requiring that their applicants have at least a few college credits, if not an actual degree. This further restricts the pool of eligible applicants. Unfavorable press coverage of scandals and corruption can further discourage people from applying.

In response, agencies are going to great pains to offer attractive schedules, benefits, and job perks and are aggressively recruiting applicants. Larger departments have officers who do nothing but travel around the country to recruit. Others have conducted studies to determine how best to attract applicants.

Testing Requirements

An applicant usually takes two tests to become an officer: a written test and a physical agility test. To ensure that their tests are valid (i.e., able to measure what they intend to measure) and reliable (the results don't vary markedly from one test to the next), most agencies use exams prepared by companies that specialize in creating exams for various occupations.

Some departments also use the written exam as an opportunity to determine an applicant's personality type. Personality tests are also routinely used in the hiring process. They consist of numerous, sometimes odd and repetitive questions that result in scores that agencies can then use to weed out the psychologically unfit.[9]

As for physical testing, every applicant must meet certain criteria. Physical agility tests vary widely from agency to agency. Some focus specifically on the candidates' ability to perform the job. State trooper applicants in Washington, for example, are required to lift a tire onto the mock hub of an automobile, among other tasks. Other departments ensure that their applicants can perform a certain number of push-ups and sit-ups and run a specified distance within a limited time period. The challenge for those involved in hiring police officers is to ensure that any exam is truly job related. In fact, tests *have* to be job related to avoid discrimination complaints. Some agencies therefore survey their officers to determine what physical work they engage in regularly, and then they tailor the physical agility exams to meet those tasks.[10]

The Interview

The vast majority of candidates are screened out during the written and physical testing phase, leaving relatively few labor-intensive, time-consuming interviews. Oral interviews are often conducted by a board of officials, including active police officers from the jurisdiction and some civilians. Psychologists or psychiatrists might serve on such boards or might conduct separate interviews. To save time and resources, it is in the interest of hiring authorities to do as much screening as possible before the interviewing phase.

A candidate can get a stellar score on a test yet be a lousy police officer. Consequently, oral interviews are intended to pick up where the written and agility tests leave off. They gauge factors like confidence, poise, reasoning abilities, oral skills, memory, and observational prowess. Candidates are often asked questions about what they would do in a specific situation. These questions can sometimes be difficult because candidates who have no background in law enforcement may be unsure of how to respond.

To assess observational skills, some elements of the interview may be staged (e.g., there may be a phrase written on a board in the interview room). Candidates may be asked later to recall certain features of the room. Officers on patrol need to be observant; hence, this interview component might be especially useful in hiring officers seeking to work patrol.

Background Investigations

By far, the most expensive and time-consuming phase of the hiring process is the background investigation. The investigator will draw on official records and will conduct in-depth interviews with friends, family members, coworkers, acquaintances, and even former acquaintances. In short, the background investigation is intended to discover those skeletons, if any, in the applicant's closet that are not revealed during other phases of the hiring process.

Polygraph Exam

Polygraphs are used to encourage honesty during questioning. The examiner begins by asking a number of reference questions, such as, "Is your name John Smith?" Then questioning about prior criminal history, drug use, and the like begins. Polygraphs are not without their faults. Evidence from polygraph exams is not allowed in court to prove guilt, for instance. On the other hand, polygraphists feel that their devices are very difficult to fool.[11] Polygraph exams continue to be used in many police hiring decisions because many law enforcement officials believe in the polygraph's usefulness.

Medical and Drug Screening

One of the last steps in the hiring process is medical and drug screening. Although polygraphs and background checks can indicate past drug use, formal drug screening provides results that are difficult to dispute. Besides detecting past or current drug use, screening also assesses medical fitness to perform the job. A person with a serious heart condition, for instance, probably wouldn't be a good fit in any police agency, considering that officers have to physically exert themselves from time to time.

Medical screening is also used to check applicants' vision and weight, among other factors. Most agencies will not hire candidates who fail to meet some uncorrected vision requirement. Likewise, many agencies will not hire overweight people. This may seem discriminatory on one level, but there are certain bona fide job requirements that an obese or legally blind individual cannot perform.

▶ The Academy and Field Training

Once a candidate successfully passes through all of the steps involved in the hiring process and is offered employment, he or she will go to an academy for training. The teaching methods and curricula of academies differ depending on the student's anticipated future position and the hiring

LEARNING OUTCOMES 2 Recount academy and field training elements of police hiring.

agency. A common thread runs through all police academies, however: They all strive to teach candidates how to be effective officers and how to develop the all-important "sixth sense" needed for successful police work. Students must "pass" through the academy without incident, or they will be terminated. This extends to field training, the "on-the-job training" new police officers receive after completing the academy.

The Academy

Academy training is regarded as one of the most important elements of the police hiring process. In this era of heightened civil liability, it is critical that recruits learn the limits of the law as it applies to police work. In addition, they need to learn proper procedures, including how and when to use force, how to drive a vehicle aggressively, how to make felony stops, how to deal with belligerent suspects, how to make arrests, how to document incidents, and how to investigate accidents. Needless to say, adequate coverage of these and other pertinent topics takes a great deal of time. The typical academy, in fact, trains recruits for approximately 400 hours.[12]

Types of Academies

There are generally three types of academies: in-house, regional, and state. Candidates for the position of trooper with the Washington State Patrol, for instance, are trained at the agency's academy in Shelton, Washington. In California, the Commission on Peace Officer Standards and Training (POST) certifies city, county, and regional academies throughout the state. More than 600 agencies in California voluntarily participate in POST. There are nearly 40 different academies certified by POST, for all different types of agencies. In other states, such as Florida, police academies are often run through community colleges and other institutions of higher learning.

In a growing trend, civilians are paying their own way through police academies in the hopes of gaining employment as an officer after completing the program.[13] This saves agencies not only the expense of paying for academy training but also the salaries that the newly hired trainees would be earning while going through their training. Some states, like New York, follow a hybrid model, allowing interested applicants to complete basic training requirements before seeking employment; once they are sworn officers, they complete additional training.[14]

Curricular Issues

Police training academies vary in terms of their curricula, but most are similar in the sense that they teach recruits the technical aspects of police work. A range of topics is usually covered, including the criminal justice system, law, patrol, investigation procedures, job proficiency (e.g., using a firearm), administration, and problems likely to be encountered on the job.[15] More recently, topics like diversity, sexual harassment, dispute resolution, victim awareness, technological applications, stress management, and courtroom demeanor have made their way into academies as well. What we have seen is something of a move away from the traditional **plebe system**, an academy model that closely parallels a military-style boot camp and that aims to produce well-groomed and disciplined officers, to a model that stresses twenty-first century problems.[16]

Modern police academy curricula have also moved somewhat beyond the **technical training model**[17] insofar as they expose trainees more to the less familiar dimensions of their jobs, such as managing stress, interacting with difficult people, and so on. The **college system** of training is gaining in popularity today.[18] This doesn't mean that the academy is run by a college. Rather, the academy's intent is to train budding officers to be professionals. To this end, besides gaining the needed technical knowledge, trainees learn problem solving, sensitivity to marginalized groups, and other valuable skills.

Research reveals that the college system approach to police academy training is still largely the exception rather than the rule. One study revealed that less than 3% of basic academy training is spent on topics other than the technical aspects of the job.[19] This concern is particularly serious in light of the recent movement toward community-oriented policing, which prides itself on relationship building, communication, and problem solving.

An overview of one of the nation's cutting-edge police academy curricula, that of the Los Angeles Police Department, can be seen in Figure 4–2. Note that the department's officers receive more than 800 hours of academy training.

Learning the Sixth Sense

Academy training also teaches recruits the so-called **sixth sense**, namely, a heightened sense of suspicion. As Peak has observed, "A suspicious nature is as important to the street officer as a fine touch is to a surgeon. The officer should not only be able to visually recognize but also be able to physically sense when something is wrong or out of the ordinary."[20] Understood differently, teaching officers to be suspicious is like teaching them to be observant. They are taught how to develop knowledge of the area they work in, the people they come into contact with, and the ordinary conditions of the area. With that knowledge, they can more capably identify things that are amiss. A person who doesn't "belong" in a certain area, for instance, may be cause for suspicion.

There is a fine line between being an effective, inquisitive officer and being too suspicious. Too much suspicion can have a number of unfortunate consequences. For example, an officer who is overly suspicious of people who fit a certain profile or social or demographic category runs the risk of infringing on people's constitutional rights. Profiling is an important topic in modern law enforcement and, according to its critics, something to be avoided at all costs. At the same time, though, there is a clear need for healthy suspicion; even the most apparently innocuous traffic stop could turn into a violent encounter in a matter of seconds. New officers need to be prepared.

Field Training and Development

Field training is not unique to policing. It is just like the on-the-job training that comes with learning any other occupation. The first formal police field training program was implemented in San Jose, California, in the late 1960s.[21] Since then, field training programs have evolved and moved in various directions. Most, however, assign a field training officer (a veteran officer) to a recent academy graduate. But as Bob Dylan so eloquently put it, "The times, they are a-changin.'" The traditional field

Academics

- Arrest procedures
- Investigation techniques
- Communications and report writing
- Traffic investigation and enforcement

Driving

- Emergency vehicle operations
- Defensive driving
- Pursuit policy
- Safe vehicle handling

Human Relations

- Cultural sensitivity training
- Sexual harassment
- Media relations
- Stress management
- Disability awareness
- Community relations
- Tactical communications
- Hate crimes, missing persons, and domestic violence

Firearms

- Weapon care and safety
- Marksmanship
- Tactical manipulation with the sidearm and shotgun
- Chemical agents handling

Law

- Search and seizure
- Evidence
- Crimes against persons and property
- Sex crimes, crimes against children, and other general criminal statutes

Physical Training

- Physical conditioning
- Physical arrest techniques
- Controls
- Weaponless defense

Agency Specific Training

- Agency policy
- Organization and structure

Tactics

- Patrol techniques and procedures
- Responding to crimes in progress
- Building searches
- Vehicle stops and searches
- Deadly force
- Shooting policy

FIGURE 4–2 **Sample Policy Academy Curriculum.**
Source: Los Angeles Police Department, "Academy training," www.joinlapd.com/academy.html (accessed December 8, 2015).

training officer program is quickly being replaced by a new model: the police training officer model.

The Field Training Officer Approach

The traditional approach to field training typically consists of three distinct phases:[22] (1) introduction, in which the new officer learns agency policies and rules; (2) training and evaluation, in which the recruit spends the most time learning the complicated tasks that police officers perform regularly; and (3) the final portion, involving firsthand observation of the new officer's actions by the **field training officer (FTO)**. The duration of FTO programs varies, but the programs typically range from 1 to 12 weeks.[23] A probationary period extending beyond that allows additional interactions between FTOs and trainees.

Toward a Police Training Officer Approach

In 1999, the Office for Community Oriented Policing Services (COPS) provided a $300,000 grant to the Reno (Nevada) Police Department to collaborate with the Police Executive Research Forum to study police training and to develop a new field training model. The collaboration produced the so-called **police training officer (PTO) program**. According to the authors of a recent report on the PTO program, "This approach is very different from traditional police training methods that emphasize mechanical repetition skills and rote memory capabilities; rather, the focus is on developing an officer's learning capacity, leadership, and problem-solving skills."[24]

The PTO model is built around John Dewey's philosophy of learning,[25] namely, that there is much more to learning than can be gleaned from a lecture. The model incorporates such concepts as Malcolm Knowles's principles of self-directed learning,[26] Howard Barrows's idea of problem-based learning,[27] and Benjamin Bloom's concern with intellectual outcomes of learning.[28] The PTO model emphasizes the following:

1. *Knowledge.* Remembering or recalling previously learned material

2. *Comprehension.* Understanding meaning well enough to be able to explain and restate ideas

3. *Application.* Applying learned material in new and different situations

4. *Analysis.* Categorizing material into segments and demonstrating their relationships

5. *Synthesis.* Grouping or combining separate ideas to form a new whole and to establish new relationships

6. *Evaluation.* Assessing the material for appropriate outcomes based on established criteria[29]

This approach may not seem that dissimilar to the traditional FTO model, but its main difference lies in the manner through which material is taught and knowledge is evaluated. Problem-based learning exercises are used throughout the process. In each phase, the recruit is tasked with a structured problem. Trainees will also develop a neighborhood portfolio, which is a detailed overview of the beat in which they work. Finally, throughout the process, trainees must demonstrate competence in a number of areas, not all of which are unique to police work. Examples include problem solving, leadership, community problems, cultural diversity, ethics, safety, and report writing. The PTO model is being developed in jurisdictions across the United States and in Canada. The new model has even given rise to the Police Society for Problem Based Learning.[30]

▶ *Diversity and Discrimination*

Both diversity and discrimination have important implications for human resources. They are of great importance

> LEARNING OUTCOMES 3
> Summarize the issues faced by female and minority police officers.

to administrators in terms of how they staff their agencies, and they are important to officers in lower ranks, too. New recruits, as we have just seen, are trained extensively in these areas so that they understand the importance of diversity and the avoidance of discrimination. Things were not always this way, however. It was not until the civil rights movement of the 1960s that diversity and discrimination were brought to the attention of politicians and the public (Figure 4–3 summarizes key issues in this section).

Equal Employment Opportunity

The notion of **equal employment opportunity** has a plain meaning: Everyone should receive an equal chance at employment. The goal of equal employment opportunity did not just emerge on its own; it was legislatively mandated. Title VII of the Civil

The EEOC	Makes it unlawful for a police department to discriminate against any individual with respect to employment because of race, color, religion, sex, age, pregnancy, or national origin
Affirmative Action	Plays a significant role in police hiring in America's 50 largest cities
Reverse Discrimination	Some police departments are now facing reverse discrimination lawsuits
Americans with Disabilities Act	Prohibits discrimination against applicants for any position if the applicant is able to perform the essential functions of the job

FIGURE 4–3 Diversity and Discrimination in Policing.

Rights Act of 1964 provides the legal basis for fair employment practices as we know them today. Section 703A of the act, for example, makes it unlawful for any employer to fail to hire, refuse to hire, discharge, or otherwise discriminate in any other manner against any individual with respect to employment compensation, terms, conditions, or privileges because of race, color, religion, sex, age, pregnancy, or national origin, among other factors.

In 1972, Title VII was revised to create the **Equal Employment Opportunity Commission (EEOC)**. The EEOC was given authority to "intervene on behalf of affected individuals" and to "file suit against businesses or governmental entities in cases of discrimination." What this means is that individuals no longer need to shoulder the burden of proving a discrimination claim; they can turn to the federal government for help.

The EEOC can also intervene in cases of alleged sexual harassment. According to Title VII, in fact, sexual harassment is a form of sex discrimination, not unlike denying employment to female candidates in favor of male candidates. Finally, the EEOC can also step in to investigate cases of employer retaliation: "An employer may not fire, demote, harass or otherwise 'retaliate' against an individual for filing a charge of discrimination, participating in a discrimination proceeding, or otherwise opposing discrimination."[31]

The push for equal employment opportunity has had interesting implications for the law enforcement profession. Policing remains, by and large, a white male–dominated occupation, but women and minorities have started to make significant inroads in terms of achieving parity in the ranks with their white male counterparts. The law enforcement profession is also in the strange position of requiring a certain physical condition for job candidates while not being allowed to discriminate based on disability.

Why is diversity essential in the police ranks? In general, it is felt that a diverse organization will be more capable of effectively addressing community needs. It is also felt that a diverse police force will be regarded more favorably by citizens, especially those in minority-dominated neighborhoods. The research supports some of these claims, but only to a modest extent. For example, researchers in Detroit found that African-American citizens had more support for black than white officers.[32] Research has also revealed that New York residents had higher regard for the police department after coming into greater contact with female police officers.[33] In contrast, a study from Washington, D.C., revealed little benefit resulted from assigning same-race officers to neighborhoods.[34]

Affirmative Action

Closely associated with equal employment opportunity is the practice of **affirmative action**. This is the practice of taking proactive steps to boost the presence of historically marginalized groups (typically minorities and women) in the ranks of an organization by giving preference to members of those groups. It is easy to see how affirmative action can further the goals of providing equal employment opportunity, but it is not part of Title VII.

There have been many court cases addressing the constitutionality of affirmative action programs. In the policing context, one researcher found that affirmative action plans played a significant role in police hiring in America's 50 largest cities.[35] It is noteworthy, however, that 23 of the affirmative action plans in these 50 cities were court mandated, not voluntary.

Minorities in Policing

It would be inaccurate to suggest that policing was exclusively a white male occupation before the 1960s. There were black police officers in Washington, D.C., as early as 1861,[36] for example, but by 1940, black officers represented less than 1% of the nation's police forces.[37] The African-Americans who did obtain work as police officers often faced discrimination on the job. For example, a study from 1959, right before the dawn of the civil rights era, revealed that several southern cities required black officers to call on white officers when they needed to arrest a white suspect.[38] Some black officers were allowed to drive only cars marked "Colored Police" and could arrest only black suspects.[39] Additionally, job assignments for black officers were not particularly desirable, dismissals were often arbitrary, there was little integration within the ranks,[40] and promotions were few and far between. For example, a study revealed that during the 1960s, only 22 police departments had promoted black officers beyond patrol positions.[41] Times have since changed, of course. Studies now show little connection between race and promotion or disciplinary decisions.[42]

While there is little direct evidence that being a minority makes one a better cop, that claim was made during the 1960s. In the wake of various race riots during that decade, the President's Commission on Law Enforcement and Administration of Justice observed the following:

> Police officers have testified to the special competence of Negro officers in Negro neighborhoods. The reasons given include: they get along better and receive more respect from Negro residents; they receive less

trouble; . . . they can get more information; and they understand Negro citizens better.[43]

Similarly, some studies have revealed that black residents wanted to see more black officers patrolling the streets because they believed that understanding would improve and that abuses would decrease.[44] On the other hand, some early studies showed that black officers either felt a need to be more forceful with black suspects[45] or were actively challenged by suspects of their own race.[46] One influential author even coined the term **double marginality** to refer to a situation in which black officers treat black suspects harshly to gain the respect of their white counterparts and to avoid giving the impression that they are biased toward members of their own race.[47]

Most recently, the President's Task Force on 21st Century Policing has highlighted the need for continued attention to diversity in recruiting. Specifically, it recommended that "law enforcement agencies should strive to create a workforce that contains a broad range of diversity including race, gender, language, life experience, and cultural background to improve understanding and effectiveness in dealing with all communities."[48] Whether it translates into measurable behavior changes remains unclear, however.[49]

Women in Policing

Women have faced much the same fate as minorities in terms of seeking law enforcement jobs. They remain significantly underrepresented in police departments to this day. Some researchers have attributed this situation to the idea that policing requires aggression, physical exertion, and "stable" emotions—supposedly masculine traits.[50] In contrast, traits often associated with women, such as compassion, empathy, and nurturing, may not find much of a home in the law enforcement world.[51] Obviously, there are exceptions to these generalities.

Historically speaking, police departments didn't start to hire women until the early twentieth century. Lola Baldwin was the first woman to hold police powers. Hired in 1905 by Portland, Oregon, Baldwin was engaged mostly in social work–like functions. Other police departments followed Portland's example: "Once the police began to think in terms of preventing juvenile delinquency, they responded to the traditional argument that women had a special capacity for child care."[52]

Alice Stebbins-Wells was hired by the Los Angeles Police Department in 1910. Even though her job also resembled social work, she led a movement for more female hiring, and by 1925, more than 200 cities had women working in police positions and even in jails.[53] In the ensuing years, women made some progress, but not much. By the mid-1960s, there were only around 1,700 female police officers in America's largest cities,[54] and most female officers were excluded from patrol duties.

It was not until 1968 that the first women were assigned to patrol work.[55] Indianapolis was the first city to put women on patrol, but other large cities, like New York; Philadelphia; Miami; Washington, D.C.; and St. Louis, quickly followed suit. By the end of the 1970s, nearly 90% of large police agencies employed female patrol officers.[56] That growth has continued at an impressive pace. Nearly all cities of more than 50,000 now have women working in the police ranks.[57] The growth is attributed partially to the fact that female and male officers perform similarly, as evidenced by some early studies on the subject.[58]

More recently, the same reasons that were once used to exclude women from the ranks of police agencies are now being used to recruit women in larger numbers. A study of patrol in New York City, for example, revealed that women are less likely than men to use firearms, to get into violent confrontations, and to become injured.[59] Some say that this means female officers are actually more emotionally stable than male officers, disavowing one of the earlier arguments that was used to keep them out of police positions.[60] A reason male and female police officers appear to perform similarly may not be so much that both sexes are equally competent but that policing may attract a certain group of women, by either self-selection, department screening, or the recruit socialization process.[61]

Diversity in the Ranks Today

So far, we have addressed only female and African-American police officers. Other minority groups have made advances as well. This can be seen clearly in Figure 4–4. Between 1987 and 2013 (the most recent year for which data are available), minorities increased their presence in the ranks of America's police departments. Women, as the accompanying "Think About It" box shows, have not made considerable advances in recent years. For example, in 2003, 11.3% of police officers were female. This number increased to only 12% by 2013.[62]

Disabled Cops

In 1990, Congress passed the **Americans with Disabilities Act (ADA)**, which forbids discrimination against the disabled. How does this apply to policing? It doesn't necessarily mean that disabled individuals can become police officers. Rather, the ADA prohibits discrimination against applicants for any position if the applicant is able to perform the essential functions of the job.

The ADA is part of the reason why medical screening occurs during the final phase of the hiring process; it prevents applicants from being rejected early on because of physical

Think About It…

Equal Employment Opportunity for Women Nearly nine out of ten police officers are male. Several explanations have been offered for the relatively low percentage of female police officers. One is that police departments continue to discriminate against women. Another is that not many women are drawn to a career in law enforcement for a variety of reasons, including its male-dominated culture. Yet another explanation is that many female candidates do not perform as well as men at certain stages of the hiring process (e.g., in physical tests of upper-body strength). *Do you think women have equal employment opportunities in the police field? If not, what can be done to improve equality of opportunity?*

disabilities. Moreover, the ADA has required police departments (and other organizations) to develop sophisticated selection procedures that mirror the job to the fullest extent possible. Selection cannot be a haphazard process.

The term *disabled* may conjure up images of wheelchairs and significant physical limitations, but disabilities can sometimes be less visible. For example, the ADA protects people with human immunodeficiency virus (HIV); a positive test is not an outright bar to employment.[63] Indeed, a sheriff's department was ordered to pay damages to a reserve officer who was discharged after testing positive for HIV.[64] The ADA also protects diabetics. In one case, an insulin-dependent diabetic was denied employment with the Toledo (Ohio) Police Department, but the court held that a blanket policy denying employment to such individuals violates the ADA.[65]

Departments have a little more leeway, though, with serious physical disabilities. For example, a court sided with a department that put an officer on disability leave after he lost his arm in a motorcycle accident.[66] The court concluded that the department was justified in its decision because the officer could no longer perform one of the key functions of the job: making an arrest.

Reverse Discrimination: A Backlash?

The push for diversity in policing, like the push for diversity in other organizations, has sometimes gone too far. **Racial quotas**, for instance, are requirements for hiring and promoting a specified number of minorities. When minorities are hired and promoted based more on race than on any other criterion, allegations of **reverse discrimination** emerge—usually from white male officers. Reverse discrimination has also been described as entailing a "white backlash."

Reverse discrimination appears to be more than a distant concern for white officers. A study from the late 1970s revealed that white officers felt that affirmative action was a

Minority representation among full-time sworn personnel in local police departments, 1987–2013

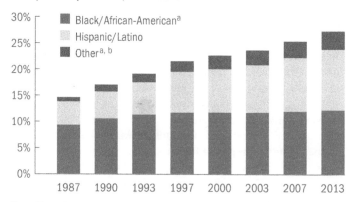

Note: Figure includes all years for which data were collected. See appendix table 18 for standard errors.

[a] Excludes persons of Hispanic or Latino origin.

[b] Includes Asian, Native Hawaiian, or other Pacific Islanders; American Indian or Alaska Natives; and persons identifying two or more races.

FIGURE 4-4 **Minority Officers in Local Police Departments.**
Source: From Local Police Departments, 2013: Personnel, Policies, and Practices by Brian A. Reaves, U.S Department of Justice.

threat to their careers.[67] Twenty years later, another study found marked resentment and bitterness on the part of white officers toward several of their black supervisors.[68] Reverse discrimination appears to be a real phenomenon. During the 1970s, for example, the Detroit Police Department adopted a policy that provided for the promotion to sergeant of one black officer for every white officer. While a court struck the policy down,[69] the U.S. Supreme Court later sanctioned temporary racial quotas in police hiring.[70]

Even in the face of conflicting court decisions, claims of reverse discrimination continue. Organizations like Adversity. net have emerged to shed light on egregious abuses of racial preference and quotas. In fact, the organization recently highlighted the case of a former Dayton (Ohio) Police Department major, a white woman who was bypassed for promotion to chief in favor of a black man. In a surprising turn of events, she was then fired so more black officers could be promoted (the department, to this day, is overwhelmingly white). The city eventually agreed to a settlement of more than $1 million.[71]

The Dayton case came on the heels of another from Milwaukee, Wisconsin, in which a jury awarded $2.2 million to 17 white police officers who, the jury felt, had been systematically bypassed for promotion in favor of minority officers.[72] Twenty of forty-one officers promoted to lieutenant were black, when the pool of applicants was more than 80% white.

▶ Realities of the Job

Once a police officer begins working, he or she is almost instantly confronted with several important "realities" of the job that may not have been made clear early on. First, police work is a stressful occupation. Stress can take its toll over the course of an officer's career. Second, fatigue is a common problem in policing, though it has historically taken a backseat to stress. Only recently have researchers started to focus their attention on the problems that can result when officers are spread too thin and forced to work long hours. Finally, as unfortunate as it sounds, sexual harassment exists in police departments just as it does in other organizations. This can be particularly difficult for female officers.

LEARNING OUTCOMES 4 — Summarize the issues police officers confront on the job.

Stress

Stress is a fact of life in many occupations, but policing has its own unique brand of stress. The nature of the job, particularly the potential for violence at any turn, takes its toll on even the most emotionally hardened officer. This toll might be manifested in the form of health-related problems,[73] family breakdown,[74] and alcoholism, to name just a few.

Nature and Symptoms of Stress

Stress has been broadly defined as anything that places an adjustive demand on the organism.[75] In other words, stressful situations require some behavioral response, and that response is usually one intended to reduce the stress being experienced. Some people thrive on what others might consider stressful situations, and stress can have both negative and positive elements. Positive stress has been called **eustress**, and negative stress has been called **distress**.[76]

Eustress is a positive form of stress that does not threaten or harm the individual but is pleasurable, challenging, or exciting. For example, the stress created by beginning a new job or a challenging assignment could qualify as eustress. The new police officer experiences eustress when going on patrol for the first time. Experienced officers usually experience eustress when beginning a new assignment, such as criminal investigation. This form of stress is generally described as positive and can actually result in higher levels of motivation.

Distress is the harmful variety of stress. It threatens the individual's functioning or can overload his or her capacity to cope with environmental stimuli. Distress may result from such things as an extraordinarily high caseload, assignment to a high-crime area, inadequate equipment, or an unsupportive supervisor. All police organizations contain job assignments or situations that are perceived as threatening by most individuals, and it is these assignments or situations that create the greatest demands.

Perhaps more than anything, stress is a problem of incompatibility between a person and his or her environment. It occurs when the individual is overwhelmed by negative environmental factors or when the environment fails to provide for or meet the individual's needs. Every person has a unique set of skills, abilities, experiences, and personality traits, and every job—within the context of the environment—requires the employee to possess a certain set of skills, abilities, experiences, and personality traits. When the employee's characteristics do not match the job's requirements, a potential result is heightened stress.

Effective stress management requires that the symptoms of stress be recognized. Within a police organization, no one party should be burdened with the responsibility for recognizing these symptoms. Rather, it is vital that everyone in administrative and management positions be able to spot the signs of stress and identify possible methods for alleviating the distress. The symptoms must be acknowledged and ameliorated before they develop into excessive problems for both the stressed person and those who must associate with him or her.[77]

The Gendered Nature of Police Stress

In one of the first research endeavors undertaken on occupational stress among men and women working in policing, researchers Merry Morash and Robin N. Haarr examined stressful situations in police work and made an effort to identify possible variations in experiences between women and men.[78] Morash and Haarr cited previous research that found that women generally reported higher stress levels than men. Still, they found that women working in policing did not report higher levels of stress than men and that both men and women share a number of work-related sources of stress. One of the most commonly shared sources of stress was identified as "a lack of influence over day-to-day operations of the police agency and "the way policing gets done." Special concerns, however, were expressed by women, such as the failure to adapt equipment and uniforms to a woman's physique, the desire to carry a firearm while off duty or undercover in a purse rather than a holster, and lack of administrative support.

The researchers also noted that an increase in women's stress levels can be related to the need for most women to spend time and energy dealing with sex, age, race, or ethnic group bias directed against others and themselves. They noted in particular language harassment through exposure to profanity and to sexual jokes. Even so, the authors concluded that "women police officers do not differ profoundly from men on variables such as workplace stress and workplace experience."

Burnout

Burnout is the progressive loss of idealism, energy, purpose, and concern that results from the conditions of work. According to one team of researchers, burnout is "a debilitating psychological condition brought about by unrelieved work stress."[79] Burnout can also be understood as the final stage of mental or physical exhaustion, in which the individual is no longer able to cope with his or her job (Figure 4–5).[80]

Critical Incidents

A major source of stress in police work concerns the possibility of becoming involved in critical or traumatic incidents. A **critical incident** is an emergency situation (a crime in progress, a traffic accident with serious injuries, a natural disaster, a terrorist attack, an officer's request for assistance, and other situations in which human life may be in jeopardy) that evokes immediate police response and that takes priority over all other police work. Examples of critical-incident stressors may include apprehending a disturbed person, serving a warrant against a dangerous person, providing riot control, or dealing with a hostage taker or a barricaded suspect.

One of the most stressful events that a police officer can experience is a shooting in which the officer critically wounds or kills another person or where a fellow officer is killed or critically wounded. Most experts agree that many good officers leave policing because of postshooting trauma; such trauma

can have long-lasting effects on the police officer. However, not every officer who is involved in a shooting has a traumatic reaction. The postshooting trauma reactions are almost equally divided among mild reactions, moderate reactions, and severe reactions.[81] Research reveals that officers involved in shootings experience emotional or psychological numbing.[82] Five phases have been identified for coping with critical incidents:

1. *Denial.* The officer does not want to believe what has happened. This stage is usually very brief in officer-involved shootings.

2. *Anger and resentment.* Anger and resentment are usually nonspecific or vaguely directed at the person who was shot. This stage is usually short lived, though it may return at various times during the adaptation process.

3. *Bargaining.* This stage involves the officer wishing the shooting had never happened. It may also be due to the officer's worry about reprisals from the department.

4. *Depression.* This stage lasts the longest. The severity of the depression depends on the basic personality of the officer, the amount of trauma involved in the incident, the agency's response to the incident, the officer's social network, and other factors.

5. *Acceptance.* This stage has been reached when the officer begins to integrate the event into his or her life or makes the transition from being totally preoccupied with the event to merely acknowledging that it took place.[83]

The symptoms of postshooting trauma are usually most intense for the first 48 to 72 hours following the incident, but the various reactions to such events can come and go for some time. For example, the officer may experience a heightened sense of danger or vulnerability, fear and anxiety about future encounters, anger or rage, nightmares, sleep difficulties (insomnia, sleep disturbances, or escaping through sleep), guilt, emotional numbing, emotional withdrawal from others, sexual difficulties, physical problems (headaches, indigestion, muscle aches, diarrhea, or constipation), or anxiety reactions (difficulty concentrating, excessive worry, irritability, or nervousness).[84] The officer may continually think about the incident and may have frequent flashbacks.

Occasionally, stress arising from critical incidents can lead to a condition known as **posttraumatic stress disorder (PTSD)**. PTSD has been defined as "a condition which sets in following a traumatic event with which the sufferer cannot cope. It has been described as an event outside the usual human experience, one which is experienced in a markedly distressing way, with intense fear, terror, bewilderment and a sense of helplessness."[85] Symptoms of PTSD can include (1) persistent and recurring memories of the event, (2) loss of interest and feelings, (3) problems sleeping and concentrating, and (4) hypervigilance.[86] In the wake of particularly traumatic incidents, it is advisable to treat potential PTSD problems before they get out of control. If early treatment is offered and utilized, many of the long-term negative effects of PTSD can be prevented and eliminated.

Fatigue

Everybody gets tired on the job from time to time. Some of us can safely doze off for a few minutes without too much

---

(1) the honeymoon/enthusiasm stage
The officer reacts enthusiastically to the challenges of the job.

(2) the fuel shortage/stagnation stage
The officer realizes that the job is not as exciting as he or she anticipated; routine sets in, and the officer may come to view the job as boring.

(3) the chronic symptoms/frustration stage
The officer has feelings of intense and seemingly irresolvable apathy and frustration.

(4) the crisis/apathy stage
Pessimism may emerge, and the officer may be plagued by feelings of self-doubt.

(5) the hitting the wall/intervention stage
The officer may reach his or her wits' end, perhaps turning to alcohol and drugs to relieve the feelings of failure and anger that have built up over time.

FIGURE 4–5 **The Five Stages of Burnout.**

concern, but others work in professions in which a nap could lead to disaster. The last thing anyone would want is for an air traffic controller to snooze on the job. The same can be said of surgeons, truck drivers, and, of course, police officers.

Police officers, like some other workers, sometimes work lengthy shifts at odd hours. While they have more or less fixed schedules, it is sometimes impractical for police officers to just walk away at quitting time. An accident, an emergency, or a high-profile arrest could require an officer to work several extra hours, contributing to a long and unpredictable work-week. As two well-known police stress researchers point out, "It is totally reprehensible that the cops we expect to protect us, come to our aid, and respond to our needs when victimized should be allowed to have the worst fatigue and sleep conditions of any profession in our society."[87]

Tired Cops

Researchers have only recently turned their attention to police fatigue.[88] Reporters, too, have expressed concern.[89] The *Boston Globe* investigated one police agency and found that 16 officers worked more than 80 hours each week. Two averaged more than 100 hours per week over a 12-month period.[90] One even worked 130 hours in a single week, which translates into less than 6 hours off on any given day. Researchers identified some officers in Florida and Massachusetts who moonlighted (e.g., as security guards) for 3,000 hours each year, above and beyond the hours spent performing their official duties.[91]

To further gauge the extent of police fatigue, criminologists Bryan Vila and Dennis Kenney surveyed a number of police agencies around the country and visited several more. Their survey revealed that while most officers work only a few overtime hours each month, some logged more than 100 hours of overtime.[92]

Nobody can blame police officers for wanting to increase their pay by working extra hours. Some, though, are forced to do so because of job demands. Either way, too much fatigue can lead to disaster. Vila and Kenney summarized some of the more serious incidents:

A Michigan police officer working nearly 24 hours straight crashes his cruiser while chasing a fleeing motorist. He is critically injured. In California, a sheriff's deputy working alone drifts off a deserted highway and is killed instantly when his patrol car crashes into a tree. An officer in Florida, who has had trouble staying awake, runs a red light in her patrol car and crashes into a van driven by a deputy sheriff, injuring him severely. A police officer driving home from work in Ohio nods off at the wheel, begins swerving in and out of traffic, and runs off the road, striking and killing a man jogging down the sidewalk.[93]

Scheduling and Workload

We have looked at the most obvious cause of police fatigue: too many hours on the job. Police fatigue may also stem from shift length and shift-assignment policies. Researchers have found that police departments that use compressed work schedules (i.e., fewer than five 8-hour days) see less fatigue among their officers.[94] It appears that four 10- to 12-hour shifts result in less fatigue than five 8-hour shifts.

Shift assignments, in addition to shift length, may have implications for police fatigue as well. Vila and Kenney noted that people are less able to cope with fatigue as they grow older. They found that older officers who can select their own shifts were less fatigued than their counterparts who had no say over scheduling matters.[95] The predictability (or unpredictability) of work hours also appears to be linked to fatigue. Surprisingly, officers who work unpredictable schedules report less fatigue. According to Vila and Kenney, "One possible interpretation of this finding could be that the officers who were having problems with fatigue were actually avoiding or minimizing overtime work—perhaps by making fewer arrests or court appearances."[96] The same officers could also have had off-duty obligations (e.g., caring for young children) that forced them to keep regular hours but that also contributed to fatigue.

Sexual Harassment

Sexual harassment, which consists of unwelcome sexual advances, requests for sexual favors, and other verbal or physical conduct of a sexual nature, is a sad reality in many of America's workplaces. Sexual harassment has occurred for generations, but the practice attracted national attention in 1991, when University of Oklahoma law professor Anita Hill testified at Clarence Thomas's Supreme Court confirmation hearing. Hill described Thomas's conduct as constituting sexual harassment, and it prompted many people to question the way women are treated in the workplace.

Sexual harassment is a form of discrimination under Title VII, as decided in 1977.[97] In 1986, the Supreme Court defined sexual harassment as falling into two categories: (1) **quid pro quo harassment** and (2) **hostile work environment**.[98] *Quid pro quo* harassment occurs when sexual favors are demanded in exchange for some perk or benefit, perhaps a promotion or a favorable job assignment. Viewed differently, *quid pro quo* sexual harassment occurs when there is a tangible economic detriment associated with refusing to succumb to sexual advances. A hostile work environment is said to exist when unwelcome sexual contact and comments have the effect of "unreasonably interfering with an individual's work performance or creating an intimidating environment."[99]

Because of the prevalence of male officers, police work has seen its share of sexual harassment. In 1993, the state of California enacted legislation requiring all peace officers to undergo sexual harassment training. The law followed several large judgments against police agencies for their officers' unscrupulous actions. In the early 1990s, the New York City Police Department went to great lengths to cover up sexual harassment allegations by a female probationary police officer. The woman alleged that she was raped and sodomized by a male officer who threatened to kill her if she reported the incident. When the facts eventually came to light, she was awarded $264,242 in damages.[100]

To this day, sexual harassment still occurs in police departments at alarming rates.[101] The author of a 1996 study interviewed 187 female police officers and found that 62% of them had seen or experienced sexual harassment during their careers as officers.[102] More recently, the National Center for Women and Policing concluded that "law enforcement agencies have tolerated workplace environments that are openly hostile and discriminatory toward female employees."[103]

Too Smart to Be a Cop?

On March 16, 1996, Robert Jordan took a test for the position of entry-level police officer with the Law Enforcement Council of Connecticut, a consortium of 14 different cities in the eastern part of the state. The test, like many of its kind, contained questions intended to assess applicants' cognitive and scholastic abilities. Jordan was informed, along with all of the other test takers, that the test "will generate an eligibility list for distribution to the participating police departments for possible future employment."

The test, developed by Wonderlic Personnel Test, Inc. (WPT), came with an official manual for each exam, including a table of recommended minimum scores for a number of occupations.[104] The company recommended a score of 22 as the minimum for a police officer. Further, WPT recommended hiring people who scored at most 4 points below and 8 points above 22.

In the fall of 1996, Jordan learned that the city of New London was going to be hiring police officers, so he requested a meeting with Keith Harrigan, the assistant city manager in charge of personnel decisions. Jordan was told he was ineligible to become a police officer because he had scored too high on the written test. New London set a test score range of 20 to 27 for police officers, and Jordan had scored above 27. Jordan promptly filed a lawsuit against the city, claiming that his equal protection rights, under the Fifth Amendment to the U.S. Constitution, had been violated. The national media picked up the story, and the headline of the day declared "Too Smart to Be a Cop."

While Jordan felt that he had been discriminated against for scoring well on the exam, the city was concerned with ensuring employment longevity for its officers and minimizing turnover. City officials felt that, given Jordan's apparently extraordinary level of intelligence, he would not have been happy as a police officer and would have quickly left his post, leaving the city with little return on its investment in his selection and training. At issue in the lawsuit, then, was whether there is a justifiable relationship between high cognitive ability and job satisfaction/longevity and, if so, whether a jurisdiction can base its hiring practices on such a relationship.

Jordan's case was heard in the U.S. District Court for the District of Connecticut.[105] Interestingly, the court sided with the city of New London, finding that the city

> followed the instructions accompanying the WPT test, on which they rationally could have relied as authoritative. Additionally, a body of professional literature concludes that hiring overqualified applicants leads to subsequent job dissatisfaction and turnover. While such studies have been challenged, it cannot be said that their conclusions have been refuted.[106]

Most equal protection lawsuits have been brought by people claiming to be victims of illegitimate discrimination. If African-Americans are hired significantly less often than Caucasians, for example, then there may be a basis for a lawsuit claiming discrimination because race is not a legitimate hiring criterion. Jordan's case was different not only because he was not a member of any historically protected group but also because the city reached its hiring decision by paying attention to what the court recognized as legitimate concerns.

This raises several interesting questions:

1. Was New London's hiring decision fair in this case?
2. Should other cities throughout the United States base their hiring decisions on test scores, like New London did in this story?
3. Is it really possible to be too smart to be a cop?
4. How effective are written tests at screening candidates for law enforcement positions?

Outline the hiring process, including testing, interviewing, and various screening procedures.

To enter the police force, candidates must move through the hiring decision, the police academy, and field training. The hiring decision follows recruitment and is based on performance in several areas, including written and physical agility tests, an interview, a background investigation, a polygraph, and medical and drug screening.

1. What are the steps involved in the hiring process?
2. What is the "sixth sense" that officers should learn?

civil service A system in which employees are hired, retained, advanced, disciplined, and discharged on the basis of merit (i.e., their abilities and qualifications).

patronage system A system of hiring in which decisions are based more on an individual's political support for an officeholder than on his or her abilities and qualifications. Patronage was common in police agencies during the political era.

civil service commission A federal, state, or local agency charged with ensuring that employees in civil service positions receive specific protections.

Recount academy and field training elements of police hiring.

Academies vary in their organization and curricular requirements. Each, however, strives to teach new hires the "sixth sense." The traditional model of postacademy training is that of the field training officer (FTO). The FTO system is gradually being replaced by a new police training officer model.

1. Distinguish between the main types of police academies.
2. What are the three phases of typical field training?

plebe system A police academy model that closely parallels a military-style boot camp and that aims to produce well-groomed and disciplined officers.

technical training model A police academy training model that emphasizes the technical aspects of police work and provides little or no training

in such nontechnical areas as stress management, interaction with difficult people, problem solving, and sensitivity to marginalized groups.

college system A police academy training model intended to enhance the professional aspects of police training curricula by exposing trainees to problem solving, sensitivity to marginalized groups, and other valuable topics in addition to required technical knowledge.

sixth sense A healthy sense of suspicion; the experience-based ability to intuit when something is amiss.

field training officer (FTO) A veteran police officer tasked with providing on-the-job training and performance critique during a rookie police officer's initial assignment following graduation from the academy.

police training officer (PTO) program A police training method that focuses on developing an officer's learning capacity, leadership, and problem-solving skills.

Summarize the issues faced by female and minority police officers.

Police departments are becoming increasingly diverse due to the Civil Rights Act of 1964, equal employment opportunity, and affirmative action—and because departments are learning the value of hiring women and minorities. However, allegations of reverse discrimination, mostly by white male police officers, have surfaced in recent years.

1. What implications has equal employment opportunity had for the law enforcement profession?
2. Why is diversity essential in the police ranks?
3. Summarize the history of minorities and women in the police field.
4. Explain the concept of reverse discrimination.

equal employment opportunity Fair employment practices mandated by Title VII of the Civil Rights Act of 1964.

Equal Employment Opportunity Commission (EEOC) The federal agency that is empowered by Title VII of the Civil Rights Act of 1964 to "intervene

on behalf of affected individuals," to "file suit against businesses or governmental entities in cases of discrimination," to intervene in cases of alleged sexual harassment, and to investigate cases of employer retaliation.[107]

affirmative action The practice of taking proactive steps to boost the presence of historically marginalized groups (typically minorities and women) in the ranks of an organization by giving preference to members of those groups.

double marginality A situation in which black officers treat black suspects harshly to gain the respect of their white counterparts and to avoid giving the impression that they are biased toward members of their own race.

Americans with Disabilities Act (ADA) U.S. legislation passed in 1990 that forbids discrimination against the disabled.

racial quota A requirement for hiring and promoting a specified number of minorities.

reverse discrimination Discrimination against nonminorities that occurs when the hiring and promotion of minorities are based more on race than on any other criterion.

LEARNING OUTCOMES 4

Summarize the issues police officers confront on the job.

Some of the realities of police work include stress, fatigue, and sexual harassment. Stress can be both positive (eustress) and negative (distress). Distress, the most destructive form of stress, can lead to numerous job-related and personal problems, including burnout. There are several sources of stress, including organizational and administrative practices, the criminal justice system, the public, stressors intrinsic to police work, and critical incidents. Fatigue is another problem for police officers. Police organizations should guard against scheduling- and workload-related fatigue. Police applicants should also be aware of occasional sexual harassment problems in police agencies, particularly for female applicants, and that some agencies have residency requirements mandating that police officers live within certain boundaries.

1. What is the difference between eustress and distress?
2. What is burnout and what are its five stages?
3. List and describe the five phases for coping with critical incidents.
4. How are scheduling and workload related to fatigue in police officers?

stress Anything that places a positive or negative adjustive demand on an organism.

eustress A positive form of stress that does not threaten or harm the individual but is pleasurable, challenging, or exciting.

distress A harmful form of stress that can threaten an individual's functioning or overload his or her capacity to cope with environmental stimuli.

burnout The progressive loss of idealism, energy, purpose, and concern that results from the conditions of work.

critical incident An emergency situation that evokes immediate police response and that takes priority over all other police work.

posttraumatic stress disorder (PTSD) A condition that sets in following a traumatic event with which the sufferer cannot cope. It has been described as an event outside the usual human experience—one that is experienced in a markedly distressing way, with intense fear, terror, bewilderment, and a sense of helplessness.[108]

sexual harassment Unwelcome sexual advances, requests for sexual favors, and other verbal or physical conduct of a sexual nature.

quid pro quo harassment A form of sexual harassment that generally involves a demand for sexual favors in exchange for some perk or benefit, such as a promotion or a favorable job assignment.

hostile work environment A form of sexual harassment involving situations in which unwelcome sexual contact and comments have the effect of "unreasonably interfering with an individual's work performance or creating an intimidating environment."[109]

References

1 Wade J. Derby, "The impact of drug decriminalization of the future of police recruiting standards," *The Police Chief*, January 2016, http://www.policechiefmagazine.org/magazine/index.cfm?fuseaction=display_arch&article_id=1582&issue_id=82008 (accessed February 1, 2016).

2 David Kravets, "FBI chief says anti-marijuana policy hinders the hiring of cyber expert," ARS Technica, http://arstechnica.com/tech-policy/2014/05/fbi-chief-says-anti-marijuana-policy-hinders-the-hiring-of-cyber-experts/ (accessed February 2, 2016).

3 K. J. Peak, *Policing America: Methods, issues, challenges*, 5th ed. (Upper Saddle River, NJ: Prentice Hall, 2006), p. 69.

4 Quoted in V. A. Leonard and H. W. More, *Police organization and management*, 3rd ed. (Mineola, NY: Foundation Press, 1971), p. 128.

5 J. Nislow, "Is anyone out there?," *Law Enforcement News*, October 31, 1999, p. 1.

6 N. Z. Dizon, "Searching for police," June 3, 2000, Associated Press news service.

7 M. Lifsher, "State strains to recruit new police," *Wall Street Journal*, November 10, 1999, p. CA1.

8 Peak, *Policing America*, p. 72.

9 For a thorough review of studies in this area, see J. G. Varela et al., "Personality testing in law enforcement employment settings: A meta-analytic review," *Criminal Justice and Behavior*, vol. 31 (2004), pp. 649–75. See also S. Daniels and E. King, "Predictive validity of MMPI-2 content scales for small-town police officer performance," *Journal of Police and Criminal Psychology*, vol. 17 (2002), pp. 54–62; W. U. Weiss et al., "Personality assessment inventory as a selection device for law enforcement personnel," *Journal of Police and Criminal Psychology*, vol. 19 (2004), pp. 23–29.

10 K. Peak, D. Farenholtz, and G. Coxey, "Physical abilities testing for police officers: A flexible, job-related approach," *Police Chief*, January 1992, pp. 51–56.

11 See, e.g., Truth or Lie Polygraph Lie Detector Examination Agency, "How can you beat the polygraph?," www.truthorlie.com/beatpoly.html (accessed December 8, 2015).

12 Peak, *Policing America*, p. 78.

13 Ibid.

14 See, e.g., New York State Division of Criminal Justice Services, "Pre-employment police basic course," http://criminaljustice.state.ny.us/ops/training/bcpo/bcpo04.htm (accessed December 8, 2015).

15 See, e.g., D. Bradford and J. E. Pynes, "Police academy training: Why hasn't it kept up with practice?," *Police Quarterly*, vol. 2 (1999), pp. 283–301; N. Marion, "Police academy training: Are we teaching recruits what they need to know?," *Policing: An International Journal of Police Strategies and Management*, vol. 21 (1998), pp. 54–79; R. F. Brand and K. Peak, "Assessing police training curriculums: 'Consumer reports,'" *Justice Professional*, vol. 9 (Winter 1995), pp. 45–58.

16 J. J. Broderick, *Police in a time of change*, 2nd ed. (Prospect Heights, IL: Waveland, 1987), p. 215.

17 Ibid.

18 Ibid.

19 Bradford and Pynes, "Police academy training."

20 Peak, *Policing America*, p. 81.

21 M. S. McCampbell, *Field training for police agencies: The state of the art* (Washington, DC: U.S. Department of Justice, National Institute of Justice, 1986).

22 K. J. Peak, S. Pitts, and R. W. Glensor, "From 'FTO' to 'PTO': A contemporary approach to post-academy recruit training," paper presented at the annual meeting of the Western and Pacific Association of Criminal Justice Educators, Reno, NV, 2006. Reprinted by permission of Ken Peak.

23 R. G. Dunham and G. P. Alpert, *Critical issues in policing: Contemporary readings* (Prospect Heights, IL: Waveland Press, 1989), pp. 111–15.

24 Peak et al., "From 'FTO' to 'PTO,'" p. 6.

25 See, e.g., J. Dewey, *How we think: A restatement of the relation of reflective thinking on the educative process* (Boston: D. C. Heath, 1933).

26 M. Knowles, *Andragogy in action: Applying modern principles of adult learning* (San Francisco: Jossey-Bass, 1981).

27 H. Barrows and R. M. Tamblyn, *Problem-based learning: An approach to medical education* (New York: Springer, 1980).

28 B. S. Bloom, *Taxonomy of educational objectives, handbook I: The cognitive domain* (New York: David McKay, 1956).

29 Peak et al., "From 'FTO' to 'PTO,'" pp. 8–9.

30 The organization's website is www.pspbl.com (accessed December 8, 2015).

31 Equal Employment Opportunity Commission, "Retaliation," www.eeoc.gov/laws/types/retaliation.cfm (accessed December 8, 2015).

32 J. Frank et al., "Reassessing the impact of citizens' attitudes toward the police: A research note," *Justice Quarterly*, vol. 13 (1996), pp. 231–34.

33 J. L. Sichel et al., *Women on patrol: A pilot study of police performance in New York City* (New York: Vera Institute of Justice, 1978).

34 R. Weitzer, "White, black, or blue cops? Race and citizen assessments of police officers," *Journal of Criminal Justice*, vol. 28 (2000), pp. 313–24.

35 S. Walker, *Employment of black and Hispanic police officers, 1983–1988: A follow-up study* (Omaha: Center for Applied Urban Research, University of Nebraska at Omaha, 1989).

36 C. S. Johnson, *Into the mainstream: A survey of best practices in race relations in the South* (Chapel Hill: University of North Carolina Press, 1947).

37 J. L. Kuykendall and D. E. Burns, "The black police officer: An historical perspective," *Journal of Contemporary Criminal Justice*, vol. 4 (1980), p. 5.

38 E. Rudwick, *The unequal badge: Negro policemen in the South—Report of the Southern Regional Council* (Atlanta: Southern Regional Council, 1962).

39 P. S. Sullivan, "Minority officers: Current issues," in *Critical issues in policing: Contemporary readings*, eds. R. G. Dunham and G. P. Alpert, pp. 331–45 (Prospect Heights, IL: Waveland, 1989). Adapted with permission from the International Association of Police Chiefs.

40 H. F. Gosnell, *Negro politicians: The rise of negro politics in Chicago* (Chicago: University of Chicago Press, 1935).

41 S. Leinen, *Black police, white society* (New York: New York University Press, 1984).

42 M. J. Hickman et al., "Does race influence the police disciplinary process?," *Justice Research and Policy*, vol. 3 (2001), pp. 97–113.

43 President's Commission on Law Enforcement and Administration of Justice, *Task force report: The police* (Washington, DC: U.S. Government Printing Office, 1967), p. 162.

44 L. W. Landrum, "The case of Negro police," *New South*, vol. 11 (1947), pp. 5–6; G. Myrdal, *An American dilemma: The Negro problem and modern democracy* (New York: Harper and Brothers, 1944).

45 W. M. Kephart, *Racial factors and urban law enforcement* (Philadelphia: University of Pennsylvania Press, 1957).

46 N. Alex, *New York cops talk back* (New York: Wiley, 1976).

47 N. Alex, *Black in blue* (Englewood Cliffs, NJ: Prentice Hall, 1969).

48 President's Task Force on 21st Century Policing, *Final report of the President's Task Force on 21st Century Policing* (Washington, DC: Office of Community Oriented Policing Services, 2015), p. 16.

49 See, e.g., M. J. Hickman and A. R. Piquero, "Organizational, administrative, and environmental correlates of complaints about police use of force," *Crime & Delinquency*, vol. 55 (2009), pp. 3–27; K. Barrick, M. J. Hickman, and K. J. Strom, "Representative policing and violence towards the police," *Policing*, vol. 8 (2014), pp. 193–204.

50 D. Parsons and P. Jesilow, *In the same voice: Women and men in law enforcement* (Santa Ana, CA: Seven Locks Press, 2001).

51 Ibid.

52 S. Walker, *A critical history of police reform* (Lexington, MA: Lexington Books, 1977), p. 85.

53 C. Owings, *Women police* (New York: F. H. Hitchcock, 1925).

54 G. E. Berkeley, *The democratic policeman* (Boston: Beacon, 1969).

55 C. Milton, *Women in policing* (Washington, DC: Police Foundation, 1972).

56 C. Sulton and R. A. Townsey, *Progress report on women in policing* (Washington, DC: Police Foundation, 1981).

57 Police Foundation, *Community policing: A binding thread through the fabric of our society* (Washington, DC: Police Foundation, 1990).

58 P. Bloch and D. Anderson, *Policewomen on patrol: Final report* (Washington, DC: Police Foundation, 1974); L. J. Sherman, "Evaluation of policewomen on patrol in a suburban police department," *Journal of Police Science and Administration*, vol. 3 (1975), pp. 434–38; J. L. Sichel et al., *Women on patrol: Pilot study of police performance in New York City* (New York: Vera Institute of Justice, 1978).

59 S. Grennan, "Findings on the role of officer gender in violent encounters with citizens," *Journal of Police Science and Administration*, vol. 15 (1988), pp. 78–85.

60 Ibid. See also M. Morash and J. R. Greene, "Evaluating women on patrol: A critique of contemporary wisdom," *Evaluation Review*, vol. 10 (1986), pp. 231–55.

61 Parsons and Jesilow, *In the same voice.*

62 B. A. Reaves, *Local police departments, 2013: Personnel, policies, and practices* (Washington, DC: Bureau of Justice Statistics, 2015), p. 4.

63 D. A. Snyder, *The Americans with Disabilities Act* (Portland, OR: Labor Relations Information Systems, 1991).

64 *Tanberg* v. *Weld County Sheriff*, 787 F.Supp. 970 (D. Colo. 1992).

65 *Bombrays* v. *Toledo*, 849 F.Supp. (N.D. Ohio 1933).

66 *Champ* v. *Baltimore County*, 884 F.Supp. 991 (1995).

67 J. Jacobs and J. Cohen, "The impact of racial integration on the police," *Journal of Police Science and Administration*, vol. 6 (1978), pp. 168–83.

68 R. N. Haarr, "Patterns of interaction in a police patrol bureau: Race and gender barriers to integration," *Justice Quarterly*, vol. 14 (1997), pp. 53–85.

69 *Detroit Police Officers Association* v. *Young*, 446 F.Supp. 979 (1978).

70 *United States* v. *Paradise*, 107 U.S. 1053 (1987).

71 For more information, see Adversity.net, "Case 49: Dayton, Ohio police dept. loses reverse discrimination suit," www.adversity.net/Dayton_OH_PD/default.htm (accessed December 6, 2010).

72 For more information, see Adversity.net, "Milwaukee police reverse discrimination," www.adversity.net/milwaukee_police/alexander_v_jones.htm (accessed December 8, 2015).

73 See, e.g., J. Grencik, "Toward an understanding of stress," in *Job stress and the police officer: Identifying stress reduction techniques*, eds. W. Kroes and J. Hurrell (Washington, DC: U.S. Department of Health, Education, and Welfare, 1975), pp. 163–81.

74 See, e.g., J. Blackmore, "Are police allowed to have problems of their own?," *Police Magazine*, vol. 1 (1978), pp. 47–55, and L. Territo and H. Vetter, *Stress and police personnel* (Boston: Allyn and Bacon, 1981).

75 J. Selye, *Stress without distress* (Philadelphia: Lippincott, 1981).

76 Ibid.

77 J. B. Kuhns, E. R. Maguire, and N. R. Leach, *Health, safety, and wellness program case studies in law enforcement* (Washington, DC: Office of Community Oriented Policing Services, 2015).

78 Merry Morash and Robin N. Haarr, "Gender, workplace problems, and stress in policing," *Justice Quarterly*, vol. 12, no. 1 (March 1995), pp. 113–40.

79 R. L. Veniga and J. Spradley, *How to cope with job burnout* (Englewood Cliffs, NJ: Prentice Hall, 1981), p. 6.

80 M. Silbert, "Job stress and burnout of new police officers," *Police Chief*, vol. 49 (1982), pp. 46–48.

81 R. M. Solomon, "Post-shooting trauma," *Police Chief*, vol. 55 (1988), pp. 40, 42, 44.

82 S. Carson, "Post-shooting stress reduction," *Police Chief*, October 1982, pp. 66–68.

83 Ibid.

84 Solomon, "Post-shooting trauma."

85 C. McHenry, "Stress in the police service: Preventing the long-term effects of trauma," *Occupational Health Review*, July–August 1995, pp. 17–20, quote on p. 18.

86 Ibid.

87 Cited in B. Vila and D. J. Kenney, "Tired cops: The prevalence and potential consequences of police fatigue," *NIJ Journal*, vol. 248 (2002), pp. 16–21, quote on p. 20.

88 B. Vila, *Tired cops: The importance of managing police fatigue* (Washington, DC: Police Executive Research Forum, 2000).

89 Vila and Kenney, "Tired cops," p. 18.

90 Ibid., p. 17.

91 Ibid.

92 Ibid., p. 18.

93 Ibid., p. 17.

94 Ibid., p. 18.

95 Ibid.

96 Ibid., p. 19.

97 *Barnes* v. *Costle*, 561 F.2d 983 (D.C. Cir. 1977).

98 *Meritor Savings Bank* v. *Vinson*, 474 U.S. 1047 (1986).

99 *Hall* v. *GHS Construction Co.*, 842 F.2d 101 (8th Cir. 1988).

100 *Sorlucco* v. *New York City Police Department*, 971 F.2d 864 (2nd Cir. 1992).

101 S. C. Collins, "Sexual harassment and police discipline: Who's policing the police?," *Policing: An International Journal of Police Strategies and Management*, vol. 27 (2004), pp. 512–38.

102 T. Mahoney, "Sexual harassment in California law enforcement: A survey of women police officers," *Journal of California Law Enforcement*, vol. 30 (1996), pp. 82–87.

103 National Center for Women and Policing, *Equity denied: The status of women in policing, 1997* (Los Angeles: Feminist Majority Foundation, 1998), p. 5.

104 For more information, see the Wonderlic website, www.wonderlic.com (accessed December 8, 2015).

105 *Jordan* v. *New London*, 1999 U.S. Dist. LEXIS 14289 (1999).

106 Ibid., pp. 6–7.

107 Equal Employment Opportunity Commission, http://eeoc.gov (accessed December 8, 2015).

108 C. McHenry, "Stress in the police service: Preventing the long-term effects of trauma," *Occupational Health Review*, July–August 1995, p. 18.

109 *Hall* v. *GHS Construction Co.*, 842 F.2d 101 (8th Cir. 1988).

5

Police Subculture

1 Describe the elements of culture.

2 Explain the sources of police subculture.

3 Summarize the components of police subculture.

DANGER AND UNPREDICTABILITY: THE HALLMARKS OF POLICE WORK

On January 7, 2016, Philadelphia officer Jesse Hartnett, 33, became the target of an assassination attempt by a man who fired 11 shots into the driver's side window of Hartnett's police cruiser.[1] Three bullets hit Hartnett in the arm, but he was able to get out his patrol car and return fire, striking his assailant in the buttocks. The alleged attacker, 30-year-old Edward Archer, was soon captured, and told police that he had acted in support of ISIS. According to a police spokesperson, Archer told investigators that "I follow Allah and I pledge allegiance to the Islamic State. That is the reason why I did what I did." Images of the shooting, taken by a nearby security camera, showed Archer wearing a long robe similar to that worn by middle-easterners, running toward the patrol car—and firing into it repeatedly. He then ran away, shooting at least one more time as he ran. Although seriously injured, Officer Hartnett survived the shooting.

The Philadelphia attack illustrates the dangers of police work, and shows how unpredictable such work can be. At the time of the attack, Officer Hartnett had been on patrol and was driving slowly down a neighborhood street

A Philadelphia Police Department vehicle on patrol in the city. In 2016, a Philadelphia police officer was shot a number of times by a man who walked up to his patrol car and fired through the window. How dangerous is police work?

without the slightest inkling of what was about to happen. Incidents like this show that policing is, at its core, a potentially dangerous line of work.

▶ Culture: What Is It?

Culture refers to a shared set of **values**, **norms**, and behaviors that form a particular way of life. Values are standards of goodness, or those things that are perceived to be important. Norms refer to

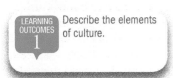

rules and expectations about which forms of behavior are acceptable and which are not. Any discussion of culture should also consider social **institutions**. Institutions can be found in organizational structures—like schools, families, and churches. Social institutions communicate values and norms throughout society and over time contribute to cultural stability. In the policing context, significant research has shown that the nature of police organizations, like other social institutions, shapes police behavior. America is considered a multicultural melting pot because there are many different cultures within our borders, organized by all manner of shared sentiments.

Culture versus Subculture

The term **subculture** refers to cultural patterns that distinguish some segment of a society's population from the rest of that population. Consequently, individuals who share values and norms that differ from those of the larger culture can be said to be members of a subculture. The term **police subculture** (sometimes called *police culture*) has been used to describe the shared values and norms and the established patterns of behavior that

are found among police officers. It describes the fact that police officers generally adhere to a set of values and beliefs that differ in certain crucial respects from those held by members of the wider American culture. Some of the values that characterize police subculture, like patriotism and a dedication to creating a better society, are positive values that many Americans share. Others, like suspicion and cynicism, are not always prized by others but may be necessary for effective (and safe) police work. It is important to understand that the values and norms that characterize police subculture are not unique when taken individually. It is their occurrence together that gives policing its distinctive nature. Police corruption and deviance, insofar as they stem from the subculture of policing, are taken up in Chapter 12. Our concern in this chapter is with the broader nature of police subculture in general.

The section that follows looks at the generic elements of any culture. After covering the basics, we then turn our attention to the sources of police subculture and to the specific components of police subculture (Figure 5–1).

Elements of Culture

Cultures are characterized by themes, or shared commonalities. Consider NASCAR racing. Some would say that there is not only a racing subculture in America but also a number of themes running through it, including fan loyalty to specific drivers, respect for the rules of racing, and a desire to own

CULTURE
A shared set of values, norms, and behaviors that form a particular way of life

SUBCULTURE
Cultural patterns that distinguish some segment of a society's population from the rest of that population

POLICE SUBCULTURE
The shared values and norms and the established patterns of behavior that are found among police officers

Some values are shared between many Americans and the police, and others are unique to the police.

(1) Shared values between many Americans and the police—patriotism, dedication to a better society

(2) Values unique to the police—suspicion, cynicism

FIGURE 5–1 The Police Subculture.

brand-name products associated with NASCAR winners. Themes tend to be shared by members of a particular culture. Culture also promotes the expression of norms and shared values in ways that are defined as acceptable. Let's look briefly at each of these concepts in greater detail (Figure 5–2).

Various Themes

John Crank, who has written extensively on the subject of police subculture,[2] refers to a "confluence of themes," "meaning that diverse aspects of organizational activity merge into a whole united by commonly held values and shared ways of thinking."[3]

Consider another type of culture: academia. The wider American culture often sees universities as places of learning dominated by liberal thinkers. But to characterize the culture of academia and all academics as "liberal" would be inaccurate. Not only do many of today's professors characterize themselves as politically conservative, but liberalism in university settings is tempered by other factors. One of those other factors is skeptical positivism (the essence of science), a theme running through academia that combines with liberal beliefs and countless other factors to create a relatively unique set of beliefs, values, and behavioral patterns. Skeptical positivism rejects beliefs based on faith or tradition alone and demands rigorous scientific proof before an idea can be accepted.

Institutional Values

Our definition of *culture* highlights the role of shared values and norms. Recall that values are what people consider important, but they can also reflect an impression of how certain things should be done. This is what is meant by **institutional values**.

There is a moral dimension to institutional values that suggests the norms we talked about earlier. Cultures contain beliefs not only about the best way to go about accomplishing tasks but also about the moral superiority of one approach over another. For example, consider how a scientific approach to a problem might differ from a faith-based approach to the same problem.

It is useful to think of organizations as promoting their particular institutional values. It is probably safe to say that most law enforcement personnel at one time felt that this was the best way to go about the business of enforcing the law.[4] An opposing view says that the traditional approach to managing police organizations is slow to adapt to new problems (such as the challenges of terrorism and homeland security) and is resistant to change.[5] Some progressive police administrators feel that decentralization, one of the hot topics in policing today, is a more effective approach. (Note that the word *progressive* is itself value laden and that "progressive" ideas should not be accepted in place of more traditional ones unless their true "value" can be demonstrated.)

Preference for centralization or decentralization may actually represent two subcultural perspectives within the larger culture of policing. What, then, would be an example of an institutional value that is ubiquitous in policing? Returning again to Crank's observations, we note the idea of personal responsibility, one of the bedrock (though unwritten) principles on which the American system of criminal justice is built. This belief in personal responsibility is clearly manifested throughout criminal justice agencies, including police departments. There is an almost unshakable faith among police administrators in preventive patrol as useful for deterring would-be criminals, even though much of the research does not necessarily support this approach. The belief seems to be that the *threat* of punishment, resulting from being caught in the act of committing a crime, serves to restrain those who would otherwise choose to break the law.

Various Themes

Various themes or aspects of a particular profession mix together to create a common set of beliefs, behaviors, and reactions to particular sets of circumstances.

Law enforcement officers, for example, often think in terms of "us against them."

Institutional Themes

A sense of agreement exists within a particular culture on how to accomplish valued objectives.

The traditional police department, for example, has a hierarchical, quasi-military structure, and an established formal chain of command with rigid bureaucratic structure.

Emotional Expression

Expression (as well as the mode of expression) of a culture's shared norms and values

In the police context, "war stories" told in the academy serve to build and reinforce cultural beliefs and preferences.

FIGURE 5–2 Three Elements of Culture.

This point also illustrates the interconnectedness between cultures. Crank's observation refers to a general set of beliefs characteristic of American culture that is not limited to criminal justice. But these beliefs have clearly shaped policing—and police subculture. What make police subculture different from the broader American culture are the many additional themes that have been grafted onto it.

Emotional Expression

Businesspeople and other workers "vent" from time to time with some of their colleagues. They complain about everything from annoying or incompetent coworkers to the direction their company is headed. Likewise, college students share with their peers concerns about college life, their professors, tests they have to take, papers they are asked to write, and even their books. Indeed, everyone expresses himself or herself in one way or another.

Expression can occur through several media. Off-duty conversations between fellow officers provide a means for release. Even if an officer's feelings are not openly shared, they can still affect the officer's perception of the world and thus his or her behavior.

To summarize, culture is complex, deeply entrenched, and shared. It is complex in the sense that it comprises various themes. Several sets of beliefs and values intersect to create individual cultures. Finally, culture is shared through a host of verbal and nonverbal channels: openly, subtly, and sometimes tacitly.

One does not need to venture far (geographically or professionally) in this country to discover how rapidly culture can change. This recognition enables us to present a more accurate, complete, and practical definition of *culture*. Crank's definition is useful in this regard: Culture is a body of knowledge that emerges through the shared application of practical skills to concrete problems encountered in daily routines and the normal course of activities.[6]

In closing, we should remark on the self-confirming nature of culture. This means that culture is self-reinforcing. It sustains itself and propagates itself largely intact from one generation to the next. It is no mystery why police officers share many of the same sentiments in different places, and even over time. The beliefs they carry emanate from shared training and common experiences and, as such, tend to transcend time and location. To be sure, cultures change and adapt, but this change does not occur quickly.

▶ Sources of Police Subculture

To this point, our discussion of culture has been generic, without much reference to the unique nature of American policing. Now it is time to get more specific: What is police subculture? What does it look like? Where does it come from? This section is concerned primarily with the last question, the sources of police subculture (Figure 5–3). After we ascertain what it is that has given rise to police subculture, we will be in a better position to grasp exactly what its components are.

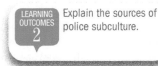
LEARNING OUTCOMES 2 — Explain the sources of police subculture.

FIGURE 5-3 Sources of Police Subculture.

Organizational Factors

Although police departments are certainly not unique in this regard, police work is usually divided into at least three shifts. In larger police departments, there are often several squads of officers working each shift. In the largest agencies, these squads are organized into platoons of 25 or more officers. Platoons might be divided up based on geographic criteria.[7] Police agencies today often use terms other than *platoon* or *squad*, but the organizational makeup remains more or less the same.[8] The result, regardless of name, is a group of officers who work the same schedule.

Perhaps the most unusual shift in policing is the one stretching from midnight or so until shortly after daybreak. Officers who work this shift generally have difficulty associating with people who work normal nine-to-five jobs because they tend to sleep during daylight hours. What's more, some officers are often required to work weekends and holidays, which further interferes with their ability to socialize with and establish friendships with people outside their professional circle.

No matter what the hours, the period at the end of a shift provides ample opportunity to rehash the day's activities, further reinforcing common bonds among police officers. Two researchers who observed a Colorado police department highlighted the importance of these end-of-shift discussions, noting that the period at the end of a shift

> provided an opportunity to discuss department policies, politics, and personalities. Rumors made their rounds at this time—with a few being squelched, several being started, and many being embellished.[9]

Of course, rumors and stories do not stay confined to specific squads or platoons. With daily interaction and transfers, which are common, they spread from one group of officers to the next, as criminologist Ted Rubinstein notes:

Occasionally, a man transfers from one squad to another, bringing with him knowledge of ex-colleagues which he offers to his new colleagues, enriching their knowledge about coworkers who are frequently seen, greeted, chatted with, but rarely known in the personal way as are the [members of the] squad.[10]

This illustrates shift work's impact on the development of police subculture. Many other features of police organizations also work together to breed a relatively unique group of individuals. We will consider the influence of administrators on subordinates, for example, but for now, let's shift gears and focus on the environment as a source of police subculture.

The Street Environment

Policing is a people profession. The daily work of most police officers involves interacting with ordinary citizens and with other professionals in the criminal justice system. No other encounters have as many culture-shaping implications as those between the police and citizens.

Crank has identified two types of encounters that are especially significant in shaping police subculture. The first of these is the **street environment**. Here, an officer's personal beliefs, the circumstances of the encounter (e.g., within view of others or not), and the attitudes each party brings to the encounter (hostility, cooperation, respect, and so on) can influence behavior in ways that are enduring and reinforcing.

Younger officers who have aspirations (some cynical older officers might say "delusions") of changing the world and of engaging in exciting crime-fighting activities are often soon disillusioned by the routine and even frustrating nature of many calls for service, especially those dealing with property crime. In this context, much attention usually focuses on the victim's experience. But the satisfaction that police officers get from taking property crime reports is usually quite low.[11]

Violent crimes can also prove less than exciting. Random acts of violence between total strangers are often the exception. Although the media may suggest otherwise, the typical violent encounters that officers respond to are those between friends and acquaintances,[12] and high on the list are domestic incidents. As Crank notes, "Instead of providing police with a satisfactory sense of work accomplished, [these encounters] reveal the seamy, coarse, and destructive side of ordinary human relations."[13]

These observations show how the environment—especially the typical kind of contact between police and citizens—bodes ominously for police subculture. Such job frustrations, coupled with other environmental elements, lead to a unique worldview and to a characteristic set of beliefs about how to deal with most members of the public and with offenders.

The street environment is an influential shaper of police subculture, but the traffic stop is at least equally influential. Since nearly every traffic stop is involuntary (i.e., drivers would rather *not* be stopped by the police), any hopes of a positive encounter between the officer and the driver are doomed from the start. As a result, traffic stop interactions negatively shape police subculture.

Administration

The administrative arrangements in the typical police department cannot help but inform police subculture. Interactions with superiors and the routine steps taken at the beginning and end of each shift work together with social and physical environments, organizational factors, and other factors to set policing apart from other professions.

The typical officer usually reports for duty at roll call. This may take place in a briefing room where officers are given their assignments, activities of the previous shift are recounted, new policies are discussed, and anything else of importance is brought up. Roll calls are usually presided over by sergeants or their equivalents. From a culture-forming standpoint, roll call is important for a number of reasons, not the least of which is it gives an opportunity to get together and commiserate, especially in the periods right before and after.[14]

At shift end, officers return to the briefing room or equivalent locations to finish their paperwork, change back into civilian attire, and prepare to head home. Debriefing also occurs at this time, particularly if a critical incident, such as a shooting or use of force, occurred during the shift. No matter the arrangement, this stage of the typical officer's day also shapes police subculture. Officers spend time together, relax, and share stories about their days.[15]

As for interactions with supervisors, one would suspect that sergeants (and other higher-ups) would have an influential role in the shaping of police subculture. Research reveals, interestingly, that this tends not to be the case. For example, police researchers David Allen and Michael Maxfield studied the arrest, citation, and warrant activities of police officers and found that sergeants had virtually no direct effects on their subordinates' activities—particularly the quantity of those activities:

> The influence of first-line supervisors in directing the behavior of officers is seriously limited. Even though supervisors emphasize a particular performance criterion or suggest that a certain level of performance be met, officers under their command do not seem to respond positively to these cues.[16]

Although supervisors may not directly influence the culture of line officers, there are other administrative factors that surely do. One of them, according to Crank, is the process of internal review, which encompasses everything from investigating officers whose activities are called into question to reviewing the performance of new and seasoned officers alike. Internal review activities—which are generally not openly welcomed by line officers—surely shape their worldviews, interactions with one another, and ultimately police subculture.

Finally, policies and procedures, sometimes known as *standard operating procedures*, also shape police subculture. Rules are put in place to protect citizens and to protect police organizations from undue scrutiny, complaints, criticisms, and lawsuits. Such rules are written by administrators, attorneys, or high-level officials, often with little input from the rank and file. Most people can sympathize with the resentment that this can breed. Students often have to follow various school procedures that may seem arcane and irrelevant. This, in turn, shapes their attitudes toward administrators, possibly their instructors, and maybe their entire educational experience. The same is true in police work.

Other Criminal Justice Agencies

Police officers' interactions with other criminal justice agencies also shape police subculture. If a prosecutor rejects a case that the investigating officer perceives to be strong, for example, this can lead to disillusionment and frustration, which the officer will likely communicate to his or her peers. The more often this occurs, the more police officers may feel that they stand alone in their crime-fighting efforts and are not being supported by other criminal justice professionals.

On the other hand, if the prosecutor elects to take a case forward, this can take a significant amount of an officer's time, including his or her off-duty time. The defense will be entitled to discovery, which usually includes examination of the police report. The defense will scrutinize the report to ensure that proper procedures were followed and may even call into question the officer's integrity and worthiness—especially if the report was poorly written. All of this can be quite stressful for the officer, thus contributing to a unique set of perceptions, beliefs, and values that characterize police subculture.

The Media

The media have perhaps the most influence on police subculture. Some members of the media are supportive of the police and represent what Crank has called the "inner circle." These are often reporters who have worked with police officers for years and have come to appreciate the difficulties involved in policing. Police officers can usually work constructively with these reporters to manage the release of information and to ensure that investigations proceed unfettered. But not all reporters are supportive, and at least a minority, it seems, are bent on casting law enforcement agencies in an unfavorable light.

The *Houston Chronicle* (a traditionally liberal newspaper) published a series of articles criticizing the Houston Police Department for its use of Tasers.[17] The department's Tasers were equipped with cameras, not unlike the cameras found in patrol cars around the country. The cameras help to ensure that officers act properly and within the law. At the same time, though, there is nothing pleasant about watching a person on the receiving end of a Taser shock. They frequently yell, howl, flail, and appear to be in great pain. The *Chronicle* posted on its website the Taser videos that it had obtained. The newspaper criticized the police department, claiming that officers were using Tasers not only to defuse hostile situations but often when use of the devices was inappropriate. The paper failed to report on any successful incidents where Taser use resulted in the apprehension of dangerous suspects without loss of life. This episode, which some saw as intentionally biased reporting, showed that the police are sometimes "damned if they do, and damned if they don't."

A police department's relationship with the media can be a double-edged sword. The media can aid in investigations, for example, by publicizing composite sketches of suspects. But they can also paint police departments in a less-than-favorable light. This is particularly true in the case of scandals. A scandal involving a small group of officers can tarnish the reputation of an entire department for years. This, in turn, takes its toll on officers who work in that department and who might come to regard members of the press skeptically.

In summary, there are five factors that have been linked to the formation of police subculture: organizational matters, the street environment, administration and administrative styles, relationships with other criminal justice agencies, and relationships with the media. This, of course, is not an exhaustive list. It would be impossible to identify all of the elements that shape police subculture in America. All of these factors interact in complex and sometimes unpredictable ways to produce a set of values and norms not found in any other occupation. What exactly are these values and norms? What is police subculture? We answer these questions in the rest of this chapter.

▶ Components of Police Subculture

In this section, we look at the values and norms that characterize police subculture in America. We examine control and territoriality;

use of force; danger, unpredictability, and suspicion; solidarity; and other components of police subculture (Figure 5–4).

Control of Territory

It is the use of coercion—or at least the *authority* to use coercion—that ultimately defines police work. Sociologist Egon Bittner once described the coercive authority of policing as the distinguishing feature that sets law enforcement apart from other professions. He called it the capacity to use force.[18] The power that officers have when it comes to the potential use of force is awesome because force can be used to deny people their freedom or even to take their lives. The ability to be coercive and to use force shapes the attitudes of police officers and sets them apart from other professionals.

Of course, force is not necessary most of the time, nor is coercion, but the maintenance of control is critical. Combined with the notion of control is territoriality, or the sense of responsibility a police officer feels for a particular area. Police officers must establish control over crime scenes and maintain social control over the neighborhoods they patrol.

Control

The term *control* sounds ominous. It suggests that police officers actively take steps to place limits on people's actions. Certainly, this does occur, especially when criminal suspects do not cooperate; however, there is more to the element of control than this. As Crank observes, "Cops may strategically use symbolic elements of their authority as coercive devices . . . displaying their weaponry in an intimidating way, for example."[19] Simply

maintaining a police presence can do wonders in the furtherance of control.

Control is somewhat synonymous with order maintenance, one of the principal police functions we identify in Chapter 7. The issue also comes up in the next chapter, where we discuss police behavior and decision making. Viewed together, these chapters make it clear that a police officer's identity and effectiveness rest significantly on his or her ability to take control, whether that control is direct (e.g., at a crime scene) or indirect (by simply maintaining a presence in the community).

Territoriality

People, like animals, are all territorial to some extent. Whether we are protecting our homes, our cars, or our personal possessions, each of us takes steps to ensure "ours" does not become "theirs" without our consent. Police officers are also territorial. Instead of using the term *territoriality*, however, Crank calls this aspect of police work **dominion**, as the term "captures the divine responsibility over secular human activity that characterizes the special relationship cops have with a piece of earthly terrain."[20] John Van Maanen made this observation about territoriality:

> [Officers] come to know, in the most familiar and penetrating manner, virtually every passageway—whether alley, street, or seldom used path—located in their sector. From such knowledge of this social stage comes the corresponding evaluations of what particular conditions are to be considered good or bad, safe or unsafe, troubled or calm, usual or unusual, and so on. . . . These evaluations are also linked to temporal properties associated with the public use of a patrolman's area of responsibility. . . . The territorial perspective carried by patrolmen establishes the basic normative standard for the proper use of space.[21]

Think About It. . .

The Police Sixth Sense Police officers are said to have a "sixth sense," a mix of suspicion, fear, and intuition that supposedly sets them apart

from ordinary citizens. Interestingly, no one has ever set out to prove that police officers are any different than ordinary citizens when it comes to a set of sixth sense–like characteristics. In *The Gift of Fear*, Gavin de Becker argues that everyone can learn to recognize risk, rely on intuition, and evaluate the potential for violence in any given encounter. Perhaps, then, cops are taught the sixth sense while ordinary citizens sometimes aren't. *Is there a police "sixth sense"? How can we know? How might one go about proving the presence or absence of a police sixth sense?*

Control—Synonymous with order maintenance, one of the principal police functions. Control is direct (at a crime scene, for example) or indirect (by simply maintaining a presence in the community).

Territoriality—Police officers tend to learn every aspect of the area to which they are assigned. As part of this learning, they come to appreciate what is normal or abnormal, safe or unsafe. An officer's sense of territory leads him or her to feel a sense of ownership over his or her geographical area of responsibility.

Use of Force—The very possibility of having to use or to face force, and the emotions that accompany the use or threat of force, is a powerful contributor to police subculture.

Danger—Much of police work is routine and predictable, but there is the potential, at any moment, for a violent altercation that could lead to the taking of a life, be it a suspect's life or the officer's.

Unpredictability—There are pros and cons to the unpredictability that is inherent in policing. For one thing, danger can erupt at any moment. Unpredictability, on the other hand, lends meaning and excitement to the job.

Suspicion—A simple equation characterizes much of police work: danger + unpredictability = suspicion. Cops know that given the potential for danger around any turn and the inherent uncertainty that go along with police work, a sense of suspicion is essential.

The Split-Second Syndrome—There are three features of policing—urgency of police–citizen encounters, the involuntariness of such encounters, and the public setting in which they take place—combine to put officers in the position of having to make quick on-the-spot decisions.

Moral Superiority—Moral superiority is concerned with a belief on the part of police officers that they represent a higher moral order.

Common Sense—Common sense arises from the doing of police work, what officers see and how officers act on and react to their working environment. It is the practical knowledge they use to do their work.

The Masculine Environment—Police officers work in a largely masculine environment. This is partly due to the fact that the profession has historically been dominated by males. Invariably, this has caused police subculture to be dominated by masculine values and orientations.

The Us-versus-Them Mentality—Police officers perception that it is "us," the police, against "them," everyone else.

Secrecy—The public does not have access to much of what happens in the world of law enforcement. Information tends to be given out on a need-to-know basis. Secrecy also insulates officers from intensive scrutiny from supervisors and the community.

Isolation—The job often requires officers to literally work in isolation. Perhaps more important, though, is the prospect of isolation from the community.

Bravery—Police officers need to possess the attribute of bravery before entering the profession. A person who does not feel comfortable in confrontational, perhaps dangerous situations (or who cannot be taught to act bravely) probably won't make a very good officer.

Art of Deception—Although somewhat controversial, some experts regard the art of deception as none other than good policing or creative detective work.

FIGURE 5–4 **Components of a Police Subculture.**

Use of Force

William Wesley was among the first police researchers to cite the importance of force as a crucial element of police culture. Others, like Bittner, also focused much of their attention on the role of force in policing. The very possibility of having to use or to face force—and the emotions that accompany the use or threat of force—is a powerful contributor to police subculture.[22]

The role force plays in shaping police culture is further magnified by the war metaphor we use to refer to crime fighting. The phrases "war on crime" and "war on drugs" are commonly used, often without much conscious thought, but the war metaphor effectively shapes police subculture. As Crank puts it, "The metaphor 'war' has had explosive mobilizing potential. It provided a way to view the police as protectors of society (read 'your wives and children'), and to view criminals as amoral enemies—less than human."[23]

It is not just force that shapes police subculture; it is specific types of force. Consider guns, perhaps the most familiar symbols of policing next to white sedans with light bars. "In the culture of policing, guns transform police work into a heroic occupation, providing both a bottom line and an unquestionable righteousness that pervades all police–citizen encounters,"[24] Crank notes. The ready availability of handguns, rifles, shotguns, and semiautomatic weapons combines with the war metaphor to create a special type of work environment, one that cannot help but mold police subculture:

> Policing in the United States is very much like going to war. Three times a day in countless locker rooms across the land, large men and a growing number of women carefully arm and armor themselves for the day's events. They begin by strapping on flak jackets. . . . Then they pick up a wide, heavy, black leather belt and hang around it the tools of their trade: gun, mace, handcuffs, bullets. When it is fully loaded, they swing the belt around their hips with the same practiced motion of the gun-fighter in Western movies, slugging it down and buckling it in front. Many officers slip an additional small-caliber pistol into their trouser pocket or a leg holster just above the ankle. Inspecting themselves in a full-length mirror, officers thread their night sticks into a metal ring on the side of their belt.[25]

Of all the items in a police officer's arsenal, though, it is the sidearm that is most apparent, most influential, and most significant in its contribution to occupational identity. The prospect of a deadly encounter, as Crank observes, is "etched into the personality of the police officer forever—an unrequested rite of passage that leaves a stain on the personality of the officer."[26]

There is an interesting paradox that arises with respect to guns. They shape police subculture perhaps more than any other factor, but (other than at practice ranges) police officers rarely fire their weapons.[27] To be sure, there are some police duties that require more frequent weapons usage, such as serving on a special weapons and tactics (SWAT) team. And there are some cities (and areas of those cities) that are far more dangerous than others. On the whole, though, gun use by police officers is infrequent.

Danger, Unpredictability, and Suspicion

Chapter 4 touched on academy training and recruits' learning of the so-called sixth sense (also see the accompanying "Think About It" box), the police officer's somewhat intuitive feelings of skepticism and suspicion. Skepticism and suspicion are essential in policing because the job can sometimes be very unpredictable. This section looks at how danger and unpredictability shape police subculture. Together they breed skepticism and suspicion at levels largely unmatched in other professions.

Danger

The potential for danger sets policing apart from other occupations (see also Figure 5–5, which includes police officers in the category of "Government").[28] It may not be the most objectively

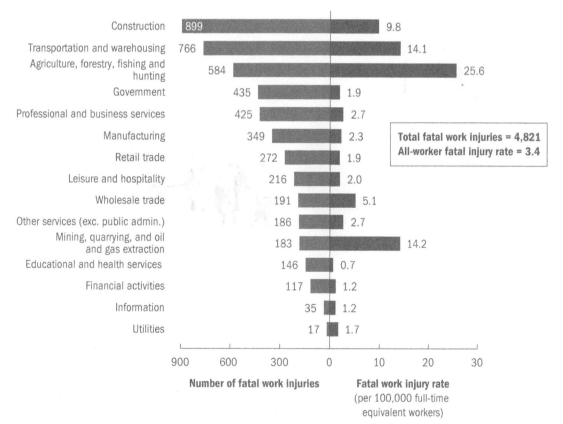

Number and rate of fatal occupational injuries by industry sector, 2014

Industry sector	Number of fatal work injuries	Fatal work injury rate
Construction	899	9.8
Transportation and warehousing	766	14.1
Agriculture, forestry, fishing and hunting	584	25.6
Government	435	1.9
Professional and business services	425	2.7
Manufacturing	349	2.3
Retail trade	272	1.9
Leisure and hospitality	216	2.0
Wholesale trade	191	5.1
Other services (exc. public admin.)	186	2.7
Mining, quarrying, and oil and gas extraction	183	14.2
Educational and health services	146	0.7
Financial activities	117	1.2
Information	35	1.2
Utilities	17	1.7

Total fatal work injuries = 4,821
All-worker fatal injury rate = 3.4

Number of fatal work injuries

Fatal work injury rate (per 100,000 full-time equivalent workers)

Private construction had the highest count of fatal injuries in 2014, but the private agriculture, forestry, fishing and hunting sector had the highest fatal work injury rate.

FIGURE 5–5 **Number and Rate of Fatal Occupational Injuries by Industry Sector, 2014.**
Source: From Census of Fatal Occupational Injuries, 2014, Bureau of Labor Statistics.

dangerous job (timber cutters and taxi drivers, for instance, die on the job considerably more often than police officers do), but this does not discount the prominent position that perceptions of danger hold in policing. Learning about the prospect of danger begins at the academy and continues through field training, where "police vicariously experience, learn, and re-learn the potential for danger through 'war stories'" told by veteran officers.[29]

In the study of victims (known as *victimology*), there is a concept called the *victimization paradox*. It refers to the fact that some people, especially women, tend to be more fearful of crime than is justified by the likelihood of actually being victimized. A similar phenomenon has been identified in policing and has been called the **paradox of policing**. University of Cincinnati criminologist Francis Cullen and his colleagues found that while the potential for danger pervades police work, policing is not particularly hazardous compared with a number of other occupations. Officers who were interviewed felt that their personal chance of being injured or killed was slim, but they still perceived policing as a dangerous occupation.[30] In other words, policing carries a high *potential* for danger, even if the chances for *actual* danger are not all that high.

A problem with the Cullen study and other studies of the relative dangerousness of police work is that they often focus on officer deaths. Deaths are relatively rare, especially in light of modern medical care, training, and personal protection equipment, such as bulletproof vests. So, if deaths are not a good measure of dangerousness, what is? Some researchers *have* looked at assaults against police officers. The Federal Bureau of Investigation (FBI), for example, found that 48,315 officers were assaulted throughout the United States in 2014.[31] This number vastly exceeded the number of killings of police officers; when limited to homicides, such killings tend to number below 50 in any given year. There were 51 in 2014, the most recent year for which data were available as of this writing.[32] See Figure 5–6 for additional details on the events surrounding killings of, and assaults against, police officers—according to the FBI.

How does police work compare with other occupations in terms of the potential for assault? Certain elements of police work are far more dangerous than others. Researchers have not fully answered this question. Even so, it is a safe bet that few other occupations carry as much potential for employee assault as does policing.

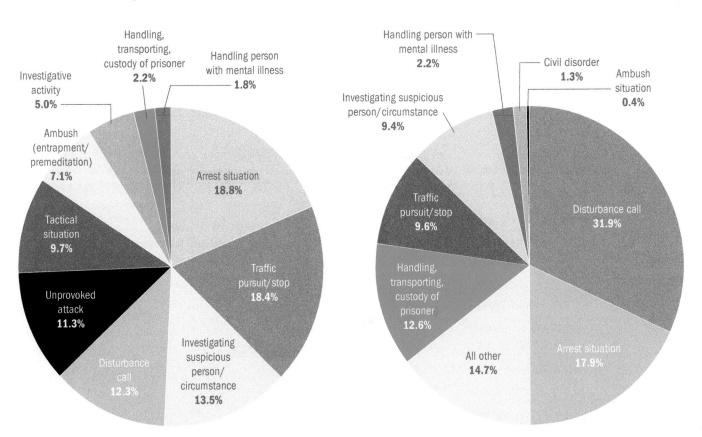

Percent of 505 officers feloniously killed[2]

Percent of 563,030 officers assaulted[3, 4]

[1] Because of rounding the percentages may not add to 100.0.

[2] The circumstance category of "All other" does not apply to the data collected for law enforcement officers feloniously killed.

[3] The circumstance categories of "Ambush (entrapment/premeditation)" and "Unprovoked attack" are included in the "Ambush situation" data collected for law enforcement officers assaulted.

[4] The circumstance categories of "Investigative activity" and "Tactical situation" are included in the "All other" data collected for law enforcement officers assaulted.

FIGURE 5–6 **Law Enforcement Officers Feloniously Killed and Assaulted: Percent Distribution[1] by Circumstance at Scene of Incident, 2005–2014.**
Source: From Law enforcement officers killed and assaulted, 2014, U.S Department of justice.

Unpredictability

The relative dangerousness of policing can be debated. Some researchers would say perceptions of dangerousness are overplayed, and officers on the streets would likely argue the opposite. But it is difficult to dispute that levels of unpredictability are high, no matter what one's perspective.

A common saying in the police literature is some variation of this: "Police work is hours of sheer boredom punctuated by moments of sheer terror." Others have referred to the "huff and puff of the chase."[33] Indeed, a number of researchers have argued that it is those unpredictable moments of terror—the adrenaline-pumping seconds—that make policing an attractive job to many people.[34]

Unpredictability need not equate with danger, however. It can simply give rise to the bizarre. Unpredictability can also take on an air of unpleasantness, and officers need a strong stomach to deal with some of what they encounter.

Suspicion

Suspicion can creep into an officer's private life and into his or her associations with others—such as neighbors and strangers—who are not employed in the same line of work. In this vein, suspicion is more than good police work or part of the working personality. Rather, it is a key factor that defines police subculture.

By outsiders, suspicion is regarded as an unfortunate byproduct of policing that slowly takes over an officer's whole personality, not just his or her working persona. Some feel that the lack of trust police officers exhibit toward others (apart from other officers) explains why they do not associate much with civilians while off the clock. Police officers regard suspicion in quite a different way. They understand that they have been *trained* to be suspicious, as failure to be "on guard" most of the time can mean the difference between life and death.[35]

The Split-Second Syndrome

If danger and unpredictability breed suspicion, then this is because of what criminologist James Fyfe has called the **split-second syndrome**.[36]

Sometimes officers' decisions are appropriate; other times they are not. If a bad decision is made, Fyfe says, it is partly due to the need to make decisions in the heat of the moment. When, for example, a police officer shoots a suspect who turns out not to be a danger, we must put ourselves in the shoes of the officer. Then it becomes a little more apparent how such decisions come to be made. Inappropriate decisions should be *expected* some of the time given the demands placed on officers to choose a course of action in a short amount of time, and "any subsequent criticism of officers' decisions—especially by those outside the police, who can have no real appreciation of the burdens upon officers—is an unwarranted attempt to be wise after the event."[37]

Solidarity

There is a tendency among police officers to stick together and to associate with one another. In terms of police subculture, this is known as **solidarity**. Solidarity itself consists of several elements, each of which is covered in the next few subsections. We will look at moral superiority, common sense, the masculine environment, the us-versus-them mentality, and secrecy. Again, we draw on John Crank's informative examination of police subculture for guidance.

Moral Superiority

In discussing police morality, Crank points out that "police see themselves as representatives of a higher morality embodied in a blend of American traditionalism, patriotism, and religion. As moral agents, police view themselves as guardians whose responsibility is not simply to make arrests but to roust out society's trouble-makers."[38] In other words, they see themselves as morally superior in some sense. This may sound pompous, but remember that policing is about enforcing the law. Laws reflect people's perceptions of right and wrong, and those who break them are on the "wrong side," at least most of the time.

There is a darker side to the police moral sense, too. It leads to a tendency to regard ordinary citizens as different and even inferior. For example, people who get speeding tickets are often admonished by the citing officer, who might conclude by saying, "Please watch your speed now." Such statements are usually offered up out of genuine concern for the driver's safety, but they can also be said with thick sarcasm laden with an air of superiority. It is these latter tendencies that Crank points to in his discussion of the "moral mandate" inherent in police work.

Related to the moral mandate is the concept of **dramaturgy**. The simple definition of *dramaturgy* is "the art of theater, or theatrics." Applied to policing, dramaturgy refers to putting on a display of high-mindedness. This display further reinforces beliefs—on the part of police *and* citizens—that law enforcement is doing the right thing and that those who work in it are the "good guys." Perhaps the classic study of this higher moral sense is John Van Maanen's 1978 paper called "The Asshole."[39] Although some people may find the title of Van Maanen's paper offensive, the paper is well known in academic circles, and we use it here in order to be true to his original presentation. Van Maanen found that police officers would brand difficult people with this quite negative term, stigmatizing them.

According to Van Maanen, the identification of an "asshole" proceeds in three steps. First, the **affront** is when an officer's authority is questioned. The second stage, **clarification**, occurs when the officer attempts to ascertain what kind of person he or she is dealing with. Finally, the **remedy** consists of the officer's response. "Assholes," according to Van Maanen, are the people most likely to be on the receiving end of some "street justice."

In reflecting on Van Maanen's work, Crank observes that the term "contained a great deal of meaning for the police. The label emerged from the need to maintain control in street encounters, and from a moral imperative to assert the authority of the state when it was questioned."[40] A problem, though, is that too many people can be branded with this label or, at best, viewed as untrustworthy. This is the result of an unfortunate reality in everyday police work:

> People lie to us eight hours a day. Everybody lies to us: offenders, victims, witnesses. They all lie to the police.

It gets so bad, you go to a party, somebody comes up to talk to you. You're thinking, "Why is this guy saying this to me? What's his game?" You can't turn it off.[41]

There are other terms besides "asshole" that police use to describe criminal suspects, other officers, citizens in general, superiors, and scores of other people and issues. Indeed, there is a police vocabulary that is unique and sometimes humorous.

Common Sense

According to Crank, common sense is "the lifeblood of the police culture."[42] What is common sense? The use of the term *common sense* in this context distinguishes between book learning and the ways in which actual police work is done:

Officers take great pride in their common sense. But their common sense does not come from the world as given. To the contrary, police common sense is expressed in their ability to see the world unseen. Common sense derives from an officer's skills in recognizing the hidden danger in the seemingly safe world inhabited by ordinary citizens.[43]

The Masculine Environment

Police officers work in a largely masculine environment. This is partly due to the fact that the profession has historically been dominated by males. Invariably, this has caused police subculture to be dominated by masculine values and orientations:

From the outset, recruits are expected to confirm their masculine images to others and to themselves by exaggerating the characteristics associated with manhood. . . . Training emphasizes physical conditioning, fighting, weaponry, all skills that are associated with traditional male roles and are practiced as play in the early childhood of American males. . . . From crude slurs against women to the demonstration of an officer's willingness to put his or her life on the line for a fellow officer, themes of masculinity are pervasive to police culture.[44]

The Us-versus-Them Mentality

Anthony Bouza, noted police scholar and former chief of the Minneapolis Police Department, vividly captured another defining component of police culture—the us-versus-them mentality:

The sense of "us vs. them" that develops between cops and the outside world forges a bond between cops whose strength is the stuff of fables. It is called the *brotherhood in blue*, and it inspires a fierce and unquestioning loyalty to all cops, everywhere. It is widened by the dependence cops have on each other for safety and backup. The response to a summons to help is a cop's life-line. An "assist police officer" is every cop's first priority. The ultimate betrayal is for one cop to fail to back up another.[45]

The us-versus-them mentality is also reflected in the points we have already made about officers associating with one another. It spills over into (and is influenced by) other components of police subculture. "It is important to bear in mind

that being a member of the police fraternity is also a highly gratifying emotional experience in which the officer sees himself as belonging to an exclusive group of men who are braver, smarter, stronger, and more self-reliant than the civilian population they serve."[46]

Secrecy

Researchers have found that secrecy goes hand in hand with solidarity. But one doesn't need to be a researcher to get a feel for how secrecy is important in police work. The veil of secrecy that tends to pervade law enforcement has been readily revealed in high-profile investigations of police corruption. The Mollen Commission's investigation of the New York City Police Department during the 1990s reached this conclusion:

[Secrecy and solidarity] facilitate corruption primarily in two ways. First, they encourage corruption by setting a standard that nothing is more important than the unswerving loyalty of officers to one another—not even stopping the most serious forms of corruption. Second, these attitudes thwart efforts to control corruption. They lead officers to protect or cover up for others' crimes—even crimes of which they heartily disapprove.[47]

Eastern Kentucky University police studies professor Victor Kappeler and his colleagues have identified a series of what they call "postulates shaping the ethos of secrecy." By "postulates," they mean statements that reflect the overall sentiments expressed by perhaps the majority of police officers. Here are some examples:

* *"Don't give up another cop."* As perhaps one of the most important factors contributing to secrecy and to a sense of solidarity, this postulate admonishes officers to never, regardless of the seriousness or nature of a case, provide information to either superiors or nonpolice that would cause harm to a fellow police officer. . . .

* *"Watch out for your partner first and then the rest of the guys working that tour."* This postulate tells police officers they have an obligation to their partners first, and then to other officers working the same shift. "Watching out," in this context, means that an officer has a duty not only to protect a fellow officer from physical harm, but also to watch out for their interests in other matters.

* *"If you get caught off base, don't implicate anybody else."* Being caught off base can involve a number of activities, ranging from being out of one's assigned sector to engaging in prohibited activities. This postulate teaches officers that if they are discovered in proscribed activities, they should accept the punishment, not implicate others.[48]

Other Components of Police Subculture

Control and territoriality, use of force, suspicion, and solidarity are key components of police culture. There are a few others, though, that do not fit neatly into any of these categories. They include isolation, bravery, and the creative use of deception.

Isolation

Police work is characterized by at least two forms of isolation. First, the job often requires officers to literally work in isolation. Consider sheriff's deputies in rural counties. They can effectively be on their own most of the time. Perhaps more important, though, is the prospect of isolation from the community. Not only are officers somewhat physically removed from the communities they serve, but they can feel isolated in terms of relationships as well. This is especially true of relationships with nonpolice:

> Social isolation becomes both a consequence and a stimulus. . . . Police officers find that constraints of schedule, of secrecy, of group mystique, and of growing adaptive suspiciousness and cynicism limit their friendships and relationships in the nonpolice world.[49]

Bravery

Bravery is one more key component of police subculture. New officers are taught the importance of not backing down, and veteran cops are constantly reminded not to appear "soft."

The Art of Deception

There is a clear dark side to deception. For one thing, most people do not enjoy being lied to. For another, deception can be criminal, such as in the case of providing perjured testimony. There is more to deception in the policing context, though, and it is not necessarily all bad.

Certain types of lies are necessary and desirable. Consider the usual buy–bust operation in which an undercover officer sells a willing buyer a quantity of illegal narcotics. This operation is common in police agencies throughout the United States and is conducted in an effort to control a number of different types of crime. Buy–bust activities rely completely on the art of deception. For obvious reasons, buy–busts would not succeed if they were conducted by uniformed officers.

What kinds of lies are appropriate? Thomas Barker, R. N. Friery, and David L. Carter identified three types of lies and then surveyed officers concerning their perceptions of each.[50] The first were so-called **accepted lies**, those that are necessary in furthering the police mission. Second were **tolerated lies**, those that are used to defend questionable discretionary decisions. Finally, **deviant lies** expressly violate the rules and legal requirements. Interestingly, 58% of the officers felt deviant lies were acceptable if the end result was satisfactory. The percentages were much higher for the other types of lies.

Deception may not exactly pervade law enforcement, but it is certainly an important component of police subculture. It is but one element in a long list of values and beliefs that tend to characterize the law enforcement profession in America. Although a distinct culture characterizes many, if not all, occupations, it is safe to say that police subculture is clearly unique.

Police Subculture and Officer Stress

A recent article in the *FBI Law Enforcement Journal* points out the negative features of police subculture, saying that it often prevents officers from seeking the help and outside support that they need in dealing with traumatic on-the-job situations and personal stress. In the words of the article:

> As a result of the difficult and often dangerous duties that police work involves, the occupational stress that officers face is cumulatively debilitating and consuming. Yet, sometimes, law enforcement agencies offer only limited resources to help officers deal with this trauma. Worse still, these organizations typically exhibit a firmly engrained policing subculture that dismisses the need for such assistance.

> Law enforcement's common but dangerous subculture poses one of the most significant risks to the health and wellness of its personnel. This subculture leads officers to feel that they need to act as though they can handle anything; it emphasizes individual strength and independence, which encourages personnel to maintain a façade of invincibility. Out of fear that they will appear weak, police officers generally do not encourage each other to talk about their problems.[51]

The article goes on to say that police officers at all levels should be encouraged to analyze police subculture, and to identify its positive and negative features. The article also encourages officers to break the bonds of police subculture and to seek out help from the people and agencies who can best provide it—even if most of those resources are outside of official channels. Although peer support is very important, the article notes that professional counseling, spirituality, and wellness programs offer additional resources that should be employed in dealing with the stress of police work.

Mark Waugh/Alamy Stock Photo

A police officer examines the scene of a violent crime. Law enforcement officers are exposed to many stressors that most other people are able to avoid. How does police subculture help in dealing with stress? How might it hinder addressing it?

This article on police subculture raises a number of interesting questions:

1. What is police subculture?
2. What are the negative aspects of police subculture?
3. What are its positive aspects?

LEARNING OUTCOMES 1

Describe the elements of culture.

Culture is a shared set of values, norms, and behaviors that form a way of life. Cultures are characterized by similar themes, institutional values (i.e., beliefs about how things should get done), and means of expression. A segment of a larger culture that shares particular values and norms is called a *subculture*.

1. What is culture?

2. What are the differences between a culture and a subculture?

3. What is the role of institutional values in the formation of a culture?

culture A set of shared values, norms, and behaviors that form a way of life.

value A standard of goodness, desirability, behavior, beauty, or interaction that serves as a guideline for living within a particular culture.

norm A rule or expectation for behavior that characterizes a particular social group.

institution An organizational structure through which values and norms are transmitted over time and from one location to another within a society.

subculture Cultural patterns that distinguish some segment of a society's population.

police subculture The shared values and norms and the established patterns of behavior that tend to characterize policing; also called *police culture*.

institutional value A sense of agreement within a particular culture about how to accomplish a valued objective.

LEARNING OUTCOMES 2

Explain the sources of police subculture.

The sources of police culture include organizational factors, the street environment, administration, other criminal justice agencies, and the media. Values within police subculture are not necessarily foreign to the wider culture, but their close association with one another and the exclusion of other wider norms and values are what give police subculture its characteristics.

1. From what sources does the police subculture arise?

2. How does the street environment influence police subculture?

street environment One of two settings identified by John Crank (the other is the traffic stop) in which police officers perform daily tasks that involve interaction with ordinary citizens and with other criminal justice professionals.

LEARNING OUTCOMES 3

Summarize the components of police subculture.

Police subculture is characterized by several factors, including control and territoriality; use of force; danger, unpredictability, and suspicion; and solidarity. Control refers not just to control over a particular area but also to an officer's sense of territoriality. Police work is potentially dangerous, and work situations are commonly unpredictable. These factors lead to suspicion and force officers to make split-second decisions. Solidarity is about sticking together. It has a number of components: moral superiority, common sense, masculine values, an us-versus-them mentality, and an aura of secrecy. Policing can be isolating; officers can be physically and socially isolated from the citizens they serve. Bravery is another essential component of police subculture. Finally, police subculture is sometimes characterized by the creative use of deception.

1. What are the key components of the police subculture? Which is most important in your view?

2. What role does territoriality play in the police subculture?

3. What is meant by the term "split-second syndrome," and how does it apply to police work?

dominion John Crank's substitute for the term *territoriality*, which refers to an officer's sense of personal ownership over the area for which he or she is responsible.

paradox of policing A phenomenon in which a police officer's fear of being injured or killed is stronger than is justified by actual rates of injury or death within the profession.

split-second syndrome A condition confronting police officers that involves three central features of policing—the urgency of police–citizen encounters, the involuntariness of such encounters, and a public setting—all of which combine to place officers in the position of having to make quick on-the-spot decisions.

solidarity The tendency among police officers to stick together and associate with one another.

dramaturgy In the law enforcement context, the act of putting on a display of high-mindedness.

affront According to John Van Maanen, the first of three steps police officers use in identifying an "asshole." It occurs when an officer's authority is questioned.

clarification According to John Van Maanen, the second of three steps police officers use in identifying an "asshole." It occurs when the officer attempts to ascertain what kind of person he or she is dealing with.

remedy According to John Van Maanen, the last of three steps police officers use in identifying an "asshole." It consists of the officer's response to an affront.

accepted lie A lie that is necessary in furthering the police mission.

tolerated lie A lie that is used to defend a questionable discretionary decision.

deviant lie A lie that expressly violates the rules and legal requirements.

References

1 Jon Hurdle and Richard Perez-Penajan, "Gunman said he shot Philadelphia officer for ISIS, police say," *New York Times*, January 8, 2016, http://www.nytimes.com/2016/01/09/us/philadelphia-police-officer-wounded-in-ambush-on-his-patrol-car.html (accessed March 16, 2016).

2 J. P. Crank, *Understanding police culture* (Cincinnati: Anderson, 1998). His book was an invaluable resource in the organization of this chapter. We cite it in several places.

3 Ibid., p. 14.

4 Ibid., p. 15.

5 See, for example, D. Guyot, "Bending granite: Attempts to change the rank structure of American police departments," *Journal of Police Science and Administration*, vol. 7 (1979), pp. 253–84.

6 Crank, *Understanding police culture*, p. 15.

7 J. Rubinstein, *City police* (New York: Farrar, Strauss, and Giroux, 1973), pp. 32–43.

8 Note that *platoon* and *squad* are terms commonly used in the military.

9 M. R. Pogrebin and E. D. Poole, "Humor in the briefing room," *Journal of Contemporary Ethnography*, vol. 17 (1988), pp. 183–210, quote on pp. 188–89.

10 Rubinstein, *City police*, p. 32.

11 Crank, *Understanding police culture*, p. 30. See also J. Van Maanen, "Observations on the making of policemen," *Human Organization*, vol. 32 (1973), pp. 407–18.

12 M. Felson, *Crime and everyday life* (Thousand Oaks, CA: Pine Forge Press, 1994).

13 Crank, *Understanding police culture*, p. 30. See also A. Niederhoffer, *Behind the shield* (Garden City, NY: Doubleday, 1967).

14 Crank, *Understanding police culture*, p. 32.

15 Ibid. See also Pogrebin and Poole, "Humor in the briefing room."

16 D. N. Allen and M. G. Maxfield, "Judging police performance: Views and behavior of patrol officers," in *Police at work: Policy issues and analysis*, ed. R. R. Bennett, pp. 65–86 (Beverly Hills, CA: Sage, 1983).

17 R. Khanna, "Questions grow over HPD's use of Taser guns," *Houston Chronicle*, January 14, 2007, http://www.chron.com/news/houston-texas/article/Questions-grow-over-HPD-s-use-of-Taser-guns-1842941.php (accessed January 13, 2016).

18 E. Bittner, *The functions of police in modern society* (Washington, DC: National Institute of Mental Health, 1970).

19 Crank, *Understanding police culture*, p. 40.

20 Ibid., p. 44.

21 Van Maanen, "Observations on the making of policemen," p. 226.

22 Rubinstein, *City police*, p. 318.

23 Crank, *Understanding police culture*, p. 69.

24 Ibid., p. 82.

25 J. H. Skolnick and D. H. Bayley, *The new blue line: Police innovation in six American cities* (New York: Free Press, 1986), pp. 141–42.

26 Crank, *Understanding police culture*, p. 86.

27 W. A. Geller and M. S. Scott, "Deadly force: What we know," in *Thinking about police*, 2nd ed., eds. C. Klockars and S. Mastrofski, pp. 446–76 (New York: McGraw-Hill, 1991), p. 449.

28 P. Ragonese, *The soul of a cop* (New York: St. Martin's Paperbacks, 1991), pp. 200–202.

29 V. E. Kappeler, R. D. Sluder, and G. P. Alpert, *Forces of deviance: The dark side of policing* (Prospect Heights, IL: Waveland, 1994), p. 100.

30 F. Cullen et al., "Paradox in policing: A note on perceptions of danger," *Journal of Police Science and Administration*, vol. 11 (1983), pp. 457–62.

31 Federal Bureau of Investigation, *Law enforcement officers killed and assaulted, 2014*, https://www.fbi.gov/about-us/cjis/ucr/leoka/2014 (accessed January 12, 2016).

32 Ibid.

33 E. Bittner, *Aspects of police work* (Boston: Northeastern University Press, 1990).

34 P. K. Manning, *Police work: The social organization of policing* (Cambridge, MA: MIT Press, 1977); J. Van Maanen, "Working the street: A developmental view of police behavior," in *The potential for reform in criminal justice*, vol. 3, ed. H. Jacob, pp. 83–129 (Beverly Hills, CA: Sage, 1974).

35 Rubinstein, *City police*, p. 224.

36 J. J. Fyfe, "The split-second syndrome and other determinants of police violence," in *Critical issues in policing*, 4th ed., eds. R. G. Dunham and G. P. Alpert, pp. 583–98 (Prospect Heights, IL: Waveland, 2001).

37 Ibid.

38 Crank, *Understanding police culture*, p. 151. See also G. W. Sykes, "Street justice: A moral defense of order maintenance policing," *Justice Quarterly*, vol. 3 (1986), pp. 497–512.

39 J. Van Maanen, "The asshole," in *Policing: A view from the street*, eds. P. K. Manning and J. Van Maanen, pp. 221–38 (Santa Monica, CA: Goodyear, 1978).

40 Crank, *Understanding police culture*, p. 160.

41 C. Fletcher, *Pure cop* (New York: Pocket Books, 1991), p. 278.

42 Crank, *Understanding police culture*, p. 164.

43 Ibid., pp. 172–73.

44 Ibid., p. 180.

45 A. Bouza, *The police mystique: An insider's look at cops, crime, and the criminal justice system* (New York: Plenum Press, 1990), p. 74.

46 P. Bonifacio, *The psychological effects of police work: A psychodynamic approach* (New York: Plenum Press, 1991), p. 39.

47 *The report of the City of New York Commission to investigate allegations of police corruption and the anti-corruption procedures of the police department* (New York: The Mollen Commission, 1994), pp. 51–52.

48 Reprinted by permission of Waveland Press, Inc., from Victor E. Kappeler et al., "Breeding deviant conformity," in *Forces of deviance: The dark side of policing* (Long Grove, IL: Waveland Press, Inc., 1998). All rights reserved.

49 C. Bahn, "Police socialization in the eighties: Strains in the forging of an occupational identity," *Journal of Police Science and Administration*, vol. 12 (1984), pp. 390–94, quote on p. 392.

50 T. Barker, R. N. Friery, and D. L. Carter, "After L.A., would your local police lie?" in *Police deviance*, 3rd ed., eds. T. Barker and D. Carter, pp. 155–68 (Cincinnati: Anderson, 1994).

51 Mark Malman, "Changing Police Subculture," *FBI Law Enforcement Bulletin*, April 2012, https://leb.fbi.gov/2012/april/changing-police-subculture (accessed March 5, 2016).

6

Police Discretion and Behavior

1 Describe police discretion and its advantages and disadvantages.

2 Differentiate between the universalistic and particularistic perspectives on police behavior.

3 Describe the factors that affect police decision making.

Danny Johnston/AP Images

THE FERGUSON EFFECT

When the FBI released a six-month report on crime rates in late 2015, it contained some shocking data. "After years of declining rates in nearly every big city, we're now seeing many cities break that trend and begin climbing back up," said University of Missouri Professor Richard Rosenfeld, one of the country's leading researchers on crime rates.[1] Although changes in crime rates are not always easy to explain, a number of police experts pointed to what they called the "Ferguson effect" in pushing rates up. The Ferguson effect is the name of a hypothesis, developed in the aftermath of riots in Ferguson, Missouri, in 2014. The riots followed the shooting of Michael Brown, an unarmed black 18-year-old, by a white police officer. (For more details on the event, see the opening story in Chapter 13.) Some claimed that Brown had his hands raised in surrender when he was shot. Although that account was later disputed, and a St. Louis County grand jury refused to indict the officer, days of rioting and looting enveloped Ferguson, a St. Louis suburb. As the violence continued, the department's police force stood down—not even making arrests while arson and looting suspects ran freely through the streets. As civil unrest spread across the country, other departments followed

Rioters in Ferguson, Missouri, in 2014. What is police discretion, and how does it affect people's lives?

LARRY W. SMITH/epa european pressphoto agency b.v./Alamy Stock Photo

Ferguson's lead and implemented a "hands-off" approach to many types of crime. The Ferguson hypothesis, proposed after crime rates jumped, suggests that criminal offenders everywhere felt emboldened to question police authority after seeing the self-restraint that police officers and their agencies exercised, fearing negative publicity, public vilification, and civil suits.

▶ Defining Discretion

Police officers have the authority to make decisions that can affect individuals in profound and lasting ways. One officer might decide to arrest someone for the first time, giving that person a criminal record. Another officer in the same situation might feel that arrest is unnecessary and might use an informal tactic instead. All criminal justice officials, including prosecutors, exercise discretion, but police are the gatekeepers to the criminal justice process, and without the decisions they make to begin the process, prosecutors and other criminal justice officials would never have the opportunity to decide the fate of criminal suspects.

What *explains* police action—the choices that individual officers make when faced with varying situations? Is there something about the job that causes police officers to behave in certain ways? Are there different kinds of officers, and might differing personalities shed some light on these questions? What about factors other than the officers themselves, such as the characteristics of the communities they serve? In this chapter, we explore how considerations like these help explain and even predict police behavior.

George Kelling, known for his "broken windows" perspective on crime prevention, once described the observations he made while walking with a Newark, New Jersey, police officer who was patrolling a neighborhood:

As he saw his job, he was to keep an eye on strangers, and make certain that the disreputable regulars observed some informal but widely understood rules. Drunks and addicts could sit on the stoops, but could not lie down.

People could drink on side streets, but not at the main intersection. Bottles had to be in paper bags. Talking to, bothering, or begging from people waiting at the bus stop was strictly forbidden. Persons who broke the informal rules, especially [the latter], were arrested for vagrancy. Noisy teenagers were told to keep quiet.[2]

This observation captures the essence of police discretion more than any formal definition can. Although it is from a study that took place more than 25 years ago, the theme remains the same. Every community has its share of problems and priorities. Police officers must respond to those priorities and manage problems as best they can. Priorities may be assigned by residents and may have little to do with serious crime. Problems may need to be addressed in one way for some people and in another way for others. Or, in the case of Kelling's observations, *where* a problem occurs—and *how* it occurs—helps officers decide on the proper course of action.

Kelling's observations describe what discretion is, but how do we formally define it? Discretion consists of a two-part decision made by a police officer in a particular situation: (1) whether to intervene and, if the decision to intervene is made, (2) how best to intervene.

Whether to intervene and how to intervene can combine into a bewildering array of possible choices. Consider the typical traffic stop. Researchers have identified about 10 different kinds of actions that officers can take once a vehicle is stopped (e.g., order the driver out of the car), 7 strategies that could be used during the stop (e.g., administer a field

Broken Windows Policing The broken windows theory is concerned with targeting low-level offenses and quality-of-life problems in an effort to prevent more serious crimes from occurring later. Such is the essence of discretion—a shift in priorities from one set of problems to another. Much of the most recent research is divided in terms of broken windows' effectiveness. One sophisticated study found that failure to address low-level problems like litter and unkempt lawns leads to future increases in serious crime. Another, however, found quite the opposite. *Effectiveness issues aside, is broken windows policing a good idea? Why or why not? Can you think of any unanticipated consequences associated with a broken windows approach to policing?*

Orange Line Media/Shutterstock

sobriety test), and 11 exit strategies that could be used (e.g., arrest). These three factors alone present a total of 770 possible action combinations.[3] Deciding whether and how to intervene can take an officer in *many* different directions, and he or she must be prepared for and trained to handle each one effectively.

Another way to conceive of discretion is to consider the distinction between the *letter* of the law and the *spirit* of the law. A police officer who follows the letter of the law issues a citation for every infraction, no matter how minor, and arrests every criminal suspect for all manner of criminal activity. In contrast, an officer who follows the spirit of the law looks at what the law intends and realizes that, from time to time, arrests and citations may not meet with the law's intent. The reality of policing is that officers frequently *must* make decisions, and often the law and an officer's decision correspond, but not always. Indeed, as we will see shortly, the two can be completely at odds with one another.

LEARNING OUTCOMES 1 — Describe police discretion and its advantages and disadvantages.

Note that we are not talking about police deviance, which is discussed in this book's last section. Perhaps it sounds a bit deviant that a police officer would ignore the letter of the law or let outside considerations enter into his or her decision-making process. And yes, it can be deviant—and possibly criminal—for

an officer to overlook certain activities. But it can also be necessary. There are many occasions when it is simply not practical or advisable to arrest all suspects. We see this particularly in the war on drugs. Is it advisable to arrest every person caught with a modest amount of marijuana for personal consumption? Some readers may feel the answer is yes, but the practical answer is certainly no. There is just not enough room in jail to arrest everyone who *could* be arrested. In this sense, police officers are de facto policy-makers. They decide, in some respects, what is and is not right. According to one scholar,

> The police are among the most important policy makers of our entire society. And they make far more discretionary determinations in individual cases than does any other class of administrators; I know of no close second.[4]

Classic Studies of Police Discretion

Discretion has been the subject of numerous scholarly examinations of police behavior. We briefly review some of the classic studies in this section, beginning with the work of William Westley (see Figure 6–1 for a summary).

Violence and the Police

In 1949, William Westley conducted one of the first studies of police behavior, in Gary, Indiana.[5] He found that socialization was a critical factor in shaping police behavior; "old-timers" worked with recruits, teaching them how to take charge of the situations they were confronted with. He also noted how recruits would come to be respected by the community if they capably took charge. Respect was, in his view, the be all and end all of police work; without it, officers could not do their jobs. Citizen challenges to police authority were regarded as something that could be responded to with force. While it is risky for officers in this day and age to respond forcibly to every threat to their authority, in 1949, it was regarded as quite acceptable—and necessary.

Westley was also perhaps the first researcher to call attention to the idea of isolation in police work. That is, he found that most officers viewed themselves as not having the support of the majority of the citizens. They felt the public could not be trusted. This, in turn, led officers to develop a tight-knit culture characterized by secrecy and looking out for one another. Indeed, nearly every study of police culture since Westley cite this pattern of behavior.

Justice without Trial

Another important classic was Jerome Skolnick's *Justice without Trial*, first published in 1966.[6] The title of Skolnick's book speaks volumes. It suggests that, in policing, decisions concerning what to do with suspects can be made with no trial at all—that is, by police officers themselves.

Skolnick also identified the concept of the symbolic assailant. This refers to a person who a police officer thinks is potentially dangerous. Perceptions of a person's relative dangerousness can come from past experience but also from so-called war stories told by other police officers. Factors such as

Brown:	Aggressiveness and selectivity used as criteria to identify several type of officers.
Manning:	Police manage their image (e.g., with crime statistics).
Muir:	Stages of ethical development and types of officers.
Rubinstein:	Officers need to establish control; organizational factors shape behavior.
Skolnick:	Symbolic assailant: tension between law and order.
Van Maanen:	Stages of police socialization.
Westley:	Officers experience isolation; socialization is important.
Wilson:	Three policing style (watchman, legalistic, and service).

FIGURE 6–1 Summary of Policing Classics.

a person's behavior, location, race, dress, age, sex, and so forth can be signals of danger, called danger signifiers. These signifiers, whether they translate into actual danger or not, are often perceived as challenges to an officer's authority that must be responded to verbally or physically. The fact that some police officers, even today, view some groups (e.g., racial minorities) as more dangerous than others may trace to this socialization process revealed in Skolnick's research.

Skolnick also focused heavily on how the conflicts of democratic society can undermine police enforcement of the rule of law. One of these conflicts is the tension between law and order. We hear both terms used together all the time. There is even a television show by the same name. But Skolnick argues that law sets forth the rules by which police must abide. Order, though, cannot always be accomplished within the limits of the law.[7]

Managing Appearances

Peter Manning, another well-known police scholar, has argued that the police have staked out a large and unmanageable domain and that their job has an impossible mandate.[8] His argument is not unlike Skolnick's: "Because their mandate automatically entails mutually contradictory ends—protecting both public order and individual rights—the police resort to managing their public image and the indexes of their accomplishment."[9] How do police manage their public image? According to Manning, one answer lies in the professionalism movement. He regards professionalism as a strategy employed by the police to defend their mandate and enhance organizational solidarity and autonomy.[10]

Another answer lies in the collection of crime statistics. Who collects such statistics? The police, of course, and Manning argues that this is no accident: "the police have claimed responsibility for crime control, using the crime rate as an index of their success."[11] This may sound somewhat conspiratorial, but it raises the question, How accurately are crime statistics recorded? It is well known that there is much error in available crime statistics. Another question is, Could statistics be manipulated to serve a particular agenda? Of course. The old adage, You can prove anything with statistics, is very true. Whether there is deliberate manipulation of crime statistics to serve particular agendas is probably unknowable, but it is at least possible. In Manning's view, then, crime statistics give

police an opportunity to make themselves look good in the eyes of the public.

Policing Styles

James Q. Wilson[12] identified a number of "policing styles."[13] A style of policing describes how a particular agency sees its purpose and chooses the methods it uses to fulfill that purpose. Wilson's three policing styles—which he does not link to any particular historical era—are the watchman (characteristic of the political era), the legalistic (professional crime fighting of the reform era), and the service (which is becoming more common today).

Police departments marked by the watchman style are concerned mainly with achieving what Wilson calls "order maintenance" through control of illegal and disruptive behavior. Compared to the legalistic style, the watchman style uses discretion liberally. Watchman-style departments keep order through informal police "intervention," which may include persuasion, threats, or even "roughing up" disruptive people. Some authors condemn this style of policing, suggesting that it is typically found in lower- or lower-middle-class communities, especially where interpersonal relations include a fair amount of violence or physical abuse.

Departments operating under the legalistic style enforce the letter of the law. For example, an officer who tickets a person going 71 miles per hour in a 70-mile-per-hour speed zone may be enforcing the law, but he or she is likely a member of a department that adheres to the legalistic style of policing. Conversely, legalistic departments routinely avoid community disputes arising from violations of social norms that do not break the law. Police expert Gary Sykes calls this enforcement style "*laissez-faire* policing" in recognition of its hands-off approach to behaviors that are simply bothersome or inconsiderate of community principles.[14]

In service-oriented departments, which strive to meet the needs of the community and serve its members, the police see themselves more as helpers than as soldiers in a war on crime. This type of department works with social services and other agencies to provide counseling for minor offenders and to assist community groups in preventing crimes and solving problems. Prosecutors may support the service style by agreeing not to prosecute law violators who seek psychiatric help or who voluntarily participate in programs like Alcoholics Anonymous, family counseling, or drug treatment. The service style is supported, in part, by citizens who seek to avoid the embarrassment that might result from a public airing of personal problems, thereby reducing the number of criminal complaints filed, especially in minor disputes. While the service style of policing may seem more appropriate to wealthy communities or small towns, it can also exist in cities whose police departments actively seek citizen involvement in identifying issues that the police can help address.

City Police

Jonathan Rubinstein's *City Police* stands out as another classic in the annals of law enforcement scholarship.[15] Rubinstein, unlike some of the other scholars we have cited, actually worked as a patrol officer in Philadelphia and was thus in a unique position relative to other scholars to report on police activity and behavior. His findings echoed Skolnick's observations concerning officers' perceptions of danger in their jobs. Rubinstein also concluded, however, that of paramount concern in any police–citizen encounter is physical control over the scene. He observed that officers must maintain alertness, watch suspects' hands closely, remain alert to the possible presence of weapons, and stand close to them so that they cannot lash out easily.

Wilson emphasized the role of organizational factors in shaping police behavior. Rubinstein, in contrast, emphasized the officer's working environment as being most influential. He found that officers learn various features of the job, such as what is and is not important, who is and is not a possible threat, and so forth, from their veteran peers. In short, Rubinstein concluded that socialization, the process of being influenced by others around them, shapes police behavior more than other factors, such as organizational structure or managerial preferences.

The "Making of Policemen"

In 1973, Van Maanen published *Observations on the Making of Policemen*, one of the first studies of police socialization as it plays out in the academy.[16] He, like Rubinstein, immersed himself in his object of study by going through the academy and serving as a police officer for a period of time in California. He identified four stages by which recruits are socialized into the police department. The first stage is the preentry choice, which Van Maanen explained sets police recruits apart from applicants for other careers. He found that those who aspire to a career in policing are attracted to the job out of a view that it is an elite occupation and that it affords one an opportunity to do something important for society, such as serve people.

Van Maanen's second stage is called admittance, where the recruit enters the academy, where he or she learns the importance of abiding by the rules and regulations of the department. As remains true today, recruits live in a military-like environment resembling a boot camp, study hard, and are punished for violating the rules. They are also regaled with war stories from seasoned officers that serve more than an entertainment function; they inform trainees about the values of their job, of sticking together, and of what it means to be a "good" cop.

The third stage is known as change. This occurs once academy training comes to a close and the officer enters the field. Typically partnered with a training officer, the new hires are continually tested and evaluated on several criteria. Can they control encounters with suspects? Do they exercise common sense? Are they sufficiently careful? Van Maanen also found that the new officers are also continually tested on their abilities to back up other officers, further reinforcing the cultural solidarity—the "looking out for one another"—that characterizes police work. This, of course, mandates helping other officers when they are in trouble.

Finally, Van Maanen called the fourth stage continuance. This occurs as officers move through the field training period and come to accept the *reality* of police work. While the potential for danger and excitement remains, much of the romanticized image of the job fades away as officers learn the bureaucratic dimensions of their chosen profession, such as following orders and completing paperwork. Officers also develop a sense of disillusionment insofar as they learn that much of the public is unsupportive of what they do and/or has no clear understanding of what police work is really like. Van Maanen found that officers employ a strategy of "lie low and hang loose" to avoid getting in trouble and to make the job tolerable.

The Police: Street-Corner Politicians

William Ker Muir, Jr., authored another important study, published in 1977. Its title, *Police: Streetcorner Politicians*,[17] like Skolnick's *Justice without Trial*, speaks volumes. Muir identified two dimensions of police ethical development: perspective (the extent to which an officer understands human suffering and is inclined to show compassion) and passion (how comfortable the officer is in using coercive means to carry out his or her responsibilities). Then, based on these dimensions, he identified four types of officers. First are the professional-style officers, those who are both compassionate and comfortable using their authority when the need arises. Enforcers, who use force whenever the opportunity arises, lack the compassion that goes along with the professional-style officers. Reciprocators, the third type of officers, are compassionate and somewhat uncomfortable with their authority role. These officers use communication to defuse volatile situations and avoid using force unless it is absolutely necessary. Finally, avoiders, not surprisingly, are officers who avoid using force. Interestingly, though, they are also devoid of compassion. These are officers who do as little as possible to maintain their positions and avoid risk-taking behavior.

Working the Street

One of the classics aimed specifically at police discretion is Michael Brown's *Working the Street: Police Discretion*, published in 1981. His was a study of three policing styles found in three different southern California cities. Like Muir, Brown identified various officer types that depended, in his view, on their aggressiveness and selectivity. Aggressiveness, Brown says, refers to officers' willingness to actively seek out problems. Selectivity is the extent to which officers are concerned only with serious crime problems.

Using these two variables, Brown identified four police styles. Old-style crime fighters are aggressive officers who concentrate on serious felony-type crimes. These are also the officers who use coercion and are inclined to bend the rules to obtain the best results. Next, clean-beat crime fighters emphasize following proper police procedures. These officers are proactive but also follow the letter of the law. Service-style officers generally avoid coercion and aggression while focusing on the most serious problems. They also avoid enforcement unless a crime is sufficiently serious to warrant it. Finally, professional-style officers are neither overly aggressive nor selective. Muir used the term *professional* for this officer because this is how he hoped the typical officer would be. Such officers enforce the law when necessary but aren't out to "get" any particular types of offenders, nor do they seek out trouble simply for the thrill of it.

The Pros and Cons of Police Discretion

One of the clear advantages associated with police discretion is that it gives law enforcement officers a measure of job satisfaction. Indeed, research reveals that job satisfaction improves with job conditions like autonomy.[18] Autonomy and discretionary decision making go hand in hand. Discretion is also advantageous because without it, the wheels of justice would grind to a halt. The system is just not equipped to deal with the massive influx of people that would result if officers arrested every identifiable lawbreaker. On a related note, discretion allows officers to treat each situation differently in accordance with realistic goals and humanitarian principles (Figure 6–2). Some people favor "throwing the book" at every offender, but for those who favor mercy from time to time, police discretion is the best solution.

The negative aspects of police discretion probably outweigh the positive ones, mainly because the public's attention is drawn to discretionary decisions when something goes wrong. Incidents of police abuse and corruption generally lead people to call for reforms aimed at reining in police behavior. For example, many police departments have adopted policies restricting pursuit driving. These are intended to limit officer discretion in the name of preserving public safety and minimizing injuries to innocent third parties. Policies restricting the use of deadly force also limit what officers can do in terms of apprehending resistant suspects. In fact, the bulk of a police department's policy manual is aimed at telling officers what they can and cannot do. When discretion runs amok, things can go wrong—resulting in needless injury or death, civil litigation, and other problems.

Discretion and Seniority

We have been discussing discretion as though it were used in the same manner by officers of all ranks. Nothing could be further from the truth. There is, as University of Nevada (Reno) professor Ken Peak has observed, an inverse relationship between discretion and seniority.[19] As an officer's rank increases, he or she is able to make fewer discretionary decisions. How is this so? The officer on the street has the greatest authority to decide who to arrest, pursue, stop, and so forth. The discretion of chiefs of police and other high-level administrators, in contrast, is limited by two factors. First, they do less ordinary police work, thus limiting the number of occasions when they may be able to employ discretion as we have defined it. Second, administrators tend to be limited by budget constraints, union pressures, governing boards, influential politicians, and others. In deciding who to hire, for instance, the chief (or whoever makes this decision) must be cognizant of diversity issues. This limits the pool of prospective officers to some extent.

This is not to say that administrators can't make decisions on their own or think outside the box. They do, but in different ways than patrol officers. For example, since money is often in short supply in some agencies, top executives have to act creatively to drum up needed revenue. The chief who sells advertising space on his department's cruisers (and some have) may be seen as a creative, forward-thinking, entrepreneurial manager. Others might regard this as unethical behavior and criticize the chief for pandering to certain interests, such as the owners of the business who buy the space. Either way, the initial decision to sell the advertising space is a discretionary one. It is safe to say, then, that while an administrative position limits one's discretionary latitude, it certainly opens the door to new

Pros	Cons
• Promotes job satisfaction	• Potential for abuse
• Promotes autonomy	• Potential for corruption
• Necessary for criminal justice system efficiency	• Potential for needless death/injury (for example, if no pursuit-driving policy)
• Promotes realistic goals	• Possible citizen complaints of unequal treatment
• Promotes humanitarian principles	• Possible litigation when things go awry

FIGURE 6–2 The Pros and Cons of Police Discretion.

types of decisions that the beat cop or frontline officer ordinarily does not get to make.

▶ *Explaining Police Behavior*

Police behavior can be explained from either a **universalistic perspective** or a **particularistic perspective**. The universalistic perspective is simply the view that all police officers are similar and that they exhibit some of the same characteristics and behavior patterns. The particularistic perspective, in contrast, considers how individual officers differ from one another. Similarly, we can ask whether law enforcement officers behave the way they do because of personal values and patterns of behavior they have acquired through socialization and introduction into police subculture or because of individual predispositions toward certain ways of thinking and acting.

The Universalistic Perspective

To say that all police officers are similar in some respects requires some attention to sociology, psychology, and organizational theory. Sociology, in this case, is concerned with the influence of peers and coworkers. Psychology is concerned with whether there is a distinct police personality. Organizational factors can influence police behavior as well.

Police officers are selected and trained in a very unique environment.[20] It is unlike that found in almost any other occupation. Academy training indoctrinates recruits into the world of policing and teaches trainees to view others in a particular way (i.e., with a measure of suspicion). The sociological perspective is also important from a demographic standpoint. To this day, the typical police officer is a white male. Women and minorities have made great strides in terms of gaining representation in the law enforcement profession, but they are not represented in the profession in accordance with their numbers in the population as a whole. Research reveals that female officers are socialized to adapt to a largely male-dominated work environment.[21] In other words, traditional police training (in the academy and on the job) has encouraged female recruits to act in a masculine fashion.

Does policing draw a particular personality type? If so, this is an example of how psychological factors may yield common bonds among police officers. There is surprisingly little research on what types of personalities are drawn to police work. Much more accepted is the view that socialization is more influential than any degree of predisposition. Not everyone agrees, however, so we will revisit the predisposition versus socialization issue shortly. It is the law enforcement equivalent of the nature-versus-nurture argument that plays out in the criminology literature and elsewhere in human development studies.

In addition, there are organizational factors that make all officers alike. The quasi-military structure of most police agencies requires a certain pattern of behavior among all employees. Everything from chain of command to rules of dress ensures that one officer closely resembles the other officers.

Community policing may be creating suborganizations within specific police departments. Ask a special weapons and tactics (SWAT) or narcotics officer in any large urban police department what he or she thinks of the officers who work in the community policing division. Some will answer that those officers are somewhat different; some may even say that they are not doing real police work. The point is that, *traditionally*, organizational factors may have led to similarities among all officers. It is quite probable that all of this is changing in contemporary policing and that a particularistic perspective is starting to take hold.

The Particularistic Perspective

The particularistic perspective is concerned with how specific officers differ from one another. We just suggested that narcotics officers may be (and almost certainly are) different in a number of respects from community police officers, although there are some officers who work both assignments at some point in their careers.

LEARNING OUTCOMES 2 — Differentiate between the universalistic and particularistic perspectives on police behavior.

Studies of police culture and personality point to a number of characteristics that police officers share, including suspiciousness, cynicism, loyalty to colleagues, and pessimism. Particularistic perspectives, however, suggest that there is no one personality or set of traits that typifies all police officers. Robert Worden has identified five attitudinal dimensions that can be used to explain differences among individual police officers. They include role orientations, perceptions of legal restrictions, perceptions of citizen respect and cooperation, perceptions of legal institutions, and views on selective enforcement.[22] Each is discussed in the following sections.

Role Orientations

Role orientation refers to an officer's individual conception of what constitutes proper and good police work. As might be expected, police officers differ in this regard. As Worden observes, "Some officers believe that the police role is defined wholly by the mandate to fight crime and enforce the law; they believe in the utility of an aggressive style of patrol, and they regard order maintenance and service tasks with distaste."[23] At the other extreme are officers who favor a broader police role that includes more than crime fighting. Some officers see order maintenance and service provision as higher callings than crime control and see themselves as positive rather than negative influences on people's lives.[24]

The officer who views his or her role as consisting mainly of crime control will be inclined to behave in a manner consistent with that view. This might translate into frequent stops of suspicious individuals, punitive responses to disputes (e.g., arresting the parties to a domestic dispute rather than counseling them), and zealous criminal investigations. Because these officers see crime control as most important, "minor disputes fall outside of their definition of police responsibilities, and more serious disputes are police business only insofar as they constitute crimes."[25] Officers with this narrow role orientation would not have an interest in mediating disputes to settle them verbally instead of with force or by arresting someone. By contrast, officers who see themselves as having a broad role orientation will use an approach that best serves the needs of the people they serve.

Perceptions of Legal Restrictions

All police officers are bound by various legal requirements, whether they agree with them or not. This does not mean, however, that they necessarily *like* operating under these legal limitations. In fact, there are clear differences among police officers in terms of their perceptions of legal restrictions. Some officers have total respect for the law, for department policy, and for the influence of the courts on their duties. These officers may be the exception,[26] however. According to Worden, "The stereotypical police officer chafes under due process provisions in the single-minded pursuit of criminal offenders. This officer bitterly resents legal and departmental restrictions concerning search and seizure, interrogation, and the use of force."[27]

An officer's perceptions of legal restrictions may also be indicative of his or her overall ideological stance. For example, some officers may occasionally bend the rules when it comes to accosting pedestrians or stopping motorists. If the justification for doing so is not in place in advance, these officers may fabricate a reason to justify their actions in hindsight. This resembles a conservative law-and-order mentality with a clear focus on crime control in lieu of due process. Indeed, studies of on-the-job performance have revealed numerous examples of this behavior.[28] At the other extreme, of course, are officers who both are cognizant of and strictly adhere to legal restrictions.

Perceptions of Citizen Support and Respect

If a suspect physically resists police intervention, the officer will surely respond in kind—that is, uncooperative suspects will be dealt with accordingly. We will see some more evidence of this toward the end of the chapter. For now, it is also important to note that there are differences among police officers in terms of their perceptions of citizen respect and cooperation. Some officers think that the public is mostly supportive. It would be easy to get this sense if one is a recruiter, a Drug Abuse Resistance Education (DARE) program officer, or an officer who works closely with citizens in a positive sense. Other officers sometimes feel that they are held in somewhat low regard by citizens, and still others feel—rightly much of the time—that they enjoy little respect and are viewed with nothing short of hostility and animosity.

Perceptions of Other Legal Institutions

Law enforcement is an institution, not unlike a religion. As an institution, it views itself somewhat differently, perhaps, than other institutions. Police officers themselves have their own divergent perceptions of legal institutions. Consider the courts, for example. Some officers view the courts as supportive and helpful. Others regard them as being soft on crime or totally out of touch with the realities of police work. In a recent case, for example, the U.S. Supreme Court decided that it is not unconstitutional for a police officer to arrest someone for a traffic violation.[29] While police officers generally applauded this clarification (and seeming expansion) of their powers, the decision did not change police work very much. It does not mean that the police will begin an aggressive campaign of arresting people for not wearing their seat belts. Police agencies have bigger fish to fry. Decisions like this, then, seem to officers to be concerned with legal minutia and do little to help the police on a practical level. Officers' perceptions of courts can be extended to include attitudes toward judges and prosecutors as well.[30]

Some officers are more proactive in their duties than others. This may also owe to their perceptions of other criminal justice institutions—including even prisons. If an officer feels that the prosecutor will reject his or her case, that the judge will hand down a lenient decision, or that there is not enough room in the local jail or nearby prison, it may influence the arrest decision. Research on traffic enforcement makes this clearer. Forty years ago, J. A. Gardiner set out to explain why police in one city issued more traffic tickets than their counterparts in a nearby city. He traced this to the fact that the first city did not require its officers to appear in court until after a not guilty plea was entered.[31] This suggests a degree of collaboration between the police and the court that influenced police behavior. In contrast, the officers in the other city, where the court was not as supportive of their efforts, were inclined to make fewer traffic stops because it would be a burden. (See Table 6–1 for a summary of the discussion in this section.)

TABLE 6–1	THE UNIVERSALISTIC VERSUS PARTICULARISTIC PERSPECTIVE ON POLICE BEHAVIOR	

Universalistic Perspective	Particularistic Perspective
Officers are socialized.	Officers take on different role orientations.
Officers are psychologically similar.	Officers act differently based on legal restrictions.
Police organizations force all officers to act similarly.	Officers act differently based on their perceptions of citizens.
Officers act differently based on their views of the criminal justice system.	Officers act differently based on their views of certain laws.

Source: Based on R. Roberg, K. Novak, and G. Cordner, "The universalistic versus the particularistic," in *Police and society,* 3rd ed. (New York: Oxford University Press, 2005), pp. 272–74.

Views on Selective Enforcement

Research reveals—and common sense suggests—that police officers also vary in terms of their selectivity—that is, their willingness to enforce the law.[32] In the case of a murder, few would argue that any officer would not want to arrest the perpetrator. But what of less serious offenses like public intoxication, prostitution, and vagrancy? Do all officers enforce laws against these behaviors equally? Of course not. To the extent that selectivity varies among individual police officers, it is reasonable to conclude that this could affect their decisions in any number of disputes:

> Officers who believe that they should be selective in enforcing the law might be expected seldom to invoke the law in resolving disputes and instead avail themselves of informal methods; officers who are nonselective might be expected to make arrests more frequently and to adopt extra-legal strategies less frequently.[33]

Socialization or Predisposition?

We earlier raised the question of whether law enforcement officers are socialized into the perspectives they hold or whether they bring with them certain predispositions in terms of their values and behavior. Although some are more susceptible to peer influence and pressure than others, it would be impossible for any officer to completely ignore his or her colleagues, superiors, and instructors.

There has been a renewed interest in the suggestion that officers bring certain predispositions into the policing profession. Research has for decades backed up this point.[34] Research also reveals that those who enter law enforcement believe in the importance of authority and seek fulfillment in their careers. A more recent study confirms these findings, leading the authors to conclude that "individual value systems are more important than occupational socialization."[35] This means that police officers' values are somewhat entrenched

before they even enter the force.[36] Chances are, though, that there is a mix of predisposition and socialization that actually takes place (see Figure 6–3).

▶ Police Decision Making

Scores of researchers have sought to identify predictors of police decision making. We can place their findings into four general categories: organizational factors, neighborhood factors, situational factors, and individual officer characteristics. Within each of these categories are several subcategories, which we explore in this section.

LEARNING OUTCOMES 3 — Describe the factors that affect police decision making.

Organizational Factors

The organization for which an officer works can shape his or her decision-making patterns. The bureaucratic structure of the typical police organization requires that its employees jump through certain hoops. Whether they like it or not, officers must follow the rules. This is true of any organization; people must follow the rules or else risk losing their job.

Bureaucratic Structure

The typical police department adheres to a fairly rigid bureaucratic model of administration. This is done primarily to guide employee behavior and to direct and control it.[37] Part of this is accomplished through written policies. Policy manuals seek to control police decision making, such as pursuit or arrest decisions.

Several researchers have criticized the bureaucratic control principle. Proponents of the community policing movement suggest that there may be a better way to run police departments, such as by decentralizing them and giving line officers

Socialization

- Police officers are socialized formally and informally into their occupations.
- Formal socialization usually plays out in the academy and during the field training period.
- Informal socialization results from the new hires' interactions with seasoned officers and their colleagues.

Predisposition

- Recently, there has been renewed interest in whether police officers are somehow predisposed either to accept a law enforcement position or to act a certain way once employed.
- Research study findings suggest that police officers' values are somewhat entrenched before they even enter the force.

Most likely it is a mix of socialization and predisposition that determine officers' values and behaviors.

FIGURE 6–3 Socialization or Predisposition.

more latitude in their decision making. More than one researcher has argued, for instance, that written policy manuals do little to affect the quality of police service.[38]

Beats and Scheduling

An officer's beat can also influence his or her behavior. In general, the larger the patrol beat, the more impersonal the relationship will be between officers and citizens.[39] In contrast, officers who patrol relatively smaller areas, such as small towns, tend to adopt more of a service orientation in their daily activities.[40] This does not mean, however, that all small areas will see a service style of policing. Some officers work dangerous beats in high-crime downtown areas on bicycle or on foot. In these places, an enforcement stance may prevail over a service orientation. Somewhat related to this is the finding that officers in larger departments are less prone to making arrests for drunk driving than their counterparts in smaller agencies.[41]

We all know that work can get boring, especially if it is routine, totally predictable, and unchanging. This extends to policing, too, but not necessarily in the way one would expect. Researchers have found that police departments that routinely rotate their officers into different beats, units, or shifts affect the relationships between their officers and citizens. In particular, frequent rotation puts distance between officers and the people they serve.[42] This has been called "stranger policing,"[43] and it is not unlike what occurs when a person frequently moves from one city or state to the next; it becomes difficult to form close relationships.

When a police officer routinely works the same beat, he or she can come to form close relationships with citizens. As one researcher puts it, "An officer's continued presence in a neighborhood increases the likelihood of repeated contact with citizens and helps officers develop empathy through an understanding of problems."[44] In fact, research also reveals that officers who routinely patrol the same area develop a sense of obligation to the area and even a desire to be protective of it. This has been called the **territorial imperative**,[45] and police departments appear to be taking advantage of it.

Neighborhood Factors

Police officers who patrol America's affluent communities rarely encounter problems. They often enjoy good relationships with the vast majority of the law-abiding citizens they see daily. Then there are the officers who patrol the worst run-down neighborhoods, which are plagued by drug problems, gang violence, and serious crime. These officers are regarded with suspicion, insulted, and even shot at periodically. It is easy to understand why the nature of the neighborhood that an officer patrols has some effect on his or her behavior.

Consider, again, the broken windows theory. It argues for a certain type of law enforcement, depending on the problems a particular neighborhood faces. James Q. Wilson and George L. Kelling argue that if signs of physical and social disorder affect a neighborhood, then officers should concentrate their efforts on those problems because failure to address quality-of-life matters like these will surely invite serious crime. The broken windows theory thus provides another illustration of how neighborhood conditions can affect police strategies, decisions, and discretion.

Racial Composition and Heterogeneity

Several researchers have looked at neighborhood racial composition and its effects on police decision making. Findings reveal a greater demand for police services in minority-dominated neighborhoods.[46] This, some have argued, has been due to a greater number of incidents as well as "a belief in the appropriateness of calling the police."[47] The relationship between neighborhood racial composition and police activity can also be understood in terms of the police being more suspicious and alert in such neighborhoods.[48]

Although it is not clear why research also suggests that the police are more active in neighborhoods characterized by extensive racial heterogeneity.[49] Heterogeneous neighborhoods are those with ethnic or racial diversity.

Socioeconomic Status

Minority-dominated neighborhoods also tend to be comparatively less well-off. Numerous studies back this up and also show that police tend to make more arrests in poorer areas.[50] Interestingly, research also reveals that police are more likely to listen to a request for arrest in wealthier neighborhoods. For example, if one of the parties to a domestic dispute insists that an officer not make an arrest, the officer would apparently be more inclined to listen to a wealthy person's views on this subject than a poor person's. This is assuming, of course, that the officer's department does not follow a mandatory arrest policy.

Crime

Informed readers know that racial composition, socioeconomic status, and crime go hand in hand. There is more crime where there are more people. Conversely, there is much less crime in rich areas. It should be no surprise, then, to find that police make more arrests in densely populated, poor, and high-crime areas. Where there is no crime, there is little need to make arrests. But there are *some* mixed findings in this area. For example, at least one author has argued that where crime is common, this may stretch police resources, forcing them to respond less vigorously than they otherwise would.[51] At the least, extensive research reveals that neighborhood crime rates can influence officer attitudes.[52]

Situational Factors

Every police–citizen encounter is different. Some occur behind closed doors, such as when an arrest warrant is served in a private residence. Others occur in full view of bystanders and even cameras. Some suspects are docile and cooperative; others put up a fight. Offenses vary, too. A person facing the prospect of life in prison for his or her third violent felony may have little to lose if he or she resists arrest, but the juvenile who is arrested for the first time may not cause any trouble. Even the means by

Mandatory Arrests for Domestic Violence In response to the problem of domestic violence, some police agencies have implemented mandatory arrest policies. The logic behind these policies is simple: By removing one of the parties from the scene through an arrest, the problem stops—at least in the short term. The question, however, is whether mandatory arrest has long-term consequences. *The issue is important because of its relevance to police discretion. Does mandatory arrest go "too far" in terms of restricting officer discretion? If so, explain. If not, in what other areas may it be beneficial to limit police discretion?*

Amelie-Benoist/BSIP SA/Alamy Stock Photo

which the police arrive at the scene can have an effect on the outcome of the situation. The point is that situational factors, in addition to community-level factors, can influence an officer's decision making.

Scene and Suspects

Whether an officer arrives at the scene on his or her initiative or as a result of a call is the first important factor in determining how the officer will act. As might be expected, if someone calls the police, it generally means that the person *wants* officers there. In contrast, if officers initiate contact with people on their own, such as by engaging in preventive patrol, the contacts can be somewhat more antagonistic. Moreover, police are more likely to make arrests and treat people harshly in the second situation.[53]

Research has also cited examples of retaliation by officers who feel offended by a suspect's behavior. For example, people who are not respectful to an officer during a traffic encounter receive more traffic citations than those who show respect.[54] This also extends to other types of police–citizen encounters. In fact, the evidence is very clear that suspect demeanor is one of the most significant predictors of police behavior: Disrespectful and uncooperative people are more likely to be arrested or cited.[55] Even studies on police corruption and brutality reveal that both occur more often when a lack of respect is displayed toward the officer.[56]

One of the research problems in this area concerns the proper measurement of suspect demeanor. Many researchers have measured demeanor in terms of criminal activity (e.g., assaulting the arresting officer), but one researcher found that legal forms of resistance (such as insulting the officer) did not lead to a higher probability of arrest.[57] Not everyone is in agreement with these findings, however.[58]

It is important to note that we are looking at all these predictors of police decision making in isolation. In reality, these factors occur together. Race combined with demeanor may have a stronger influence on an officer's decision. Socioeconomic status may interact with the crime rate—and even race—and also exert a substantial influence.

Suspect demographic characteristics, notably race, gender, and age, have also been shown to influence police decision making. The effects of race are consistent with the neighborhood factors we have already touched on: Minorities tend to be treated differently from whites.[59] "Some researchers contend that this situation is the result of the fact that African-Americans, and possibly other minorities, may be more likely to resist police authority or display a 'bad' attitude or outright hostility, from an officer's point of view."[60] One recent study reveals, interestingly, that race is more important in shaping an officer's level of suspicion toward someone than his or her initial decision to stop or arrest the person.[61]

Consider racial profiling. Although it is difficult to measure accurately whether profiling actually occurs, many believe it is rampant, and at least a few studies support such claims.[62] To the extent that profiling occurs, it provides perhaps the clearest evidence that race can influence officer's decision making. But is that because police officers are racially biased? Is it misguided stereotyping, or is it just good policing? The answers to these questions remain somewhat elusive. Some law enforcement officials say more minorities appear to be stopped because they are where crime is; civil libertarians argue otherwise.

Gender has also been considered as a possible predictor of police decision making, although researchers have not been drawn to it as much as race. Who is more likely to be arrested, men or women? At least one study reveals, not too surprisingly, that women are less likely to be arrested than men, particularly when they display ladylike characteristics or behaviors.[63] In contrast, when women step outside the bounds of what is considered proper behavior, they are arrested more often.

Controversially, some researchers have studied police sexual violence, finding that it may be more common than once expected.[64] Others have explained this as resulting from the greater opportunities (e.g., isolation from others, such as during a traffic stop) and the power and authority of police work. Indeed, some researchers have even found that attractive women are more likely to be stopped for traffic violations, mainly so that the officer can make personal contact.[65]

Finally, the suspect's age may be associated with police decision making as well. In general, young people tend to be rebellious and thus disrespectful toward police. The research bears this out,[66] particularly as it influences officer behavior. Also, younger people are more likely than older people to be arrested or dealt with harshly.[67] This may create a two-way relationship—that is, if young people are dealt with more harshly because they are disrespectful, then disrespect may be exacerbated by the fact that young people are treated harshly.[68] Of course, these are generalizations. There are different types of officers out there, as we have already made clear. Research reveals, in fact, that community police officers may be more inclined than their traditional counterparts to deal with young people informally.[69]

Relationships between Parties

The evening news makes it appear as though most crime is violent and that it occurs between strangers. Neither is correct. Most crime is nonviolent, and much of it occurs between people who know each other to some extent. When thinking about police decision making, it is also important to consider the relationship between both parties to the incident: victims and offenders. If two people know each other, does it always make sense to arrest one of the parties when, perhaps, the matter could be settled informally? The answer is often no. Several studies reveal that as relational distance between the parties increases, arrest is more likely.[70] Research also reveals that when the victim prefers that no arrest be made, officers are often influenced by such sentiments.[71]

Offense Seriousness

For obvious reasons, the seriousness of the offense will bear significantly on officer behavior. A serious crime, such as a homicide, will surely result in an arrest if a suspect is identified and located. Minor offenses and infractions are more often dealt with informally, perhaps with just a warning. An interesting question has arisen in this context, however. Do police officers make more arrests in cases of serious crime simply because the crime is serious, or is something else at work? The answer lies in what constitutes proper legal justification, or probable cause, to make an arrest. Probable cause is more likely to be present in cases of serious crime, especially violent crime, because there may be signs of physical injury, a weapon that can be located, witness accounts, and so forth. In contrast, minor offenses like shoplifting a trivial amount of merchandise may be more difficult to prove, thus making it harder for an officer to justify an arrest.[72]

Location

Consider this hypothetical scenario. An officer stops a motorist for drunk driving. He then administers a field sobriety test in broad daylight in view of several pedestrians. The driver has apparent difficulty passing the exam, but the officer lets her drive away. Would this happen? Certainly not, for two reasons. First, it would be dangerous to allow an intoxicated motorist to drive off. It would also be against department rules for a police officer to allow a visibly intoxicated motorist to drive home on her own. Second, the presence of bystanders would make it even more controversial to send the motorist on her way. The location of this incident in plain view of other people would be sure to influence the officer's decision to some extent. Step

outside this scenario to any other high-profile public contact between a police officer and a citizen. Officers know in these moments that they must be careful to follow proper policy to avoid complaints, litigation, and so forth. Alternatively, when police–citizen contacts take place behind closed doors or out of public view, there is more of an opportunity to treat the matter informally.

Bystanders

Closely related to the public–private distinction is the issue of whether bystanders are present. Bystanders are, of course, more likely to be present in public places. Thus, when they are under citizen scrutiny, officers will act differently than when they are not. A different sort of situation arises when the observers are other police officers, in which case an officer's decision making will likely be influenced differently. The motivation to look good in the eyes of one's peers, for instance, may prompt an officer to act differently than he or she would otherwise behave. Researchers have found that officers who work together, as opposed to alone, are sometimes more prone to make arrests or to treat citizens harshly.[73] The combination of working in public and having bystanders present can have a profound influence on police decision making.

Individual Officer Characteristics

Thus far, we have focused only on how neighborhood and situational factors affect officers' decisions. What about the officers themselves? How do differences among them affect their decision making? A number of individual officer characteristics have been linked to police decision making. These include factors such as education, age, experience, gender, ambition, and attitude toward the job.

Education, Age, and Experience

Does a well-educated officer act differently than, say, an officer with just a high school diploma? Unfortunately, researchers have yet to determine whether education affects an officer's decision to behave one way over another. The same can be said of age and experience, which tend to go hand in hand.

Younger officers are generally more aggressive and may work harder than their older counterparts, but seasoned officers may be "better" at their jobs, meaning the quality of their work could be higher.[74]

Gender

Few researchers have looked recently at gender as a possible predictor of police decision making. Some studies from the late 1980s, when women were first beginning to gain a significant presence in law enforcement, revealed that female officers tend to act less aggressively than their male counterparts.[75] On the whole, women tend to be less aggressive than men, which probably explains the differences in their decision making in the law enforcement context.

Ambition and Attitudes

An officer's ambition can clearly affect his or her decision making. One study revealed, for example, that officers who made the most arrests felt they needed to do so in order to gain a promotion.[76] Some of the officers who made more than their share of arrests were also motivated by the possibility of making more money from the overtime they needed to work to process all of their arrestees.

Attitudes toward the job, particularly toward different types of police work, have also been linked to decision making.

Researchers have found that an officer's perception of community policing can affect his or her arrest patterns.[77] In general, officers who view community policing favorably tend to be more selective in their arrest decisions. Circumstances, preferences, and neighborhood characteristics can call for an intervention other than arrest. Figure 6–4 summarizes the explanations of police decision making discussed in this section.

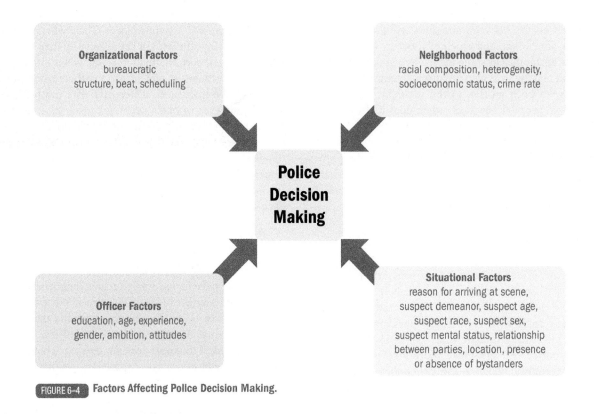

FIGURE 6-4 Factors Affecting Police Decision Making.

Depolicing and Rising Crime

This chapter began with a discussion of the "Ferguson effect," or the idea that less aggressive policing in the wake of widespread civil protests may embolden criminals and lead to higher rates of crime. In October 2015, FBI director, James B. Comey, spoke at the University of Chicago Law School and gave additional support for the belief that "depolicing" is contributing to rising crime.[78]

Comey began by noting that violent crime rates have been trending up in major cities across the country. He offered various reasons as to why that's happening, but then he added: "Nobody says it on the record, nobody says it in public, but police and elected officials are quietly saying it to themselves. And they're saying it to me, and I'm going to say it to you. And it is the one explanation that does explain the calendar and the map and that makes the most sense to me. Maybe something in policing has changed."

Comey went on to ask: "In today's YouTube world, are officers reluctant to get out of their cars and do the work that controls violent crime? Are officers answering 911 calls but avoiding the informal contact that keeps bad guys from standing around, especially with guns?" He continued, "I spoke to officers privately in one big city precinct who described being surrounded by young people with mobile phone cameras held high, taunting them the moment they get out of their cars. They told me, 'We feel like we're under siege and we don't feel much like getting out of our cars.'"

The question, Comey said, "is whether these kinds of things are changing police behavior all over the country." His answer? "I do

FBI Director James B. Comey, speaking at the University of Chicago Law School in 2015. What is depolicing?

Keith Srakocic/AP Images

have a strong sense that . . . a chill wind that has blown through American law enforcement . . ."

He concluded his talk by saying: "Lives are saved when . . . potential killers are confronted by a police officer, a strong police presence and actual, honest-to-goodness, up-close 'What are you guys doing on this corner at 1 o'clock in the morning' policing.'"

We need to be careful, the FBI director said, that good policing "doesn't drift away from us in the age of viral videos, or there will be profound consequences."

This story raises several interesting questions:

1. Is Director Comey right? Has a "chill wind" blown through American law enforcement in recent years?
2. What sort of a "chill wind" is Comey talking about?
3. Some say that close scrutiny of law enforcement activities and practices is a positive force for change, and that it will produce better enforcement efforts—ones that are in close keeping with the civil rights of all citizens. Do you agree?

Describe police discretion and its advantages and disadvantages.

Police discretion is the latitude an officer has in making the decision to act one way instead of another. Discretion is helpful because the police cannot be everywhere and arrest every offender. It is risky because it can lead to unequal treatment, favoritism, and even corruption.

1. What is police discretion? Is it beneficial or harmful? Explain your response.

2. What experiences in a police officer's background are likely to influence his or her discretionary decisions?

3. Should police discretion be limited? If so, how?

Differentiate between the universalistic and particularistic perspectives on police behavior.

Police behavior can be perceived as being either universalistic (all officers share some of the same characteristics and attitudes) or particularistic (officers differ from one another in various respects). It is likely that officers are socialized to behave in certain ways (the socialization perspective), but there is also evidence that policing attracts a certain kind of person (the predisposition perspective).

1. What are the differences between the universalistic and particularistic perspectives on police behavior?

2. Which do you believe is more important in predicting police behavior: socialization or predisposition?

3. What kinds of personalities are most likely to be attracted to police work?

universalistic perspective The view that all police officers are similar and that they exhibit some of the same characteristics and behavior patterns.

particularistic perspective The view that individual officers differ from one another in various ways, including values, role orientation, and preferred styles of policing.

Describe the factors that affect police decision making.

Police decision making can be understood in terms of (1) organizational factors, (2) neighborhood factors, (3) situational factors, and (4) individual officer characteristics. Organizational factors that can influence officer's decision making include the bureaucratic structure of an agency, beats, and scheduling. Neighborhood factors include racial composition, heterogeneity, socioeconomic status, and crime. Situational factors include the reason the officer arrives at the scene (on his or her initiative or following a call for assistance), the suspect's demeanor and demographic characteristics, the relationship between the parties, the seriousness of the offense, the location of the contact, and the presence or absence of bystanders. Individual characteristics that can influence officer's decision making include the officer's education, age, experience, gender, ambition, and attitudes toward the job.

1. What organizational factors have been identified as possible predictors of police decision making?

2. What neighborhood factors have been identified as possible predictors of police decision making?

3. What situational factors have been identified as possible predictors of police decision making?

4. What individual characteristics have been identified as possible predictors of police decision making?

territorial imperative The sense of obligation, even protectiveness, that develops in officers who routinely patrol the same area.

References

1 Jon Schuppe, "As violence spikes in some cities, is 'Ferguson effect' to blame?," *NBC News*, June 2, 2015, http://www.nbcnews.com/news/us-news/violence-spikes-some-cities-ferguson-effect-blame-n368526 (accessed March 16, 2016).

2 J. Q. Wilson and G. L. Kelling, "Broken windows: The police and neighborhood safety," *Atlantic Monthly*, March 1982, pp. 28–29.

3 D. H. Bayley and E. Bittner, "Learning the skills of policing," in *Critical issues in policing: Contemporary readings*, eds. R. G. Dunham and G. P. Alpert, pp. 87–110 (Prospect Heights, IL: Waveland, 1989).

4 K. C. Davis, *Police discretion* (St. Paul, MN: West, 1975), p. 73.

5 W. A. Westley, "Violence and the police," *American Journal of Sociology*, vol. 59 (1953), pp. 34–42; see also W. A. Westley, *Violence and the police* (Cambridge, MA: MIT Press, 1970).

6 J. H. Skolnick, *Justice without trial*, 3rd ed. (New York: Macmillan College Publishing, 1994).

7 Ibid., p. 226.

8 See P. K. Manning and J. Van Maanen, eds., *Policing: A view from the street* (Santa Monica, CA: Goodyear, 1978).

9 P. K. Manning, "The police: Mandate, strategy, and appearances," in *The police and society: Touchstone readings*, 2nd ed., ed. V. E. Kappeler (Prospect Heights, IL: Waveland, 1999), p. 101.

10 Ibid., p. 109.

11 Ibid., p. 108.

12 To learn more about Wilson, see "Presidential Medal of Freedom recipient James Q. Wilson," http://www.anderson.ucla.edu/media-relations/2003/james-q-wilson-pres-medal-of-freedom (accessed January 14, 2016).

13 James Q. Wilson, *Varieties of police behavior: The management of law and order in eight communities* (Cambridge, MA: Harvard University Press, 1968).

14 Gary W. Sykes, "Street justice: A moral defense of order maintenance policing," *Justice Quarterly*, vol. 3, no. 4 (December 1986), p. 505.

15 J. Rubenstein, *City police* (New York: Farrar, Straus, and Giroux, 1973).

16 J. Van Maanen, "Observations on the making of policeman," *Human Organization*, vol. 32 (1973), pp. 407–18.

17 W. K. Muir, *Police: Streetcorner politicians* (Chicago: University of Chicago Press, 1977).

18 J. Zhao, Q. Thurman, and N. He, "Sources of job satisfaction among police officers: A test of demographic and work environment models," *Justice Quarterly*, vol. 16 (1999), pp. 153–73.

19 K. Peak, *Policing America: Methods, issues, challenges*, 5th ed. (Upper Saddle River, NJ: Prentice Hall, 2006).

20 D. Black, *The manners and customs of the police* (New York: Academic Press, 1980).

21 S. E. Martin, *Breaking and entering: Policewomen on patrol* (Berkeley: University of California Press, 1980).

22 R. Worden, "Situational and attitudinal explanations of police behavior: A theoretical reappraisal and empirical assessment," *Law and Society Review*, vol. 23 (1989), p. 687.

23 Ibid.

24 S. O. White, "A perspective on police professionalization," *Law and Society Review*, vol. 7 (1982), p. 61.

25 Worden, "Situational and attitudinal explanations of police behavior," p. 687.

26 White, "A perspective on police professionalization," p. 61.

27 Worden, "Situational and attitudinal explanations of police behavior," p. 688.

28 See, e.g., M. K. Brown, *Working the street* (New York: Russell Sage Foundation, 1981), p. 162.

29 *Atwater v. City of Lago Vista* 121 S.Ct. 1536 (2001).

30 Worden, "Situational and attitudinal explanations of police behavior," p. 689.

31 J. A. Gardiner, *Traffic and the police: Variations in law enforcement policy* (Cambridge, MA: Harvard University Press, 1969).

32 See, e.g., Brown, *Working the street*.

33 Worden, "Situational and attitudinal explanations of police behavior," p. 690.

34 M. Rokeach, M. Miller, and J. Snyder, "The value gap between police and policed," *Journal of Social Issues*, vol. 27 (1971), pp. 155–71.

35 M. Caldero and A. P. Larose, "Value consistency within the police: The lack of a gap," *Policing: An International Journal of Police Strategies and Management*, vol. 24 (2003), pp. 162–80, quote on p. 162.

36 For an examination of this issue, see also J. Crank and M. Caldero, *Police ethics: The corruption of noble cause* (Cincinnati: Anderson, 1999).

37 G. Alpert and W. Smith, "Developing police policy: An evaluation of the control principle," in *Policing perspectives: An anthology*, eds. L. Gaines and G. Cordner, pp. 353–62 (Los Angeles: Roxbury, 1998). See also J. Auten, "Preparing written guidelines," *FBI Law Enforcement Bulletin*, vol. 57 (1988), pp. 1–7.

38 G. Cordner, "Written rules and regulations: Are they necessary?," *FBI Law Enforcement Bulletin*, July 1989, pp. 17–21. See also T. Adams, *Police field operations* (Englewood Cliffs, NJ: Prentice Hall, 1990).

39 R. Roberg, K. Novak, and G. Cordner, *Police and society*, 4th ed. (New York: Oxford University Press, 2008), p. 285.

40 S. D. Mastrofski, "Policing the beat: The impact of organizational scale on patrol officer behavior in urban

residential neighborhoods," *Journal of Criminal Justice*, vol. 9 (1981), pp. 343–58.

41 S. D. Mastrofski, R. Ritti, and D. Hoffmaster, "Organizational determinants of police discretion: The case of drinking-driving," *Journal of Criminal Justice*, vol. 15 (1987), pp. 387–402.

42 Brown, *Working the street*, p. 58; P. V. Murphy and T. Pate, *Commissioner* (New York: Simon and Schuster, 1977), p. 39.

43 Murphy and Pate, *Commissioner*.

44 L. W. Brooks, "Police discretionary behavior: A study of style," in *Critical issues in policing: Contemporary readings*, 4th ed., eds. R. G. Dunham and G. P. Alpert (Prospect Heights, IL: Waveland, 1989), p. 123.

45 E. M. Davis, *Staff one: A perspective on effective police management* (Englewood Cliffs, NJ: Prentice Hall, 1978), p. 135.

46 S. Walker, *The police in America*, 2nd ed. (New York: McGraw-Hill, 1991); P. F. Nardulli and J. M. Stonecash, *Politics, professionalism, and urban services: The police* (Cambridge, MA: Oelgeschlager, Gunn, and Hain, 1981).

47 Nardulli and Stonecash, *Politics, professionalism, and urban services*, pp. 86–88.

48 Roberg et al., *Police and society*, p. 286.

49 D. A. Smith, "The neighborhood context of police behavior," in *Crime and justice: An annual review of research*, vol. 8, eds. A. J. Reiss and M. Tonry (Chicago: University of Chicago Press, 1986).

50 E. C. Riksheim and S. M. Chermak, "Causes of police behavior revisited," *Journal of Criminal Justice*, vol. 21 (1993), pp. 353–82; D. A. Smith, "The organizational aspects of legal control," *Criminology*, vol. 22 (1984), pp. 19–38; Smith, "The neighborhood context of police behavior"; D. A. Smith and J. R. Klien, "Police agency characteristics and arrest decisions," in *Evaluating performance of criminal justice agencies*, eds. G. D. Whitaker and C. D. Phillips (Beverly Hills, CA: Sage, 1984).

51 D. A. Klinger, "Negotiating order in patrol work: An ecological theory of police response to deviance," *Criminology*, vol. 35 (1997), pp. 277–306.

52 L. W. Brooks, A. Piquero, and J. Cronin, "Workload rates and police officer attitudes: An examination of 'busy' and 'slow' precincts," *Journal of Criminal Justice*, vol. 22 (1994), pp. 277–86.

53 L. W. Sherman, "Causes of police behavior: The current state of quantitative research," in *The ambivalent force*, 3rd ed., eds. A. S. Blumberg and E. Niederhoffer (New York: Holt, Rinehart, and Wilson, 1985), p. 187.

54 J. Van Maanen, "The asshole," in *Policing: A view from the streets*, eds. P. K. Manning and J. Van Maanen, pp. 221–38 (Santa Monica, CA: Goodyear, 1978).

55 See, e.g., D. Black and A. Reiss, "Police control of juveniles," *American Sociological Review*, vol. 35 (1970), pp. 63–77; R. Ericson, *Reproducing order: A study of police patrol work* (Toronto: University of Toronto Press, 1982); D. A. Smith, "The neighborhood context of police behavior," in *Crime and justice: An annual review of research*, vol. 8, eds. A. J. Reiss and M. Tonry (Chicago: University of Chicago Press, 1986); C. A. Visher, "Gender, police arrest decisions, and notions of chivalry," *Criminology*, vol. 21 (1983), pp. 5–28.

56 K. M. Lersch and J. R. Feagin, "Violent police–citizen encounters: An analysis of major newspaper accounts," *Critical Sociology*, vol. 22 (1996), pp. 29–49.

57 D. Klinger, "Demeanor or crime: Why 'hostile' citizens are more likely to be arrested," *Criminology*, vol. 32 (1994), pp. 475–93.

58 See, e.g., R. J. Lundman, "Demeanor or crime? The Midwest City police–citizen encounter," *Criminology*, vol. 32 (1994), pp. 631–56, and R. E. Worden and R. L. Shepard, "Demeanor, crime, and police behavior: A reexamination of the police services study data," *Criminology*, vol. 34 (1996), pp. 83–105.

59 V. E. Kappeler, R. D. Sluder, and G. P. Alpert, *Forces of deviance: Understanding the dark side of policing* (Prospect Heights, IL: Waveland, 1994); W. Chambliss, "Policing the ghetto underclass: The politics of law and law enforcement," in *Public policy: Crime and criminal justice*, eds. B. Handcock and P. Sharp, pp. 146–65 (Upper Saddle River, NJ: Prentice Hall, 1997); M. Maurer, *Young black men and the criminal justice system: A growing national problem* (Washington, DC: Sentencing Project, 1993).

60 Roberg et al., *Police and society*, p. 288.

61 G. P. Alpert, J. M. Macdonald, and R. G. Dunham, "Police suspicion and discretionary decision making during citizen stops," *Criminology*, vol. 43 (2005), pp. 407–34.

62 For some examples, see D. A. Harris, "The stories, the statistics, and the law: Why 'driving while black' matters," *Minnesota Law Review*, vol. 84 (1999), pp. 265–326, and E. Spitzer, *The New York City Police Department's 'stop and frisk' practices: A report to the people of the State of New York from the Office of the Attorney General* (Albany: New York Attorney General's Office, 1999).

63 C. A. Visher, "Gender, police arrest decisions, and notions of chivalry," *Criminology*, vol. 21 (1983), pp. 5–28.

64 P. B. Kraska and V. E. Kappeler, "To serve and pursue: Exploring police sexual violence against women," *Justice Quarterly*, vol. 12 (1995), pp. 85–112.

65 Kappeler et al., *Forces of deviance*.

66 See, e.g., D. Black, *The behavior of law* (New York: Academic Press, 1976).

67 K. J. Novak et al., "Revisiting the decision to arrest: Comparing beat and community officers," *Crime and Delinquency*, vol. 48 (2002), pp. 70–98.

68 Y. G. Hurst and J. Frank, "How kids view cops: The nature of juvenile attitudes toward the police," *Journal of Criminal Justice*, vol. 28 (2000), pp. 189–202.

69 See, e.g., S. D. Mastrofski, R. E. Worden, and J. B. Snipes, "Law enforcement in a time of community

policing," *Criminology*, vol. 33 (1995), pp. 539–63; G. Cordner, "Community policing: Elements and effects," *Police Forum*, vol. 5 (1995), pp. 1–8.

70 Black and Reiss, "Police control of juveniles"; D. Black, "The social organization of arrest," *Stanford Law Review*, vol. 23 (1971), pp. 1087–111; R. J. Friedrich, "The impact of organizational, individual, and situational factors on police behavior" (PhD diss., University of Michigan, 1977).

71 Black and Reiss, "Police control of juveniles"; Black, "The social organization of arrest"; L. W. Brooks, "Determinants of police officer orientations and their impact on police discretionary behavior" (PhD diss., University of Maryland, 1986); Friedrich, "The impact of organizational, individual, and situational factors on police behavior"; D. A. Smith, "Police response to interpersonal violence: Defining the parameters of legal control," *Social Forces*, vol. 65 (1987), pp. 767–82; D. A. Smith and C. Visher, "Street level justice: Situational determinants of police arrest decisions," *Social Problems*, vol. 29 (1981), pp. 167–78; C. A. Visher, "Gender, police arrest decisions, and notions of chivalry," *Criminology*, vol. 21 (1983), pp. 5–28; Worden, "Situational and attitudinal explanations of police behavior."

72 See, e.g., Black, *The manners and customs of the police*.

73 Roberg et al., *Police and society*, p. 291.

74 See, e.g., Brooks, "Police discretionary behavior," p. 126; Sherman, "Causes of police behavior," pp. 189–92.

75 See, e.g., S. E. Martin, "Female officers on the move?," in *Critical issues in policing: Contemporary readings*, eds. R. G. Dunham and G. P. Alpert, pp. 312–30 (Prospect Heights, IL: Waveland, 1989); S. A. Grennan, "Findings on the role of officer gender in violent encounters with citizens," *Journal of Police Science and Administration*, vol. 15 (1988), pp. 78–85.

76 W. F. Walsh, "Police officer arrest rates," *Justice Quarterly*, vol. 3 (1986), pp. 271–90.

77 Mastrofski et al., "Law enforcement in a time of community policing."

78 James B. Comey, "Remarks delivered at the University of Chicago Law School, Chicago, IL, October 23, 2015," FBI press release, https://www.fbi.gov/news/speeches/law-enforcement-and-the-communities-we-serve-bending-the-lines-toward-safety-and-justice (accessed March 3, 2016).

7

Core Police Functions

1 Identify the different types of police missions.

2 Describe the types of patrol, methods of patrol, the response role, and the traffic function.

3 Describe the function of peacekeeping and order maintenance.

4 Summarize the evolution of investigations, including investigative goals, processes, and undercover work.

PREDICTIVE POLICING

Crime prevention is one of the many responsibilities of any police department. Recent technologies, like those involved in predictive policing (discussed in greater detail in Chapter 9), seem to have given law enforcement officers an edge over street criminals. Predictive policing "is the application of statistical methods to identify likely targets for police intervention (the predictions) to prevent crimes or solve past crimes, followed by conducting interventions against those targets."[1] The technique typically uses computer technology to predict where crimes will occur before they do. One such technology is PredPol, which runs crime reports through a mathematical algorithm to discover locations with a high probability of crime. For departments who are already using it, like those in Miami, Seattle, Los Angeles, and Santa Cruz, the software spits out 10 to 20 "hotspots" that are the most likely to experience crime over the next shift. Using predictive technology, police departments can send additional patrols and resources into an area where the occurrence of crime is likely. The sophistication of predictive policing technology is growing rapidly, and it is being applied to an ever-increasing set of crime types. In New Orleans, for example, a software company named Palantir claims to be able to use its technology to specifically identify approximately 1% of a city's population who will be likely to inflict or to become victims of gun violence.

Although few question its usefulness to law enforcement, some question whether predictive policing is "fair." Andrew Ferguson, a law professor at the University of the District of Columbia notes that predictive policing can

New technologies can assist law enforcement agencies to better enforce the law. Some, however, worry that innovations like predictive policing can violate the rights of individuals by leading to arrests that might not otherwise have been made. What do you think?

"distort the law" regarding the Fourth Amendment prohibition of illegal search and seizures—meaning that it can provide reasonable suspicion where it might otherwise be lacking, and lead to police stops-and-frisks that might not otherwise take place.[2] In short, does predictive policing somehow violate the civil rights of suspects, by pointing a finger at them even before they have a chance to take action?

Others counter that the only difference between the new analytical models and "old fashioned" policing is that the models give law enforcement agencies the option to base their predictions on hard data, rather than the instinct that comes from experience. Whatever the case, new technologies in the area of policing are sure to change the methods by which crimes are investigated and solved—as well as prevented.

▶ The Police Mission

LEARNING OUTCOMES 1 Identify the different types of police missions.

The police mission in this country is essentially five-fold: (1) to enforce and support the law, (2) to investigate crimes and apprehend offenders, (3) to prevent crime, (4) to help ensure domestic peace and tranquility, and (5) to provide local communities, states, and the nation as a whole with needed enforcement-related services.

The first police mission is the one that comes immediately to mind for most people. The police operate under an official public mandate to enforce the law. Not surprisingly, police officers see themselves as crime fighters, a view generally shared by the public and promoted by the popular media. Although it is the job of the police to enforce the law, it is not their *only* job. Most officers spend the majority of their time answering nonemergency public-service calls,[3] controlling traffic, or writing tickets. Most are not involved in intensive, ongoing crime-fighting activities. Research shows that only about 10% to 20%

of all calls to the police involve situations that actually require a law enforcement response—that is, situations that might lead to arrest and eventual prosecution.[4]

Second, police are charged with investigating crimes and apprehending offenders. Some offenders are apprehended during the commission of a crime or immediately afterward. Fleeing Oklahoma City bomber Timothy McVeigh, for example, was stopped by an Oklahoma Highway Patrol officer on routine patrol only 90 minutes after the destruction of the Alfred P. Murrah Federal Building for driving a car with no license plate.

The third police mission, crime prevention, refers to a proactive approach to the problem of crime (see Figure 7–1). Crime prevention involves "the anticipation, recognition and appraisal of a crime risk and initiation of action to remove or reduce it."[5] In preventing crime, police agencies seek to act before a crime happens, thus preventing victimization from taking place. Although the term *crime prevention* is relatively new, the idea is not. Securing valuables, limiting access to sensitive

Crime-Prevention Techniques	Access control, including barriers to entryways and exits; surveillance, including video systems; theft-deterrence devices like locks, alarms, and tethers; security lighting; visibility landscaping
Crime-Prevention Programs	Organized efforts that focus resources on reducing a specific form of criminal threat
Preventive Patrol	The practice of canvassing (that is, scrutinizing) neighborhoods in an effort to discourage people from committing crime

FIGURE 7-1 Prevention Efforts.

areas, and monitoring the activities of suspicious people are techniques used long before Western police forces were established in the 1800s. Modern crime-prevention efforts aim not only to reduce crime and criminal opportunities and to lower the potential rewards of criminal activity but also to lessen the public's fear of crime.[6]

Enforcing the law, apprehending offenders, and preventing crime are all daunting tasks for police departments because there are many laws and numerous offenders. Still, crimes are clearly defined by statute and are therefore limited in number. Peacekeeping, the fourth element of the police mission, is a virtually unbounded police activity involving not only the control of activities that violate the law (and hence the community's peace) but many others as well. Law enforcement officers who supervise parades, public demonstrations, and picketing strikers, for example, attempt to ensure that the behavior of everyone involved remains "civil" and does not unduly disrupt community life. Robert H. Langworthy, who has written extensively about the police, says that keeping the peace is often left up to individual officers.[7] Basically, he says, departments depend on patrol officers "to define the peace and decide how to support it," and an officer is doing a good job when his or her "beat is quiet, meaning there are no complaints about loiterers or traffic flow, and commerce is supported."

Then there is service, perhaps the most extensive and far-reaching police mission. As writers for the National Institute of Justice note, "Any citizen from any city, suburb, or town across the United States can mobilize police resources by simply picking up the phone and placing a direct call to the police."[8] "Calling the cops" has been described as the cornerstone of policing in a democratic society.[9] About 70% of the half-million daily calls to 911 systems across the country are directed to the police, although callers can also request emergency medical and fire services.[10] Calls received by 911 operators are prioritized and then relayed to patrol officers, specialized field units, or other emergency personnel.

There is much more to enforcement, investigation and apprehension, crime prevention, order maintenance, and community service than we have presented thus far. Enforcement,

for example, can be accomplished through several means, such as preventive patrol, broken windows law enforcement, and emergency response. Investigation can be—and often is—performed by trained detectives, but traffic cops also perform this role, such as when they investigate traffic accidents. The police service mission is extensive and includes many functions that most people are not aware of. Thus, our goal in this chapter is to present these and other police functions in more detail.

▶ Patrol

Most of us are familiar with policing because of the patrol function. Movies and television dramas seem to focus more heavily on the investigation function, but

 LEARNING OUTCOMES 2 Describe the types of patrol, methods of patrol, the response role, and the traffic function.

in real life most of us see patrol officers far more often than we see detectives. That is because patrol officers are the most visible aspect of the police department, engaging in preventive patrol, incident response, and traffic enforcement.

Types of Patrol

Preventive patrol refers to the practice of canvassing (i.e., scrutinizing) neighborhoods in an effort to discourage people from committing crime. **Deterrence theory**, a perspective holding that crime will be less likely when the potential for getting caught outweighs any likely benefits from breaking the law, underlies this practice. Preventive patrol can occur through a number of other means, several of which we will consider here. We will also consider two interesting questions: How much patrol is really preventive, and is preventive patrol effective?

Directed patrol is, as the term suggests, patrol with direction. Unlike random patrol, directed patrol involves concentrating the police presence in areas where certain crimes are a significant problem. Two terms used in conjunction with directed patrol are **hot spots** and **hot times**. Hot spots are concentrated areas of significant criminal activity, such as a street corner known for its prostitution traffic. Hot times are those times of day when crime is particularly problematic, such as after dark on a Friday night.

Other terms that frequently arise with reference to directed patrol include **crime peaks**, or those times of day when certain crimes increase; **saturation patrol**, which occurs when several police officers flood a certain area in an effort to catch criminals and to deter would-be offenders; and **focused patrol**, in which police focus their efforts on certain problems, locations, or times.

Police departments today are able to identify hot spots and hot times with crime mapping. Using dispatch data, for example, police departments can plot the concentration of certain offenses on a map, including the times during which they occur. This allows officials to see firsthand where the problems are so they can allocate personnel to the areas where they are needed the most. Directed patrol is one way of making the most out of a police department's limited resources.

Patrol Methods and Techniques

Foot patrol was how policing was accomplished in America's early cities. It continues to be practiced in a number of areas, especially in strip malls, downtown shopping districts, tourist destinations, and other areas where many people are concentrated in a limited space. Being on foot, though, can clearly limit an officer's ability to give chase if the need arises. Even so, criminologist and author John Fuller has this to say about foot patrol: "An aggressive, street-smart police officer, working an active post, can develop as many (or more) quality cases and arrests working foot patrol as he can working motorized patrol."[11]

Today, automobile patrol has effectively replaced foot patrol. The shift was inevitable once the automobile was invented and people began to spread out and move away from downtown areas. The act of driving itself can be a distraction, possibly diminishing even the most well-trained officer's ability to detect crimes in progress. Automobile patrol is also expensive; it requires not just an officer but also a fully equipped vehicle (with all the attendant maintenance costs) for him or her to drive.

A number of other patrol methods are common and familiar. Bicycle patrol, for example, can be found in a number of relatively small towns and areas with fair weather. As police cyclist instructor Kathleen Vonk notes, "Officers on bike patrol have pursued and caught armed robbers, home invasion criminals, car thieves, criminals breaking into cars and criminals in possession of stolen property. They have assisted in searches for missing children. [And] housing officers have used bicycles in the areas where both stealth and speed are essential, pursuing and arresting many drug dealers, street thugs, and trespassers."[12] Additionally, "The bicycle officer is an important public relations tool and is instrumental in bringing the citizenry closer to the police. An officer on bicycle, wearing the more casual 'uniform' of a polo-type shirt and shorts, is far more approachable

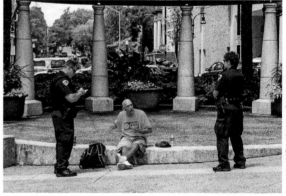
than an officer zipping by in an air-conditioned cruiser with the windows up."[13]

Mounted patrol is also common in some areas. As one researcher recalls, "Folklore of the frontier lawman on horseback in the American Old West evokes an image of peace and justice. That image of an officer on horseback remains a part of modern law enforcement. In the United States today, more than 600 organized mounted police patrol units form a visible pedestal and serve citizens throughout their jurisdiction. An officer on horseback invites constructive community contact in its own unique way."[14] As one scholar has observed, "The horse gives the police a more visible presence in a crowd, and the horse gives the officer a better view of problems."[15] Mounted patrol is also relatively economical compared to automobile patrol. See Figure 7–2 for a summary of patrol methods.

Types of Police Patrol

- **Foot.** The oldest method of patrol, predating the invention of the automobile. Foot patrol's advantages lie in the close proximity it provides to citizens, which tends to enhance rapport between people and officers.

- **Automobile.** Automobile patrol reverses the advantages and disadvantages of foot patrol. On the one hand, it improves officer mobility. On the other hand, it distances officers from the people they serve.

- **Bicycle.** Bicycles give officers much more mobility than foot patrol and can also be advantageous from the standpoint of community relations.

- **Mounted.** Like bicycle patrol, mounted patrol puts officers in closer contact with citizens. In addition, mounted patrol provides effective crowd control. Horses are large and heavy and put officers well above the crowd, thereby permitting them to push unruly groups back if the need arises.

- **Air.** Air patrol is done for everything from traffic enforcement in rural areas to investigation of possible marijuana-growing operations (with thermal imagery) in inner cities.

- **Water.** Water patrol can be found on lakes and waterways throughout the United States.

- **K9-Assisted Patrol.** Police officers who work with K9 units (police dogs) do everything from searching for elusive suspects to detecting drugs, bombs, and other threats to public safety.

- **Special Terrain Vehicle Patrol.** Some all-terrain vehicle (ATV) parks, for instance, are patrolled by officers on off-road motorcycles. Some of the typical offenses found while patrolling are noise violations, fire hazards, illegal dumping, illegal shooting, trespassing with motor vehicles, illegal hunting, abandoning stolen vehicles, and undocumented alien trafficking.

FIGURE 7–2 Types of Police Patrol.

How Much Patrol Is Really Preventive?

The public has something of a romanticized image of preventive patrol—that of police officers diligently scanning up and down every side street, alleyway, and lot as they drive through their beat. Then there is the real world, which unfortunately does not bode particularly well for the prospects of preventive patrol. Consider, for instance, the number of police officers on patrol in relation to crime rates: Several large cities across the country have approximately the same number of police officers per citizen, but very different levels of crime. For example, according to the latest data, St. Louis has 42 full-time sworn police officers per 10,000, while Seattle had 21.[16] At first glance, one may be inclined to conclude that St. Louis is a safer city, but such is not the case. It was one of the most crime-ravaged cities in America during 2010.[17]

There are more reasons why preventive patrol may not do a good job of disrupting crime. First, the police presence in America is spread very thin. Even if we could double the size of our nation's police force, the number of police officers per 10,000 citizens would remain quite small. Next, according to Sam Walker, a prominent criminal justice professor, "many actual or potential offenders do not perceive police patrol as a

meaningful threat."[18] Even with a substantial and visible police presence, some people cannot be deterred from committing crimes. Walker draws this conclusion: "Many crimes are inherently not 'suppressible' by patrol. Because they usually occur indoors and in the heat of passion, the amount of police patrol out on the street is not going to affect them."[19]

COPS Funding

Former president Bill Clinton signed the Violent Crime Control and Law Enforcement Act in September 1994. Title I of the act, known as the Public Safety Partnership and Community Policing Act of 1994, permitted the use of $8.8 billion to fund local law enforcement agencies in the fight against crime and to help improve their community policing capabilities. To spend this massive sum of money, the U.S. Department of Justice created a new agency known as the **Office of Community Oriented Policing Services (COPS Office)**. Its job was to administer and supervise the spending.

Since its creation, the COPS Office has awarded grants to law enforcement agencies throughout the United States. More than $7 billion has been spent. These grant awards have included funds for the hiring of additional police officers, for innovative community policing programs, and for improvement of law enforcement technology. COPS funds have also been used to fund regional community policing institutes, research, and training and technical assistance. All in all, the COPS Office has provided funding for the hiring of more than 100,000 new police officers throughout the United States.

How Effective Is Patrol?

How effective is patrol? This is not an easy question to answer because it is difficult to get in the heads of would-be criminals to determine whether the police presence affects their decision making. Researchers have, however, examined the effects on crime of putting more officers on America's streets. They began in Kansas City, Missouri, and then expanded their horizons to hundreds of other cities and counties throughout the United States.

One of the most important policing studies relevant to police hiring is the now-famous Kansas City (Missouri) Preventive Patrol Experiment.[20] Conducted during 1972 and 1973, the experiment divided the South Patrol District of Kansas City into three groups of patrol beats. *Proactive beats* received two to three times the normal level of patrol. *Reactive beats* received no patrol, only responses to calls for service. *Control beats* kept police patrol levels to normal.

The experiment revealed that the level of patrol had no effect on crimes suppressible by patrol. These included burglaries, auto thefts, larcenies involving auto accessories, robberies, and vandalism. That is, public safety was neither improved nor decreased in either of the three beats. In addition, citizens weren't even aware of the differences! Citizens' attitudes toward the police, their feelings of security, and their decisions to report crime did not vary noticeably from one beat to the next. The lessons of Kansas City, therefore, are often touted as evidence that more police will not reduce crime,[21] but they should not be construed as the gospel truth. For example, the authors of the experiment's final report pointed out that their findings may have been misinterpreted—that there was more to the experiment than just a look at whether additional hiring is necessary.[22] Also, some academics have been highly critical of the experiment.[23]

Since the results of the Kansas City experiment were published, multiple studies have examined the police–crime relationship.[24] They have sought to determine whether there is a relationship between the police presence and crime. Whether a police–crime relationship exists is actually one of the most significantly researched questions in criminal justice.

In 1998, a study was published wherein the author reviewed 22 previous studies of the police–crime relationship.[25] He concluded that 18 of the 22 studies found either no relationship between police and crime or a positive relationship. A positive relationship is not what one would expect because it suggests that as the police presence increases, so does crime. A similar review published in 1996 reviewed 36 previous studies.[26] The authors of that review reported that only 10 of the 36 previous studies found a relationship between the police presence and crime, that is, a relationship showing a decrease in crime when the police presence increases. In short, both studies appear to show that there is *very little* research concluding that

it is desirable to hire more police officers. But some time has passed, and some more sophisticated research techniques have been used, leading some researchers to conclude that previous research in this important area of criminal justice is flawed.

Criminologists Thomas Marvell and Carl Moody have claimed that previous researchers have failed to address the possibility not only that an enhanced police presence may affect crime but also that crime may affect the police presence.[27] Clearly this is plausible. We know, for example, that voters commonly express frustration when public safety is threatened, thereby calling on politicians to give more resources to law enforcement. In a sophisticated analysis that controlled for this possibility, Marvell and Moody were able to show that a heightened police presence does reduce crime. They concluded that "higher police levels reduce most types of crime, particularly at the city level. The size of the impact is often substantial."[28]

Researchers have also examined the effects of COPS funding on crime. All the spending has led researchers to ask, Has it reduced crime? One important study answered the question with a yes.[29] A few others have followed suit, but at least one study, one of the more sophisticated studies to date, revealed that COPS grants have made virtually no dent in the crime problem.[30] Thus, police officers may prevent some crimes, but certainly not all them.

The Response Role

Perhaps one of the reasons why preventive patrol may not be the most effective approach to law enforcement is that officers are routinely responding to calls, which may limit the time they have to patrol neighborhoods and prevent crime.

Think About It…

Preventive Patrol How effective is preventive patrol? This is not an easy question to answer because it is difficult to get into the heads of would-be criminals to determine whether police presence affects their decision making. *What are some possible limitations of studies that look at the aggregate relationship between the police presence and crime? What is the best way to know whether preventive patrol "works"?*

Brad Sauter/Shutterstock

Routine Incident Response

Routine incident response is the second most common activity of patrol officers.[31] As noted by the National Institute of Justice, "The specific police objective will vary depending on the nature of the situation, but generally, the objective is to restore order, document information or otherwise provide some immediate service to the parties involved."[32]

One important measure of police success that is strongly linked to citizen satisfaction is **response time**: the time it takes for police officers to respond to calls for service. It is measured from the time a call for service is received by a dispatcher until an officer arrives on the scene. In 2001, for example, police response time in New York City averaged 7.2 minutes for all types of calls, 29% faster than the previous year and the quickest response time in a decade.[33] The average response time for critical calls in New York City decreased 20%, to 4.8 minutes. Response times in 2001 were cut by an average of nearly three minutes over the previous year, even in the face of an increased number of calls and budget cutbacks that resulted in fewer officers on patrol.

Emergency Response

In a bizarre case from Pomona, California, police officers on routine patrol responded to a dispatcher's instructions to assist in an emergency at a local coin-operated laundry.[34] On arrival, they found a two-year-old girl trapped inside an industrial-size washing machine. The officers used their batons to smash the locked glass-paned door. The girl, unconscious and nearly drowned when pulled from the machine, was taken to a local hospital, where she was expected to recover. Her mother, 35-year-old Erma Osborne, was arrested at the scene and charged with child endangerment when the on-site video surveillance cameras showed her placing her daughter in the machine and shutting the door. This is but one disturbing example of the many emergencies police officers throughout the United States respond to.

Although police respond to emergencies far less frequently than to routine incidents,[35] emergency response is a vital aspect of what police agencies do. Emergency responses take priority over all other police work, and until order is restored, the officers involved will not turn to other tasks. An important part of police training involves emergency response techniques, including first aid, hostage rescue, and the physical capture of suspects. Perhaps the ultimate critical incident these days is a terrorist attack. Figure 7–3 further distinguishes between routine response and emergency response.

The Traffic Function

Most civilians are more familiar with the traffic enforcement function of police work than with any other dimension of the job—often because they've been on the receiving end of the enforcement. Traffic enforcement is generally concerned with enforcing laws pertaining to motor vehicles and their operation. It also involves the relief of congestion and the reduction of

Routine Responses   Emergency Responses

Police officers on patrol frequently respond to routine incidents, many of which are minor traffic accidents. Responding officers must collect information and, typically, file a written report.

Emergency Response, often called *critical incident response*, is used for crimes in progress, traffic accidents with serious injuries, natural disasters, terrorist attacks, officer requests for assistance, and other situations in which human life may be in jeopardy.

FIGURE 7–3 Routine versus Emergency Responses.

accidents. To do each of these tasks, officers may run radar surveillance, conduct checkpoints to apprehend drunk drivers, perform license and safety checks, direct traffic, enforce anticruising ordinances, ensure that people wear their seat belts, target illegal street racers, nab red-light runners, and keep an eye out for road rage. According to one writer, "Among the most common problems facing law enforcement today are those relating to traffic issues in their community. Citizens may call to complain about speeding cars in their neighborhood or voice concern over a nearby school crosswalk."[36] Perhaps the most controversial aspect of traffic enforcement these days involves stopping a motorist for reasons *other* than legitimate law violations, a practice known as *profiling*.

Think About It...

Rapid Response A common assumption is that if the police could reach crime scenes more quickly, they would have a better chance of apprehending lawbreakers. This is the essence of rapid response. One study found that probability of arrest increased when police travel time decreased, but other studies found virtually no relationship between travel time and the probability of arrest, possibly because people are slow to report crime. *How do the findings from rapid response research mesh with your previous understanding of its effectiveness? If rapid response is not effective across the board, are there areas, times, and contexts in which it could be very important? Explain.*

Michael Matthews/Alamy Stock Photo

Pretext Stops and Profiling

The U.S. Supreme Court has held that police officers can stop cars based on the belief that a crime has been committed, which includes any traffic violation.[37] Once a motorist has been stopped, the officer can order him or her to stand outside of the vehicle without any justification,[38] search the vehicle with consent,[39] seize items that are in "plain view,"[40] frisk the driver and search the passenger compartment of the vehicle out of concerns for safety,[41] and search the entire car if probable cause to arrest or search is developed.[42]

Whether every motorist is stopped for a legitimate reason, though, is sometimes questionable. In addition, even if an officer has legal grounds to stop a motorist, the question of pretext presents itself: Should police with other motivations in mind (e.g., to gain consent to search) be allowed to use traffic laws to stop people? In other words, should officers be able to conduct **pretext stops** (Figure 7–4), which are stops based on more than one motive? In a pretext stop, the officer stops the vehicle for a legitimate reason but is also suspicious about the driver. To the extent that pretext stops occur, too many of them can amount to **racial profiling**, which has been defined as "the use of discretionary authority by law enforcement officers in encounters with minority motorists, typically within the context of a traffic stop, that results in the disparate treatment of minorities."[43]

A driver's race obviously does not create justification to stop. Yet there are many people who have argued that the police use existing traffic laws, which are many and easy to violate, to single out certain drivers based on their race.[44] The Supreme Court has yet to decide directly on the constitutionality of this type of conduct, but at least one of its decisions has come close. In *Whren* v. *United States*,[45] Washington, D.C., police made a traffic stop and observed two bags of crack cocaine in the hands of a passenger who was seated in the front of the car. The police testified that they stopped the driver because he violated traffic laws. In contrast, the defendants claimed that the stop was made based on their race and that the police used alleged traffic violations as a reason to stop them.

The Supreme Court concluded that the "constitutional reasonableness of traffic stops" does not depend "on the actual motivations of the individual officers." The Court also concluded that the only relevant inquiry is whether the officer has cause to stop the car. It rejected the argument that the Fourth Amendment requires a court to consider whether "the officer's conduct deviated materially from usual police practices, so that a reasonable officer in the same circumstances would not have made the stop for the reasons given." Simply put, the Supreme Court has stated that officers' individual motivations—whether racial or otherwise—are irrelevant. The only question worth answering, according to the Court, is whether the officer has cause to stop the vehicle. Needless to say, this decision did not satisfy critics of racial profiling.

Is racial profiling really a problem? Some studies suggest that it is. For example, in a study of drivers' characteristics during traffic stops, Robin Engel and Jennifer Calnon reached this conclusion: "The findings show that young black and Hispanic males are at increased risk for citations, searches, arrests, and use of force after other extralegal and legal characteristics are controlled."[46] Their findings are supported by other researchers.[47]

There is some concern that conclusions like these are difficult to make sense of without first considering the demographic composition of the area studied. We might expect, for example, that more blacks than whites will be stopped in an area with a large percentage of black residents. Most of us would agree that such an apparent disparity could be explained by the demographics of the area. The problem, though, is settling on the appropriate base for comparison. For example, we could look at census data to ascertain the racial composition of a particular neighborhood, but just because someone is stopped in their vehicle in that area doesn't mean they live there. The mobility of automobiles makes it difficult to find something with which to compare police traffic stop data. An alternative is driver's license databases, but even they are limited because not every driver has a license. There are ways around these types of research problems. For example, researchers can look at different officers within the same department. If one stops significantly more minorities than others, then arguably something other than legitimate enforcement is going on.

As most of us are aware, profiling has become a hot topic in the war on terror. Before September 11, 2001, critics were up in arms over the profiling of black motorists. Now the focus has shifted to people of Middle Eastern descent. But surprisingly, there is now a measure of support for profiling: "After years of enduring harsh criticism and suspicion from the public for alleged racial profiling practices, law enforcement in the aftermath of the World Trade Center disaster has suddenly found itself on the high road, as some who once considered the practice taboo are now eager for police to bend the rules when

Justification for Pretext Traffic Stops

There are numerous opportunities for the police to detect contraband during the course of a vehicle stop. And since almost every driver commits traffic law violations at some point, there is usually ample justification for stopping motorists.

Concern with Pretext Traffic Stops

There is the possibility of racial profiling: Many people have argued that the police use existing traffic laws, which are many and easy to violate, to single out certain drivers based on their race.

FIGURE 7–4 Pretext Traffic Stops.

it comes to Middle Easterners."[48] One researcher reported on a *Los Angeles Times* poll, conducted after September 11, that found that more than two-thirds of those questioned favored "randomly stopping people who may fit the profile of suspected terrorists."[49]

Accident Investigation

The traffic function involves much more than enforcement. Officers also respond to accidents. Motor vehicle crashes are all too common and exceedingly costly: "Although the traffic fatality rate has dropped dramatically since the mid-1960s, traffic crashes account for 95% of all transportation-related deaths and 99% of transportation-related injuries. Traffic crashes are the leading cause of death for people ages 4 to 34. The total economic costs of motor vehicle crashes in the United States approach $900 billion annually."[50] In addition, traffic crashes are the leading cause of line-of-duty deaths for police officers.

After victims' needs have been met and the scene has been secured, officers turn to investigating the accident. The causes of some accidents are immediately apparent and require little investigation. Some even occur in plain view of an officer. The causes of many accidents, though, may not be immediately apparent. To ascertain the cause, the officer takes statements from witnesses, physically examines the vehicles involved, measures the skid marks, takes note of the final positions of vehicles on the roadway, and so on. The officer takes photographs and notes in an effort to carefully document all pertinent aspects of the accident scene. All of this helps the officer "reconstruct" the accident in order to determine who, if anyone, was at fault.

Pursuits

Every now and then, suspects flee the police, and pursuits ensue. In some areas of the country, pursuits seem to be a frequent occurrence in light of all the media attention they receive. Some characteristics of police pursuits are listed in Table 7–1. The public seems to thrive on "the chase." There is a thrill in it for police officers, too, but there is also a dark side: Every pursuit carries with it the potential for danger to third parties. When innocent motorists or pedestrians are injured or killed in the course of a pursuit, lawsuits are often filed, and sometimes the plaintiffs prevail. In Washington, D.C., a jury awarded $1 million to a woman who was seriously injured when her car was struck during a high-speed police pursuit.[51] Virtually all police administrators are committed to avoiding the costs associated with such litigation.

Before initiating a high-speed pursuit, the officer must weigh two competing objectives. As Geoffrey Alpert—one of the nation's leading authorities on police pursuits—puts it, "The basic dilemma associated with high-speed pursuit of suspects

TABLE 7–1 | CHARACTERISTICS OF POLICE PURSUITS

Reason for Pursuit	Number (Percentage) of Incidents		
	Metro-Dade (Miami) Florida	Omaha, Nebraska	Aiken County, South Carolina
Traffic violation	**448 (45%)**	**112 (51%)**	**5 (36%)**
DUI/reckless driving		8 (4%)	1 (7%)
"Suspect" vehicle		7 (3.5%)	2 (14%)
Driver known from previous incident		3 (1.5%)	
Felonies	**344 (35%)**	**89 (40%)**	**6 (43%)**
Armed robbery	117		2
Vehicular assault	67		
Aggravated assault	37		
Stolen vehicle	37	36	3
Burglary	24		
Other felonies	62	53	1
Accidents			
Personal injury	428 (41%)	31 (14%)	2 (12%)
Property damage	213 (20%)	91 (40%)	4 (24%)
Arrests	**784 (75%)**	**118 (52%)**	**14 (82%)**

Source: From *Police Pursuit: Policies and Training* by Geoffrey P. Alpert, U.S. Department of Justice.

is deciding whether the benefits of potential apprehension outweigh the risks of endangering police officers, the public, and suspects in the chase."[52] This dilemma becomes especially pronounced in the context of minor offenses. Research reveals that the majority of violators who flee from the police were suspected of committing offenses for which arrest would not be customary.[53]

Most police agencies have some sort of policy governing police pursuits, and these policies have a direct impact on the incidence of pursuits. A study revealed, for instance, that when the Metro-Dade (Florida) Police Department adopted a "violent felony only" pursuit policy, the number of pursuits declined markedly.[54] In contrast, Omaha, Nebraska, adopted a more lax pursuit policy and witnessed an increase in pursuits of 600% in the space of one year.[55] Clearly, then, agencies can manage the incidence of police pursuits by altering their policies.

Assuming the officer decides to engage in a pursuit, what are the likely outcomes? First, research reveals that injuries are more likely to occur when people suspected of violent felonies flee the police.[56] Injuries are also likely when pursuits occur on surface streets (rather than highways) in urban and suburban (rather than rural) areas.[57]

The Washington, D.C., case described at the beginning of this section might not have occurred but for apparent negligence on the part of the pursuing officer. The D.C. police department has one of the most restrictive pursuit policies in the country, permitting officers to chase only those suspected of committing violent felonies, but the officer gave chase through a residential area after a suspect with expired license plates. Was the jury's decision a just one? Perhaps it would help to know that the woman who was injured lost three fingers and other parts of her left hand—and she was an innocent bystander to the chase.

Numerous technologies have been developed to assist police with interrupting high-speed pursuits. Most readers are probably familiar with spike strips. Recent versions of these feature hollow spikes that slowly release the air from the fleeing suspect's tires to bring the vehicle to a safe stop. The spikes can be retracted remotely so that pursuing vehicles can pass over them safely. Another device, called "StarChase," launches a GPS dart at the fleeing vehicle. When the dart attaches, officers can fall back and safely track the fleeing motorists' whereabouts from a distance.[58]

▶ Peacekeeping and Order Maintenance

Peacekeeping and order maintenance are also critical police missions. The mere thought that police officers might be close can discourage crime and deviance, thereby fostering peace and order. On the other hand, it is sometimes necessary to take visible steps to maintain peace and order. Police officers dressed in riot gear during a high-profile public protest are an example of this. The presence of police officers at sporting events, such as on the sidelines in a football game, is

LEARNING OUTCOMES 3 · Describe the function of peacekeeping and order maintenance.

another. In either case, police officers take *proactive* steps to maintain peace and order. There is also a *reactive* element to peacekeeping and order maintenance, such as when neighborhood disorder and quality-of-life problems surface in the wake of civil disobedience and during crisis situations.

Managing Disorder and Quality-of-Life Issues

Many police departments focus on quality-of-life offenses as a crime-reduction and peacekeeping strategy. **Quality-of-life offenses** are minor law violations, sometimes called *petty crimes*, that demoralize residents and businesspeople by creating disorder. Examples of petty crimes include excessive noise, graffiti, abandoned cars, and vandalism. Other quality-of-life offenses reflect social decay and include panhandling and aggressive begging, public urination, prostitution, roaming youth gangs, public consumption of alcohol, and street-level substance abuse. Homelessness, while not necessarily a violation of the law unless it involves some form of trespass,[59] is also typically addressed under quality-of-life programs. Through police interviews, the homeless may be relocated to shelters or hospitals or arrested for some other offense. Some researchers claim that reducing the number of quality-of-life offenses in a community can restore a sense of order, reduce the fear of crime, and lessen the number of serious crimes that occur. However, quality-of-life programs have been criticized by those who say that the government should not be taking a law enforcement approach to social and economic problems.[60]

The Broken Windows Model

A similar approach to keeping the peace can be found in the **broken windows model** of policing.[61] This model is based on the notion that physical decay in a community, such as litter and abandoned buildings, can breed disorder and can lead to crime by signaling that laws are not being enforced (Figure 7–5).[62] Such decay, the theory postulates, pushes law-abiding citizens to withdraw from the streets, which then sends a signal that lawbreakers can operate freely.[63] The broken windows model suggests that by encouraging the repair of run-down buildings and controlling disorderly behavior in public spaces, police agencies can create an environment in which serious crime cannot easily flourish.[64] While desirable, public order has its own costs. Noted police author Charles R. Swanson says, "The degree to which any society achieves some amount of public order through police action depends in part upon the price that society is willing to pay to obtain it."[65] Swanson describes the price to be paid in terms of (1) police resources paid for by tax dollars and (2) "a reduction in the number, kinds, and extent of liberties" that are available to members of the public.[66]

Civil Disobedience and Crisis Situations

Civil disobedience involves law-breaking to prove a point or to protest against something (Figure 7–6). As Karen Hess and Henry Wrobleski observe, "Civil disobedience occurs daily

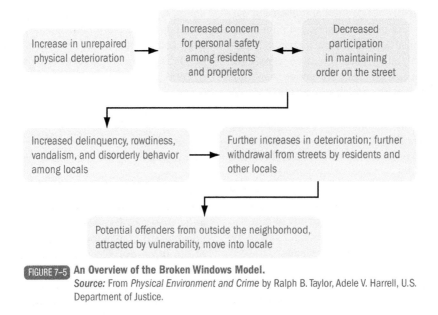

FIGURE 7-5 An Overview of the Broken Windows Model.
Source: From *Physical Environment and Crime* by Ralph B. Taylor, Adele V. Harrell, U.S. Department of Justice.

FIGURE 7-6 Civil Disobedience and Crisis Situations.

around the world, from the fight against apartheid in South Africa, to the quest for autonomy of ethnic groups in Europe, to demonstrations in Washington, DC, against racism or for a more responsive government."[67] Police officers need to be equipped to deal with such situations.[68]

A problem with policing civil disobedience is that much of it is based on a desire to protest some perceived inequity, a right protected by the First Amendment. So important is this right that even the President's Task Force on 21st Century Policing called attention to it: "Citizens have a constitutional right to freedom of expression, including the right to peacefully demonstrate."[69] The Task Force called for "positive communication and engagement strategies that can protect constitutional rights of demonstrators and the safety of citizens and the police."[70]

Crisis situations also keep the police busy. Ever wonder why the police don't just swarm a building where a person is being held hostage? The obvious answer is that doing so would be dangerous, but why? Because an assault by police threatens the lives of hostages as well as the hostage takers. Hostages could be killed by those holding them before they can be rescued, or they might be killed or injured in the battle between police and the hostage takers. An assault, of course, can also result in loss of life or injury to police personnel. Often, time is on the side of hostage negotiators.

▶ Investigations

Criminal investigation is one of the most important police functions—and certainly the most romanticized. Investigation is carried out largely by detectives—sworn officers who have moved up from patrol to something of a "glamour" job wherein they spend their days solving crimes. Detective work would be unnecessary if patrol officers were able to catch all crimes in progress. Of course, they hardly ever do this, in part because they are spread so thin—hence the need for a dedicated criminal investigations division.

Large police agencies often have hundreds of detectives in various divisions covering offenses that run the gamut from homicide to check fraud. Indeed, a study by the RAND Corporation revealed that police departments in every city with a population of more than 250,000 people—and 90% of those in smaller cities—have dedicated detectives.[71]

The Evolution of Investigations

At the heart of any investigation is the practice of **criminalistics**, which refers to the scientific study and evaluation of evidence associated with the commission of a crime. Today, this term carries connotations of recent technological advancements that detect nearly invisible **trace evidence** (e.g., blood stains that someone tried to clean up) or other evidence of a crime that would escape all but the most skilled investigator. But criminalistics is about as old as policing itself. Henry Fielding's Bow Street Runners and Sir Robert Peel's bobbies experienced some early investigative success. The bobbies, for instance, were occasionally removed from their patrol duties to perform investigations.

Anthropometry and Dactylography

Some fundamentals of detective work were developed well over 100 years ago. **Anthropometry** (also known as *Bertillon measurements*), a technique for identifying people based on their body measurements, was developed in 1882. Alphonse Bertillon, who developed this technique, concluded that if just 11 measurements were taken on a person, the odds of finding someone with similar measurements were 4,191,304 to 1.[72] The problem, though, was in attempting to use these measurements to identify those who would be most likely to commit crime.

Bertillon successfully identified some criminals, but his ideas fell out of favor because they were inaccurate and a bit complicated. They were replaced with the more accurate identification practice of **dactylography**, or fingerprinting. Dactylography was proposed for criminal investigation around 1880 in England,[73] but knowledge of fingerprints far predated the routine use of such prints to identify criminals. In the first century, for example, a Roman lawyer by the name of Quintilianus used a bloody fingerprint from what was apparently a crime scene to defend a child who was accused of murdering his father.[74]

Throughout the 1880s, fingerprinting continued to gain popularity as a valid technique for identifying criminal perpetrators. Once it was accepted practice (in the mid-1890s), it was successfully used in a number of high-profile contexts. For example, in 1904, Detective Sergeant Joseph Faurot of the New York City Police Department went to England to study fingerprinting. On his return, he used his newfound knowledge to successfully identify a man accused of burglarizing a suite in the Waldorf-Astoria Hotel. The man claimed to be a respected businessman by the name of James Jones, but Faurot learned, as a result of fingerprints, that he was actually Daniel Nolan, a man with 12 prior convictions for similar crimes.[75]

In another high-profile case, as Will West was being processed into the federal prison in Leavenworth, Kansas, a guard noted that there was already a photograph on file for him. West claimed to have never been in the prison before. After measurements and fingerprints were taken, it became clear that he had been mistaken for another man, William West, who had been in the same prison for some time. The concern was that Will West had tried to change his name to avoid harsh punishment for being a repeat offender, which was, of course, not the case. The two were so close in both physical appearance and Bertillon measurements—not to mention the similarity of their names—as to be virtually indistinguishable. Ultimately, it was their fingerprints that permitted authorities to distinguish one man from the other. This case earned fingerprinting a permanent place in the criminal investigator's tool kit.

Firearms Identification and Beyond

Firearms identification, or ballistics, burst onto the criminalistics scene during the mid-1800s. In 1835, Henry Goddard, who was one of the last Bow Street Runners, was the first to successfully identify a murderer from a spent bullet removed from the victim's body. He noticed that the bullet had similar characteristics as bullets fired from the suspect's gun. When confronted with the evidence, the suspect quickly confessed.[76] Near the turn of the twentieth century, Paul Jeserich, a German chemist, testified against a murder defendant on the grounds that the bullet pulled from the victim matched that fired from the defendant's gun.[77] Firearms identification gained popularity in the early 1900s. The first permanent crime laboratory was established at the Northwestern University Law School and was headed by a former army physician, Calvin Goddard, who is credited with making firearms identification a science through his development of the bullet comparison microscope.[78]

August Vollmer is credited with helping initiate the police professionalism movement, but he also made his mark in early criminal investigations. Vollmer teamed up with a chemist from the University of California, Berkeley, to help identify a poison that was allegedly used to murder someone. He also trained his officers in the identification and preservation of evidence and established a forensics lab in Los Angeles. Vollmer's partnership with the university prompted a number of scientists to become interested in criminal investigations.

Other influential figures of the early twentieth century included Albert Osborn, who wrote *Questioned Documents*,[79] an important work intended to assist in the identification of fabricated and falsified papers and records, and Leone Lattes, who pioneered a blood-typing procedure that assisted in the identification of criminals.[80]

Determining whether a crime has been committed	The reporting of an alleged crime and the completion of a report by the responding officer does not necessarily mean that a crime has actually been committed. Consider, for instance, a reported sexual assault. Has it actually occurred, or is it a falsified claim made by a vindictive lover? Thorough investigations are often needed to sort out the truthfulness of such reports when the credibility of the victim is in doubt.
Obtaining information and evidence	This is perhaps the most labor-intensive and least glamorous aspect of detective work. Untold hours of interviewing and questioning can lead to a dead end.
Apprehending suspects	Detectives, as sworn police officers, may elect to arrest the individual they feel was responsible for the crime. Alternatively, they may seek a warrant that would permit any duly authorized peace officer to make the arrest.
Recovering stolen property	In cases of theft, detectives may spend a great deal of time recovering stolen property so it can be used as part of a criminal prosecution before being returned to its rightful owner.
Successfully presenting the case to the prosecutor	One of the detective's foremost responsibilities is presenting an airtight case to the prosecutor so that the correct person can be held to answer for the offense in question.

FIGURE 7-7 Investigative Goals.

Investigative Goals and Process

In the world of mystery novels and television shows, the goal of investigations is to discover "whodunit." In the real world, though, the goals of detective work are much more complex (see Figure 7–7).

Criminal investigations typically progress through two stages: (1) the preliminary investigation and (2) the follow-up investigation. The preliminary investigation is the investigation that plays out immediately after the incident is reported.

In the vast majority of police departments, either line officers or detectives do all this work. In larger agencies, though, dedicated crime scene investigators get involved, especially in the search for **forensic evidence**. Generally speaking, *evidence* is anything useful in a court of law that tends to prove or disprove the facts at issue. *Physical evidence* is evidence that consists of physical material or traces of physical activity. The term *forensic* refers to that which (1) is of interest to the legal system or (2) must be adapted or suited to use through argumentation—that is, something that is not self-evident. For purposes of policing, forensic evidence, therefore, is physical evidence whose usefulness in a court of law would not be immediately apparent to an untrained observer. Argument, usually through the application of accepted scientific techniques, is necessary to demonstrate the legal value of forensic evidence. This is where crime scene investigators come on board. They often take trace evidence to a laboratory where further testing is performed with the intent of identifying the perpetrator.

The job of crime scene investigators has of course been prominently featured on television programs like *CSI*. The show and its progeny portray the crime scene investigator's life as something of an exciting frontline occupation. In reality, it is often anything but exciting. Much investigation work is tedious and plays out behind the scenes. It is also performed more often by trained scientists than by police officers. These individuals, often labeled *forensic experts*, are adept at linking nearly all conceivable forms of evidence to an alleged perpetrator. Examples of such experts include forensic pathologists, toxicologists, anthropologists, odontologists, psychiatrists, and serologists, to name just a few.

The follow-up investigation proceeds through a few more steps, each with a common theme as noted in Figure 7–8.

Undercover Work

Undercover work is closely aligned with investigations. Indeed, many detectives might as well be working undercover because they usually dress in street clothes. For the most part, though, undercover work is common in the investigation and detection of vice crimes, particularly those involving the illicit drug trade.

For obvious reasons, effective drug enforcement would be impossible if it were performed solely by uniformed officers. Police need to infiltrate the criminal underworld in order to successfully nab high-profile criminals. This is seductive work for a number of officers because of the thrill and autonomy it provides. As police scholar Ken Peak has observed, "Since only a few officers are actually selected for undercover assignments, these officers enjoy a professional latitude in their roles, minimal departmental supervision, the ability to exercise greater personal initiative, and a higher degree of professional autonomy than regular patrol officers."[81] What attracts police officers to undercover work, though, can also be their undoing. Several potential problems are associated with working undercover.

Preliminary Investigation Steps

Attending to emergencies, such as a fleeing suspect

↓

Securing the scene

↓

Measuring, photographing, and videotaping the crime scene

↓

Searching for evidence

↓

Identifying, collecting, and examining physical evidence (e.g., suspected weapons, bloodstains, fingerprints, and hair samples)

↓

Questioning victims, witnesses, possible witnesses, and suspects

↓

Recording all statements given for later inclusion in the written report[i]

Follow-Up Investigation Steps

Continuing the investigation. This stage, which begins when preliminary work is done, includes conducting follow-up interviews; developing a theory of the crime; analyzing the significance of information and evidence; continuing the search for witnesses; contacting crime lab technicians and assessing their analyses of the evidence; conducting surveillance, interrogations, and polygraph tests, as appropriate; and preparing the case for the prosecutor.

↓

Reconstructing the crime. The investigator seeks a rational theory of the crime, using inductive reasoning. The collected information and evidence are carefully analyzed to develop a theory. Often, a rational theory of a crime is developed with some assistance from the careless criminal. Verbrecherpech, or "criminal's bad luck," is an unconscious act of self-betrayal. One of the major traits of criminals is vanity; their belief in their own cleverness is the key factor in their leaving a vital clue. Investigators look for mistakes.

↓

Focusing the investigation. When this stage is reached, all investigative efforts are directed toward proving that one suspect or group of suspects is guilty of the crime. This decision is based on the investigator's analysis of the relationship among the crime, the investigation, and the habits and attitudes of the suspect or suspects.[ii]

FIGURE 7-8 **Preliminary and Follow-Up Investigation Steps.**
Source: [i.] K.M. Hess and H.M. Wrobleski, *Police Operations: Theory and Practice,* 4th ed. (Belmont, CA: Wadsworth, 2006), p. 319. [ii.] P.B. Weston and K.M. Wells, *Criminal Investigation: Basic Perspectives,* 4th ed. (Englewood Cliffs, NJ: Prentice Hall, 1986), pp. 5-10.

Problems with Undercover Work

The lack of supervision and the procedural flexibility that go with undercover work can diminish some officers' respect for procedural rules or tempt them with a number of criminal "perks." The money that changes hands in the illegal drug trade, for example, can be all too enticing to civil servants who aren't necessarily well paid.

Undercover work also calls for long and unpredictable hours, which can place not just a physiological strain on officers but also a strain on their personal relationships. One study revealed, for instance, that the number of undercover assignments experienced in an officer's career was associated with problems like drug use, alcohol abuse, and disciplinary actions.[82] While many officers emerge from undercover work unscathed, not all do. For example, a California police officer who went deep undercover with the notorious Hell's Angels motorcycle gang ultimately became hooked on drugs, resigned from the force, robbed banks, and was sentenced to prison.[83]

High-Tech Innovation Meets Law Enforcement

Drones became important assets in the wars in Iraq and Afghanistan. They have also been used for years to assist in patrolling the U.S.–Mexico border. More recently, they have been entering into domestic law enforcement use, such as for search-and-rescue operations or performing reconnaissance ahead of raids. Ordinary citizens can readily access drones, too, albeit cheaper and less sophisticated versions of what government officials typically use. Drones have become so popular that privacy advocates have sounded the call for tight regulations.

The Federal Aviation Administration has enacted a number of rules restricting the activities of what it calls "unmanned aircraft, and now requires drone owners to register such devices.[84]" States, however, are also leading the charge with new laws and legislative proposals intended to place limits on drone use. Some efforts have also been made to curtail unrestricted law enforcement use, such as by requiring police agencies to secure warrants based on probable cause before flying drones over private property. Other proposals have called for warrant requirements *any time* a drone is used. Some enforcement agencies have faced so much backlash from concerned citizens that they have returned their new equipment to the manufacturers.[85]

High courts have yet to answer questions about the constitutionality of drone use, but that will likely change in the

Paul Fleet/Shutterstock

not-too-distant future. But even if legislatures and courts place strict limitations on drone use in domestic law enforcement, civilian use remains an issue. Citizens are not bound by the same constitutional restrictions as the government. That, coupled with the increased accessibility to the technology (many drones are homemade), means it is not difficult to imagine a situation in which drones armed with high-definition cameras fly across neighborhoods engaged in all manner of surveillance.

This article raises several important questions:

1. Should drones be used by domestic law enforcement? If so, for what kinds of purposes?
2. What are the constitutional issues involved when drones are used by enforcement agencies?
3. Can the use of drones effectively deter criminals?
4. Can technology ever replace good old-fashioned police work?
5. What limits, if any, should be placed on law enforcement drone activities?

Identify the different types of police missions.

The police mission involves five elements: (1) enforce and support the law, (2) investigate crimes and apprehend offenders, (3) prevent crime, (4) help ensure domestic peace and tranquility, and (5) provide local communities, states, and the nation with needed enforcement-related services.

1. What are the main crime-prevention activities the police engage in?

2. What is the most important element of the police mission? Why?

Describe the types of patrol, methods of patrol, the response role, and the traffic function.

Preventive patrol refers to the practice of canvassing neighborhoods in an effort to discourage people from committing crime. Directed patrol addresses crime in hot spots. Crackdowns, where police officers target a particular area, are the most common example of this. Proactive patrol refers to targeting specific offenses or offenders. Examples include targeting drunk drivers or identifiable repeat offenders. Incident response, which often involves patrol units, includes both emergency response and routine incident response. Traffic enforcement consists of enforcing applicable traffic laws, relieving congestion, and reducing accidents.

1. Distinguish among preventive patrol, the response role, and the traffic function in policing. Summarize the leading issues associated with each.

2. Distinguish between directed patrol and proactive policing. In your opinion, which approach is better?

3. How does the use of racial profiling impact policing? Are there some situations in policing in which race might provide valuable clues in crime prevention or offender apprehension?

preventive patrol The practice of canvassing neighborhoods in an effort to discourage people from committing crime.

deterrence theory A perspective that holds that crime will be less likely to occur when the potential for getting caught outweighs any likely benefits from breaking the law.

directed patrol A form of patrol that involves concentrating the police presence in areas where certain crimes are a significant problem.

hot spot A concentrated area of significant criminal activity, such as a street corner known for its prostitution traffic.

hot time A period during the day when crime is particularly problematic, such as after dark on a Friday night.

crime peak A time of day when a particular crime increases in frequency.

saturation patrol A form of patrol that involves concentrating the police presence in a certain area in an effort to catch criminals and to deter would-be offenders.

focused patrol A form of patrol that focuses police efforts on certain problems, locations, or times.

foot patrol The oldest method of police patrol, which entails officers walking through neighborhoods. Foot patrol tends to enhance rapport between citizens and officers, but it clearly limits an officer's ability to give chase if the need arises.

Office of Community Oriented Policing Services (COPS Office) An agency within the U.S. Department of Justice tasked with administering and supervising federal funds allocated to improve community policing capabilities.

response time The time it takes for police officers to respond to a call for service.

pretext stop A traffic stop based on more than one motive. For example, an officer stops a vehicle for a legitimate reason but is also suspicious about the driver.

racial profiling The use of discretionary authority by law enforcement officers in encounters with minority motorists, typically within the context of a traffic stop, that results in the disparate treatment of minorities.

Describe the function of peacekeeping and order maintenance.

Peacekeeping and order maintenance policing involve the management of disorder, quality-of-life policing, and the management of civil disobedience and crisis situations.

1. How does the peacekeeping and order maintenance role frequently manifest itself?

2. What is meant by the "broken windows" model of policing? How can the broken windows model lead to lower crime rates?

3. What is a quality-of-life offense? How does the concept of quality-of-life offenses fit in with the broken windows model of policing?

quality-of-life offense A minor law violation that demoralizes residents and businesspeople by creating disorder. Sometimes called *petty crime*.

broken windows model A model of policing based on the notion that physical decay in a community (e.g., litter and abandoned buildings) can breed disorder and lead to crime by signaling that laws are not being enforced. Such decay is thought to push law-abiding citizens to withdraw from the streets, which signals that lawbreakers can operate freely. The model suggests that by encouraging the repair of run-down buildings and by controlling disorderly behavior in public spaces, police agencies can create an environment in which serious crime cannot easily flourish.

civil disobedience Law-breaking used as a political tactic to prove a point or to protest against something.

LEARNING OUTCOMES 4

Summarize the evolution of investigations, including investigative goals, processes, and undercover work.

Police investigative goals include determining whether a crime has actually been committed, gathering information and evidence, apprehending suspects, recovering stolen property, and successfully presenting the case to the prosecutor. Criminal investigations typically progress through two stages: (1) the preliminary investigation and (2) the follow-up investigation—each of which has its own substages. Undercover work is common in policing today, but as this chapter notes, it is especially challenging because it may tempt officers to break the law and can strain personal relationships.

1. What are the investigative goals identified by this chapter?

2. What is involved in the investigative process?

3. What stages characterize the investigative process?

4. What are the possible problems associated with undercover work?

5. Is undercover work more dangerous than other kinds of police work? Why or why not?

6. Are undercover officers more likely to go rouge than other officers? Why or why not?

7. How can potential problems associated with undercover work best be addressed?

criminalistics The use of technology in the service of criminal investigation; the application of scientific techniques to the detection and evaluation of criminal evidence.

trace evidence Minute, nearly invisible evidence of a crime that would escape all but the most skilled investigators.

anthropometry A technique developed by Alphonse Bertillon in 1882 for identifying people based on their body measurements. Also called *Bertillon measurements*.

dactylography An early name for fingerprinting.

forensic evidence Physical evidence whose usefulness in a court of law may not be immediately apparent to an untrained observer but can be demonstrated through the application of accepted scientific techniques.

References

1 Priscillia Hunt, Jessica Saunders, and John S. Hollywood, *Evaluation of the shreveport predictive policing experiment* (Santa Monica, CA: Rand, 2014).

2 Henrick Karoliszyn, "Can a computer predict crime?" *The crime report*, January 11, 2016.

3 C. D. Hale, *Police patrol: Operations and management* (Englewood Cliffs, NJ: Prentice Hall, 1994).

4 V. Kappeler et al., *The mythology of crime and criminal justice* (Prospect Heights, IL: Waveland, 1996).

5 See, e.g., http://pdf.plano.gov/planning/neigh_serv/ServicesandProgramsBrochure.pdf (accessed January 15, 2016).

6 See S. P. Lab, *Crime prevention at a crossroads* (Cincinnati: Anderson, 1997).

7 R. H. Langworthy and L. P. Travis III, *Policing in America: A balance of forces*, 2nd ed. (Upper Saddle River, NJ: Prentice Hall, 1999), p. 194.

8 L. Mazerolle et al., "Managing citizen calls to the police: An assessment of nonemergency call systems," *Criminology*, vol. 2, no. 1 (2002), pp. 97–124.

9 Ibid.

10 Terence Dunworth, "Criminal justice and the IT revolution," in *Criminal justice 2000* (Washington, DC: National Institute of Justice, 2000), pp. 371–426, available at www.ncjrs.gov/criminal_justice2000/vol_3/03h.pdf (accessed January 15, 2016).

11 J. Fuller, "Rethinking foot patrol," *Police and Security News*, May–June 2004, pp. 63–66, quote on p. 63.

12 K. D. Vonk, "Bike patrol successes," *Law and Order*, April 2003, pp. 82–86, quote on p. 85.

13 J. Bellah, "Low-speed ahead," *Law Enforcement Technology*, October 2001, pp. 76–82, quote on p. 78.

14 J. C. Fine, "Police on horseback: A new concept for an old idea," *FBI Law Enforcement Bulletin*, July 2001, pp. 6–7, quote on p. 6.

15 S. Slahor, "MEU: Mounted units for crowd control," *Law and Order*, October 2001, pp. 234–37, quote on p. 237.

16 http://www.governing.com/gov-data/safety-justice/police-officers-per-capita-rates-employment-for-city-departments.html (accessed January 15, 2016).

17 *City crime rankings*, 2014 (Washington, DC: CQ Press, 2013), available at http://www.cqpress.com/pages/cc2014 (accessed January 15, 2016).

18 S. Walker, *Sense and nonsense about crime and drugs: A policy guide*, 5th ed. (Belmont, CA: Wadsworth, 2001), p. 81.

19 Ibid.

20 George L. Kelling, Tony Pate, Duane Diekman, and Charles E. Brown, *The Kansas City Preventive Patrol Experiment: A summary report* (Washington, DC: The Police Foundation, 1974).

21 Samuel Walker, *Sense and nonsense about crime and drugs: A policy guide*, 5th ed. (Belmont, CA: Wadsworth, 2001), p. 81.

22 George L. Kelling, Tony Pate, Duane Diekman, and Charles E. Brown, "The Kansas City Preventive Patrol Experiment: A summary report," in *What works in policing*, ed. David Bayley (New York: Oxford University Press, 1998), p. 49.

23 R. C. Larson, "What happened to patrol operations in Kansas City? A review of the Kansas City Preventive Patrol Experiment," *Journal of Criminal Justice*, vol. 3 (1975), pp. 267–97.

24 Illustrative examples include R. W. Bahl, R. G. Gustely, and M. J. Wasylenko, "The determinants of local government police expenditure: A public employment approach," *National Tax Journal*, vol. 31 (1978), pp. 64–79; D. H. Bayley, *Patterns of policing: A comparative international analysis* (New Brunswick, NJ: Rutgers University Press, 1985); R. A. Carr-Hill and N. H. Stern, "An economic model of the supply and control of recorded offenses in England and Wales," *Journal of Public Economics*, vol. 2 (1973), pp. 289–313; C. Cornwell and W. M. Trumbell, "Estimating the economic model of crime with panel data," *Review of Economics and Statistics*, vol. 72 (1994), pp. 360–66; I. Ehrlich, "Participation in illegal activities: A theoretical and empirical investigation," *Journal of Political Economy*, vol. 81 (1973), pp. 521–67; J. A. Fox, "Crime trends and police expenditures: An investigation of the lag structure," *Evaluation Quarterly*, vol. 3 (1979), pp. 41–58; D. F. Greenberg, R. C. Kessler, and C. Loftin, "The effect of police employment on crime," *Criminology*, vol. 21 (1983), pp. 375–94; S. Hakim, "The attraction of property crimes to suburban localities: A revised economic model," *Urban Studies*, vol. 17 (1980), pp. 265–76; C. R. Huff and J. M. Stahura, "Police employment and suburban crime," *Criminology*, vol. 17 (1980), pp. 461–70; K. C. Land and M. Felson, "A general framework for building dynamic macro social indicator models, including an analysis of changes in crime rates and police expenditures," *American Journal of Sociology*, vol. 82 (1976), pp. 565–604; S. Levitt, "Using electoral cycles in police hiring to estimate the effect of police on crime," *American Economic Review*, vol. 87 (1997), pp. 270–91; C. Loftin and D. McDowall, "The police, crime, and economic theory: An assessment," *American Sociological Review*, vol. 47 (1982), pp. 393–401; Thomas B. Marvell and Carlisle E. Moody, "Specification problems, police levels and crime rates," *Criminology*, vol. 34 (1996), pp. 609–46; T. V. Kovandzic and J. J. Sloan, "Police levels and crime rates revisited: A county level analysis from Florida (1980–1998)," *Journal of Criminal Justice*, vol. 30 (2002), pp. 65–76.

25 S. Cameron, "The economics of crime deterrence: A survey of theory and evidence," *Kyklos*, vol. 41 (1988), pp. 301–23.

26 Marvell and Moody, "Specification problems, police levels, and crime rates."

27 Ibid.

28 Ibid, p. 640.

29 Jihong "Solomon" Zhao, Matthew C. Scheider, and Quint Thurman, "Funding community policing to reduce crime: Have COPS grants made a difference?" *Criminology and Public Policy*, vol. 2 (2002), pp. 732.

30 See J. L. Worrall and T. V. Kovandzic, "COPS grants and crime revisited," *Criminology*, vol. 45 (2007), pp. 159–90; but also see W. N. Evans and E. Owens, "Cops and crime," *Journal of Public Economics*, vol. 91 (2007), pp. 181–201.

31 Much of this material is adapted from Walker, *Sense and nonsense about crime and drugs*.

32 Ibid., p. 86.

33 W. K. Rashbaum, "Response time to police calls is 29% faster," *New York Times*, September 26, 2002, p. B1.

34 Details for this story come from K. Streeter, "Girl, 2, rescued from washer," *Los Angeles Times*, May 26, 2003, http://articles.latimes.com/2003/may/26/local/me-laundry26 (accessed January 15, 2016).

35 See M. S. Scott, *Problem-oriented policing: Reflections on the first 20 years* (Washington, DC: Office of Community Oriented Policing Services, 2000), p. 87, from which much of this material is adapted.

36 G. Carrick, "Traffic safety in the new millennium," *Law and Order*, April 2003, pp. 44–50.

37 *Whren* v. *United States*, 517 U.S. 806 (1996).

38 *Maryland* v. *Wilson*, 519 U.S. 408, 410 (1997), and *Pennsylvania* v. *Mimms*, 434 U.S. 106, 111 (1977).

39 *Ohio* v. *Robinette*, 519 U.S. 33 (1996).

40 *Horton* v. *California*, 496 U.S. 128, 133–37 (1990).

41 *Michigan* v. *Long*, 463 U.S. 1032, 1035 (1983).

42 *New York* v. *Belton*, 453 U.S. 454, 460 (1981).

43 C. Batton and C. Kadleck, "Theoretical and methodological issues in racial profiling research," *Police Quarterly*, March 2004, pp. 30–64.

44 See, e.g., "Driving while black: Study shows minorities more likely to question why police stopped them, how they were treated," *Ohio State Research*, February 10, 2003, available at http://researchnews.osu.edu/archive/dwbstudy.htm (accessed January 15, 2016).

45 *Whren* v. *United States* (1996).

46 R. S. Engel and J. M. Calnon, "Examining the influence of drivers' characteristics during stops with the police: Results from a national survey," *Justice Quarterly*, March 2004, pp. 49–90, quote on p. 49.

47 J. Rojek, R. Rosenfeld, and S. Decker, "The influence of driver's race on traffic stops in Missouri," *Police Quarterly*, March 2004, pp. 126–47, quote on p. 143.

48 J. Nislow, "Are Americans ready to buy into racial profiling?" *Law Enforcement News*, October 15, 2001, p. 11.

49 Ibid.

50 J. Lowy, "Traffic accidents in the U.S. cost $871 billion a year, federal study finds," *Associated Press*, May 29, 2014, http://www.pbs.org/newshour/rundown/motor-vehicle-crashes-u-s-cost-871-billion-year-federal-study-finds/ (accessed January 15, 2016).

51 H. E. Cauvin, "D.C. ordered to pay in police chase: Woman maimed in crash is awarded almost $1 million," *Washington Post*, December 14, 2006, p. B1.

52 G. P. Alpert, *Police pursuit: Policies and training* (Washington, DC: National Institute of Justice, 1997), p. 1.

53 G. P. Alpert et al., *Police pursuits: What we know* (Washington, DC: Police Executive Research Forum, 2000).

54 Alpert, *Police pursuit*, p. 4.

55 Ibid.

56 Ibid., p. 3.

57 Ibid.

58 See www.starchase.com (accessed January 15, 2016).

59 Other violations may be involved as well. On December 29, 2000, for example, Judge John S. Martin, Jr., of the Federal District Court in Manhattan, ruled that homeless people in New York City could be arrested for sleeping in cardboard boxes in public. Judge Martin held that a city sanitation department regulation barring people from abandoning cars or boxes on city streets could be applied to the homeless who were sleeping in boxes.

60 For example, Norman Siegel, executive director of the New York Civil Liberties Union, as reported in "Quality of life offenses targeted," *Western Queens Gazette*, November 22, 2000, www.qgazette.com/News/2000/1122/Editorial_pages/e01.html (accessed January 15, 2016).

61 The broken windows thesis was first suggested by G. L. Kelling and J. Q. Wilson in "Broken windows: The police and neighborhood safety," *Atlantic Monthly*, March 1982.

62 For a critique of the broken windows thesis, see B. E. Harcourt, *Illusion of order: The false promise of broken windows policing* (Cambridge, MA: Harvard University Press, 2001).

63 P. Schuler, "Law professor Harcourt challenges popular policing method, gun violence interventions," *Chicago Chronicle*, March 20, 2003.

64 G. L. Kelling, C. M. Coles, and J. Q. Wilson, *Fixing broken windows: Restoring order and reducing crime in our communities* (repr., New York: Touchstone, 1998).

65 C. R. Swanson, L. Territo, and R. W. Taylor, *Police administration: Structures, processes, and behavior*, 4th ed. (Upper Saddle River, NJ: Prentice Hall, 1998), p. 1.

66 Ibid.

67 K. M. Hess and H. M. Wrobleski, *Police operations: Theory and practice*, 4th ed. (Belmont, CA: Wadsworth, 2006), pp. 188–89.

68 C. A. Rohr, "Training for managing crowds and responding to civil disobediences," *Police Chief*, October 2001, pp. 10–11, especially p. 10.

69 President's Task Force on 21st Century Policing, *Final report of the President's Task Force on 21st Century Policing* (Washington, DC: Office of Community Oriented Policing Services, 2015), p. 20.

70 Ibid.

71 P. W. Greenwood and J. Petersilia, *The criminal investigation process*, vol. 1, *Summary and policy implications* (Santa Monica, CA: RAND, 1975).

72 J. Thorwald, *The century of the detective* (New York: Harcourt, Brace, and World, 1965), pp. 9–10.

73 Ibid., p. 62.

74 A. L. Califana and J. S. Levkov, *Criminalistics for the law enforcement officer* (New York: McGraw-Hill, 1978), p. 20.

75 J. Thorwald, *The marks of Cain* (London: Thames and Hudson, 1965), pp. 78–79.

76 Ibid., pp. 87–88.

77 Ibid., p. 164.

78 C. R. Swanson, N. C. Chamelin, and L. Territo, *Criminal investigation*, 4th ed. (New York: Random House, 1988), p. 19.

79 A. S. Osborn, *Questioned documents: A study of questioned documents with an outline of methods by which the facts may be discovered and shown* (Rochester, NY: The Lawyers' Co-operative Publishing Co., 1910).

80 P. R. DeForest, R. E. Gaensslen, and H. C. Lee, *Forensic science: An introduction to criminalistics* (New York: McGraw-Hill, 1983), p. 19.

81 K. J. Peak, *Policing America: Methods, issues, challenges*, 5th ed. (Upper Saddle River, NJ: Prentice Hall, 2006).

82 M. Girodo, "Drug corruption in undercover agents: Measuring the risk," *Behavioral Sciences and the Law*, vol. 3 (1991), pp. 299–308.

83 G. T. Marx, "Who really gets stung? Some issues raised by the new police undercover work," in *Moral issues in police work*, eds. F. Ellison and M. Feldberg (Totowa, NJ: Bowman and Allanheld, 1988), pp. 99–128.

84 www.faa.gov/about/initiatives/uas/uas_faq (accessed November 6, 2016).

85 Seattle is one such city. See www.slate.com/articles/technology/future_tense/2013/02/domestic_surveillance_drone_bans_are_sweeping_the_nation.html (accessed November 6, 2013).

Community Policing and Community Involvement

1 Describe community justice and problem-oriented policing.

2 Discuss the emergence of community policing and the extent of its application in American policing.

3 Distinguish between citizen involvement in policing and civilianization.

4 Define *third-party policing* and provide some examples.

ENCOURAGING COPS TO LIVE IN THE CITIES THEY SERVE

Chapter 1 began with a story about the 2015 report of the *President's Task Force on 21st Century Policing.*[1] That story focused on the important law enforcement role of police officers as *guardians* of public safety, and contrasted it with the more traditional, and often-times problematic, concept of police as *warriors* against evil-doers. The President's report also recognized that the police can't "go it alone," and stressed the importance of community partnerships as the backbone of successful police work. The report offered police administrators what it termed "Practical Next Steps to Get Started." The recommended steps toward better community involvement are:

- Conduct community surveys, forums, and town hall meetings on a regular basis, not just in a crisis.
- Encourage regular officer participation in neighborhood or school meetings.
- Form community advisory groups (general or population specific).
- Participate in positive interactions with the community that do not involve an enforcement action or investigation.
- Involve community members in discussing policing tactics and designing problem-solving strategies.
- Adjust patrol schedules to allow time for interactions with the community.

Jim West/Alamy Stock Photo

- Measure and reward nonenforcement community contacts.

We begin this chapter with section of background information that puts recent developments in context. The rest of the chapter is organized into three key sections on community policing, citizen involvement in policing, and third-party policing. Whereas Chapter 7 covered the traditional aspects of policing, this chapter shifts attention to relatively innovative, creative, and otherwise nontraditional forms of police work.

▶ *Community Justice and Problem-Oriented Policing*

The idea of reaching out to the community in an effort to improve relationships with citizens and to put citizens in closer touch with criminal justice professionals is part of a larger community justice movement that has been under way for some time now. Prosecutors, for example, have begun to pursue many of the same proactive, preventive, and creative crime-control strategies as those in which the police are engaged. In "community prosecution," as attorneys call it, prosecutors do much more than just charge suspected criminals and bring them to court.

Closely connected to community involvement and community policing is the idea of problem-oriented policing, which emerged at roughly the same time as the strategies we cover in this chapter. It is worth discussing separately, however, because it is the glue that holds a number of recent developments together. The idea that policing (and criminal justice in general) should be geared toward the identification and solution of root problems in the community is a relatively recent one. Still, it explains why police want to strengthen ties with the communities they serve and why police departments want to provide citizens with a window into the law enforcement world.

Community Justice

Community justice is a relatively new and innovative set of ideas about how the goals of the criminal justice system can be achieved. Further,

LEARNING OUTCOMES 1 — Describe community justice and problem-oriented policing.

community justice assumes that custom-fit crime control is better than the traditional approach, which is increasingly criticized as unimaginative. In addition, community justice emphasizes that criminal justice agencies (police, courts, and corrections) cannot accomplish crime control alone; community participation is essential.

Outside of the policing context, community justice has manifested itself in our nation's courts, particularly through the creation of so-called community courts and other problem-solving courts, including drug courts, domestic violence courts, teen courts, and reentry courts. Corrections agencies are also doing community justice as we have just defined it. Approaches like restorative justice fit the community justice model, as do partnerships between probation, parole, and private companies, such as treatment facilities.

Problem-Oriented Policing

Problem-oriented policing is, as the term suggests, policing that is oriented toward problem solving. Problem-oriented policing involves identifying areas, times of days, specific crimes, individuals, and the like that are particularly troublesome and then crafting a creative solution to these problems.[2]

Problem-oriented policing is the brainchild of law professor (emeritus) Herman Goldstein and shares much in common with some of the policing strategies discussed in the previous chapter.[3] For example, problem-oriented policing resembles directed patrol because it emphasizes direction and purpose, not just random and reactive patrol. Problem-oriented policing also resembles community policing because it usually relies on input from citizens to help identify problems. Indeed, some of the time the terms *community policing* and *problem-oriented policing* are used interchangeably. Much of the time, though, problem solving is viewed as a separate strategy unto itself.

There are at least two ways to distinguish between community policing and problem-oriented policing. First, problem-oriented policing is, as Arizona State University criminology professor Mike Reisig has observed, "an analytic framework used by police to identify and solve problems that result in repeated calls for service."[4] This often occurs independent of contact with citizens. In contrast, for policing to be truly community oriented, it must include some degree of citizen involvement. Another, perhaps more controversial way to distinguish between both approaches is to say that community policing focuses on citizen involvement and satisfaction as an end in itself, and problem-oriented policing is concerned with achieving a swift reduction in crime.

Despite problem-oriented policing's differences from community policing and community justice, it is still useful to think of it as a part of both movements because problem solving is a central feature of community policing and community justice. All three approaches necessitate an understanding of the geographic area, an in-depth understanding of the problems, and some degree of familiarity with the people in the areas where the problems occur. It is possible, of course, for problem-oriented policing to have no community involvement (direct or indirect), but true problem-oriented policing almost requires some outreach and relationship building with the community. See Figure 8–1 for a summary of the relationships between community justice, community policing, and problem-oriented policing.

Community Justice
Favors original, nontraditional approaches to crime control that draw heavily on input and cooperation from members of the community

Community Policing
Simply a part of this larger community justice movement

Problem-Oriented Policing
Geared toward identifying and solving particular and specific problems—from serious ones, such as gang shootings in one part of town, to minor ones, such as panhandlers bothering visitors at a local park

FIGURE 8–1 Relationships between Community Justice, Community Policing, and Problem-Oriented Policing.
Source: John L. Worrall, *Crime Control in America: What Works?*, 3rd ed., © 2015. Reprinted and electronically reproduced by permission of Pearson Education, Inc., New York, NY.

▶ Community Policing

Community policing emerged in the wake of the reform era discussed in Chapter 1. The reform era hasn't disappeared; there is much that occurs in the world of policing that is consistent with the ideas set forth by August Vollmer, O. W. Wilson, and others. Some not-so-desirable aspects of police professionalism, however, have been replaced with something new.

What were some of the not-so-desirable aspects of reform era policing? First, as we have seen, police research has revealed that preventive patrol wasn't particularly effective. Also, as we have already seen, the 1960s witnessed a great deal of strain in relationships between the police and the public. At the same time, the police came to realize that they couldn't reduce crime by their own efforts alone. Community era reformers sought authorization from community members and extensive citizen support; a broad mandate that stressed the provision of services; a decentralized, responsive organizational structure; and improved relationships with citizens. These strong ties would be achieved through foot patrol, problem solving, quality-of-life preservation, and a host of other tactics—all of which were designed to ensure citizen satisfaction.

LEARNING OUTCOMES 2 — Discuss the emergence of community policing and the extent of its application in American policing.

The sentiments of the community era were perhaps most clearly expressed in an important article authored by John Angell, a community policing innovator, during the early 1970s.[5] He argued that traditional police departments—and particularly their paramilitary organization and structure—are culture bound, that police bureaucracy is inconsistent with the humanistic democratic values of the United States, that it demands that employees demonstrate "immature" personality traits, and that it cannot cope with environmental pressures. The community model, he said, would (1) improve community relations, which suffered under the bureaucratic paramilitary model of law enforcement; (2) improve officers' morale by allowing them a measure of flexibility in the performance of their duties; and (3) improve interagency coordination.

There is more to the emergence of community policing than we have presented thus far. Some have argued, for instance, that it has emerged for less-than-noble purposes. It is also important to define community policing and, from a research standpoint, to gauge its true extent. We conclude by exploring the various forms of community policing and looking at the compatibility of community policing and the "war on terror."

The Birth of Community Policing

The history of community policing is rich and nuanced. There has been a tendency to assume that community policing has emerged for simple reasons, such as poor police–citizen relations, but there is a great deal more to the origins of the new policing paradigm. Together, the explanations fall into two categories: (1) those concerned directly with crime control and (2) those involving other intentions.

Crime Control

A few writers have called attention to the many noble reasons for the present community policing era. In a discussion concerning the "drive for change," one researcher identifies three reasons for the changes that have occurred and those that are taking place now.[6] The first reason, not surprisingly, is citizen disenchantment with police services: "Minority citizens in inner cities continue to be frustrated by police who whisk in and out of their neighborhoods with little sensitivity to community norms and values."[7]

The second reason concerns social science research undertaken in the 1970s. Specifically, "research about preventive patrol, rapid response to calls for service, and investigative work—the three mainstays of police tactics—was uniformly discouraging."[8] The third reason for reform suggests that "patrol officers have been frustrated with their traditional role"[9] and that they began to demand improved methods of interacting with citizens. It is sometimes felt that such an approach improves police officer morale. Other authors have suggested that community policing can be traced to two interrelated problems: the isolation of police officers in patrol cars from citizens and the public's fear of victimization and perceptions of a rising crime rate.[10] More specifically, the authors claim that community policing "rose like a phoenix from the ashes of burned cities."[11]

Other Intentions

Is there more to the community policing movement than meets the eye? Some scholars believe there is. For example, some have argued that police organizations may have adopted community policing for selfish reasons, such as to make rank-and-file officers more content with their jobs.[12] A professional ethic or a desire to emulate progressive police agencies could also be responsible for the current and widespread diffusion of community policing.

Perhaps more cynically, community policing may be a means of changing the goals of police work (e.g., from crime control to service), of shaping public opinion instead of responding to it,[13] or of deflecting attention away from law enforcement officials.[14] Fiscal constraints may have served as a powerful motivator. Political culture and community characteristics could also explain the origins of community policing.[15]

How might community policing shape public opinion? By presenting officers in a favorable light, by making them look good in the eyes of citizens, historically strained relationships can improve. What about deflecting attention? Part of community policing puts crime control at least *partly* in the hands of citizens (as in neighborhood watch). Some have said, therefore, that community policing passes the buck. And what about fiscal constraints? Some have argued that community policing is a cheap alternative to more expensive innovations because, at its core, it is a philosophy, and a philosophical change is free. These and many other reasons to initiate community policing are summarized in Figure 8–2. Whatever the reasons for its present popularity, community policing owes its origins to multiple demands and historical contingencies.

Definitions of Community Policing

We are guilty of having talked about community policing without really defining it, but that is for good reason: It is difficult to define. Community policing is a relatively new approach to law enforcement that is premised on the assumption that the police and citizens must work together to control crime.[16] Unfortunately, this short definition fails to adequately capture all of the

1. Citizen disenfranchisement with police services
2. Research showing the ineffectiveness of random patrol and quick response times
3. Patrol officers' frustration with the traditional reactive police role
4. Isolation of officers from citizens, largely owing to increased use of patrol vehicles
5. Narrow crime-fighting police image
6. Overreliance on bureaucratic and paramilitary structure
7. Overreliance on high-tech gadgetry that diminishes personal interactions
8. Insulation of police administration from community input and accountability
9. Concern about human rights
10. Failure of police to reach out to the community
11. Desire to appear "with it" and professional
12. Desire to emulate other agencies
13. Need to change the goal of police work from crime control to service
14. Need to reduce police officers' workloads
15. Desire to deflect attention from the police department to the community
16. Need to save money
17. Needs or wants of the community
18. Political culture of the surrounding area
19. Desire to improve the police image
20. Desire to increase control over the community by adopting multiple strategies

FIGURE 8–2 Twenty Reasons to Initiate Community Policing Services.

Definition	Community policing is difficult to define; however, it is a reorientation of policing philosophy and strategy away from the view that police alone can reduce crime, disorder, and fear. The strategy is based on the view that police don't help their communities very much by placing primary reliance on random preventive patrolling, rapid response to calls for service irrespective of their urgency, postincident investigations to identify offenders, and other primarily reactive criminal justice system tactics.
Five Perspectives	1. *Deployment perspective*—emphasizes the fact that police officers are deployed in a way that moves them closer to citizens 2. *Community revitalization*—emphasizes the importance of the police and citizens working closely together to improve neighborhoods and make them safer places 3. *Problem-solving perspective*—an approach in which citizens and police work together to identify and respond to neighborhood problems 4. *The customer*—emphasizes the importance of the police listening to citizens and serving their needs 5. *Legitimacy*—emphasizes bolstering the credibility of the police through police-citizen partnerships
Four Dimensions	1. The *philosophical dimension* includes the ideas and beliefs surrounding a new paradigm of policing. Three ideas underlying community policing are citizen input, an enhanced and broadened police function, and personal service. 2. The *strategic dimension* consists of "the key operational concepts that translate philosophy into action." Community policing strategies include reoriented operations (e.g., from cruiser patrol to foot patrol), geographic permanency (assigning patrol officers to the same areas for extended periods of time), and an emphasis on crime prevention (e.g., police officers acting as mentors and role models). 3. The *tactical dimension* is best understood as the inevitable outcome of the successful implementation of the first two dimensions. "The tactical dimension of community policing ultimately translates ideas, philosophies, and strategies into concrete programs, practices, and behaviors." This dimension stresses constructive interactions between the police and citizens, improved partnerships between law enforcement officials and the public, and problem solving. 4. Finally, the organizational dimension, though not necessarily a fundamental part of community policing, is essential to its development. The structure of police agencies and their management and information services need to be adjusted to accommodate community policing through such changes as decentralization, strategic planning, and program evaluation.
Extent	The extent of community policing is widespread in that it is supported in the Violent Crime Control Act of 1994, which led to the creation of the COPS Office in the U.S. Department of Justice, and to date, billions of dollars in grants to local law enforcement agencies have been allocated to enhance their community policing capabilities.

FIGURE 8–3 **Community Policing.**
Sources: W. A. Geller and G. Swanger, *Managing Innovation in Policing: The Untapped Potential of the Middle Manager* (Washington, DC: Police Executive Research Forum, 1995); G. W. Cordner, "Community policing: Elements and effects," in *Critical Issues in Policing: Contemporary readings*, 3rd ed., R. G. Dunham and G. P. Alpert (Prospect Heights, IL: Waveland, 1997), p. 452.

various aspects of community policing. A more comprehensive definition is illustrated in Figure 8–3.

Community Policing Perspectives and Dimensions

According to the Police Executive Research Forum, community policing consists of five different "perspectives,"[17] which are noted in Figure 8–3. Professor Gary Cordner has identified the philosophical, strategic, tactical, and organizational dimensions of community policing and has described some of the common elements within each,[18] which have also been noted in Figure 8–3.

The Extent of Community Policing

The rhetoric of community policing has become more or less institutionalized in American policing. But is there more to community policing than the term itself? Is community policing really being done, or do police departments just *say* they're doing it? Two research focuses help us answer these questions:

(1) research on structural changes to police departments and (2) research on whether police officers themselves are supportive of community policing.

Structural Change

Researchers have questioned whether police departments have actually changed their structure in ways that are consistent with the spirit of community policing. A recent study on trends in police agencies' implementation of community policing from 1995 to 2000 is particularly revealing.[19] The authors of that study conclude, "Among organizational changes to support community policing activities, the most rapidly growing were those intended to signal change: revised mission statements and new performance review criteria for community police officers."[20] In other words, the study found that police departments were focusing on making mostly symbolic changes to show their acceptance of community policing.[21]

The author of another recent study reached the same conclusion: "The police still cling to an institutional definition that stresses crime control and not prevention."[22] He also concludes that "by all available evidence, police organizations (their structures, division of labor, and the like) have not been radically or even significantly altered in the era of community and problem-oriented policing."[23] In short, many police agencies have adopted the cosmetic tenets of community policing but without altering their basic organizational structure in a meaningful way that actually changes the substance of their performance.[24] Additional research appears to confirm the discouraging news that structural change linked to community policing is frustratingly slow and is failing to result in functional change.[25]

Attitudinal Change

If American police agencies are slow to change in response to community policing, what about police officers themselves? Here is one author's answer to this important question:

> Police have a remarkable ability to wait out efforts to reform them. Important aspects of police culture mitigate against change. Police resist the intrusion of civilians (who "can't really understand") into their business. They fear that community troublemakers will take over the program and that people will seek to use police for their private purposes or for personal revenge. When police dislike changes proposed from within, they snort that the top brass are "out of touch with the street."[26]

In short, police officers are resistant to change and, as the preceding passage suggests, will actively take steps to thwart change. In fairness to law enforcement officials, other types of agencies—especially public agencies—also respond slowly to change. Nevertheless, it seems that community policing is being resisted by police officers themselves.

Two researchers recently described the efforts to do community policing in two midsize U.S. cities.[27] Those cities' police departments attempted four types of community policing: participatory management, community policing training, the decentralization of certain police operations, and the creation of special community policing units. The authors then tracked the opinions of the officers in both cities over a six-year period. They found that (1) a specialized community policing unit, not full-scale implementation of community policing, is desirable because not all officers will buy in and that (2) despite the presence of different community policing approaches, much law enforcement business proceeded as it always had (e.g., routine patrol remained unchanged).

In another related study, researchers sought to determine whether community policing affects police officers' decisions to use coercion during encounters with suspected criminals.[28] Studying two cities, they focused in particular on whether community policing assignments, community policing

training, and community partnerships affected officers' patterns of using coercion. Their analysis showed that none of these variables had much effect on officers' decisions to use coercion, again lending support to previous studies that showed that police are resistant to change. These findings have been echoed in more recent studies.[29]

Critical Views of Community Policing

Some authors note that "community policing has become the dominant theme of contemporary police reform in America,"[30] yet problems have plagued the movement since its inception (see Figure 8–4). As noted in Figure 8–4, recent findings continue to show that the attitudes of African-Americans toward the police remain poor. The wider reach of these studies, however, led evaluators to discover that this dissatisfaction may be rooted in overall quality of life and type of neighborhood.[31] Because most African-Americans continue to experience a lower quality of life than most other U.S. citizens and because they often live in neighborhoods characterized by economic problems, drug trafficking, and street crime, recent studies conclude that it is these conditions of life rather than race that are most predictive of citizen dissatisfaction with the police.

Those who study community policing have often been stymied by ambiguity surrounding the concept of community.[32] Sociologists, who sometimes define a community as "any area in which members of a common culture share common interests,"[33] tend to deny that a community needs to be limited geographically. Police departments, on the other hand, tend to define communities "within jurisdictional, district or precinct lines, or within the confines of public or private housing developments."[34] Robert Trojanowicz, a well-regarded community policing scholar, once cautioned police planners that "the impact of mass transit, mass communications and mass media have widened the rift between a sense of community based on geography and one [based] on interest."[35]

1.
The range, complexity, and evolving nature of community policing programs make their effectiveness difficult to measure.

2.
Citizen satisfaction with police performance can be difficult to conceptualize and quantify. Most early studies examined how citizens' attitudes developed through face-to-face interaction with individual police officers. They generally found a far higher level of dissatisfaction with the police among African-Americans than among most other groups.

3.
Sense of community is based more on interests than geography.

4.
Continuing evidence shows that not all police officers or managers are willing to accept nontraditional images of police work. Similarly, many officers are loathe to take on new responsibilities as service providers whose role is defined more by community needs and less by strict interpretation of the law.

FIGURE 8–4 Critical Views of Community Policing.

Researchers who follow the police definition of *community* recognize that there may be little consensus within and between members of a local community about the community's problems and about appropriate solutions. Robert Bohm and colleagues at the University of Central Florida have found, for example, that while there may be some "consensus about social problems and their solutions . . . the consensus may not be community-wide." It may, in fact, exist only among "a relatively small group of 'active' stakeholders who differ significantly about the seriousness of most of the problems and the utility of some solutions."[36]

Finally, there is continuing evidence that not all police officers or managers are willing to accept nontraditional images of police work. One reason is that the goals of community policing often conflict with standard police performance criteria (such as arrests), leading to a perception among officers that community policing is inefficient at best and a waste of time at worst.[37] Some authors have warned that police subculture (see Chapter 5) is so committed to a traditional view of police work, which is focused almost exclusively on crime fighting, that efforts to promote community policing can demoralize an entire department, rendering it ineffective at its basic tasks.[38] As the Christopher Commission found following the Rodney King riots, "Too many . . . patrol officers view citizens with resentment and hostility; too many treat the public with rudeness and disrespect."[39] Some analysts warn that only when the formal values espoused by today's innovative police administrators begin to match those of rank-and-file officers can any police agency begin to perform well in terms of community policing.[40]

Think About It . . .

Foot Patrol The notion of putting officers in close contact with citizens is desirable not just because of today's preference for community policing but also because foot patrol is useful in some areas where car patrol is impossible. It is quite likely that foot patrol works in some areas better than others. For example, pedestrian malls and downtown areas lend themselves more readily to foot patrol than suburban and rural areas do. Clearly, it would be impractical to put officers on foot patrol in rural areas where they have to cover thousands of square miles. *Where might foot patrol be most effective? Explain.*

Tom Carter/Alamy Stock Photo

Some public officials, too, are unwilling to accept community policing. For example, former New York City Mayor Rudolph W. Giuliani criticized the police department's Community Police Officer Program, saying that it "has resulted in officers doing too much social work and making too few arrests."[41] Similarly, many citizens are not ready to accept a greater involvement of the police in their personal lives. Although the turbulent, protest-prone years of the 1960s and early 1970s are long gone, some groups remain suspicious of the police. No matter how inclusive community policing programs become, it is doubtful that the gap between the police and the public will ever be entirely bridged. The police role of restraining behavior that violates the law will always produce friction between police departments and some segments of the community.

Examples of Community Policing

Community policing is practiced in more forms than we can possibly list here. The majority of community policing programs, though, can be placed into one of three categories. First, some are intended to encourage citizens to take an interest in crime control. Others seek to communicate with and inform citizens. Finally, some programs expand police presence in the community, such as putting police in schools or on specialized patrols. These three categories are discussed in Figure 8–5. The following sections examine some of the more popular community policing methods and the research on their effectiveness.

Citizen Contact Patrol

One community policing approach that appears promising consists of door-to-door contacts by police officers. This is known as citizen contact patrol.[42] This occurs when police officers knock on people's doors, introduce themselves, give out information, and otherwise try to make policing more personal in nature. Police have also used this so-called citizen contact patrol to obtain information about who is carrying guns on the street,[43] to provide citizens with burglary reduction tips,[44] and to offer advice to citizens about how to deal with domestic violence problems.[45]

Researchers have found that such door-to-door visits result in decreased victimization. For example, at least two studies show that door-to-door visits by police led to reductions in victimization.[46] Two other studies found reductions in victimization following door-to-door contacts, but the contacts were supplemented with either storefronts (discussed later in this section)[47] or buy–bust operations.[48] But three additional studies show that door-to-door contacts led to no reductions in victimization.[49] Needless to say, these findings are conflicting. They also make it difficult to draw conclusions about the effect of door-to-door contacts by police on crime.

To sift through some of these conflicting studies, it is useful to consider some of their specific findings. For example, one of the studies showed that door-to-door contacts reduced victimization but largely for vehicular burglaries and minor property crimes.[50] Another researcher concluded that door-to-door contacts worked best in middle-class, predominantly white neighborhoods.[51]

Mobilizing Citizens

Formal meetings between police and community members: identify and deal with specific crime problems and locations. These meetings must be distinguished from neighborhood watch programs.

Informing Citizens

Crime-control newsletters: Often contain information on recent developments at the police department, crime statistics for the area, tips for avoiding victimization, and so on.

Websites: Allow citizens to complete hot-spot reports of criminal activity online and to submit noncriminal complaints electronically. At the same time, citizens can learn about new approaches taken by the department, see pictures of dangerous fugitives, view active warrants, and otherwise develop familiarity with their local police department.

Television: Some police departments—mostly in the largest jurisdictions—actually have their own community-access channel that broadcasts programs like "John TV," which shows the faces and names of men suspected of soliciting prostitutes. Other programming includes television shows and TV advertisements designed to improve public relations and public attitudes toward the local police force.

Engaging with Citizens

Improved police presence: For example, police officers are coming to occupy a significant position in our nation's schools. Police who work in schools are often called school resource officers. They are represented by the National Association of School Resource Officers. Police are also collaborating more with schools, and some schools are opting to hire private security personnel to patrol campuses in an effort to preserve a safe learning environment and provide security in response to incidents like the infamous Columbine High School shooting.

FIGURE 8-5   Examples of Community Policing.

On the one hand, a citizen contact approach to the crime problem has a slim chance of succeeding where it is needed the most. On the other hand, it does not appear that citizens in more disadvantaged areas received the treatment to begin with, so we cannot conclude with certainty that citizen contact patrol is a crime control failure. Nor can we conclude that it is a success.

Organizing Neighborhood Watch Programs

Most people are familiar with neighborhood watch programs. All one needs to do is drive through a suburban neighborhood, and one will encounter signs highlighting "Block Watch" and similar programs. These and other neighborhood watch programs are sometimes started by neighborhood residents; other times, they are started at the urging of local police departments. Most of the research in this area is concerned with the ability of the police to organize neighborhood watch programs for the purpose of reducing criminal activity.

Think About It . . .

Neighborhood Watch Neighborhood watch programs are a very popular example of community policing. Throughout suburban neighborhoods across the country, one encounters signs announcing "Block Watch" and similar programs, which are sometimes started by neighborhood residents and sometimes at the urging of local police departments. Many communities still rely on neighborhood watch despite evidence that it is not particularly effective. *Why? Can you think of other law enforcement initiatives that continue to be pursued despite evidence that they don't work? If so, which ones?*

Sascha Burkard/Shutterstock

Unfortunately, the literature devoted to neighborhood watch is almost uniformly unsupportive of this approach to America's crime problem. One study out of Minneapolis sought to determine whether neighborhood watch (with and without police participation) reduced crime. Random assignment was used, adding a level of sophistication to the study, but researchers found no effect on crime.[52] One earlier study showed a link between neighborhood watch and a reduction in burglary for a period of 18 months,[53] but this study appears isolated. For example, researchers in Cincinnati, Ohio, found that neighborhood watches and other community-based organizations had no effect on crime.[54]

Researchers have attributed these findings to reluctance among citizens to organize neighborhood watch programs in poor, high-crime areas.[55] This reluctance stems from either fear of the police or distrust between neighbors.[56] To make matters worse, researchers have found that in the areas where neighborhood watch programs flourish (usually middle-class neighborhoods), the programs *increase* rather than decrease fear of crime. This effect was also witnessed in a study of "apartment watch," the equivalent of neighborhood watch for apartments.[57] The scientific literature thus appears to show that police officers who work with citizens to organize neighborhood watch programs in high-crime urban areas could better spend their time on other activities.

Storefronts and Substations

Most of us have happened on a police information booth in a shopping mall or police officers occupying a building in a strip mall. These storefronts and substations are consistent with the spirit of community policing; they bring police officers into closer contact with citizens. The logic is that members of the public might be more likely to talk with police officers in a place that they frequent instead of having to physically go to the police station, which might be inconveniently located.

Somewhat discouragingly, most research suggests that the presence of police offices in storefronts and strip malls does not affect crime.[58] Indeed, there is not much convincing evidence that such police substations are necessary to begin with; they tend to pop up in areas where they are needed the least. Placing police officers in strip malls and storefronts might improve public perceptions of the police,[59] but there is no evidence that much else is accomplished. Part of the reason for this might be that substations are largely informational and passive. That is, they are more often concerned with providing information about crime control to the public; comparatively little attention is given to proactive crime control. Some substations are staffed by civilian personnel or volunteers, making it doubtful that they could do much to affect crime rates.

Specialized Patrols

Another community policing strategy consists of specialized patrols. The most common is foot patrol. This is where officers get out of their cars and patrol their beats on foot in an effort to develop closer relationships with citizens.

Naturally, foot patrol works better in some areas than in others. Pedestrian malls and downtown areas obviously lend themselves more readily to foot patrol than suburban and rural areas do. Other specialized patrols include bicycle patrol and horse patrol.

The most researched type of specialized patrol is foot patrol, so we will focus on it here. Much research suggests that citizens are more likely to notice police when they patrol on foot,[60] and some research suggests that citizens are more satisfied with police following the implementation of foot patrol.[61] But does this approach reduce crime? One study suggests that foot patrol was associated with a reduction in such public order offenses as vagrancy, disorderly conduct, and vandalism.[62] Another suggested that foot patrol in Flint, Michigan, reduced crime, but the authors of the study did not control for other factors that have been linked to reported crime.[63] In one of the most recent and sophisticated studies on the subject, researchers found that targeted foot patrols in crime hot spots led to significant reductions in violent crime that lasted well after the intervention ended.[64]

Community Policing and Antiterrorism

Community policing stresses improved relationships between police and citizens. The ongoing "war on terror," however, seems to place a strain on those relationships. The typical response to terrorism, particularly high terrorist alert levels, is to put more police on the streets, make more liberal use of searches, and otherwise inconvenience people in the name of national security. These tactics are somewhat at odds with building relationships and improving police–community bonds and contacts. Some have argued, though, that community policing is *not* at odds with antiterrorism efforts. According to Chuck Wexler, director of the Police Executive Research Forum,

> The events of September 11, 2001, have changed the role of local police in America—perhaps forever. Local law enforcement faces the challenges of assuming more responsibility in countering domestic terrorism threats while continuing to address crime and disorder. Success will depend on their ability to build on strong community policing networks for information exchange and to maintain a collaborative problem-solving approach to crime amid high anxiety and crisis. Now more than ever, departments need to adhere to community problem-solving principles to decrease crime and disorder in their communities, increase their departments' efficiency, and strengthen their relationships with citizens.[65]

Not everyone is so convinced, however. In fact, some have argued that police departments that haven't historically favored community policing are using the "war on terror" as a reason to scrap it.[66] But they also argue that even in the face of resistance, community policing is needed to succeed against terrorism:

> Few people outside the field know about the pitched battle for the heart and soul of policing that has raged

over the past decade [the traditional bureaucratic model versus community policing]. It is said that people get the police they deserve. If we are to maintain recent reductions in violent crime and uncover the terrorists living among us, while preserving the civil rights that make our society special, we must insist on community policing now more than ever.[67]

▶ Citizen Involvement and Civilianization

Thus far, we have examined community policing strategies that are operated largely by the police. The strategies covered are best considered one-way because the police develop or coordinate them. Moreover, they are one-way in the sense that the police are the ones who go out into the community to work with citizens in numerous ways. An alternative to these approaches is to bring citizens to the police. While programs of this type are still run and coordinated by the police, they are different in that they allow citizens to view and participate in the world of law enforcement.

Citizen Patrol and Citizen Police Academies

There are hundreds, if not thousands, of **citizen patrols** around the United States.[68] An example of a volunteer citizen patrol that has received some attention is the Neighborhood Patrol Officers Program in Fort Worth, Texas.[69] Started in 1991, the program provided eight hours of training to volunteers on such topics as rules of conduct, liability issues, and legal considerations. Once training was completed, volunteers were issued an identification badge, a T-shirt, a hat, and a jacket. They also received police radios. Once trained and equipped, the volunteers used their own vehicles to patrol neighborhoods, looking for evidence of criminal activity.

LEARNING OUTCOMES 3 — Distinguish between citizen involvement in policing and civilianization.

Many police departments also operate so-called **citizen police academies.**[70] Although the programs differ to some extent, all of them possess a common element: Citizens are given an opportunity to learn about the policing profession and even to experience some of the same sensations that uniformed officers experience.[71] Sometimes citizens even learn to use firearms and otherwise defend themselves from victimization.

It is tempting to ask whether citizen police academies work, but in order to answer this question, we must first understand their purpose. While some critics find it difficult to fathom any crime-reduction benefits due to citizen police academies, that is not their direct goal. Rather, the academies are intended to affect citizens' perceptions of the police rather than to reduce crime, and that is what the research suggests they accomplish. The authors of one recent study found that citizen police academy participants viewed the police more favorably after completing the program.[72] Similar findings were reported in at least two other studies.[73]

Other researchers have been critical of citizen police academies. One researcher found that academy participants tend to be mostly community "elites" and that minorities are drastically underrepresented.[74] The argument has also been raised that citizen police academies—like citizen patrol programs—perpetuate a traditional law enforcement strategy and may in fact be antithetical to the spirit of community policing.[75] This argument becomes quite convincing when police departments teach civilians many law enforcement "tricks of the trade," such as self-defense techniques.

What can be gleaned from the literature on citizen police academies? They appear to improve public perceptions of and attitudes toward the police, but people who participate in the academies may already be more prone to viewing the police favorably prior to enrolling in the curriculum. As far as the effect of citizen police academies on crime, there is no evidence that there is any. In fact, there is a total lack of research on the subject. Regardless of this, the practice of giving citizens a window into the law enforcement world is intended to do little more than improve the image of the police, and while there is nothing particularly wrong with that, an improved police image has no effect on crime.

Civilianization

Civilianization has been defined as a "law enforcement agency's hiring of nonsworn personnel to replace or augment its corps of sworn officers, typically with the aims of reducing costs and improving service"[76] (see Figure 8–6). This definition makes it clear that civilianization is something distinct from private security, private policing, and privatization in general.

Citizen patrol and citizen police academies have largely different motivations than civilianization. Both get citizens involved in policing-related functions by having them either actively patrol neighborhoods or experience policing life through a short mock academy. Civilianization, in contrast, is done largely because it saves money. It is more expensive to have a sworn officer handle department communications when a civilian could just as easily be hired. A civilian doesn't need to go through the police academy or use the expensive specialized equipment that a sworn officer needs.

At the same time, civilianization may not be *all* about cost savings. Expanded citizen hiring is a sign of a progressive, change-oriented agency. As American University professor Brian Forst has observed, "While some tradition-bound police executives have been reluctant to transfer a variety of support functions to civilians, it has become increasingly clear that civilians tend to perform certain specialized roles more effectively than sworn officers."[77] Dispatch functions were largely performed by sworn officers during the 1960s; now dispatch is almost exclusively performed by nonsworn personnel. Hiring more civilians also creates an air of openness consistent with the community policing ideals of involving more and more citizens in crime-control functions.

Citizen Patrol

Typically, citizen patrols are composed of volunteers who engage in preventive patrol. These volunteers are often provided with some type of government vehicle and patrol the streets during daylight hours. Sometimes, however, citizens volunteer to drive their own vehicles and operate independently of the police.

Civilianization

Civilians are hired as nonsworn personnel (communications specialists, criminalists, computer specialists, lawyers, and a host of other support positions) to replace or augment its corps of sworn officers, with the aim of reducing costs and improving service.

Citizen Police Academy

Citizens are given an opportunity to learn about the policing profession, which often consists of a watered-down version of a police academy where citizens are taught the nature, operations, and complexity of the policing profession.

FIGURE 8-6 Citizen Involvement in Policing.

▶ *Third-Party Policing*

We introduced private policing and security in Chapter 3. One could conceive of these approaches as policing by third parties—that is, by parties other than citizens or the police. When we talk about **third-party policing**, however, we are referring to something entirely different. Basically, it amounts to formal methods of policing that invoke the use of the **civil law** rather than the criminal law (see Figure 8–7).

Michael Buerger and Lorraine Mazerolle, the scholars who first conceived the term *third-party policing*, distinguish it from community policing and problem-oriented policing because of its intended targets: "In community- and problem-oriented policing, the police assume an active quasi-enforcement and managerial role in addition to their more established, hortatory [encouraging] role as dispensers of expert advice."[78] They go on to argue that community policing and problem-oriented policing are simply augmented versions of traditional policing that rely heavily on citizens and guardians (those responsible for places, like landlords) for influence and control over criminals and would-be criminals. Third-party policing is different from this because "it focuses on the places that the guardians control by promoting certain collective responses as a way of controlling individual behavior."[79] In other words, third-party policing is more place oriented than person oriented.

Third-party policing should not be confused with environmental criminology, which is concerned with designing "places" to make them less vulnerable to crime (e.g., access control with a tall security gate). Third-party policing is place oriented, but it is not concerned with design. Instead, it is about providing guardians with the information and tools they need to take a certain element of law enforcement into their own hands.

LEARNING OUTCOMES 4

Define *third-party policing* and provide some examples.

There is a possible "dark side" to third-party policing, however. It is not just about encouraging guardians to target problems at the places they are responsible for. It is also about coercing them to do so. Once again according to Buerger and Mazerolle, "Third-party policing constitutes a return to a compliance model of policing, although the police do not resume inspectorial functions. . . . Rather, these functions are performed by nominal partners of the police, or remain an implied threat behind police negotiations with guardians."[80]

The characteristics of third-party policing

Defined as police efforts to persuade or coerce nonoffending persons to take actions that are outside the scope of their routine activities, and that are designed to indirectly minimize disorder caused by other persons or to reduce the possibility that crime may occur.

Pertains to formal methods of policing that invoke the use of the **civil law** rather than the criminal law.

Example of how civil law is used

Civil law approach to policing: Not just the police but other officials relying on civil process, such as nuisance abatement and code enforcement, to reduce crime and disorder.

Third-Party Policing

Examples of third-party policing programs

The Beat Health Program (Oakland, California) Police officers make the first contacts with the targeted nonoffending parties. Initial contacts are as collegial as possible. The teams attempt to build rapport with the property owners. Any owners who fail to cooperate, however, quickly encounter the more coercive arm of third-party policing.

Minneapolis Repeat Call Address Policing (RECAP) Program

- Police officers present call histories to owners and managers of problem properties.
- They explain that improvements would be mutually beneficial
- Benefits to businesses: Attract more customers and thereby increase profits if police are not seen arresting people on the property.
- Benefits to owners of rental properties: Better tenants would be more likely to pay their rent and increase the profitability of the property.

Police departments are increasingly wising up to the idea that, in some instances, civil law can work just as well for crime control as does the criminal law. Beyond the policing realm, other criminal justice officials, particularly prosecutors, are coming to the same realization. Prosecutors sometimes work closely with the police because they bring to the table the legal knowledge and ability to pursue appropriate actions in court. Although third-party policing is catching on, it hasn't been subject to extensive evaluation. Much more research remains to be done in order to identify best practices.

FIGURE 8-7 Third Party Policing.

In our definition of *third-party policing*, the "nonoffending" persons are the guardians. They are basically persuaded by police to do something about identified problems "or else." Simply put, "third-party policing establishes a control over nonoffending persons and persuades (or coerces) them to engage in activities thought to control crime."[81]

At its core, some would say that third-party policing is about turning certain enforcement functions over to those who haven't traditionally done them. Others, though, would argue that this is simply good law enforcement and that it is intended to bring guardians out of the shadows to take control over their properties. The police might, for instance, coerce a slumlord to fix a problem at one of his or her apartment complexes or face possible civil consequences.

Beyond the Criminal Law

Police routinely use the criminal law, local ordinances, curfew statutes, and the like to target crime. Third-party policing goes beyond the criminal law, invoking primarily civil law provisions. These, according to Buerger and Mazerolle, are "controls imported from the regulatory wing of the civil law [that] include provisions that allow the police to target deviant places, typically crackhouses, blighted homes, and false-front stores (such as 'bodegas') that sell drugs or traffic in black-market food stamps."[82] In truth, the civil law has always been available to the police, but the recent proliferation of problem-oriented and community policing has caused police officials to use more creative methods of crime control.

Civil law provisions, like those governing building codes, have been used periodically in law enforcement and, indeed, throughout the public sector to target problems. A dilapidated building that is replete with code violations can be shut down or condemned, something officials have done for years. Recently, though, scores of cities have capitalized on existing civil ordinances and created more of their own. An example is San Diego's creative ordinances aimed at the problem of illegal street racing. One of them provides that

a motor vehicle shall be declared a nuisance and forfeited subject to this division if . . . [i]t is used in violation of California Vehicle Code sections 23109(a) or (c); and . . . it is being driven by the registered owner of the vehicle, the registered owner is a passenger, the registered owner's immediate family member is driving or riding in the car, or the driver or passenger lives at the same address as the registered owner.[83]

A Digital Partnership with the Community

A number of police departments around the country have partnered with the website CrimeReports.com to make available the latest crime data to their residents. CrimeReports.com is a free online service that allows anyone to stay up to date about criminal incidents in areas from which the website receives data. Police departments supply the data, and the website automatically publishes the information. People can then use any computer with an Internet connection or a mobile device to access and browse the crime information, which is presented in the form of an interactive map.

Marmaduke St. John/Alamy Stock Photo

One view of this type of community notification is that it embodies the spirit of community policing by bringing members of the community and the police into close contact. An opposing view is that the effort is largely symbolic—meaning that the department is giving the *appearance* of working closely with the community when in fact it is simply making use of a Web service that is readily available.

These competing views raise several interesting questions:

1. Is a Web-based approach to community policing sufficient? Is it meaningful and useful reform?
2. Is community policing an honest effort to improve police–community relations, or is it merely a symbolic gesture?
3. Where is the line between real and symbolic community policing drawn?
4. Is it realistic to expect the police and the community to work together in the name of crime prevention?
5. Is community policing effective, or is its actual intent something other than crime reduction?

CHAPTER 8   Community Policing and Community Involvement

LEARNING OUTCOMES 1

Describe community justice and problem-oriented policing.

The contemporary notion of community justice encompasses community policing and several other recent law enforcement innovations, such as citizen patrol. Problem-oriented policing is best viewed as part of community policing. Both policing styles rely on citizen involvement.

1. What is community justice?
2. What is problem-oriented policing?
3. How are community justice and problem-oriented policing related?

community justice A relatively new and innovative set of ideas about how the goals of the criminal justice system can be achieved. It favors original, nontraditional approaches to crime control that draw heavily on input and cooperation from the community.

problem-oriented policing A method of policing that is geared toward identifying and solving problems within a community that are particularly troublesome and then crafting creative solutions to them. Also called *problem-solving policing*.

LEARNING OUTCOMES 2

Discuss the emergence of community policing and the extent of its application in American policing.

Community policing is often promoted as an effective crime-control technique, but it exists for several other reasons as well. For example, it serves to address citizen dissatisfaction, and it saves money. *Community policing* can be defined in various ways, but the essence of it is a partnership in which the police and the community work together to reduce crime.

1. What is community policing?

2. How did the concept of community policing develop?
3. What are the positive aspects of community policing, and why is it being widely promoted today?
4. What are some potentially negative aspects of community policing for law enforcement agencies?

community policing A collaborative effort between the police and the community that identifies problems of crime and disorder and involves all elements of the community in the search for solutions to these problems.

LEARNING OUTCOMES 3

Distinguish between citizen involvement in policing and civilianization.

Citizen involvement in policing is common today and occurs largely through citizen patrol and citizen police academies. Civilianization refers to the hiring of nonsworn personnel to perform certain limited functions within police departments.

1. What is the difference between citizen involvement in policing and civilianization?
2. What kinds of duties are best suited to civilians working in police departments?

3. What purposes do citizen police academies serve? Why do departments that utilize citizens for volunteer purposes find such academies important?

citizen patrol A preventive patrol program staffed by citizen volunteers.

citizen police academy A training experience that offers citizens an opportunity to learn about the policing profession and even to experience some of the same situations that uniformed officers experience.

civilianization "A law enforcement agency's hiring of nonsworn personnel to replace or augment its corps of sworn officers" in an effort to reduce costs and improve service.

LEARNING OUTCOMES 4

Define *third-party policing* and provide some examples.

In third-party policing, the police apply pressure to nonoffending third parties (such as landlords) to improve their properties and thereby promote crime control and crime prevention.

1. What is third-party policing?
2. How can third-party policing help police departments? How might it harm them?
3. How can third-party policing help communities? How might it hurt?

4. Can you think of any potentially useful third-party policing strategies that this book doesn't discuss?

third-party policing A recently coined term that describes police efforts to persuade or coerce nonoffending persons to take actions that are outside the scope of their routine activities and that are designed to indirectly minimize disorder caused by other persons or to reduce the possibility that crime may occur.

civil law The branch of modern law that governs relationships between parties.

142   Chapter 8   Community Policing and Community Involvement

References

1 The President's Task Force on 21st Century Policing, *Final report* (Washington, DC: The White House, May 2015).

2 V. G. Strecher, *Planning community policing* (Prospect Heights, IL: Waveland, 1997).

3 H. Goldstein, *Problem oriented policing* (New York: McGraw-Hill, 1990); H. Goldstein, "Improving policing: A problem-oriented approach," *Crime and Delinquency*, vol. 25 (1979), pp. 236–58.

4 M. D. Reisig, "Community and problem-oriented policing," *Crime and Justice: A Review of Research*, vol. 39 (2010), pp. 2–53, quote on p. 2.

5 J. E. Angell, "Toward an alternative to the classic police organizational arrangements: A democratic model," *Criminology*, vol. 9 (1971), pp. 185–206.

6 G. L. Kelling, "Police and communities: The quiet revolution," in *Criminal justice in America: Theory, practice, and policy*, eds. B. W. Hancock and P. M. Sharp, pp. 134–44 (Upper Saddle River, NJ: Prentice Hall, 1996).

7 Ibid., p. 138.

8 Ibid.

9 Ibid.

10 R. Trojanowicz et al., *Community policing: A contemporary perspective*, 2nd ed. (Cincinnati: Anderson, 1988).

11 Ibid., p. 53.

12 D. Hayeslip and G. Cordner, "The effects of community-oriented patrol on police officer attitudes," *American Journal of Police-Special Issue on Foot Patrol and Community Policing*, vol. 4 (1987), pp. 95–119.

13 P. K. Manning, "Community policing as a drama of control," in *Community policing: Rhetoric or reality?*, eds. J. R. Greene and S. D. Mastrofski, pp. 27–45 (New York: Praeger, 1988).

14 D. Garland, "The limits of the sovereign state: Strategies of crime control in contemporary society," *British Journal of Criminology*, vol. 36 (1996), pp. 445–71.

15 J. Zhao, *Why police organizations change* (Washington, DC: Police Executive Research Forum, 1996).

16 See, e.g., W. G. Skogan and S. M. Hartnett, *Community policing: Chicago style* (New York: Oxford University Press, 1997).

17 Police Executive Research Forum, *Themes and variations in community policing* (Washington, DC: Police Executive Research Forum, 1996).

18 G. W. Cordner, "Community policing: Elements and effects," in *Critical issues in policing: Contemporary readings*, 3rd ed., eds. R. G. Dunham and G. P. Alpert (Prospect Heights, IL: Waveland, 1997), p. 452.

19 J. A. Roth, J. Roehl, and C. C. Johnson, "Trends in the adoption of community policing," in *Community policing: Can it work?*, ed. W. G. Skogan, pp. 3–29 (Belmont, CA: Wadsworth, 2003).

20 Ibid., p. 24.

21 See also J. Zhao, Q. Thurman, and N. Lovrich, "Community oriented policing across the U.S.: Facilitators and impediments to implementation," *American Journal of Police*, vol. 14 (1995), pp. 11–28; J. Zhao, N. Lovrich, and Q. Thurman, "The status of community policing in American cities," *Policing: An International Journal of Police Strategies and Management*, vol. 22 (1999), pp. 152–70.

22 J. R. Greene, "Community policing and organization change," in Skogan, *Community policing*, p. 49.

23 Ibid.

24 See, e.g., D. Guyot, "Bending granite: Attempts to change the rank structure of American police departments," *Journal of Police Science and Administration*, vol. 7 (1979), pp. 253–384.

25 E. R. Maguire, "Structural change in large municipal police organizations during the community-policing era," *Justice Quarterly*, vol. 14 (1997), pp. 547–76. See also J. A. Roth, ed., *National evaluation of the COPS program: Title 1 of the 1994 Crime Act* (Washington, DC: National Institute of Justice, 2000).

26 Skogan, *Community policing*, p. xxviii.

27 D. P. Rosenbaum and D. L. Wilkinson, "Can police adapt? Tracking the effects of organizational reform over six years," in Skogan, *Community policing*, pp. 79–108. See also D. P. Rosenbaum, S. Yeh, and D. L. Wilkinson, "Estimating the effects of community policing reform on police officers," *Crime and Delinquency*, vol. 40 (1994), pp. 331–53.

28 W. Terrill and S. D. Mastrofski, "Working the street: Does community policing matter?," in Skogan, *Community policing*, pp. 109–35. See also W. Terrill and S. D. Mastrofski, "Situational and officer based determinants of police coercion," *Justice Quarterly*, vol. 19 (2002), pp. 101–34.

29 R. L. Wood, M. Davis, and A. Rouse, "Diving into quicksand: Program implementation and police subcultures," in Skogan, *Community policing*, pp. 136–61.

30 J. Zhao, N. P. Lovrich, and Q. Thurman, "The status of community policing in American cities: Facilitators and impediments revisited," *Policing*, vol. 22, no. 1 (1999), p. 74.

31 Michael D. Reisig and Roger B. Parks, "Experience, quality of life, and neighborhood context: A hierarchical analysis of satisfaction with police," *Justice Quarterly*, vol. 17, no. 3 (2000), p. 607.

32 Mark E. Correia, "The conceptual ambiguity of community in community policing: Filtering the muddy waters," *Policing*, vol. 23, no. 2 (2000), pp. 218–33.

33 Adapted from D. R. Fessler, *Facilitating community change: A basic guide* (San Diego, CA: San Diego State University, 1976), p. 7.

34 D. W. Flynn, *Defining the "community" in community policing* (Washington, DC: Police Executive Research Forum, 1998).

35 R. C. Trojanowicz and M. H. Moore, *The meaning of community in community policing* (East Lansing: Michigan State University's National Neighborhood Foot Patrol Center, 1988).

36 R. M. Bohm, K. M. Reynolds, and S. T. Holms, "Perceptions of neighborhood problems and their solutions: Implications for community policing," *Policing*, vol. 23, no. 4 (2000), p. 439.

37 Ibid., p. 442.

38 M. K. Sparrow, "Implementing community policing," *Perspectives on Policing*, no. 9 (Washington, DC: National Institute of Justice, 1988).

39 "L.A. police chief: Treat people like customers," *USA Today*, March 29, 1993, p. 13A.

40 R. Wasserman and M. H. Moore, "Values in policing," *Perspectives in policing*, no. 8 (Washington, DC: National Institute of Justice, 1988), p. 7.

41 "New York City mayor sparks debate on community policing," *Criminal Justice Newsletter*, January 18, 1994, p. 1.

42 M. A. Wycoff, A. M. Pate, W. Skogan, and L. W. Sherman, *Citizen contact patrol in Houston: Executive summary* (Washington, DC: Police Foundation, 1985).

43 L. W. Sherman, J. W. Shaw, and D. P. Rogan, *The Kansas City Gun Experiment* (Washington, DC: National Institute of Justice, 1995).

44 G. Laycock, "Operation identification, or the power of publicity?," *Security Journal*, vol. 2 (1991), pp. 67–72.

45 R. C. Davis and B. G. Taylor, "A proactive response to family violence: The results of a randomized experiment," *Criminology*, vol. 35 (1997), pp. 307–33.

46 Wycoff et al., *Citizen contact patrol in Houston*; W. Skogan, *Disorder and decline: Crime and the spiral decay in American neighborhoods* (New York: Free Press, 1990).

47 A. M. Pate and W. Skogan, *Coordinated community policing: The Newark experience* (Washington, DC: Police Foundation, 1985).

48 C. D. Uchida, B. Forst, and S. O. Annan, *Modern policing and the control of illegal drugs: Testing new strategies in two American cities.* (Washington, DC: National Institute of Justice, 1992).

49 Sherman et al., *The Kansas City Gun Experiment*; Uchida et al., *Modern policing and the control of illegal drugs*; Davis and Taylor, "A proactive response to family violence."

50 Wycoff et al., *Citizen contact patrol in Houston*.

51 Skogan, *Disorder and decline*.

52 Anthony M. Pate, Marlys McPherson, and Glenn Silloway, *The Minneapolis Community Crime Prevention Experiment: Draft evaluation report* (Washington, DC: Police Foundation, 1987).

53 B. Lindsay and D. McGillis, "Citywide community crime prevention: An assessment of the Seattle Program," in *Community crime prevention: Does it work?*, ed. D. Rosenbaum, pp. 46–67 (Beverly Hills, CA: Sage, 1986).

54 B. W. Smith, K. J. Novak, and D. C. Hurley, "Neighborhood crime prevention: The influences of community-based organizations and neighborhood watch," *Journal of Crime and Justice*, vol. 20 (1997), pp. 69–86; see also D. P. Rosenbaum, "The theory and research behind neighborhood watch: Is it a sound fear and crime reductions strategy?," *Crime and Delinquency*, vol. 33 (1987), pp. 103–34.

55 Dennis Rosenbaum, Dan A. Lewis, and Jane A. Grant, "Neighborhood-based crime prevention: Assessing the efficacy of community organization in Chicago," in Rosenbaum, *Community crime prevention*.

56 See, e.g., T. Bennett, *Evaluating neighborhood watch* (Basingstoke: Gower, 1990).

57 C. Meredith and C. Paquette, "Crime prevention in high-rise rental apartments: Findings of a demonstration project," *Security Journal*, vol. 3 (1992), pp. 161–68.

58 M. A. Wycoff and W. G. Skogan, *Community policing in Madison: Quality from the inside out: An evaluation of implementation and impact* (Washington, DC: Police Foundation, 1993); Uchida et al., *Modern policing and the control of illegal drugs*; Pate and Skogan, *Coordinated community policing*.

59 See, e.g., W. G. Skogan and M. A. Wycoff, "Storefront police offices: The Houston Field Test," in Rosenbaum, *Community crime prevention*, pp. 179–99.

60 A. M. Pate, "Community-oriented policing in Baltimore," in *Police and policing: Contemporary issues*, ed. D. J. Kenney, pp. 112–35 (New York: Praeger, 1989); Police Foundation, *The Newark Foot Patrol Experiment* (Washington, DC: Police Foundation, 1981).

61 G. Kelling, *Foot patrol* (Washington, DC: National Institute of Justice, 1987); but see F. Esbensen, "Foot patrols: Of what value?," *American Journal of Police*, vol. 6 (1987), pp. 45–65; Pate, "Community-oriented policing in Baltimore," and Police Foundation, *The Newark Foot Patrol Experiment*.

62 Esbensen, "Foot Patrols."

63 R. C. Trojanowicz, "Evaluating a neighborhood foot patrol program: The Flint, Michigan, Project," in Rosenbaum, *Community crime prevention*, pp. 157–178.

64 Jerry H. Ratcliffe, Travis Taniguchi, Elizabeth R. Groff, and Jennifer D. Wood, "Philadelphia Foot Patrol Experiment: A randomized controlled trial of police patrol effectiveness in violent crime hotspots," *Criminology*, vol. 49 (2011), pp. 795–832.

65 C. Wexler, "Foreword," in *Solving crime and disorder problems: Current issues, police strategies, and organizational tactics*, eds. M. Reuland, C. S. Brito, and L. Carroll (Washington, DC: Police Executive Research Forum, 2001), p. vii.

66 B. Bucqueroux and D. Diamond, "Community policing is our best bet against terror," *Subject to Debate*, January 2002, pp. 1, 6, esp. p. 6.

67 Ibid.

68 U.S. Department of Justice, *Citizen patrol projects: National evaluation program phase 1 summary report* (Washington, DC: U.S. Department of Justice, 1976).

69 J. Hilson, "Fort Worth's citizens on patrol program," *TELEMASP Bulletin* 1 (1994), full issue.

70 See, e.g., V. W. Bumphus, L. K. Gaines, and C. R. Blakely, "Citizen police academies: Observing goals, objectives, and recent trends," *American Journal of Criminal Justice*, vol. 24 (1999), pp. 67–79.

71 See, e.g., G. A. Aryani et al., "Citizen police academy: Success through community partnership," *FBI Law Enforcement Bulletin*, vol. 69 (2000), pp. 16–21.

72 J. Palmiotto and N. P. Unninthan, "Impact of citizen police academies on participants: An exploratory study," *Journal of Criminal Justice*, vol. 30 (2002), pp. 101–6.

73 J. A. Schafer and E. M. Bonello, "Citizen police academy: Measuring outcomes," *Police Quarterly*, vol. 4 (2001), pp. 434–48; E. G. Cohn, "Citizen police academy: A recipe for improving police-community relations," *Journal of Criminal Justice*, vol. 24 (1996), pp. 265–71.

74 W. T. Jordan, "Citizen police academies: Community policing or community politics," *American Journal of Police*, vol. 25 (2000), pp. 93–118.

75 Ibid.

76 B. Forst, "The privatization and civilianization of policing," in *Boundary changes in criminal justice organizations*, ed. C. M. Friel (Washington, DC: National Institute of Justice, 2000), p. 23.

77 Ibid., p. 25.

78 Ibid.

79 Ibid., p. 403.

80 Ibid.

81 Ibid., p. 408.

82 Ibid.

83 San Diego Municipal Code, Chapter 5, article 2, division 52.5301.

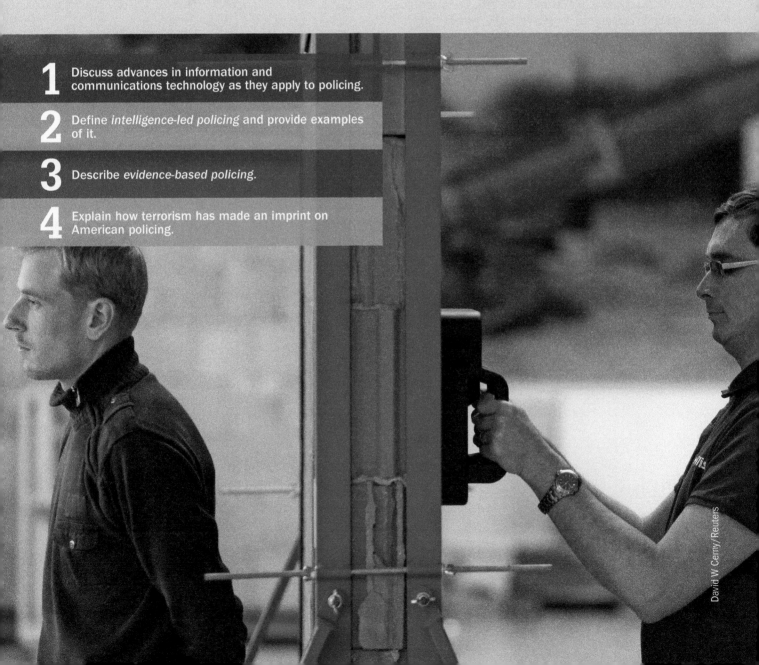

9

Policing in the Modern Era

1 Discuss advances in information and communications technology as they apply to policing.

2 Define *intelligence-led policing* and provide examples of it.

3 Describe *evidence-based policing*.

4 Explain how terrorism has made an imprint on American policing.

David W Cerny/Reuters

POLICING AND EMERGING TECHNOLOGY

In 2015, South Carolina Governor Nikki Haley signed the nation's first state law[1] directing every police department in the state to implement the use of body-worn cameras. Interestingly, however, South Carolina's Freedom of Information Act limits public access to only footage shot by cruiser-mounted cameras, effectively keeping video captured by cop-worn cameras beyond public reach. Prior to passage, state lawmakers cited "privacy and safety concerns" as they amended the bill to specifically exempt police body-cam videos from the state's public-records law. While some people have touted police body cameras as a tool to ensure transparency in police actions, legislators were concerned with preserving the privacy of victims and of criminal suspects pending the resolution of criminal cases. Under the law, criminal defendants and civil litigants still have access to all recordings, but the public (and the media) will not. Police departments in the state are authorized to release body-camera video at their own discretion.

While we might all want to be able to examine video footage of particular police incidents, there are, in fact, substantial reasons why footage from police-worn cameras shouldn't always be public. For one thing, crime victims might sometimes avoid calling the police for fear they'll be recognized on video, and subject to retaliation. In addition, cameras might record evidence or other material that police may have a legitimate interest in not releasing.

Charlie Neuman/ZUMA Press Inc/Alamy Stock Photo

This chapter begins with an examination of the many advances in information and communications technology, including crime-mapping programs and Compstat. Next, it introduces the concept of evidence-based and intelligence-led policing. Intelligence-led policing is about gathering information, analyzing it, and using the results to target specific crime problems. Evidence-based policing, on the other hand, is about using well-established techniques in the social sciences to evaluate the effectiveness and efficiency of police programs and initiatives. Finally, the chapter concludes with a look at the police response to terrorism. A focus on terrorism fits well in this chapter because *policing* the terrorist threat relies heavily on technology and intelligence-led policing.

▶ *The Imprint of Technology on Policing*

LEARNING OUTCOMES 1

Discuss advances in information and communications technology as they apply to policing.

Advances in information and communications technology have worked wonders for law enforcement. As the President's Task Force on 21st Century Policing reported, "Implementing new technologies can give police departments an opportunity to fully engage and educate communities in a dialogue about their expectations for transparency, accountability, and privacy."[2] From helping investigators reconstruct crime scenes to facilitating information sharing between agencies, technology has also transformed the way police do business.[3] This section briefly examines some of the more interesting developments in this area (Figure 9–1).

Crime Mapping

It used to be that patterns of criminal activity were identified on **pin maps**. Colored stick pins would literally be stuck in various places on a map of a city, county, district, precinct, or other area. Different colors corresponded to different types of crimes. This approach, while crude, permitted police to identify problem areas and patterns of criminal activity. The problem was that the maps were one-dimensional and could easily get crowded with pins, especially in the case of minor crimes that occurred with great frequency. The maps were also static, meaning that they could not easily be manipulated to serve different purposes, such as tracking certain types of crime over time. Pin maps were large and could take up significant wall space. But then came crime-mapping software (see Figure 9–2).

Crime-mapping or geographic information system (GIS) software made it relatively easy to create and update crime maps. The practice is now commonplace in policing. How common? The vast majority of police departments employ mapping programs in some form or fashion; most larger departments have crime analysis units, sometimes with several staff whose sole job is to assist with identifying crime trends and hot spots or times. As the National Institute of Justice observed,

- Combining geographic data with police report data and then displaying the information on a map is an effective way to analyze where, how and why crime occurs.

Computer-Aided Drafting	Permits drafting of crime scenes on a computer that can then be viewed three-dimensionally. CAD software has also been developed for animation purposes, enabling viewers to get a feel for the perpetrators' movements.
Computer-Assisted Training	Training now consists of simulators that fully encase trainees in a particular surrounding rather than simply putting them in front of a television screen. This makes the training more realistic, as threats can come from any direction on the job.
Computerized Crime Mapping	Combines geographic information systems with crime statistics generated by a police department so that the crimes can be plotted on a map, resulting in a clean image with details concerning the frequency with which certain crimes take place in given areas. Additionally, computerized crime maps can be overlaid with other information, such as demographic or law enforcement data (e.g., unemployment levels or known gang territories).
Geographic Profiling	Using crime-mapping technology, geographic profiling allows investigators to identify the likely whereabouts or residences of repeat or serial offenders.
Crime Intelligence Systems	SRA International, a provider of crime intelligence software, created GangNet Solution, a browser-based investigative, analysis, and statistical resource for recording and tracking gang members and their activities. The database system enables information sharing on relationships between individuals involved in gangs, which gives law enforcement officials a tool to identify individuals, vehicles, tattoos, gang symbols, and locations, and to facilitate work on gang-related cases. Additional features, such as mapping and facial recognition, are continuously being added to the system[i].
Compstat	This is defined as a goal-oriented strategic management process that uses computer technology, operational strategy and managerial accountability to structure the manner in which a police department provides crime-control services.

FIGURE 9-1 The Impact of Technology on Policing.

- Examining where past victims and offenders lived and where crimes occurred helps police determine which neighborhoods attract offenders and where unknown offenders may reside.

- Using GIS software helps researchers visualize data, assess human behavior over geographic space, follow spatial patterns, and validate theories.[4]

Agencies are also making their crime statistics more accessible to citizens than ever. The previous chapter's closing story featured the website crimereports.com. A related site that is really gaining traction as of this writing is crimemapping.com. Depending on where you live, you might be able to map the incidence of specific offenses in areas of interest to you, down to the street level. Such sites will continue to grow in popularity. Indeed, the Bureau of Justice Statistics recently reported that nearly two in three police departments make crime statistics available through their websites or other means.[5] It won't be long before nearly all do.

Geographic Profiling

Geographic profiling makes use of crime-mapping technology. In particular, it maps connected criminal acts in an effort to determine the offender's residence location. It is used for a range of criminal acts, including murder, rape, robbery, and auto theft.

Geographic profiling can be made particularly effective when it is combined with databases used to track serial offenders. For example, the Washington State Attorney General's Office uses the **Homicide Investigation and Tracking System (HITS)**, which ties various databases together—including gang files, sex offender registries, parole records, and department of motor vehicle records—so that they can be searched simultaneously. According to University of Nevada at Reno criminologist Ken Peak,

> When an agency in the state has a major crime in its jurisdiction, the case is loaded into a central system, which scans every database and linking file for connections by comparing eyewitness descriptions of a suspect and vehicle. It then builds a dataset containing profiles of the offender, the victims, and the incidents. The dataset then goes into a geographic information system, where the program selects and maps the names and addresses of those suspects whose method of operation fits the crime being investigated.[6]

Crime Intelligence Systems

Today, nearly every patrol officer has a laptop computer in his or her car that is linked to various databases, such as vehicle registration records and criminal history information. Recently, though, the databases have become increasingly sophisticated.

FIGURE 9–2 Crime Map Depicting Motor Vehicle Thefts.
Source: Produced by the Maptitude mapping software, © 2008 Caliper Corporation. Reprinted with permission.

One of them, known as **CalGang** (in California) or GangNet (in other states), contains detailed information on known gang members that officers in the field can quickly access.

Predictive Analytics

Predictive analytics is the use of data, machine learning, and data mining to predict future outcomes based on historical data. The practice is commonplace in the business world; only recently has the law enforcement profession come to explore its potential. In a policing context, the concern is with predicting future crime based on past data. The practice is known as **predictive policing**. It involves the use of analytical techniques to identify likely targets for criminals and prevent crime. A study by the RAND Corporation identified four methods of predictive policing (also see the story at the end of this chapter):

1. *Methods for predicting crimes:* These are approaches used to forecast places and times with an increased risk of crime.

2. *Methods for predicting offenders:* These approaches identify individuals at risk of offending in the future.

3. *Methods for predicting perpetrators' identities:* These techniques are used to create profiles that accurately match likely offenders with specific past crimes.

4. *Methods for predicting victims of crimes:* Similar to those methods that focus on offenders, crime locations, and times of heightened risk, these approaches are used to identify groups or, in some cases, individuals who are likely to become victims of crime.[7]

How successful is predictive policing? The practice is cutting-edge, so few studies are available. One study published in the prestigious *Journal of the American Statistical Association*[8] pitted a predictive policing algorithm against professional crime analysts in an effort to determine which could most accurately predict crime in areas throughout Los Angeles. For one part of the study, researchers gave crime analysts a map of the police district and asked them to identify one precise location (approximately a half block in size) where a crime would be most likely to occur within the next 12 hours. The computer algorithm was programmed to answer the same question. It correctly predicted the location of the next crime 4.7% of the crime, compared to just 2.1% for the crime analyst. In other words, the computer was twice as effective as a professional crime analyst in predicting crime.[9] The percentages were still low, though, as would be expected. Human behavior is exceedingly difficult to predict, so it is doubtful crime analysts' job security will be threatened anytime soon.

Automated License Plate Recognition

According to the most recent Law Enforcement Management and Administrative Statistics (LEMAS) survey, about one in six police departments uses automated license plate recognition (ALPR).[10] Agencies have for years been using in-car cameras (approximately two in three agencies do so), but license plate readers are used for different reasons. Whereas in-car cameras are primarily used to promote officer safety and reduce complaints against police,[11] license plate readers are more proactive, constantly scanning for stolen vehicles and people of interest. According to one study, ALPR systems can capture upward of 1,800 plates per minute, even for cars that are moving quickly.[12] The systems are expensive, however, running between $10,000 and $22,000 per patrol car. Nevertheless, their benefits may outweigh their costs, at least according to a government report:

> ALPR technology is a significant tool in the arsenal of law enforcement and public safety agencies. It automates a tedious, distracting, and manual process that officers regularly complete in their daily operations, and vastly improves their efficiency and effectiveness in identifying vehicles of interest among the hundreds or thousands they observe in routine patrol. Moreover, it generates a rich and enduring record of vehicle sightings, complete with time, date, and geographic location information for each observation. This data can substantially enhance the investigative capacity of law enforcement, and greatly contribute to intelligence collection and analysis functions.[13]

As with any other technology, ALPR systems have their critics. For example, the American Civil Liberties Union has claimed the devices ". . . have the potential to create permanent records of virtually everywhere any of us has driven, radically transforming the consequences of leaving home to pursue private life, and opening up many opportunities for abuse."[14] As such, it has recommended a number of rules for ALPR use, including no storage of data on innocent persons and use only by authorized law enforcement personnel.[15]

Websites and Social Media

Nearly every law enforcement organization maintains a website. Some are bare bones; others offer a connection between law enforcement and the community. The Police Executive Research Forum (PERF) recently conducted a survey of 500 police departments around the country in an effort to determine what besides websites agencies were using to stay "connected" with their constituents.[16] Of the responding agencies, all reported maintaining a website. As for other social media:

- 82% use Facebook
- 69% use Twitter
- 48% use YouTube
- 34% use LinkedIn

According to the report, "[p]olice departments are using social media for a variety of reasons for two basic purposes: *disseminating* their own messages to the public, and *gathering* information from social media platforms to prevent and investigate crimes."[17] This was echoed in another study of police departments' use of Facebook: ". . . these tools allow departments to build public relations by conveying information about police effectiveness, reporting human-interest stories, and soliciting feedback from community members."[18] A 2015 study by the International Association of Chiefs of Police (IACP) found that, more than anything, departments use social media to assist in criminal investigations; Facebook, Twitter, and YouTube were most commonly used in this regard.[19]

Compstat

During the early years of his tenure as police commissioner of New York City, William Bratton called for weekly meetings with representatives from each of the NYPD's eight bureaus. Deputy Commissioner Jack Maple, in conjunction with other high-ranking officials, placed pressure on the bureaus to generate crime statistics, which had not been kept up to date at the time. Precincts began to measure criminal activity more carefully, then the results were computerized and assembled into a document known as the *Compstat book*.[20] The crime figures reported in the Compstat book were eventually used to hold precinct commanders responsible for the crime rates in their areas.

Compstat is an acronym for "computer statistics" or, in some locations, "compare statistics." The NYPD program has been widely imitated around the country,[21] and the programs have several different designations. Generally speaking, Compstat emphasizes four important elements:

1. Accurate and timely intelligence
2. Effective tactics
3. Rapid deployment
4. Relentless follow-up and assessment[22]

The logic behind the intelligence aspect is that "information describing how and where crimes are committed, as well as who criminals are, must be available to all levels of policing."[23] "Tactics are designed to respond directly to facts discovered during the intelligence gathering process."[24] Rapid deployment is important and often involves quick and effective coordination because "the most effective plans require that personnel from several units and enforcement functions work together as a team."[25] Relentless follow-up is necessary to ensure desired outcomes. Figure 9–3 lists the general elements of the Compstat model.

The last step, relentless accountability, is extremely important and is usually accomplished most effectively in intensive management meetings. According to Jack Maple, former deputy commissioner of the NYPD, "the first step to crime reduction itself—the gathering and analyzing of accurate, timely intelligence—has to be quickened by the heat of accountability."[26]

One important aspect of Compstat is crime mapping. Because crime data must be portrayed clearly and rapidly, computer technology is essential. According to one source, "A powerful software tool, MapInfo 94, became the NYPD's crime radar screen, with attention-grabbing colors and shapes. Red dots indicated drug complaints from the public, blue dots showed drug arrests, green triangles represented shooting incidents, and yellow dots indicated homicides."[27] Computerized images generated by MapInfo 94 brought together all the data in the Compstat books. Previously, crime statistics had not been kept or presented in any single source. As another researcher observed, "These visual presentations are a highly effective complement to the Compstat report, since they permit precinct commanders and executive staff members to instantly identify and explore trends, patterns, and possible solutions for crime and quality-of-life problems."[28]

Innovative problem-solving tactics: Police responses are selected because they offer the best prospects of success, not because they are "what we have always done." Innovation and experimentation are encouraged and use of the best available knowledge about practices is expected.

Data-driven analysis of problems and assessment of department's problem-solving efforts: Data are made available to identify and analyze problems and to track and assess the department's response. Data are made accessible to all relevant personnel on a timely basis and in a readily usable format.

Mission clarification: Top management clarifies and exalts the core features of the department's mission. Management demonstrates commitment and states its goals. The organization and its leaders can be held accountable for specific goals—such as reducing crime by 10% in a year.

Organizational flexibility: The organization develops the capacity and habit of changing established routines as needed to mobilize resources when and where they are needed for strategic application.

Internal accountability: Operational commanders are held accountable for knowing their commands, being well acquainted with the problems in the command, and accomplishing measurable results in reducing those problems—or at least demonstrating a diligent effort to learn from that experience.

Geographic organization of operational command: Operational command is focused on the policing of territories, so central decision-making authority over police operations is delegated to commanders with territorial responsibility for districts. Functionally differentiated units and specialists—patrol, community-policing officers, detectives, narcotics, vice, juvenile, and traffic—are either placed under the command of the district commander, or arrangements are made to facilitate their responsiveness to the commander's needs.

FIGURE 9-3 **Core Elements of the Compstat Model.**
Source: J. J. Willis, S. D. Mastrofski, and D. Weisburd, *Compstat in Practice: An In-depth Analysis of Three Cities* (Washington, DC: Police Foundation, 2004). Reprinted by permission of the Police Foundation.

Crime statistics are the most popular measure of success for precinct commanders. However, Sam Houston State University criminologists Randall Garner and Larry Hoover question the appropriateness of crime statistics as the sole measure of success.[29] They cite quality-of-life issues and citizen complaints as barometers of police performance that agencies experimenting with Compstat may wish to consider. The appropriate measure of success, they suggest, "communicates what issues are valued most in the department."[30] They also raise concerns about the NYPD version of Compstat, which they regard as confrontational. While the NYPD's program has established greater accountability, increased awareness, improved problem-solving endeavors, and increased managerial control, they caution that weekly meetings may be too shortsighted and aggressive an approach to reducing crime and may overemphasize outcomes rather than underlying causes of problems. Indeed, one researcher has observed that "Compstat's approach ignores

Think About It...

Compstat The effect of Compstat on crime has not received much research attention. Some researchers have attributed drops in crime to Compstat and similar managerial approaches, but to date, few researchers have applied rigorous scientific methods to the question of whether Compstat directly affects crime. *Is it possible to conclude that Compstat, independent of all other possible explanations, reduces crime? Can Compstat alone reduce crime, or are more means necessary? Explain.*

Mikael Karlsson/ Alamy Stock Photo

decades of expert research that has shown that crime levels are determined by vast social forces beyond police control—poverty, racism, [and] demographics."[31]

Computer-Aided Drafting

Computer-aided drafting (CAD) is not a law enforcement technology per se, but it has been adapted to meet the needs of police officers and criminal investigators. Gone are the days of convincing jury members to convict based on tedious one-dimensional drawings and photographs. For instance, a three-dimensional crime scene image puts jurors at the crime scene almost as if they were actually there.

As this technology continues to develop, it is becoming more portable. For example, the U.S. Department of Energy has been working on a device that officers in the field can use to beam the information they gather (via pictures, laser range finders, Global Positioning System devices, and so on) to the crime lab for instant expert advice and accurate recording of the crime scene.[32]

CAD programs offer several advantages. First, they create images that are professional in their appearance, an improvement over traditional methods of drafting crime scene images by hand and relying on simple photographs. This is of great importance if the images are to be shared with jurors in a criminal trial. In this vein, the next CAD advantage is that the software minimizes duplication of effort; there is no need to draft separate images for investigators and jurors. With a few keystrokes, a large image can be printed for sharing with a jury.

The software makes crime scene investigation much cheaper, too. Gone are the days when draftspeople or engineers needed to take precise measurements of every detail of a crime scene. Delays in crime scene reconstruction are now largely a thing of the past. Perhaps most important, it is easy to alter images as new information becomes available, thus eliminating the need to redraw the entire image.

Computer-Assisted Training

Computers also enhance the training of law enforcement officers. Veteran officers may have had the opportunity to participate in one of the old "shoot/don't shoot" training exercises in front of a television screen with a noninteractive video. Those days are largely over; computers have helped make such exercises much more realistic and dramatic.

One of the new technologies in this area, the **firearms training system (FATS)**, is about as realistic as shooting a simulated firearm can get. It is a full-size, fully interactive device, not unlike flight and driving simulators. Moreover, the technology is also relatively affordable and portable.

VirTra Systems, which markets FATS devices, uses a 300-degree immersive training platform that surrounds the trainee with a realistic judgmental use-of-force scenario in one of its products.[33] Another company has gone so far as to develop a simulator that actually pelts the trainee with large-caliber nylon balls when he or she makes a mistake, further approximating reality. One such device, the Professional Range Instruction Simulator (PRISim), has been described as "training

so real, you will not call it a simulator."[34] AIS Solutions, the company behind the device, says this:

> PRISim™ puts trainees into the middle of an interactive theatre to cause responses to potentially deadly mistakes, indecision, sudden fear, partial understanding, blindside surprise, eye-blink response and life or death choices. The PRISim™ system gives trainees the coaching they could never get in actual field operations and provides situational experiences far beyond the capability of conventional training. . . . The PRISim™ Shoot-Back cannon is a devastatingly effective tool to train effective use of cover. An instructor-aimed cannon is mounted above the centre of the screen to fire 17mm caliber nylon projectiles synchronized with the video scenario. The cannon fires accurate single, 3-round burst or full auto hostile fire.[35]

▶ Intelligence-Led Policing

In 2005, the U.S. Department of Justice embraced **intelligence-led policing** as an important technique that American law enforcement agencies can employ in the battle against terrorism.[36] Intelligence-led policing can also be used to target other pressing problems, such as property crime, narcotics violations, and organized crime. Not every agency has the staff or resources needed to create a dedicated intelligence unit. Even without an intelligence unit, however, a law enforcement organization should have the ability to effectively utilize the information and intelligence products that are developed and disseminated by organizations at all levels of government. In other words, even though a police agency may not have its own resources for analyzing all the information it acquires, it should still be able to mount an effective response to credible threat information that it receives. The following sections take a closer look at the nature of intelligence, why it is important, the intelligence process, and the nature of intelligence-led policing, especially in comparison to some other approaches we discuss elsewhere in this book.

LEARNING OUTCOMES 2 — Define *intelligence-led policing* and provide examples of it.

Intelligence

What is intelligence? It is tempting to liken it to information, but they are not the same. Rather, **intelligence** is the result of information and the analysis of that information.[37] One definition of *intelligence* within a law enforcement context is the "formal process of taking information and turning it into knowledge while ensuring that the information is collected, stored, and disseminated appropriately."[38] Police expert David Carter's *Law Enforcement Intelligence: A Guide for State, Local, and Tribal Law Enforcement Agencies* defines criminal intelligence as "a synergistic product intended to provide meaningful and trustworthy direction to law enforcement decision makers about complex criminality, criminal enterprises, criminal extremists, and terrorists."[39]

In other words, intelligence is information that has been analyzed and integrated into a useful perspective. The information used in the development of effective intelligence is typically gathered from many sources, as noted in Figure 9–4. Law enforcement intelligence, or **criminal intelligence**, is the result of a "process that evaluates information collected from diverse sources, integrates the relevant information into a cohesive package, and produces a conclusion or estimate about a criminal phenomenon by using the scientific approach to problem solving."[40] While criminal investigation is typically part of the intelligence-gathering process, the intelligence function of a police department is more exploratory and more broadly focused than a single criminal investigation.[41]

Key to these definitions is the idea that without analysis there is no intelligence. What, then, is analysis? It is not just information processing by trained crime analysts. Instead, "analysis requires thoughtful contemplation that results in conclusions and recommendations."[42] With this in mind, it is useful to distinguish between various types and levels of intelligence.

Tactical and Strategic Intelligence

Carter points out that there are two types of intelligence: tactical and strategic. **Tactical intelligence** "includes gaining or developing information related to threats of terrorism or crime and using this information to apprehend offenders, harden targets, and use strategies that will eliminate or mitigate the threat."[43] **Strategic intelligence**, in contrast, provides information to decision makers about the changing nature of threats for the purpose of "developing response strategies and reallocating resources"[44] to accomplish effective prevention.

Levels of Intelligence

There are four levels of intelligence. Level 1 intelligence is the highest. According to one study, "the law enforcement agency at [level 1] employs an intelligence manager, intelligence officers, and professional intelligence analysts."[45] The secretive Financial Crimes Enforcement Network (FINCEN) fits into this category. "Level 2 intelligence includes police agencies that produce tactical and strategic intelligence for internal consumption. . . . These agencies generally use intelligence to support investigations rather than to direct operations."[46] The typical agency at this level is a state police agency that may have intelligence units or officers on the payroll. Level 3 intelligence, the second most common form, includes local law enforcement agencies with anywhere from a few dozen to hundreds of sworn personnel. These agencies sometimes produce their own intelligence but often rely on other higher-level (state or federal) agencies that specialize in intelligence gathering.

Decision Making
It is common for law enforcement agencies to gather information and to decide what to do with it. Having the most accurate and complete intelligence aids in decision making.

Strategic Targeting
Intelligence enables administrators to carefully target their efforts to achieve the best results with limited funds. Strategic targeting is about focusing on the individuals, groups, or locations where success is most likely.

Intelligence Gathering
newspapers
surveillance
covert operations
financial records
electronic eavesdropping
interviews
interrogations

Planning
Planning also depends on intelligence. Unfortunately, planning in many agencies is done without sufficient intelligence, such as the nature of specific crime problems facing an area.

Crime Prevention
Every police agency hopes to prevent crime rather than just respond to it. Intelligence from previous crimes may arm decision makers with the information they need to prevent similar crimes from occurring. Analysts can compare the indicators from local neighborhoods to anticipate crime trends, and agencies can take preventive measures to intervene or mitigate the impact of those crimes.

FIGURE 9–4 **Sources of Intelligence.**

Level 3 agencies should not always rely on outside help, however. According to one study,

> While smaller agencies may not be able to devote a full-time position to the criminal intelligence function . . . [they] need to understand the proactive concept of criminal intelligence and recognize that most law enforcement agencies, regardless of size, are susceptible to organized criminal activity that may extend beyond jurisdictional boundaries. Their personnel should be trained to recognize and report indications of organized crime, gang activity, and criminal extremist and terrorist activity. The information should be shared with intelligence-trained personnel from neighboring agencies.[47]

Finally, level 4 intelligence characterizes the vast majority of law enforcement agencies in the United States. "If they assign someone to intelligence operations, that person generally has multiple responsibilities and is often a narcotics officer, gang officer, or counter-terrorism officer."[48]

Why Intelligence Is Important

Law enforcement agencies at all levels depend on intelligence and cannot function adequately without it.

The Intelligence Process

The Global Intelligence Working Group produced the **National Criminal Intelligence Sharing Plan (NCISP)**. It was approved and released by the U.S. attorney general in October 2003.

Several recommendations for improved intelligence gathering were offered, and the group also organized the process into six steps (Figure 9–5). Note that the process is circular and that it starts with planning and direction. According to a recent report, *planning and direction* require

> an agency to identify the outcomes it wants to achieve from its collection efforts. This identification directs the scope of the officers' and agents' investigations—for example, a straightforward inquiry to identify crime groups operating in a jurisdiction or a more complex inquiry to determine the likelihood that criminal extremists will attack a visiting dignitary.[49]

Next, *collection* refers to gathering and processing information. This can be accomplished through several strategies, including physical surveillance, electronic surveillance (e.g., wiretapping), confidential informants, newspaper reports, and so on. Third, *processing* consists of sifting through all this information to organize and collate it. *Analysis* converts the information to intelligence. As one official put it, "Without the explicit performance of this function, the intelligence unit is nothing but a file unit."[50] Analysis includes crime analysis (e.g., crime-pattern analysis with mapping software), but it also includes investigative analysis (bank record analysis) and strategic analysis (risk assessment). The next step is *dissemination*, which is the process of getting intelligence to the decision makers who need it. Finally, *reevaluation* is concerned with reanalysis of intelligence products to determine their accuracy and effectiveness. According to a report on the subject, "One way to reevaluate intelligence is to include a feedback form with each product that is disseminated."[51]

The Nature of Intelligence-Led Policing

We have spent significant time discussing intelligence in general, but what exactly is intelligence-led policing? The term originated in the United Kingdom.[52] Specifically, the Kent Constabulary came up with the concept in response to a rise in property crime—a rise that occurred while police resources were being cut. Originally called the *Kent Policing Model*, this approach prioritized calls for service and referred nonemergency calls to other agencies, when appropriate. This freed up resources so that officers could focus on the property crimes that were on the rise. The result was a property crime drop of 24% over three years. According to one assessment of this effort,

> [I]ntelligence-led policing focuses on key criminal activities. Once crime problems are identified and quantified through intelligence assessments, key criminals can be targeted for investigation and prosecution. Because the groups and individuals targeted in Kent were those responsible for significant criminal activity, the ultimate reduction in crime was considerable.[53]

Since it has been imported into the United States, intelligence-led policing has remained largely the same, with

Think About It...

Directed Patrol *Directed patrol* refers to patrol with direction—that is, patrol targeted at specific areas and problems. Directed patrol is heavily influenced by the gathering of intelligence. That is, with the right data, law enforcement officials can decide where to concentrate their efforts. *Assuming police have a particular problem area in mind, is directed patrol the ideal approach? Should you worry about displacement of the problem into surrounding neighborhoods or cities? Why or why not?*

EuroStyle Graphics/Alamy Stock Photo

Reevaluation

Planning and Direction

Collection

Processing/ Collation

Analysis

Dissemination

FIGURE 9–5 The Intelligence Process.
Source: Office of Justice Programs, *National Criminal Intelligence Sharing Plan* (Washington, DC: U.S. Department of Justice, 2003), p. 6.

A fusion center is a "collaborative effort of two or more agencies that provide resources, expertise, and information to the center with the goal of maximizing their ability to detect, prevent, investigate, and respond to criminal and terrorist activity." Fusion centers can identify potential threats through data analysis and enhance investigations through analytical support (e.g., flow charting and geographic analysis).[54]

Intelligence-Led versus Problem-Oriented Policing

Intelligence-led policing sounds similar to problem-oriented policing (see Chapter 8), but the two are somewhat different. Problem-oriented policing seeks to control crime through the study of problems. Common to problem-oriented policing, too, is the scanning, analysis, response, assessment (SARA) model.

Intelligence-led policing basically takes problem-oriented policing to the next level; it does the same for community-oriented policing. These strategies "have been used for crime analysis, which is statistical and incident-based, rather than strategic intelligence analysis, which looks at large-scope problems or models."[55] In other words, intelligence-based policing takes problem-oriented policing beyond the level of a single police agency. Intelligence-led policing may also sound something like Compstat. As Table 9–1 shows, they are similar but not quite the same.

some minor twists. For example, it has benefited from so-called **fusion centers**. These are essentially intelligence-gathering units—often collaborative efforts that serve various agencies. As David Lambert explains,

TABLE 9–1 | COMPARISON OF COMPSTAT AND INTELLIGENCE-LED POLICING

Compstat	Commonalities	Intelligence-Led Policing
• Single jurisdiction	• Both have a goal of prevention	• Multiple jurisdictions
• Incident driven	• Both require	• Threat driven
• Street crime and burglary	—Organizational flexibility	• Criminal enterprises and terrorism
• Crime mapping	—Consistent information input	• Commodity flow; trafficking and transiting logistics
• Time sensitive (24-hour feedback and response)	—A significant analytic component	• Strategic
• Disrupt crime series (e.g., burglary ring)	• Both are driven from the bottom up with respect to operational needs	• Disrupt enterprises
• Drives operations:		• Drives operations:
—Patrol		—JTIF
—Tactical unit		—Organized crime investigations
—Investigators		—Task forces
• Analysis of offender MOs		• Analysis of enterprise MOs

Source: Office of Community Oriented Policing Services, Intelligence-led Policing: The Integration of Community Policing and Law Enforcement Intelligence, part 4 (Washington, DC: COPS Office, n.d.), p. 43, www.cops.usdoj.gov/pdf/e09042536_Chapter_04.pdf (accessed July 24, 2011).

▶ Evidence-Based Policing

At the close of the twentieth century, noted police researcher **Lawrence W. Sherman** addressed an audience of criminal justice policy-makers, scholars, and practitioners at the Police Foundation in Washington, D.C., and called for a new approach to American policing that would use research to guide and evaluate practice. "Police practices should be based on scientific evidence about what works best," Sherman told his audience. Sherman's lecture, titled "Evidence-Based Policing: Policing Based on Science, Not Anecdote,"[56] popularized the term evidence-based policing, which, says Sherman, "is the use of best available research on the outcomes of police work to implement guidelines and evaluate agencies, units, and officers."[57] In other words, **evidence-based policing** uses research into everyday police procedures to evaluate current practices and to guide officers and police executives in future decision making. In any discussion of evidence-based policing, it is important to remember that the word *evidence* refers to scientific evidence, not criminal evidence.

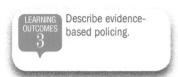

LEARNING OUTCOMES 3 — Describe evidence-based policing.

"The basic premise of evidence-based practice," says Sherman, "is that we are all entitled to our own opinions, but not to our own facts."[58] Our own facts, or our beliefs about the way things should be done, says Sherman, often turn out to be wrong. During the civil rights movement of the 1960s and 1970s, for example, police executives in many areas took a heavy-handed approach in their attempts to control demonstrators. Images of tear gas–filled streets, high-pressure fire hoses aimed at marchers, and police dogs biting fleeing demonstrators symbolize that era for many people. This heavy-handed approach had unintended consequences and served to inflame protesters. Situations that might have otherwise been contained with simple crowd-control tactics and the use of physical barriers became largely uncontrollable. Sherman reminds us that "the mythic power of subjective and unstructured wisdom holds back every field and keeps it from systematically discovering and implementing what works best in repeated tasks."

Some suggest that evidence-based policing offers a long-term approach for creating cost-effectiveness in policing that, in the current economic environment, "is the only alternative to current ways of operating."[59] "In an age of austerity and budget cuts," argue British writers Neil Wain and Alex Murray, it is necessary for police departments to invest wisely in programs and initiatives that have a proven track record at reducing or preventing crime.

Today's evidence-based policing model has been called the single "most powerful force for change" in policing today.[60] Leading the movement toward evidence-based policing are organizations like the FBI's Futures Working Group, the Campbell Crime and Justice Group, and the Center for Evidence-Based Crime Policy at George Mason University. FBI Supervisory Special Agent Carl J. Jensen III, a member of the Futures Working Group, notes that in the future "successful law enforcement executives will have to be consumers and appliers of research." They won't need to be researchers themselves, Jensen notes, "but they must use research in their everyday work."[61] The Campbell Crime and Justice Group emphasizes the use of experimental studies in crime and justice policy making.

The Institute of Criminology at Cambridge University has identified the following questions in the area of policing as goals to be answered by evidence-based studies:[62]

- How can policing produce greater public safety without eroding civil liberties?
- How can more value for the money be returned from investments in policing to cut the costs of crime?
- Can crime be better forecast for preventive policing by time and place?
- Can unsuccessful police methods be distinguished from cost-effective ones?
- Can better policing reduce the high costs of a growing prison population?
- Can evaluation tools used in evidence-based medicine be adopted by police?
- What are the possibilities for a police service based on cost-effectiveness?
- What are the prospects for developing the knowledge base for such evidence?

In 2010, innovative British police professionals and academics founded the British Society of Policing to promote and facilitate the increased use of the best available research evidence to solve policing problems and the production of new research by police practitioners and researchers and to communicate research evidence to police practitioners and the public. An evidence-based policing matrix is available at http://gemini.gmu.edu/cebcp/Matrix.html. The matrix, provided by the Center for Evidence-Based Crime Policy, is a research-to-practice translation tool that visually identifies strong evidence-based policing practices.

The federal government's CrimeSolutions.gov initiative offers perhaps the most current example of how research can inform evidence-based policing—and criminal justice in general. The site uses research to rate the effectiveness of various programs aimed at preventing and reducing crime. Trained reviewers evaluate previously published research for rigor, then the site ranks the underlying programs as effective, promising, or having no effects. The site is pitched as

> . . . a central, reliable resource to help [practitioners] understand what works in justice-related programs and practices . . . [It's] purpose is to assist in practical decision-making and program implementation by gathering information on specific justice-related programs and practices and reviewing the existing evaluation and meta-analysis research against standardized criteria.[63]

Smart Policing

Evidence-based policing contributes to what some people have termed "smart policing." The term *smart policing* has been used to describe the shift in attitude that came about as a result of the economic squeeze that law enforcement administrators began facing in the early 2000s.[64]

According to the Smart Policing Initiative (SPI), **smart policing** is "a systemwide and strategic view of police operations that includes consideration of causal factors of crime, system impact of police actions, partnerships with community organizations to support crime-prevention activities, and more effective policing that stresses integration of analytics, evidence-based practices, and emerging technology tools into ongoing police operations."[65] Smart policing also encourages a focus on outcomes, including achieving less crime and safer communities in more cost-effective ways.

The goal of smart policing is to "develop tactics and strategies that are effective, efficient, and economical—as measured by reduced crime and high case closure rates." The SPI, which is a collaborative effort between the Bureau of Justice Assistance, the nonprofit CNA Corporation, and dozens of police departments, says that "effective policing requires a tightly focused, collaborative approach that is measurable; based on sound, detailed analysis; and includes policies and procedures that promote and support accountability." Hence, the SPI works to build evidence-based law enforcement strategies that are effective, efficient, and economical.

Hot-spot policing, in which agencies focus their resources on known areas of criminal activity, is one example of smart policing techniques. Predictive policing, another example of smart policing, provides the ability to anticipate or predict crime through the use of statistical techniques and helps to guide enforcement operations.[66] Two programs that support effective policing are the SPI and the National Law Enforcement and Corrections Technology Center (NLECTC). The NLECTC works to identify emerging technologies and to assess their efficiency. Visit the SPI on the Web at www.smart-policinginitiative.com.

▶ *Policing in an Age of Terrorism*

September 11, 2001, and the events in its wake have made clear the changed role of American police agencies in a new era

of international terrorism. While the core mission of American police departments has not changed, law enforcement agencies at all levels now devote an increased amount of time and other resources to preparing for possible terrorist attacks and to gathering the intelligence necessary to thwart them.

Local police departments play an especially important role in responding to the challenges of terrorism. They must help prevent attacks and respond when attacks occur, offering critical evacuation, emergency medical, and security functions to help stabilize communities following an incident. A PERF survey of 250 police chiefs found that the chiefs strongly believe that their departments can make valuable contributions to terrorism

prevention by using community policing networks to exchange information with citizens and to gather intelligence.[67]

The Council on Foreign Relations, headquartered in New York City and Washington, D.C., agrees with PERF that American police departments can no longer assume that federal counterterrorism efforts alone will be sufficient to protect the communities they serve. Consequently, says the council, many police departments have responded by doing the following:

- Strengthening liaisons with federal, state, and local agencies, including fire departments and other police departments

- Refining their training and emergency response plans to address terrorist threats, including attacks with weapons of mass destruction

- Increasing patrols and shoring up barriers around landmarks, places of worship, ports of entry, transit systems, nuclear power plants, and so on

- More heavily guarding public speeches, parades, and other public events

- Creating new counterterrorism divisions and reassigning officers to counterterrorism from other divisions, such as drug enforcement

- Employing new technologies, such as X-ray-like devices, to scan containers at ports of entry and sophisticated sensors to detect a chemical, biological, or radiological attack[68]

The extent of local departments' engagement in such preventive activities depends substantially on budgetary considerations and is strongly influenced by the assessed likelihood of attack. The NYPD, for example, which has firsthand experience in responding to terrorist attacks (23 of its officers were killed when the World Trade Center towers collapsed), has created a special bureau headed by a deputy police commissioner responsible for counterterrorism training, prevention, and investigation.[69] One thousand officers have been reassigned to antiterrorism duties, and the department is training its entire 39,000-member force in how to respond to biological, radiological, and chemical attacks.[70] The NYPD has assigned detectives to work abroad with law enforcement agencies in Canada, Israel, Southeast Asia, and the Middle East to track terrorists who might target New York City,[71] and it now employs officers with a command of the Pashto, Farsi, and Urdu languages of the Middle East to monitor foreign television, radio, and Internet communications. The department has also invested heavily in new hazardous materials protective suits, gas masks, and portable radiation detectors.

In November 2004, in an effort to provide the law enforcement community and policy-makers with guidance on critical issues related to antiterrorism planning and critical-incident response, the IACP announced its **Taking Command Initiative**. The IACP describes the initiative as "an aggressive project to assess the current state of homeland security efforts in the United States and to develop and implement the actions necessary to protect our communities from the specter of both crime and terrorism."[72] Initial deliberations under the initiative led the IACP to conclude that "the current homeland security strategy is handicapped by a fundamental flaw: It was developed without sufficiently seeking or incorporating the advice, expertise, or consent of public safety organizations at the state, tribal or local level."[73] The IACP report identified five key principles of an effective homeland security strategy.

The IACP recognizes that workable antiterrorism programs at the local level require the effective sharing of critical information between agencies. FBI-sponsored **Joint Terrorism Task Forces (JTTFs)** facilitate this by bringing together federal and local law enforcement personnel to focus on specific threats. The FBI currently has established or authorized JTTFs in each of its 56 field offices. In addition to the JTTFs, the FBI has created Regional Terrorism Task Forces (RTTFs) to share information with local enforcement agencies. Through the RTTFs, FBI special agents assigned to terrorism prevention and investigation meet twice a year with their federal, state, and local counterparts for common training, discussion of investigations, and intelligence sharing. The FBI says that "the design of this nontraditional terrorism task force provides the necessary mechanism and structure to direct counterterrorism resources toward localized terrorism problems within the United States."[74] Six RTTFs are currently in operation: the Inland Northwest, South Central, Southeastern, Northeast Border, Deep South, and Southwest.

Given the changes that have taken place in American law enforcement since the terrorist attacks of September 11, 2001, some say that traditional distinctions between crime, terrorism, and war are fading and that, at least in some instances, direct military action and civil law enforcement are becoming integrated. The critical question for law enforcement administrators in the near future may be one of discerning the role that law enforcement is to play in the emerging global context.

Federal Agencies and Antiterrorism

The FBI's counterterrorism efforts became especially important following the September 11, 2001, attacks on American targets. Two months after the attacks, then–U.S. Attorney General John Ashcroft announced a major reorganization and mobilization of the FBI and other federal agencies, such as the Immigration and Naturalization Service. Speaking at a press conference in Washington, D.C., Ashcroft said,

> Our strategic plan mandates fundamental change in several of the most critical components of American justice and law enforcement, starting with the organization that is at the center of our counterterrorism effort, the Federal Bureau of Investigation. In its history, the FBI has been many things: the protector of our institutions when they were under assault from organized crime; the keeper of our security when it was threatened by international espionage; and the defender of our civil rights when they were denied to some Americans on the basis of their race, color or creed. Today the American people call upon the Federal Bureau of Investigation

to put prevention of terrorism at the center of its law-enforcement and national-security efforts.[75]

Following the attorney general's lead, the FBI reshaped its priorities to focus on preventing terrorist attacks. This effort is managed by the Counterterrorism Division at FBI headquarters and is emphasized at every field office, resident agency, and legal attaché (Legat) office. Headquarters administer a national threat warning system that allows the FBI to instantly distribute important terrorism-related bulletins to law enforcement agencies and public-safety departments throughout the country. "Flying Squads" provide specialized counterterrorism knowledge and experience, language capabilities, and analytic support as needed to FBI field offices and Legats. To combat terrorism, the FBI's Counterterrorism Division collects, analyzes, and shares information and critical intelligence with various federal agencies and departments—including the CIA, the National Security Agency, and the Department of Homeland Security—and with law enforcement agencies throughout the country.

An essential weapon in the FBI's battle against terrorism is the JTTF. A national JTTF, located at the FBI's Washington headquarters, includes representatives from the Departments of Defense and Energy, the Federal Emergency Management Agency, the CIA, U.S. Customs and Border Protection, the U.S. Secret Service, and U.S. Immigration and Customs Enforcement. In addition, through 66 local JTTFs, representatives from federal agencies, state, and local law enforcement personnel, and first responders coordinate efforts to track down terrorists and to prevent acts of terrorism in the United States.

In a speech delivered in late 2015, FBI Director James B. Comey summarized recent changes in the agency's (and the government's) anti-terrorism focus:

> . . . al Qaeda, . . . the primary tumor of terrorism which before 9/11, and in the years shortly after 9/11, was based in the Afghanistan and Pakistan region. It was focused on the spectacular attacks aimed at landmarks, aimed especially at this great city, focused on airplane-based attacks, sophisticated multi-pronged efforts involving carefully selected operatives, long-tail surveillance, careful operational security, and the execution of the next big thing . . . That culture of core al Qaeda, and its approach to attacks lasted, frankly, until the rise of the group that we call ISIL . . . [W]ith the rise of ISIL, we were suddenly confronted with a terrorist group that had significant land that it controlled, significant resources, and an entirely different way of approaching terrorism . . . Their mission was two-pronged: to bring fighters and their families to the Iraq–Syria border region where they claim their so-called caliphate, and if they couldn't attract fighters to them, they wanted people to kill where they were. Not sophisticated, airplane-focused, landmark-focused attacks, just kill anybody wherever you are. That was their twin-pronged call, their siren song . . . The paradigm of al Qaeda still exists in the world, but ISIL has become the leader in the global jihad through the crowdsourcing of terrorism.[76]

Information Sharing and Antiterrorism

The need to effectively share criminal intelligence across juris-dictions and between law enforcement agencies nationwide became apparent with the tragic events of September 11, 2001. Consequently, governments at all levels are today working toward the creation of a fully integrated criminal justice information system. Although a fully integrated nationwide criminal justice information system does not yet exist, efforts to create one began with the 2003 National Criminal Intelligence Sharing Plan (NCISP). The NCISP was developed under the auspices of the U.S. Department of Justice's Global Justice Information Sharing Initiative and was authored by its Global Intelligence Working Group.[77] Federal, local, state, and tribal law enforcement representatives all had a voice in the development of the plan. The NCISP provides specific steps that can be taken by law enforcement agencies to participate in the sharing of critical law enforcement and terrorism prevention information. Plan authors note that not every agency has the staff or resources needed to create a formal intelligence unit. Even without a dedicated intelligence unit, however, the plan says that every law enforcement organization must have the ability to effectively consume the intelligence available from a wide range of organizations at all levels of government.[78]

Efforts to share crime- and terrorism-related intelligence can result in what some have called **boundaryless policing**.[79]

Examples of boundaryless policing can be found today in so-called Regional Information Sharing Systems, or RISS. A nationwide communications and information-sharing network, RISS serves thousands of law enforcement member agencies from all 50 states, the District of Columbia, the U.S. territories, Canada, Australia, and England. A private, secure intranet (riss.net) connects six RISS centers and their participating law enforcement member agencies.[80] The RISS ATIX,[81] a special aspect of the RISS Program that began operating in 2003, allows for the secure exchange of information between government and nongovernment officials who are responsible for planning and implementing terrorism-related prevention, response, mitigation, and recovery efforts.

The federally funded SLATT Program provides specialized training for active state and local law enforcement personnel in combating terrorism and extremist criminal activity.[82] The SLATT Program has been central to antiterrorism research and training since the bombing of the Alfred P. Murrah Federal Building in Oklahoma City in 1995. SLATT focuses on the prevention of terrorism by training state and local law enforcement officers to understand, detect, deter, and investigate acts of terrorism in the United States by both international and domestic terrorists. Following the attacks of September 11, 2001, SLATT increased its training in the area of international terrorism. Other examples of information sharing in the war on terror, most spearheaded by the FBI, appear in Figure 9–6.

Integrated Automated Fingerprint Identification System (IAFIS)

* IAFIS—which had 42,203 transactions per day during its inaugural year in 1999—now has the capability to process up to 400,000 ten-print fingerprint and latent searches daily.
* The growth in fingerprint transaction volume is due to about 20,000 Department of Defense submissions per day, both domestically and overseas; and about 40,000 US-Visit Customs and Border Protection transactions per day, representing noncriminal fingerprint submissions of individuals at ports of entry into the United States.

Next Generation Identification (NGI)

* With the NGI program's implementation of advanced fingerprint identification technology in February 2011, there is an automated system true match rate of more than 99%, exceeding the previous IAFIS true match rate of approximately 92%. Processing speeds have also improved dramatically; the average response rate for criminal submissions was just eight minutes and 42 seconds in fiscal year 2010—down from two hours pre-9/11.

Biometric Technology Center

* To house the ever-expanding biometric business, the FBI has begun constructing the Biometric Technology Center, which is scheduled to be completed in late spring 2014.
* The new building will serve three purposes: it will provide additional space for CJIS to accomplish needed biometrics services; it will house the FBI's Biometric Center of Excellence, which will provide training, conference space, and office and developmental facilities; and it will accommodate joint biometric research and development efforts between the FBI and the Department of Defense.

National Crime Information Center (NCIC)

* Over the past ten years, NCIC transaction levels have increased from an average of three million daily to eight million daily. The largest increase is to support Department of Homeland Security checks at U.S. ports of entry.
* Following 9/11, the NCIC's Violent Gang and Terrorist Organization File took on added significance, becoming a central collection point for information about terror suspects and forming the basis for the Terrorist Screening Center and its centralized terrorist watchlist.

National Instant Criminal Background Check System (NICS)

* CJIS has vastly improved the NICS program, enabling it to handle transactions that have grown from 8.5 million in 2001 to well over 14 million NICS background checks for gun transfers completed in fiscal year 2010.
* To date, NICS has prevented 850,186 prohibited persons from obtaining guns.

Law Enforcement National Data Exchange (N-DEx)

* Launched in 2008, N-DEx provides a secure, online national information sharing system to the criminal justice community for their data, including incident, arrest, booking, incarceration, probation, and parole reports.
* As of May 10, 2011, N-DEx possesses more than 100 million searchable records with 500 million entities (persons, places, and things) from 4,000 agencies available to more than 20,000 users.

Law Enforcement Online (LEO)

* LEO today supports virtual command centers that provide critical Internet-based, real-time monitoring of the detached parts of an operation, from a local agency's function to national security needs. This capability is used in a wide variety of circumstances—from criminal investigations to major sporting events such as the Super Bowl, and from counterterrorism exercises and investigations to major international meetings.

CJIS Division Intelligence Group (CDIG)

* Established 2006, CDIG provides investigative and intelligence support to local, state, tribal, and federal law enforcement agencies, including the Department of Defense, DHS, and other U.S. intelligence community members.
* Since its inception, CDIG has disseminated a wide variety of intelligence documents, including intelligence information reports, intelligence assessments, threat assessments, intelligence notes, and security risk assessments.

FIGURE 9-6 **Information Sharing in the War on Terror.**
Source: Federal Bureau of Investigation, Criminal Justice Information Services Division, https://www.fbi.gov/about-us/ten-years-after-the-fbisince-9-11/just-the-facts-1/criminal-justice-information-services-division (accessed January 25, 2016).

Encryption Technologies and Personal Rights

In early 2016, Apple and the FBI entered into a contentious and very public argument over privacy rights. As the fight played out on national media, a federal magistrate in California ordered Apple to help the FBI get secure information off of an iPhone previously owned and used by San Bernardino terrorist Syed Farook. Farook and his wife, Tashfeen, were killed in a gun battle with police after shooting and killing 14 employees at a holiday party just before Christmas, 2015.

The strong encryption built into the iPhone left the FBI helpless to recover its contents. Although Apple executives agreed with the FBI that terrorism must be combatted, the company's refusal to crack its own code was based on its belief that users of Apple devices were entitled to privacy in their communications, and that, once the code was broken, any and all communications over iPhones or iPads would be "fair game" to government agencies wanting to unlock them.

About the time that the Apple/FBI rift became public, FBI Director James B. Comey spoke to members of the House Judiciary Committee in Washington, D.C. What follows is an extract of that talk:[83]

> In recent years, new methods of electronic communication have transformed our society, most visibly by enabling ubiquitous digital communications and facilitating broad e-commerce. As such, it is important for our global economy and our national security to have strong encryption standards. The development and robust adoption of strong encryption is a key tool to secure commerce and trade, safeguard private information, promote free expression and association, and strengthen cyber security. We are on the frontlines of the fight against cyber crime, and we know first-hand the damage that can be caused by those who exploit vulnerable and insecure systems. We support and encourage the use of secure networks to prevent cyber threats to our critical national infrastructure, our intellectual property, and our data so as to promote our overall safety.
>
> American citizens care deeply about privacy, and rightly so. Many companies have been responding to a market demand for products and services that protect the privacy and security of their customers. This has generated positive innovation that has been crucial to the digital economy. We, too, care about these important principles. Indeed, it is our obligation to uphold civil liberties, including the right to privacy.

> We have always respected the fundamental right of people to engage in private communications, regardless of the medium or technology. Whether it is instant messages, texts, or old-fashioned letters, citizens have the right to communicate with one another in private—without unauthorized government surveillance—not simply because the Constitution demands it, but because the free flow of information is vital to a thriving democracy.
>
> The benefits of our increasingly digital lives, however, have been accompanied by new dangers, and we have been forced to consider how criminals and terrorists might use advances in technology to their advantage. For example, malicious actors can take advantage of the Internet to covertly plot violent robberies, murders, and kidnappings; sex offenders can establish virtual communities to buy, sell, and encourage the creation of new depictions of horrific sexual abuse of children; and individuals, organized criminal networks, and nation-states can exploit weaknesses in our cyber-defenses to steal our sensitive, personal information. Investigating and prosecuting these offenders is a core responsibility and priority of the Department of Justice. As national security and criminal threats continue to evolve, the Department has worked hard to stay ahead of changing threats and changing technology.
>
> We must ensure both the fundamental right of people to engage in private communications as well as the protection of the public. One of the bedrock principles upon which we rely to guide us is the principle of judicial authorization: that if an independent judge finds reason to believe that certain private communications contain evidence of a crime, then the government can conduct a limited search for that evidence.
>
> The more we as a society rely on electronic devices to communicate and store information, the more likely it is that information that was once found in filing cabinets, letters, and photo albums will now be stored only in electronic form. We have seen case after case—from homicides and kidnappings, to drug trafficking, financial fraud, and child exploitation—where critical evidence came from smart phones, computers, and online communications.
>
> When changes in technology hinder law enforcement's ability to exercise investigative tools and follow critical leads, we may not be able to root out the child

(*continued*)

Encryption Technologies and Personal Rights (*Continued*)

predators hiding in the shadows of the Internet, or find and arrest violent criminals who are targeting our neighborhoods. We may not be able to identify and stop terrorists who are using social media to recruit, plan, and execute an attack in our country. We may not be able to recover critical information from a device that belongs to a victim who cannot provide us with the password, especially when time is of the essence. These are not just theoretical concerns. . . .

We are seeing more and more cases where we believe significant evidence resides on a phone, a tablet, or a laptop—evidence that may be the difference between

an offender being convicted or acquitted. If we cannot access this evidence, it will have ongoing, significant impacts on our ability to identify, stop, and prosecute these offenders.

We would like to emphasize that the Going Dark problem is, at base, one of technological choices and capability. We are not asking to expand the government's surveillance authority, but rather we are asking to ensure that we can continue to obtain electronic information and evidence pursuant to the legal authority that Congress has provided to us to keep America safe.

The everyday use of encryption technologies raises several important questions:

1. What are the societal and personal needs of strong encryption technologies, like those discussed in this story?
2. Should encrypted communications be subject to enforced decryption in the face of valid court orders supporting law enforcement's need to examine the contents of those communications?

Discuss advances in information and communications technology as they apply to policing.

Advances in information and communications technology that have affected police agencies include computer-aided drafting, computer-assisted training, crime mapping, geographic profiling, and crime intelligence systems. Compstat, an innovative police management strategy, stresses intelligence gathering, rapid deployment of police resources, effective tactics, and follow-up.

1. How has information and communications technology improved law enforcement?

2. What is Compstat? How did it develop?

3. What is crime mapping? How can crime mapping be utilized to improve law enforcement outcomes?

4. What is "HITS," and how can it improve the outcome of efforts made by law enforcement agencies to prevent crime?

pin map An early crime-mapping technique that used colored pins to track criminal events on a map of the police department's jurisdictional area.

geographic profiling Using crime-mapping technology to identify the likely whereabouts or residences of repeat or serial offenders.

Homicide Investigation and Tracking System (HITS) A geographic profiling system that ties various databases together (gang files, sex offender registries, parole records, and department of motor vehicle records) to facilitate simultaneous database searches.

CalGang A sophisticated software database of known gang members that field officers in California can access quickly. GangNet is a modified version of the software that is used nationwide.

predictive policing The use of analytical techniques to identify likely targets for criminals and prevent crime.

Compstat A goal-oriented police management process that relies heavily on computer technology and accountability of top-level administrators.

computer-aided drafting (CAD) A technology, adapted to meet the needs of police officers and criminal investigators, that facilitates the drafting of crime scenes on a computer so that they can be viewed three-dimensionally.

firearms training system (FATS) A full-size, fully interactive training device, not unlike flight and driving simulators, that exposes police trainees to realistic shooting scenarios. The realism is enhanced by fully encasing the trainees in a particular surrounding rather than simply putting them in front of a television screen.

Define *intelligence-led policing* and provide examples of it.

Intelligence-led policing is a method of policing that focuses resources on key criminal activities. Once crime problems are identified and quantified through intelligence assessments, key areas of criminal activity can be targeted for investigation and prevention efforts.

1. What is criminal intelligence? How does it differ from information?

2. What is intelligence-led policing? Provide some examples.

3. What is the difference between strategic intelligence and tactical intelligence? How can both forms of intelligence be used by law enforcement agencies?

4. What is National Criminal Intelligence Sharing Plan? What event provided the impetus for its creation?

intelligence-led policing The collection and analysis of information to produce an intelligence end product designed to inform police decision making at both the tactical and the strategic level. Also called *intelligence-driven policing*.

intelligence Information that has been analyzed and integrated into a useful perspective.

criminal intelligence A synergistic product intended to provide meaningful and trustworthy direction to law enforcement decision makers about complex criminality, criminal enterprises, criminal extremists, and terrorists. Also, a process that evaluates information collected from diverse sources, integrates the relevant information into a cohesive package, and produces a conclusion or estimate about a criminal phenomenon by using the scientific approach to problem solving.

tactical intelligence A type of intelligence that includes gaining or developing information related to threats of terrorism or crime and using this information to apprehend offenders, harden targets, and use strategies that will eliminate or mitigate the threat.

strategic intelligence A type of intelligence that provides information to decision makers about the changing nature of threats, enabling them to develop response strategies and reallocate resources for effective threat prevention.

National Criminal Intelligence Sharing Plan (NCISP) A formal intelligence-sharing initiative that addresses the security and intelligence needs recognized after the tragic events of September 11, 2001. It describes a nationwide communications capability that will link together all levels of law enforcement personnel, including officers on the streets, intelligence analysts, unit commanders, and police executives, for the purpose of sharing critical data.

fusion center An intelligence-gathering unit, often constituted as a collaborative effort that serves various agencies.

Describe *evidence-based policing*.

Evidence-based policing, a concept originally developed by noted police researcher Lawrence W. Sherman at the close of the twentieth century, refers to the application of social science analytical techniques in an effort to measure the effectiveness and efficiency of law enforcement policies and programs. The basic premise of evidence-based practice, says Sherman, "is that we are all entitled to our own opinions, but not to our own facts."

1. What is evidence-based policing?

2. What does the term *evidence* mean within the context of evidence-based policing?

3. Why is evidence-based policing especially important today?

Lawrence W. Sherman A noted police researcher, and contemporary proponent of evidence-based policing.

evidence-based policing The use of the best available research on the outcomes of police work to implement guidelines and evaluate agencies, units, and officers.

smart policing A systemwide and strategic view of police operations that includes consideration of causal factors of crime, system impact of police actions, partnerships with community organizations to support crime-prevention activities, and more effective policing that stresses integration of analytics, evidence-based practices, and emerging technology tools into ongoing police operations.

Explain how terrorism has made an imprint on American policing.

While the core mission of American police departments has not changed, law enforcement agencies at all levels now devote an increased amount of time and other resources to preparing for possible terrorist attacks and to gathering the intelligence necessary to thwart them.

1. In what ways has terrorism affected American policing?

2. What is boundaryless policing, and how can law enforcement agencies benefit from the concept?

3. Which federal agency sponsors Joint Terrorism Task Forces? What do such task forces do?

4. What is the Taking Command Initiative? Which organization sponsors it? What is the purpose of the initiative?

Taking Command Initiative A project undertaken by the International Association of Chiefs of Police to assess the current state of homeland security efforts in the United States and to develop and implement the actions needed to protect American communities from the specter of both crime and terrorism.

Joint Terrorism Task Force (JTTF) An FBI-sponsored group composed of federal, state, and local law enforcement personnel who are brought together to focus on a specific threat.

boundaryless policing Any of various technology-based intelligence efforts designed to combat crime and terrorism.

References

1 South Carolina General Assembly, 121st Session, 2015–2016, A71, R100, S47, http://www.scstatehouse.gov/sess121_2015-2016/bills/47.htm (accessed March 15, 2015).

2 President's Task Force on 21st Century Policing, *Final Report of the President's Task Force on 21st Century Policing* (Washington, DC: Office of Community Oriented Policing Services, 2015), p. 31.

3 P. J. Solar, *How technology is changing law enforcement: The latest high-tech innovations offer benefits and challenges for crime fighters*, http://www.policemag.com/blog/technology/story/2015/12/how-technology-is-changing-law-enforcement.aspx (accessed January 21, 2016).

4 National Institute of Justice, *Mapping and analysis for public safety*, http://www.nij.gov/topics/technology/maps/pages/welcome.aspx (accessed January 22, 2016).

5 B. A. Reaves, *Local police departments, 2013: Equipment and technology* (Washington, DC: Bureau of Justice Statistics, 2013), p. 7.

6 K. J. Peak, *Policing in America: Methods, issues, challenges*, 5th ed. (Upper Saddle River, NJ: Prentice Hall, 2006), pp. 430–31.

7 W. L. Perry, B. McInnis, C. C. Price, S. C. Smith, and J. S. Hollywood, *Predictive policing: The role of crime forecasting in law enforcement operations* (Santa Monica, CA: RAND Corporation, 2013), p. xiv.

8 G. O. Mohler, M. B. Short, S. Malinowski, M. Johnson, G. E. Tita, A. L. Bertozzi, and P. J. Brantingham, "Randomized controlled field trials of predictive policing," *Journal of the American Statistical Association*, vol. 110 (2015), pp. 1399–1411.

9 S. Wolpert, "Predictive policing substantially reduces crime in Los Angeles during months-long test," UCLA Newsroom, October 7, 2015, http://newsroom.ucla.edu/releases/predictive-policing-substantially-reduces-crime-in-los-angeles-during-months-long-test (accessed January 22, 2016).

10 B. A. Reaves, *Local police departments, 2013: Equipment and technology* (Washington, DC: Bureau of Justice Statistics, 2013), p. 3.

11 L. J. Westphal, "The in-car camera: Value and impact," *Police Chief*, November 9, 2004, http://www.policechiefmagazine.org/magazine/index.cfm?fuseaction=display&article_id=358 (accessed January 21, 2016).

12 D. J. Roberts and M. Casanova, *Automated License Plate Recognition (ALPR) use by law enforcement: Policy and operational guide, summary* (Washington, DC: U.S. Department of Justice, 2012), p. 2.

13 Ibid., p. 10.

14 https://www.aclu.org/feature/you-are-being-tracked (accessed January 21, 2016).

15 Ibid.

16 Police Executive Research Forum, *Future trends in policing* (Washington, DC: Office of Community Oriented Policing Services, 2014).

17 Ibid., p. 27.

18 J. D. Lieberman, D. Koetzle, and M. Sakiyama, "Police departments' use of Facebook: Patterns and policy issues," *Police Quarterly*, vol. 16 (2013), pp. 438–62.

19 International Association of Chiefs of Police, *2015 Social Media Survey Results*, http://www.iacpsocialmedia.org/Portals/1/documents/FULL%202015%20Social%20Media%20Survey%20Results.pdf (accessed January 22, 2016).

20 E. Silverman, *NYPD battles crime: Innovative strategies in policing* (Boston: Northeastern University Press, 1999).

21 D. Weisburd et al., *Compstat and organizational change: Findings from a national survey* (Washington, DC: Police Foundation, 2001). For a review of Compstat-like strategies in six cities, see also M. H. Moore and A. A. Braga, "Measuring and improving police performance: The lessons of Compstat and its progeny," *Policing: An International Journal of Police Strategies and Management*, vol. 26 (2003), pp. 439–53.

22 E. Brady, "Compstat: Mapping, accountability, equal less crime," *USA Today*, December 1, 1997, p. 18A.

23 K. Harries, *Mapping crime: Principle and practice* (Washington, DC: National Institute of Justice, 1999), p. 79.

24 Ibid.

25 Ibid.

26 J. Maple, *The crime fighter* (New York: Doubleday, 1999), p. 93.

27 Silverman, *NYPD battles crime*, p. 104.

28 Harries, *Mapping crime*, p. 80.

29 R. Garner and L. Hoover, "The Compstat craze: Emphasizing accountability in policing," paper presented at the annual meeting of the Academy of Criminal Justice Sciences in New Orleans, 2000.

30 Ibid., p. 11.

31 D. Pederson, "Bullets in the big easy," *Newsweek*, December 23, 1996, p. 29.

32 J. Raymond, "Forget the pipe, Sherlock: Gear for tomorrow's detectives," *Newsweek*, June 22, 1998, p. 12.

33 VirTra Systems, http://www.virtra.com/ (accessed January 21, 2016).

34 Advanced Interactive Solutions, "PRISim," www.ais-solutions.co.uk/prisim.php (accessed January 21, 2016).

35 Ibid.

36 The concept of intelligence-led policing appears to have been first fully articulated in A. Smith, ed., *Intelligence-led policing* (Richmond, VA: International Association of Law Enforcement Intelligence Analysts, 1997).

37 M. Peterson, *Intelligence-led policing: The new intelligence architecture* (Washington, DC: Bureau of Justice Assistance, 2005), p. 3.

38 Ibid., p. 11.

39 I. D. L. Carter, *Law enforcement intelligence: A guide for state, local, and tribal law enforcement agencies* (Washington, DC: U.S. Department of Justice, 2004), p. 7.

40 Ibid.

41 Much of the information and some of the wording in this section is taken from Carter, *Law enforcement intelligence*.

42 Peterson, *Intelligence-led policing*, p. 3.

43 Carter, *Law enforcement intelligence*, p. 8.

44 Ibid.

45 Peterson, *Intelligence-led policing*, p. 12.

46 Ibid.

47 R. Wright, "Management of the intelligence unit," in *Intelligence 2000: Revising the basic elements*, eds. M. B. Peterson, R. Wright, and B. Morehouse, p. 69 (Lawrenceville, NJ: International Association of Law Enforcement Intelligence Analysts and Law Enforcement Intelligence Units, 2001).

48 Peterson, *Intelligence-led policing*, p. 13.

49 Ibid., p. 6.

50 Ibid., p. 7.

51 Ibid.

52 This section draws from Peterson, *Intelligence-led policing*, p. 9.

53 Ibid.

54 D. Lambert, "Intelligence-led policing in a fusion center," *FBI Law Enforcement Bulletin*, December 2010, www.fbi.gov/stats-services/publications/law-enforcement-bulletin/Dec2010/intelligence_feature (accessed January 14, 2011).

55 Ibid., p. 11.

56 "Evidence-based policing," Police Foundation press release, March 17, 1998, www.policefoundation.org/docs/evidence.html (accessed January 5, 2009).

57 Lawrence W. Sherman, *Evidence-based policing* (Washington, DC: Police Foundation, 1998), p. 3.

58 Much of the information in this section comes from Sherman, *Evidence-based policing*.

59 Neil Wain and Alex Murray, "Gathering evidence," PoliceProfessional.com, March 24, 2001, http://gemini.gmu.edu/cebcp/BritishSocietyEBPolicing.pdf (accessed May 18, 2011).

60 Carl J. Jensen III, "Consuming and applying research: Evidence-based policing," *Police Chief*, vol. 73, no. 2 (February 2006), http://www.policechiefmagazine.org/magazine/index.cfm?fuseaction=display_arch&article_id=815&issue_id=22006 (accessed January 21, 2016).

61 Ibid.

62 University of Cambridge, "Evidence-based policing: Possibilities and prospects," revised and final program announcement, June 30, 2008.

63 https://www.crimesolutions.gov/about.aspx (accessed January 25, 2016).

64 Smart Policing Initiative, "Background," www.smartpolicinginitiative.com/background (accessed May 2, 2014).

65 Steve Rickman, "Defining the Smart Policing Initiative," www.smartpolicinginitiative.com/spi-events/defining-smart-policing-initiative (accessed January 21, 2016).

66 Charlie Beck, "Predictive policing: What can we learn from Wal-Mart and Amazon about fighting crime in a recession?," *The Police Chief*, April 2012, www.policechiefmagazine.org/magazine/index.cfm?fuseaction=display_arch&article_id=1942&issue_id=112009 (accessed January 21, 2016).

67 Police Executive Research Forum, *Local law enforcement's role in preventing and responding to terrorism* (Washington, DC: Police Executive Research Forum, October 2, 2001).

68 Council on Foreign Relations, "Terrorism questions and answers: Police departments," www.cfr.org/publication/10214/police_departments.html?breadcrumb=default (accessed January 21, 2016).

69 Ibid.

70 M. Weissenstein, "NYPD shifts focus to terrorism, long considered the turf of federal agents," Associated Press, March 21, 2003.

71 Ibid.

72 International Association of Chiefs of Police, *From hometown security to homeland security: IACP's principles for a locally designed and nationally coordinated homeland security strategy* (Alexandria, VA: International Association of Chiefs of Police, 2005).

73 Ibid.

74 R. J. Jordan, Federal Bureau of Investigation, Congressional statement on information sharing before the U.S. Senate Committee on the Judiciary, Subcommittee on Administrative Oversight and the Courts, Washington, DC, April 17, 2002, www2.fbi.gov/congress/congress01/mcchesney111301.htm (accessed January 21, 2016).

75 U.S. Department of Justice, "Attorney General Ashcroft and Deputy Attorney General Thompson announce reorganization and mobilization of the nation's justice and law enforcement resources," press release, November 8, 2001.

76 https://www.fbi.gov/news/speeches/standing-together-against-terrorism-and-fear-tossed-by-the-waves-but-never-sunk (accessed January 25, 2016).

77 The plan was an outgrowth of the IACP Criminal Intelligence Sharing Summit held in Alexandria, Virginia, in March 2002. Results of the summit are documented in International Association of Chiefs of Police, *Recommendations from the IACP intelligence summit, criminal intelligence sharing* (Washington, DC: COPS Office, 2002).

78 Office of Justice Programs, *The national criminal intelligence sharing plan* (Washington, DC: U.S. Department of Justice, 2003).

79 The term comes from Bud Levin, as quoted in Gene Stephens, "Policing the future: Law enforcement's new challenges," *The Futurist*, March–April 2005, p. 55.

80 Visit RISS at www.riss.net (accessed January 21, 2016).

81 http://www.riss.net/Resources/ATIX (accessed January 21, 2016).

82 State and Local Anti-Terrorism Training Program, www.slatt.org/default.aspx (accessed January 21, 2016).

83 James B. Comey, Director, Federal Bureau of Investigation, "Statement Before the House Judiciary Committee," Washington, DC, March 1, 2016.

10

Policing and the Law

1 Discuss the influence of the Fourth Amendment on searches and seizures.

2 Discuss the constitutional rules governing confessions and interrogations.

Mikael Karlsson/Alamy Stock Photo

PLAYING BY THE RULES: A JOB REQUIREMENT

Not only do police officers enforce the law, but they are also held accountable under it. The principle that no one—not even those who make and enforce the law—is immune from the law's reach is known as the *rule of law*. In societies where the rule of law operates, fairness and equal treatment before the law are accorded to everyone—no matter their social status or political position.

In a society like ours, effective police officers must be aware of how the law governs their everyday activities. When they make arrests, search suspects, and interrogate them—and even when they make simple observations and draw certain actionable conclusions—various constitutional considerations come into play. Those constitutional issues, which are sometimes collectively referred to as *the law of search and seizure*, are the focus of this chapter.

Consider the Supreme Courts' decision in *Riley* v. *California*[1], a case dealing with the question of whether a police officer's warrantless search of an arrestee's cell phone violated the Fourth Amendment. Riley was arrested for weapons violations following a traffic stop. A police officer then searched him, which is permissible under a popular exception to the Fourth Amendment's warrant requirement (search incident to arrest), discussed in greater detail later in this chapter. As part of the search, the officer also examined Riley's cell phone and found information linking him to a recent gang shooting. Later at the police station, a gang unit detective further examined the phone, confirming the arresting officer's suspicions that Riley was involved in the recent shooting. Riley attempted to exclude the evidence obtained from his cell phone, arguing that the officers engaged in an unreasonable search. In a unanimous and

Mark Bugnaski/AP Images

somewhat unexpected decision, the Supreme Court agreed. It decided in part that "a search of digital information on a cell phone does not further . . . government interests . . . and implicates substantially greater individual privacy interests than a brief physical search." The *Riley* decision was heralded as a huge victory for privacy advocates, including the American Civil Liberties Union and other organizations concerned with potential overreach by authorities in a digital age.

In this chapter, we will examine the rules governing searches and seizures, as well as those pertaining to confessions and interrogations. The rules we will be discussing stem largely from court interpretations of the Fourth and Fifth Amendments to the U.S. Constitution, and it would be a good idea to review both amendments before proceeding. While the language in these amendments may seem to be relatively straightforward, it has been scrutinized in scores of federal court cases.

▶ *Search and Seizure*

The issue of how to properly conduct searches and seizures ranks as among the most important in law enforcement today. Serving search warrants, arresting suspects, making traffic stops, stopping suspicious individuals on foot, inventorying impounded vehicles, and a host of other activities require an intimate knowledge of the Fourth Amendment. Fourth Amendment violations can result in lawsuits, complaints, difficulty convicting defendants, the release of criminals into the community, and even criminal charges against law enforcement officers.

When the Fourth Amendment Applies

The **Fourth Amendment** states the following:

> The right of the people to be secure in their persons, houses, papers, and effects, against unreasonable searches and seizures, shall not be violated, and no Warrants shall issue, but upon probable cause, supported by Oath or affirmation and particularly describing the place to be searched, and the persons or things to be seized.

The Fourth Amendment applies when a search or seizure is being contemplated (search warrants are discussed later in this chapter) or takes place. **Searches** are, as the term suggests, activities performed in order to find evidence to be used in a criminal prosecution. To define when a *Fourth Amendment search* takes place, however, two important elements must be considered: (1) whether the search is a product of **government action** and (2) whether the government action infringes on the individual's **reasonable expectation of privacy**. We will return to this topic shortly.

The term **seizure** has a dual meaning in policing. First, property can be seized, and a search often results in the seizure of evidence. For example, if the police successfully serve a search warrant to look for illegal weapons at 345 Oak Street, any illegal weapons they find there will be seized. But people can also be seized. Seizures of people can occur almost anywhere and at any time. An arrest, for example, is considered a seizure within the meaning of the Fourth Amendment.

The next stage in the Fourth Amendment analysis requires that we focus on the **reasonableness** of the search or seizure. Once Fourth Amendment protections have been triggered, we must ask whether the officers acted in line with Fourth Amendment requirements. If a person has been arrested, for example, the question is whether the police had adequate reason to believe that the person arrested in fact committed the crime. When courts focus on the reasonableness of a search or seizure, they speak in terms of **justification**. If the police engage in searches or seizures without justification, they violate the Fourth Amendment.

The only justification mentioned in the Fourth Amendment is probable cause. Consequently, lay readers may be inclined to think that any search or seizure based on a lesser degree of certainty than probable cause would violate the Fourth Amendment. For a time, this was the case, but in recent decades, the U.S. Supreme Court has carved out exceptions to the Fourth Amendment's probable cause requirement. The Court has ruled that there are certain situations in which the police can seize people or look for evidence with a lesser degree of certainty than probable cause. These situations are described later in this chapter.

Defining Search and Seizure

Not every act of looking for evidence can be considered a search within the meaning of the Fourth Amendment, nor is every act of "grabbing" something or someone considered a seizure. For example, private citizens may look for evidence,

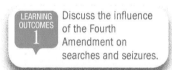 LEARNING OUTCOMES 1 Discuss the influence of the Fourth Amendment on searches and seizures.

but their actions are not bound by the Fourth Amendment because private citizens are not government actors. The Fourth Amendment protects citizens from *government* action. As such, one requirement in determining when a search occurs is to ascertain *who* is looking for evidence. And although the Fourth Amendment restricts government action, it is not the case that government actors always engage in searches when looking for evidence. There are many things the police can do to look for evidence—such as looking in open fields and public areas, examining items that have been discarded, observing people and things in public view, and so on—without being bound by the Fourth Amendment.

What Is a Search?

The Fourth Amendment's protection against unreasonable searches and seizures has been limited by the courts to behavior that is governmental in nature. When a private individual seizes evidence or otherwise conducts a search, Fourth Amendment protections are not triggered.[2]

For a Fourth Amendment search to occur, the government actor must also infringe on a person's reasonable expectation of privacy. What is a reasonable expectation of privacy? Prior to 1967, the definition of *search* was closely tied to property interests. Police action was deemed a search only if it physically infringed on an individual's property. Essentially, the activity

had to amount to what would otherwise be considered common law trespass for it to be considered a search. Any police activity that was not trespassory in nature was not considered a search. This definition became outdated in the landmark decision in *Katz* v. *United States* (1967).[3]

In *Katz*, federal agents placed a listening device outside a phone booth in which Katz was having a conversation. Katz made incriminating statements during the course of his conversation, and the Federal Bureau of Investigation (FBI) sought to use the statements against him at trial. The lower court ruled that the FBI's activities did not amount to a search because there was no physical entry into the phone booth. The U.S. Supreme Court reversed the lower court's decision, holding that the Fourth Amendment "protects people, not places," so its reach "cannot turn upon the presence or absence of a physical intrusion into any given enclosure."[4] Instead, the Fourth Amendment definition of *search* turns on the concept of privacy. In the Court's words, "The Government's activities in electronically listening to and recording words violated the privacy upon which [Katz] justifiably relied while using the telephone booth and thus constituted a 'search and seizure' within the meaning of the Fourth Amendment."[5]

Despite the seemingly profound change in the *search and seizure* definition following *Katz*, several subsequent decisions have interpreted the *Katz* ruling rather narrowly. For example, the Supreme Court has since ruled that a Fourth Amendment search or seizure occurs only when there has been an infringement on an expectation of privacy that society (through the eyes of a court) is willing to accept as reasonable.[6] It further stated that "[w]hat a person knowingly exposes to the public, even in his own home or office, is not subject to Fourth Amendment protection."[7] Protection is afforded only for "what he seeks to preserve as private."[8]

What Is a Seizure?

The Supreme Court has concluded that the seizure of tangible property occurs "when there is some meaningful interference with an individual's possessory interest in that property."[9] A seizure of a person occurs when a police officer, by means of physical force or show of authority, intentionally restrains an individual's liberty in such a manner that a reasonable person would believe that he or she is not free to leave.[10] Another way to understand a Fourth Amendment seizure is by asking the question, Would a reasonable person believe that he or she is free to decline the officer's requests or otherwise terminate the encounter?[11] If the answer is no, a seizure has occurred.

There can be several types of seizures of a person, just as there can be many different types of searches. For example, a person can be arrested, perhaps the most significant form of seizure. But a stop-and-frisk situation also amounts to a seizure, as we will see later. A seizure can also occur without any physical contact; for example, an officer can block a person's path, which could amount to a seizure. Add to that the number of possible search scenarios, including searches with and without warrants, and things get even more complex. Figure 10–1 summarizes the differences between searches and seizures.

Search

Government actor must infringe on a person's reasonable expectation of privacy. Fourth Amendment protections only extend to government officials such as a police officer working in his or her official capacity.

Private citizens are not government actors, unless they act at the behest of a governmental official (e.g., an officer asks a private citizen to conduct the search *for* him or her).

Seizure

Meaningful interference with an individual's possessory interest in that property. A seizure of a person occurs when a police officer, by means of physical force or show of authority, intentionally restrains an individual's liberty in such a manner that a reasonable person would believe that he or she is not free to leave.

FIGURE 10-1 **Search and Seizure.**

Justification

To this point, we have addressed only the threshold question of whether the Fourth Amendment applies; that is, has a search or a seizure occurred? If the answer is no, the matter would go no further, and justification would not matter because a search or seizure did not occur. However, if, in the case of a search, the government's action infringes on a person's reasonable expectation of privacy, the next issue involves deciding whether the police acted within the limits of the Fourth Amendment.

The police must have justification, or cause, before they can conduct a search or a seizure. Justification must be in place a priori, that is, before a person or evidence is sought in an area protected by the Fourth Amendment. The police cannot conduct illegal searches to obtain evidence and then argue *after the fact* that what they did was appropriate.

Justification can be viewed as something of a sliding scale that hinges on the type of intrusion the police make. Generally, the more intrusive the police action, the higher the level of justification required. Likewise, the lower the level of intrusion, the lower the justification the police need. Three primary levels of justification recognized by the courts are considered in this chapter: (1) **probable cause**—the standard for searches and seizures; (2) **reasonable suspicion**—the standard for stop-and-frisk activities; and (3) **administrative justification**—the standard for administrative searches.

Probable Cause

Probable cause has been defined by the U.S. Supreme Court as more than bare suspicion; it exists when "the facts and circumstances within [the officers'] knowledge and of which they [have] reasonably trustworthy information [are] sufficient to warrant a prudent man in believing that the [suspect] had committed or was committing an offense."[12] The Court had noted in an earlier case, "The substance of all the definitions of probable cause is a reasonable ground for belief of guilt."[13] A more practical definition of probable cause is that it consists of more than 50% certainty. Probable cause lies somewhere below absolute certainty and proof beyond a reasonable doubt (the latter is

necessary to obtain a criminal conviction) but above a hunch or reasonable suspicion (the latter is required to conduct a stop-and-frisk). See Figure 10–2 for an overview of the components of probable cause.

Reasonable Suspicion

While the justification required to conduct a search or a seizure is probable cause, much police activity does not reach the level of intrusion that occurs when a search or seizure is carried out. For example, the police routinely confront people on the street to question them or pull over automobiles to enforce traffic laws. If probable cause were required under such circumstances, there would be very little the police could do in terms of investigating suspicious activity.

Recognizing how essential these lesser intrusions are to the police mission, the Supreme Court established a different level of justification for such activities in *Terry* v. *Ohio* (1968).[14] The standard the Court created was "reasonable suspicion." Reasonable suspicion is something below probable cause but above a hunch.

The facts of the *Terry* case are interesting: An officer's attention was drawn to two men on a street corner who appeared to the officer to be "casing" a store for a robbery. The officer approached the men and asked them to identify themselves and then proceeded to pat the men down. Finding a gun on each man, he placed the men under arrest. They later sought to have the guns excluded as evidence from trial (the exclusionary rule is discussed in the next chapter), but the U.S. Supreme Court eventually held that the officer's actions were valid in the interests of "effective crime prevention and detection."[15] It also stated that because "street encounters between citizens and police officers are incredibly rich in diversity,"[16] a lower standard than probable cause is required.

As a level of justification lying below probable cause, reasonable suspicion is "considerably less than proof of wrongdoing by a preponderance of evidence"[17] but more than a mere hunch. Think of reasonable suspicion as more than 0% certainty (i.e., more than a mere hunch) and less than 51% certainty (i.e., less than probable cause).

Prior record
Flight from the scene
Suspicious conduct
Admission
Incriminating evidence
Unusual hour
Suspect resembling perpetrator
Evasive and untruthful responses to questions
Obvious attempt to hide something
Presence in a high-crime area or near the crime scene
Furtive gestures
Knowing too much

FIGURE 10-2 **Components of Probable Cause.**

Administrative Justification

A third level of justification has arisen by virtue of the fact that government entities occasionally conduct searches in circumstances other than criminal investigations. There are occasions where some sort of search is necessary, but that search is not conducted in an effort to detect evidence of a crime, such as a cache of illegal weapons. We have seen that searches and seizures aimed at obtaining evidence intended to be used in a criminal proceeding cannot occur without appropriate justification: probable cause for a search or seizure or reasonable suspicion for a stop-and-frisk. The Supreme Court has created a different level of justification for noncriminal, or administrative, searches.

Administrative searches attempt to achieve a balance between protecting individuals' privacy interests and protecting public safety. Where public-safety concerns outweigh individual privacy interests, an administrative search may be permissible. One such search that has routinely been sanctioned by the courts is a sobriety checkpoint set up for the purpose of protecting the public by removing drunk drivers from roadways. Other examples of permissible administrative searches are discussed later in this chapter. For a summary of the various levels of proof, see Figure 10–3.

The Rules of Search and Seizure

Assuming that a case arises wherein the Fourth Amendment applies and officers have proper justification, what's next? The answer depends on whether the action in question is a search, a seizure, a stop, or an administrative search. It also depends on whether a warrant is required.

Arrest Warrant Requirements

The Fourth Amendment does not *require* an arrest warrant for all arrests, but the U.S. Supreme Court has adopted the view that arrest warrants are preferable. They can be obtained when the police know who they want to arrest but the person is not immediately available (e.g., he or she has escaped confinement). In contrast, if a police officer observes a person rob a bank, then it would obviously be impractical to require the officer to obtain an arrest warrant before arresting the suspect.

When are arrest warrants required? Essentially, the rule is this: An arrest made in a public place does not require an arrest warrant (but does require probable cause); an arrest made in a private place usually requires a warrant, unless special circumstances exist. In its landmark decision in *Payton* v. *New York* (1980),[18] the U.S. Supreme Court held that the Fourth Amendment prohibits warrantless, nonconsensual

Think About It...

Drug Courier Profiling
In *United States* v. *Montoya De Hernandez*, the U.S. Supreme Court ruled that "the detention of a traveler at the border, beyond the scope of a routine customs search and inspection, is justified at its inception if customs agents, considering all the facts surrounding the traveler and her trip, reasonably suspect that the traveler is smuggling contraband in her alimentary canal." Profiling is also used in airports and other ports of entry to detect suspected terrorists. *What are the characteristics of suspected terrorists? How many otherwise law-abiding people are stopped and inconvenienced? Do the benefits of the practice outweigh the costs? Explain.*

United States Customs and Border Patrol

entries into private homes for the purpose of making an arrest. The Court has also required that arrests made in third-party homes require a warrant to search the property for the person to be arrested. To enter without a warrant could amount to a search without proper justification, in violation of the Fourth Amendment.[19]

Assuming that an arrest warrant is required, it must conform to certain requirements. First, a neutral and detached magistrate must authorize the warrant. Second, a showing of probable cause must be made. Finally, the warrant should be sufficiently particular so as to minimize the possibility of arresting the wrong person.

Neutral and Detached Magistrate. The U.S. Supreme Court has said,

> The point of the Fourth Amendment . . . is not that it denies law enforcement the support of the usual inferences reasonable men draw from evidence. Its protection consists in requiring that those inferences be drawn by a neutral and detached magistrate instead of being judged by the officer engaged in the often competitive enterprise of ferreting out crime.[20]

Most judges are considered neutral and detached. Even so, the Supreme Court has focused on this first critical warrant requirement in a number of cases. For example, the Court has declared that a state attorney general cannot issue a search warrant.[21] State attorneys general are chief prosecutors and thus inclined to side with law enforcement officers. Similarly, in another case the Court decided that the president, acting through the attorney general of the United States, cannot authorize electronic surveillance without judicial approval.[22]

Proof beyond a reasonable doubt = around 95% certainty
Probable cause = more than 50% certainty
Preponderance of the evidence = civil equivalent of probable cause
Reasonable suspicion = between 1% and 50% certainty
Administrative justification = balancing approach
Hunch = no justification or certainty at all

FIGURE 10–3 A Comparison of Levels of Proof.

	Neutral and Detached Magistrate	Probable Cause	Particularity
Arrest Warrant Requirements	A neutral and detached magistrate must authorize the arrest warrant.	The officer applying for the warrant must simply show probable cause that the person to be arrested committed the crime but not that the suspect will be found at a particular location.	If the suspect's name is known, then simply supplying the suspect's name is enough to meet the particularity requirement. There are some situations, however, where the suspect's name is *not* known. In such situations, a sufficiently specific description of the suspect supports issuance of a "John Doe" warrant. As long as other officers may locate the suspect with reasonable effort, the suspect's name is not required.
Search Warrant Requirements	Similar to the arrest warrant requirements, a neutral and detached magistrate must authorize the search warrant.	Unlike the arrest warrant requirements, the probable cause showing in a search warrant is twofold. First, the officer applying for the search warrant must show probable cause that the items to be seized are connected with criminal activity. Second, the officer must show probable cause that the items to be seized are in the location to be searched.	If a warrant does not "particularly" describe the place to be searched and the items to be seized, then it is not automatically deemed in violation of the Fourth Amendment. If there is a reasonable basis for the officers' mistaken belief, then the warrant will most likely be upheld.

FIGURE 10–4 Arrest and Search Warrant Requirements.

Probable Cause. The probable cause showing in an arrest warrant is not particularly complex. The Court has stated, "If there is sufficient evidence of a citizen's participation in a felony to persuade a judicial officer that his arrest is justified, it is constitutionally reasonable to require him to open his doors to the officers of the law."[23]

Particularity. There are two ways to satisfy the Fourth Amendment's particularity requirement with regard to arrest warrants, which are highlighted in Figure 10–4.

Search Warrant Requirements

Search warrants have the same three requirements as arrest warrants. The neutral and detached magistrate requirement remains the same, but there *are* differences in terms of probable cause and particularity, which have been highlighted in Figure 10–4.

Searches and Seizures without Warrants

Searches without warrants are far more common than those with warrants. Police can, for example, rely on the hot-pursuit doctrine to chase a fleeing suspect into a private area and make an arrest without a warrant. Requiring officers to secure warrants in all such instances would be impractical. Similarly, it would endanger the public's safety if police were required to obtain a warrant in the face of a clear and sudden threat to public safety. Warrantless searches thus come in several varieties: (1) searches incident to arrest, (2) searches based on exigent circumstances, (3) automobile searches, (4) plain-view searches, and (5) consent searches (see Figure 10–5).

Searches Incident to Arrest. The first type of permissible warrantless search is known as a **search incident to arrest**. The U.S. Supreme Court has said that a warrantless search incident to arrest is permitted "to remove any weapons that the [arrestee] might seek to use in order to resist arrest or effect his escape" and to "seize any evidence on the arrestee's person in order to prevent its concealment or destruction."[24]

Probable cause to arrest must always precede a search incident to arrest.[25] This is to restrict officers from engaging in "fishing expeditions," searches based on less than probable cause that could potentially result in establishing the probable cause needed to make an arrest.

If probable cause to arrest is in place, the officer is not required to formally arrest the suspect before engaging in the search,[26] but the search should take place *soon* after the arrest if one is made. In other words, the search must be *contemporaneous* to the arrest. In *Preston* v. *United States* (1964),[27] the case that established this rule, Justice Hugo Black observed that the "justifications [for the search incident to arrest] are absent where a search is remote in time or place from the arrest."[28] In *Preston*, police officers arrested the occupants of a car and took them to jail. After this, the officers searched the car, which had been towed to an impound lot. In reversing the lower court's ruling, the Supreme Court noted that the possibilities of destruction of evidence or danger to the officers were no longer in place, as the suspects were no longer present to pose a threat.[29]

What is the scope of a search incident to arrest? In *Chimel* v. *California* (1969),[30] the Court held that "a warrantless search

Searches Incident to Arrest	Search made at the time of or shortly following an arrest, done out of a concern for the safety of the arresting officer and others.
Searches Based on Exigent Circumstances	Search based on (1) **Hot pursuit**—police have probable cause to believe that the person they are chasing has committed a crime and is on the premises entered. (2) Police have reason to believe that the suspect will escape or that further harm will occur if not immediately apprehended. (3) **Evanescent evidence**—evidence likely to disappear during time necessary to obtain a warrant.
Automobile Searches	Search admissible when (1) there is probable cause to believe that the vehicle contains evidence of a crime and (2) securing a warrant is impractical.
Plain-View Searches	Search authorized when (1) the police are lawfully in the area where the evidence is located, (2) the item is "immediately apparent" as being subject to seizure, and (3) the discovery of the evidence is "inadvertent."
Consent Searches	If a person gives consent to search, he or she effectively waives Fourth Amendment protection. *Consent must be voluntary and not the result of duress or coercion.

FIGURE 10–5 Searches and Seizures Without Warrants.

'incident to a lawful arrest' may generally extend to the area that is considered to be in the 'possession' or under the 'control' of the person arrested."[31] It went on to create the so-called **arm-span rule**. In the Court's words, a search incident to arrest is limited to the area "within [the] immediate control" of the person arrested, that is, "the area from within which he might have obtained either a weapon or something that could have been used as evidence against him."[32]

In *Maryland* v. *Buie* (1990),[33] the Court further expanded the scope of the incident search in two ways. It held that the police may, as part of a search incident to arrest, look in areas immediately adjoining the place of arrest for other individuals who might attack the officers; no justification is required. The key is that such a search must occur immediately following an arrest. Next, the Court held that at any point up to the time the arrest is completed, the police may engage in a **protective sweep** (i.e., "a cursory visual inspection of those places in which a person might be hiding"), but reasonable suspicion must exist for such a sweep to be justified. No justification is required *after* arrest, but reasonable suspicion is required to engage in a sweep up to the point of the arrest.

If a suspect is arrested during a traffic stop, police may search him or her *and* the vehicle; however, they may search the vehicle without a warrant only if it is reasonable to assume that the arrestee could access the vehicle or that the vehicle

contains evidence of the offense for which the individual was arrested.[34] In 2014, the Supreme Court reached its most recent search incident to arrest decision (see also this chapter's opening story), holding in *Riley* v. *California*[35] that police may not generally conduct a warrantless search of a cell phone pursuant to lawful arrest.

Searches Based on Exigent Circumstances. Searches (and, by extension, arrests) based on **exigent circumstances** are permissible without warrants. Generally, three types of exigencies (emergencies) have been recognized: (1) hot pursuit, (2) the likelihood of a suspect's escaping or presenting a danger to others, and (3) evanescent evidence.

The Supreme Court established a **hot-pursuit exception** to the Fourth Amendment's warrant requirement in *Warden* v. *Hayden* (1967).[36] In that case, the police were called by taxicab drivers who reported that their taxi company had been robbed. The police then located and followed the suspect to a house and were granted entry by the suspect's wife. When they entered, they found the suspect upstairs, pretending to be asleep. However, as they were searching the house for the suspect, the police found and seized clothing, a shotgun, and a pistol, which were used as evidence against the suspect at trial. The Court found that the warrantless entry was "reasonable" because the "exigencies of the situation made that course imperative."[37] Several reasons were offered for the decision. First, as Justice William Brennan stated, "The Fourth Amendment does not require police officers to delay in the course of an investigation if to do so would gravely endanger their lives or the lives of others."[38] Second, "[s]peed . . . was essential, and only a thorough search of the house for persons and weapons could have insured that Hayden was the only man present and that the police had control of all weapons which could be used against them or to effect an escape."[39]

Despite its sweeping language in the *Hayden* decision, the Supreme Court has imposed a number of restrictions on searches and seizures premised on hot pursuit. One court has observed that "[a] hot pursuit, by itself, creates no necessity for dispensing with a warrant."[40] Similarly, the Ninth Circuit has stated that police officers must reasonably believe (1) "that the suspect either knows or will learn at any moment that they are in immediate danger of apprehension," (2) that "evidence is being currently removed or destroyed and it is impractical to avert the situation without immediately arresting the suspects or seizing the evidence," or (3) that "a suspect is currently endangering the lives of themselves or others."[41]

Third, the police must begin hot pursuit from a lawful starting point. If officers are unlawfully on someone's private property, they will not succeed in claiming hot pursuit to justify any further warrantless action. However, in *United States* v. *Santana* (1976),[42] the Supreme Court upheld the warrantless arrest of a woman in her house when the police *observed* a crime on private property from a public vantage point. In that case, police officers observed Santana standing in the open doorway of her house with a brown paper bag that they believed to contain narcotics. They pursued her into the house and arrested her. This decision suggests that the police can pursue from a public vantage point a suspect whom they observe on private property.

Fourth, the hot-pursuit doctrine applies only to "serious" offenses. These include felonies and some serious misdemeanors.[43] This is perhaps the most important restriction on the hot-pursuit doctrine—and, indeed, on exigent circumstance searches in general.

A fifth restriction on hot pursuits concerns the scope of the search. Generally, the scope of a search based on hot pursuit is broad. In *Hayden*, the Supreme Court stated, "The permissible scope of search must, at the least, be as broad as may reasonably be necessary to prevent the dangers that the suspect at large in the house may resist or escape."[44] However, the search must be "prior to or immediately contemporaneous with" the arrest of the suspect. Also, officers may search only where the suspect or weapons might reasonably be found.

Moving beyond hot pursuit, it is also permissible for police officers to dispense with the warrant requirement when it is likely that a suspect could escape or endanger others, even in the absence of hot pursuit.[45] This means they can chase and apprehend the suspect without the need to first secure a warrant.

Evanescent evidence refers to evidence that is likely to disappear if the officers took the time to obtain a warrant.[46] Examples of evanescent evidence are alcohol in a person's bloodstream or drugs that are in the process of being destroyed, such as by flushing them down the toilet.[47]

In *Missouri* v. *McNeely*,[48] the Supreme Court ruled that the natural dissipation of alcohol in a person's bloodstream does not necessarily constitute an exigency justifying a warrantless search. The Court stopped short of deciding that *all* blood draws must be supported by a warrant, but it certainly sent a message that a warrant should be obtained whenever practical.

In *Kentucky* v. *King*,[49] the Supreme Court held that police can make a forcible warrantless entry into a private residence if they have reason to believe evidence is being destroyed. In that case, officers smelled marijuana outside an apartment, knocked loudly, and announced their presence. They then heard what they believed was the sound of evidence being destroyed. They announced their intent to enter, kicked in the door, and found drugs in plain view—and other evidence during the course of a protective sweep. The Supreme Court ruled that the evidence was admissible.

Automobile Searches. The warrantless search of an automobile is permissible when (1) there is probable cause to believe that the vehicle contains evidence of a crime and (2) securing a warrant is impractical.[50] This rule resulted from a Prohibition-era case involving the vehicle stop of a suspect who was known to have previously engaged in the sale of bootleg whiskey. A warrantless search of the car revealed 68 bottles of illegal liquor. The Supreme Court upheld the warrantless search on the grounds that the evidence would have been lost if the officers had been required to secure a warrant. It pointed out that the inherent mobility of motor vehicles made it impractical to obtain a warrant, that people enjoy a lesser expectation of privacy in their vehicles, and that vehicles are subject to extensive government regulation, essentially making driving a privilege.

Several subsequent decisions have dealt with the definition of an automobile, the role of probable cause, whether warrants are required, and the scope of automobile searches. Concerning the first of these issues, any vehicle that serves a transportation function is considered to be an automobile. Four factors are used to determine whether a vehicle serves a transportation function: (1) whether it is mobile or stationary, (2) whether it is licensed, (3) whether it is connected to utilities, and (4) whether it has convenient access to the road. If, for example, a trailer is on blocks, unlicensed, connected to utilities, and in a trailer park, then it will almost certainly be treated as a residence for Fourth Amendment purposes.

Next, despite the fact that a vehicle search is permissible without a warrant, the search must still be based on probable cause. Even when probable cause to search exists, this does not automatically create probable cause to arrest; likewise, probable cause to arrest may not give rise to probable cause to search.

Given the circumstances surrounding most vehicle stops, it would seem foolish to require that the police obtain warrants before engaging in automobile searches. In *Husty* v. *United States* (1931),[51] a police officer, acting on a tip from an informant, found contraband in Husty's unattended car. Given that the car was unattended, one can argue that a warrant should have been secured, but the Court ruled that the officer "could not know when Husty would come to the car or how soon it would be removed."[52] Contrast *Husty* with *Coolidge* v. *New Hampshire* (1971).[53] In the *Coolidge* case, the Court ruled that the automobile exception did not apply to a warrantless search and seizure of two cars located on the defendant's property because the police had probable cause to act more than two weeks before the search.

Finally, what about the scope of an automobile search? In *United States* v. *Ross* (1982), the Supreme Court declared that as long as the police have justification to conduct a warrantless vehicle search, they may conduct a search "that is as thorough as a magistrate could authorize in a warrant."[54] The only limitation is "defined by the object of the search and the places in which there is probable cause to believe that it may be found."[55] Accordingly, if the contraband sought is small (e.g., a syringe), the scope of the vehicle search exception is almost limitless.

Plain-View Searches. Plain-view searches can also be conducted without a warrant. In *Coolidge* v. *New Hampshire*,[56] the Supreme Court created the **plain-view doctrine** and held that seizure of evidence authorized when (1) the police are lawfully in the area where the evidence is located, (2) the item is "immediately apparent" as being subject to seizure, and (3) the discovery of the evidence is "inadvertent."[57] Police are lawfully in the area where the evidence is located when they have a warrant or are otherwise authorized to be there (e.g., due to a hot-pursuit exigency). "Immediately apparent" means that the police must have probable cause that the item of interest is subject to seizure.[58] The inadvertency requirement was eliminated by the Court's subsequent ruling in *Horton* v. *California* (1990).[59]

Consent Searches. Consent searches are also permissible without a warrant—and even without probable cause. Consent cannot be "the result of duress or coercion, express or implied."[60] When does duress or coercion take place? There is no clear answer to this question. Instead, the Supreme Court has opted for a "totality of circumstances" test. This requires considering factors such as whether a show of force was made; whether the person's age, mental condition, or intellectual capacities inhibited understanding; whether the person was in custody; and whether consent was granted.

Importantly, consent to search may be valid even if the consenting party is unaware of the fact that he or she can refuse consent.[61] As the Court stated in *Ohio* v. *Robinette* (1996),[62] "[J]ust as it 'would be thoroughly impractical to impose on the normal consent search the detailed requirements of an effective warning,' so too would it be unrealistic to require police officers to always inform detainees that they are free to go before

a consent to search may be deemed involuntary."[63] Nevertheless, the issue of one's awareness of the right to refuse consent is still factored into the totality of circumstances of analysis,[64] although ignorance of the right to refuse is not enough in and of itself to render consent involuntary.

To err on the side of constitutionality, many police departments have suspects complete consent-to-search forms. An example of one such form, from the Alabama Court of Criminal Appeals, is reprinted in Figure 10–6.

The scope of a consent search is limited to the terms of the consent. In other words, the person giving consent defines the limits of the search. This was the decision reached in *Florida* v. *Jimeno* (1991).[65] For example, if a person says, "You may look around," that does not necessarily mean that the police can look *anywhere* for evidence of criminal activity.

Another issue concerning the scope of a consent search is whether the consent can be withdrawn once given. In *State* v. *Brochu* (1967),[66] the Maine Supreme Court held that a defendant's consent to search his house for evidence of his wife's murder did not extend to another search carried out the day after he was arrested as a suspect. Thus, although the man did not expressly request that the search end, the Maine court still decided that consent had been terminated.

Other Search-and-Seizure Issues

Earlier we talked about standards of justification, including reasonable suspicion. We pointed out that reasonable suspicion, which is a lesser standard of proof than probable cause, permits stop-and-frisk activities by police.[67] In this section, we look first at what constitutes a **stop-and-frisk**. Then we examine a few special-needs searches that must be based on administrative justification, which were also introduced earlier.

Stop-and-Frisk

In *Terry* v. *Ohio*,[68] the famous stop-and-frisk case mentioned earlier, the U.S. Supreme Court failed to provide a clear definition of a stop, but it did offer one in a later case, *United States* v. *Mendenhall* (1980):

> [A] person has been "seized" within the meaning of the Fourth Amendment only if, in view of all the circumstances surrounding the incident, a *reasonable person*

I, _____, having been informed of my constitutional right not to have a search made of the premises hereinafter mentioned without a search warrant and of my right to refuse consent to such a search, hereby authorize Officers _____ and _____ of the city of _____, state of Alabama, to conduct a complete search of

_____.

These officers are authorized by me to take from this location any property that they may desire. This written permission is being given by me to the above-mentioned officers voluntarily and without threats or promises of any kind.

Dated, signed, and witnessed

_____

FIGURE 10–6 **A Consent-to-Search Form.**
Source: Used with permission from the Institute for Criminal Justice Education, Inc. (ICJE).

would have believed that he was not free to leave. Examples of circumstances that might indicate a seizure, even where the person did not actually attempt to leave, would be the threatening presence of several officers, the display of a weapon by an officer, some physical touching of the person of the citizen, or the use of language or tone of voice indicating that compliance with the officer's request might be compelled.[69]

The Court's decision in this case stemmed from a confrontation between plainclothes Drug Enforcement Administration agents and a 22-year-old woman named Mendenhall in the Detroit airport. They had asked the woman for her ticket and identification. The name on the ticket did not match the name on the woman's identification, so the agents asked her to accompany them into a nearby private room. The Court did not actually decide whether Mendenhall had been "stopped," but it nevertheless articulated the "free to leave" test cited in the above quote.

The duration of a stop must also be given consideration. Sometimes a stop is drawn out until it evolves into an arrest, which would require probable cause rather than reasonable suspicion. At the other extreme, so-called nonstops, or consensual encounters, require no justification at all. See Figure 10–7 for a list of factors used to distinguish between a stop and a consensual encounter.

Frisks are often associated with stops. A frisk is a pat down of a person's outer clothing conducted out of a concern for the officer's safety. The officer is not permitted to reach into the person's pockets at the outset or to grope or manipulate the target area.[70] In one relevant case,[71] police officers observed an individual driving a vehicle with expired plates. The officers stopped the vehicle in order to issue the driver a traffic summons. When the officers asked the driver to step out of the car, they observed a large bulge in the pocket of his jacket. Fearing that the bulge might be a weapon, one of the officers frisked the driver. It turned out that the bulge was a .38-caliber revolver. The driver claimed at his trial that the gun was seized illegally, but the U.S. Supreme Court upheld the frisk. Even though a bulge in one's pocket is not necessarily indicative of a weapon, the Court felt that under these particular circumstances it was.

1. Degree of threatening behavior on the part of the officer.
2. Number of officers present.
3. Display of a weapon by the officer.
4. Physical touching of the person by the officer.
5. Orders by the officer, as opposed to requests.
6. Intimidating language or tone of voice used by the officer.
7. Length of time involved.
8. Intrusive actions (such as a full body search).
9. Use of lights or siren.
10. Blocking of the person's path.
11. Coercive police behavior.
12. Location of the encounter away from public view.

FIGURE 10–7 **Factors Used to Distinguish between a Stop and a Consensual Encounter.**
Source: J. L. Worrall, *Criminal Procedure: From First Contact to Appeal,* 5th ed., © 2015. Reprinted and electronically reproduced by permission of Pearson Education, Inc., New York, NY.

Special-Needs Searches

Special-needs searches (sometimes called *regulatory or administrative searches*) are those whose primary purpose is noncriminal. They are based on administrative justification, which was introduced earlier. Because such searches nonetheless intrude on people's privacy and can lead to the discovery of evidence, the Fourth Amendment is implicated. However, instead of focusing on probable cause or reasonable suspicion, the courts use a "balancing test" that weighs citizens' privacy interests with public-safety interests. When the latter outweighs the former, administrative searches are allowed—subject to certain limitations, such as department policy. There are many types of special-needs searches. We consider two that are most relevant in the policing context: inventories and checkpoints.

Inventories. There are two types of inventories: **person inventories** and **vehicle inventories**. The general rule is that the police may search an arrestee and his or her personal items, including containers found in his or her possession, as part of a routine inventory incident to the booking and jailing procedure. Neither a search warrant nor probable cause is required.[72] As for vehicle inventories,[73] the U.S. Supreme Court held that warrantless inventories are permissible on administrative or regulatory grounds; however, they must (1) follow a *lawful* impoundment, (2) be of a routine nature and follow standard operating procedures, and (3) not be a "pretext concealing an investigatory police motive."

Checkpoints. Many types of **checkpoints** have been authorized. First, brief border detentions are constitutionally permissible.[74] That is because it is in the interest of "national self-protection" to permit government officials to require "one entering the country to identify himself as entitled to come in, and his belongings as effects which may be lawfully brought in."[75] Second, the U.S. Supreme Court has upheld the establishment of roadblocks near the Mexican border designed to discover illegal aliens.[76] Third, warrantless, suspicionless sobriety checkpoints have also been authorized.[77]

The administrative search rationale is *not* acceptable for detecting evidence of criminal activity. This was the decision reached in *City of Indianapolis* v. *Edmond* (2000),[78] in which the Court examined whether a city's suspicionless checkpoints for detecting illegal drugs were constitutional. Here is how the Supreme Court described the checkpoints:

The city of Indianapolis operated a checkpoint program under which the police, acting without individualized suspicion, stopped a predetermined number of vehicles at roadblocks in various locations on city roads for the primary purpose of the discovery and interdiction of illegal narcotics. Under the program, at least one officer would (1) approach each vehicle, (2) advise the driver that he or she was being stopped briefly at a drug checkpoint, (3) ask the driver to produce a driver's license and the vehicle's registration, (4) look for signs of impairment, and (5) conduct an open-view examination of the vehicle from the outside. In addition, a narcotics-detection dog would walk around the outside of each stopped vehicle.[79]

The Court held that stops like those conducted during Indianapolis's checkpoint operations require individualized suspicion. In addition, "because the checkpoint program's primary purpose [was] indistinguishable from the general interest in crime control,"[80] it was deemed to violate the Fourth Amendment.

In *Illinois* v. *Lidster* (2004),[81] the Supreme Court decided that officers at checkpoints are also authorized to ask questions related to crimes occurring at the same area earlier. In that case, police briefly detained motorists to ask them if they had any information about a hit-and-run accident between a vehicle and a bicycle that took place at the same location a week earlier. A driver entered the checkpoint, swerved, and nearly hit an officer. He was stopped and subjected to a field sobriety test. He was eventually convicted of drunk driving but challenged the constitutionality of the checkpoint. The Court rejected the challenge, thus permitting yet another type of checkpoint.

▶ Confessions and Interrogations

Just as the police need to be cognizant of Fourth Amendment requirements, they also need to be aware of the rules governing confessions and interrogations. It is possible to violate a suspect's rights by failing to adhere to legal requirements spelled out in the Constitution and interpreted by the courts.

LEARNING OUTCOMES 2 Discuss the constitutional rules governing confessions and interrogations.

Accordingly, this section briefly reviews the leading constitutional rules governing confessions and interrogations.

Three Approaches to Confession Law

The primary focus in this section is on the **Fifth Amendment**, but for the sake of placing Fifth Amendment confession law into context, it is important to briefly consider the extent to which confessions are protected by other constitutional provisions. Figure 10–8 illustrates the key learning points associated with three different approaches to confessions and interrogations: the **due process voluntariness approach**, the Sixth Amendment approach, and **Miranda rights**.

This section focuses primarily on the Supreme Court's landmark decision in *Miranda* v. *Arizona*[82] and the many decisions that have flown from it. In *Miranda*, the Supreme Court announced that suspects must be advised of their Fifth Amendment right not to incriminate themselves when *custodial interrogation* takes place. More specifically, the Court announced that *Miranda* warnings (shown in Figure 10–9) must be given when "a person has been taken into custody or otherwise deprived of his freedom of action in any significant way."

Miranda is often interpreted as requiring a code of conduct for police interrogation. However, and very importantly, it is only a rule governing the admissibility of evidence. The judiciary is forbidden under the separation-of-powers doctrine from setting policy for the executive branch. As the Supreme Court observed in *United States* v. *Patane*,[83] "[T]he police do not violate a suspect's constitutional rights (or the *Miranda* rule) by negligent or even deliberate failures to provide full *Miranda*

warnings. Potential violations occur, if at all, only upon the admission of unwarned statements into evidence." In other words, the failure to give *Miranda* warnings does not, by itself, constitute a violation of constitutional rights. It only impacts the admissibility of statements given by the defendant.

Custody

An arrest is a clear-cut case of police custody, but what about a lesser intrusion, such as an order not to leave the scene? Unfortunately, there is no easy answer to this question. Instead, courts focus on the circumstances surrounding each individual case. The Supreme Court has stated, however, that "the only relevant inquiry [in analyzing the custody issue] is how a reasonable man in the suspect's position would have understood his situation."[84]

The second major component of *Miranda* is interrogation. Custody by itself is not enough to require that *Miranda* warnings be given. For a person to be afforded Fifth Amendment protection—and particularly to be advised of his or her right to remain silent—then that person must be subjected to interrogation.

Interrogation

Miranda defined *interrogation* as "questioning initiated by law enforcement officers." Then, in *Rhode Island* v. *Innis* (1980), the Court noted that interrogation "must reflect a measure of compulsion above and beyond that inherent in custody itself."[85] Thus, any questions that tend to incriminate, that is, those that are directed toward an individual about his or her suspected involvement in a crime, are considered interrogation.

Unfortunately, many "questions" are not always readily identifiable as such. In *Innis*, the Supreme Court noted that in addition to "express questioning," the "functional equivalent" of a question is also possible. The **functional equivalent of a question**, according to the Court, includes "any words or actions on the part of the police (other than those normally attendant to arrest and custody) that the police should know are reasonably likely to elicit an incriminating response from the suspect."[86]

Think About It…

Marmaduke St. John/Alamy Stock Photo

Miranda In simple terms, the *Miranda* decision sent a message to the police that they cannot question people who are in custody, most often under arrest, without first advising them that they don't have to talk. If they do, then any resulting confession cannot be used against such people during a criminal trial. Some believe that the *Miranda* decision should be abolished because it could cause convictions to be lost. They also claim that there are other constitutional protections that ensure suspects' rights are not violated. *Is Miranda a loophole? Why or why not? Can you think of other supposed loopholes in the criminal justice process? Explain.*

The Due Process Voluntariness Approach

A suspect's involuntary statement is not admissible in a criminal trial (or in any other criminal proceeding) to prove guilt. A confession is involuntary when, under the "totality of circumstances that preceded the confessions," the defendant is deprived of his or her "power of resistance." Courts take a case-by-case approach to determine voluntariness, focusing on two issues: (1) the police conduct in question and (2) the characteristics of the suspect.

Example: if the suspect is a minor and the police act with brutality, any subsequent confession will be deemed involuntary.

The Sixth Amendment Approach

Massiah v. *United States* (1964) led to the rule that the Sixth Amendment's guarantee to counsel in all "formal criminal proceedings" is violated when the government "deliberately elicits" incriminating responses from a person.

Two key elements:
(1) **deliberate elicitation:** an effort by a government actor to draw incriminating statements from a suspect who is not represented by counsel
(2) **formal criminal proceedings:** include the formal charge, preliminary hearing, indictment, information, and arraignment.

Example: If a police officer questions a person who has already been indicted and counsel is not present, the officer violates the person's Sixth Amendment rights.

The *Miranda* Approach

Miranda v. *Arizona* (1966) led to the rule that the prosecution may not use statements by the defendant stemming from custodial interrogation, unless it shows the use of procedural safeguards to secure privilege against self-incrimination.

*If the person being questioned is not in custody, *Miranda* rights do not apply. Simple police questioning—even full-blown interrogation—is not enough to trigger the protections afforded by the Fifth Amendment. The person subjected to such questioning *must* be in police custody.

Example: If police arrest and interrogate suspect without reading them their *Miranda* rights, anything suspect says cannot be used in court.

FIGURE 10–8   Three Approaches to Confession Law.

You have the right to remain silent. Anything you say can and will be used against you in a court of law. You also have the right to an attorney. If you cannot afford an attorney, one will be provided to you at no cost. Do you understand these rights as they have been read to you?

FIGURE 10–9   *Miranda* Rights.

Controversy over Miranda

The *Miranda* decision was not without controversy. Shortly after the *Miranda* decision, Congress passed the Crime Control Act of 1968, which, among other things, attempted to overrule the *Miranda* decision. The statute, codified as **18 U.S.C. Section 3501**, states that in any federal prosecution a confession "shall be admissible in evidence if it is voluntarily given." Under the law, suspects need not be advised of their right to counsel, their right not to incriminate themselves, and so on.

For several years, Section 3501 remained dormant, but critics of *Miranda* continued to look for ways to bring it before the Court. That opportunity arose in 2000. The case involved Charles Dickerson, who had been indicted for bank robbery and related crimes. He moved to suppress a statement he made to agents from the FBI on the grounds that he had not received his *Miranda* warnings. The district court granted Dickerson's motion to suppress but also noted that the confession was voluntary despite the apparent *Miranda* violation. The Court of Appeals for the Fourth Circuit held (in a 2–1 decision) that "Congress, pursuant to its power to establish the rules of evidence and procedure in the federal courts, acted well within its authority in enacting Section 3501, [and] Section 3501, rather than *Miranda*, governs the admissibility of confession in federal court."[87] The case then went before the U.S. Supreme Court.[88] In a 7–2 opinion for the Court, Chief Justice Rehnquist wrote,

> We hold that *Miranda*, being a constitutional decision of this Court, may not be in effect overruled by an Act of Congress, and we decline to overrule *Miranda* ourselves. We therefore hold that *Miranda* and its progeny in this Court govern the admissibility of statements made during custodial interrogation in both state and federal courts.[89]

The Court further noted, "We do not think there is such justification for overruling *Miranda*. *Miranda* has become embedded in routine police practice to the point where the warnings have become part of our national culture."[90]

Other *Miranda* Issues

Subsequent Supreme Court cases have hinged on the substance and adequacy of the *Miranda* warnings and waivers. For example, if *Miranda* rights are not given "adequately," then the police risk having a confession thrown out of court.[91] Also, like many rights, *Miranda* rights can be waived; that is, suspects can elect *not* to remain silent.[92] To be safe, many police departments require that suspects complete a *Miranda* waiver before interrogation commences. Finally, suspects need not be advised of their *Miranda* rights when doing so could compromise public safety.[93] The following sections examine these issues more closely.

Substance and Adequacy of the Warnings

There is a long line of cases involving people who have sought to have their confessions excluded at trial because all or some of the *Miranda* warnings were not read adequately. For example, in *California* v. *Prysock*,[94] the juvenile defendant was told, "You have the right to talk to a lawyer before you are questioned, have him present with you while you are being questioned, and all during the questioning."[95] The defendant was then told that he had the right to a court-appointed lawyer but not that one would be provided for him if he were indigent.

The defendant challenged his conviction, but the Court concluded that the warnings given to him were sufficient and that "*Miranda* itself indicates that no talismanic incantation was required to satisfy its strictures."[96]

In another interesting case, *Duckworth* v. *Eagan*, the following warnings were given:

> Before we ask you any questions, you must understand your rights. You have the right to remain silent. Anything you say can be used against you in court. You have the right to talk to a lawyer for advice before we ask you any questions, and to have him with you during questioning. You have this right to the advice and presence of a lawyer even if you cannot afford to hire one. We have no way of giving you a lawyer, but one will be appointed for you, if you wish, if and when you go to court. If you wish to answer questions now without a lawyer present, you have the right to stop answering questions at any time. You also have the right to stop answering at any time until you've talked to a lawyer.[97]

Even though the warnings in this version suggested that counsel would be provided only at court, the Supreme Court held, in a 5–4 decision, that these warnings "touched all the bases required by *Miranda*."[98] Thus, as long as all the essential *Miranda* information is communicated, simple departures will not render a confession thereby obtained inadmissible in a criminal trial.

Another factor involving the substance and adequacy of the *Miranda* warnings concerns the role of additional, unnecessary information. If more information than the original *Miranda* warnings is provided to a suspect, will any subsequent confession be inadmissible? For example, must the defendant be advised of the consequences of deciding to answer questions? The case, *Colorado* v. *Spring*,[99] is a useful point of departure. There, the defendant was arrested and questioned on suspicion of transporting stolen firearms. He was also questioned about a homicide. He admitted that he had been given his *Miranda* warnings and that he understood them; however, he argued that the statements he made about the homicide were not admissible because he had not been informed that he was going to be questioned about the homicide (i.e., he was arrested on suspicion of transporting stolen firearms). Unfortunately for the defendant, the majority held that "a suspect's awareness of all the possible subjects of questioning in advance of interrogation is not relevant to determining whether the suspect voluntarily, knowingly, and intelligently waived his Fifth Amendment privilege."[100]

A similar issue came up in *Florida* v. *Powell*,[101] a case in which the following was added to the *Miranda* warning: "You have the right to use any of these rights at any time you want during this interview." The Supreme Court held that advising a suspect that he or she has the right to talk with an attorney before answering any questions *and* that the suspect can invoke that right at any time during questions conformed with *Miranda*.

Waiver of Miranda

In *Miranda*, the Supreme Court stated that if a person talks after he or she has been read the warnings, "a heavy burden rests on the government to demonstrate that the defendant knowingly and intelligently waived his privilege against self-incrimination and his right to retained or appointed counsel."[102] Furthermore, "a valid waiver will not be presumed simply from the silence of the accused after warnings are given or simply from the fact that a confession was in fact eventually obtained."[103] According to the Supreme Court,

> Whatever the testimony of the authorities as to waiver of rights by an accused, the fact of lengthy interrogation or incommunicado incarceration before a statement is made is strong evidence that the accused did not validly waive his rights. In these circumstances, the fact that the individual eventually made a statement is consistent with the conclusion that the compelling influence of the interrogation finally forced him to do so. It is inconsistent with any notion of a voluntary relinquishment of the privilege. Moreover, any evidence that the accused was threatened, tricked, or cajoled into a waiver will, of course, show that the defendant did not voluntarily waive his privilege.[104]

In recent years, the courts have interpreted this language loosely. That is, whereas *Miranda* declared that a waiver should be viewed with considerable caution, later decisions have suggested that the burden of demonstrating a valid waiver is not difficult to meet. For example, in *Colorado* v. *Connelly*,[105] the Court held that the government need only show the validity of a waiver by a "preponderance of evidence." And in *Fare* v. *Michael C.*, the Court held that the "totality of the circumstances approach is adequate to determine whether there has been a waiver."[106] A similar conclusion was reached in *Berghuis* v. *Thompkins*[107] when the Supreme Court held that "where the prosecution shows that a *Miranda* warning was given and that it was understood by the accused, an accused's uncoerced statement establishes an implied waiver of the right to remain silent."

Before moving on, it is worth mentioning that in addition to the requirement that a valid *Miranda* waiver must be knowing and intelligent, it must also be voluntary. The test for voluntariness is similar to the due process voluntariness test discussed earlier in this chapter. Threats, physical force, and the like can lead to defendants issuing involuntary confessions. However, in *Fare* v. *Michael C.*, the Court held that the confession obtained from a 16-year-old was not involuntary. In a strongly worded dissent, Justice Powell argued that the juvenile in this case "was immature, emotional, and uneducated, and therefore was likely to be vulnerable to the skillful, two-on-one, repetitive style of interrogation to which he was subjected."[108] A safe rule is that the police must engage in seriously questionable conduct for the voluntariness requirement of a *Miranda* waiver to be violated.

Questioning after Assertion of One's Right to Remain Silent

As a general rule, questioning must cease once the accused asserts his or her right to remain silent. However, there is at least one circumstance in which the police can question a suspect after he or she has asserted the *Miranda* rights. In *Michigan* v. *Mosley*,[109] the Supreme Court permitted questioning after an assertion of *Miranda*. In that case, two hours after the defendant had stated that he did not want to talk, a different police officer confronted him in a different room about another crime and read him the *Miranda* rights for a second time. After this, the man made incriminating statements. In a 7–2 decision, the Court held that the suspect's *Miranda* rights had been "scrupulously honored." The Court said that the second officer's actions were acceptable because "the police here immediately ceased the interrogation, resumed questioning only after the passage of a significant period of time and the provision of a fresh set of warnings, and restricted the second interrogation to a crime that had not been a subject of the earlier interrogation."[110]

In *Bobby* v. *Dixon*,[111] police did not warn Dixon of his *Miranda* rights before questioning him about his suspected involvement in a forgery case. In a subsequent interrogation during which he *was* informed of his *Miranda* rights, Dixon confessed to a murder. Both crimes arose out the same act (Dixon and an acquaintance were accused of burying a man alive and stealing his identity), but Dixon was questioned separately about his involvement in each. Dixon's conviction was upheld. The Court stated, "Dixon received *Miranda* warnings before confessing to Hammer's murder; the effectiveness of those warnings was not impaired by the sort of 'two-step interrogation technique'" used in the investigation.

The common thread running throughout the last two cases is that the second set of questions either involved a separate crime or led to a confession to a second crime. What if police had continued to ask questions about the same crime? Had they done so immediately, the questioning would have been inappropriate. But the issue is less than black and white according to the Supreme Court's recent decision in *Maryland* v. *Shatzer*.[112] In that case, police (albeit a different officer) resumed questioning about the same crime more than *two weeks* after the suspect was released following initial questioning. The suspect was reread his *Miranda* rights, which he then waived. He confessed to various crimes of sex abuse. The Supreme Court decided that his confession was admissible, in part because "[h]is change of heart [was] . . . likely attributable to the fact that further deliberation in familiar surroundings [had] caused him to believe (rightly or wrongly) that cooperating with the investigation [was] in his interest."

The Public Safety Exception to Miranda

On some occasions, custodial interrogation is permissible without the *Miranda* warnings. Specifically, if public safety is in jeopardy, no *Miranda* warnings are required—at least in the short term. This was the decision reached in *New York* v. *Quarles*.[113] There, the Court held that the warnings need not be given if the suspect could have endangered public safety.

The facts from *Quarles* are as follows: After receiving information that a man with a gun had just entered a supermarket, Officer Kraft, along with three other officers, entered the store. Kraft spotted the defendant, drew his gun, and ordered the man to stop and put his hands over his head. When the officers frisked the man, they found an empty shoulder holster on him. When they asked where the man had put the gun, he replied, "The gun is over there." Officer Kraft retrieved the revolver and then placed the man under arrest and read him the *Miranda* warnings. The trial court and the lower appellate courts excluded the gun on the grounds that it was obtained in violation of *Miranda* (i.e., the man had not been advised of his right to remain silent at the time the gun was found).

The Supreme Court disagreed. Justice Rehnquist wrote the majority opinion, arguing that rigid application of *Miranda* is not always warranted, particularly when public safety is a concern:

> [T]he need for answers to questions in a situation posing a threat to public safety outweighs the need for the prophylactic rule protecting the Fifth Amendment's privilege against self-incrimination. We decline to place officers such as Officer Kraft in the untenable position of having to consider, often in a matter of seconds, whether it best serves society for them to ask the necessary questions without the *Miranda* warnings and render whatever probative evidence they uncover inadmissible, or for them to give the warnings in order to preserve the admissibility of evidence they might uncover but possibly damage or destroy their ability to obtain that evidence and neutralize the volatile situation confronting them.[114]

The Court also made it clear that the appropriate test for determining whether a threat to public safety exists is an objective one—that is, one based on what a reasonable person in the same circumstances would believe: "[W]here spontaneity rather than adherence to a police manual is necessarily the order of the day, the application of the [public safety] exception . . . should not be made to depend on *post hoc* findings at a suppression hearing concerning the subjective motivation of the arresting officer."[115] The majority in *Quarles* apparently believed that an objective threat to public safety existed. Insofar as the officers did not know where the gun was located, not knowing "obviously posed more than one danger to the public safety: an accomplice might make use of it [or] a customer or employee might later come upon it."[116]

The *Quarles* decision is a controversial one. As Justice O'Connor noted in disagreement with the newly issued public safety exception to *Miranda* (though not with the majority's ultimate decision),

Miranda has never been read to prohibit the police from asking questions to secure the public safety. Rather, the critical question *Miranda* addresses is who shall bear the cost of securing the public safety when such questions are asked and answered: the defendant or the state. *Miranda*, for better or worse, found the resolution of that question implicit in the prohibition against compulsory self-incrimination and placed the burden on the State.[117]

Quarles, by contrast, appears to place the burden on the defendant. It does so, in Justice O'Connor's view, not by ensuring that public safety is preserved but by creating a *Miranda* loophole that helps ensure that otherwise inadmissible evidence can be used against the defendant.

The Importance of Documenting a Confession

This section has been concerned mainly with the methods by which the police can extract incriminating information from criminal suspects. Assuming that the police are successful in terms of eliciting an incriminating response, it is not enough for the suspect to say, "I did it," or to offer some other form of a verbal confession. In fact, if the police hand the suspect a pencil and paper and say, "Write down your confession," this will not be enough, either. Instead, the police must follow specific procedures for documenting and reporting a confession.

The police should document every interrogation and even keep an interview log, which is a document containing information about the individuals involved in the interrogations and actions taken by both sides.[118] A list of topics to be recorded in an interview log can be found in Figure 10–10.

Also, the police should secure a signed statement from the accused. The statement should identify the suspect, the investigators, and the crime involved and should describe—in language that the suspect can understand—the details of the crime, what the suspect did, and how he or she did it. The statement should then be carefully reviewed with the suspect, even read aloud, so that its contents are clear. Finally, it should be signed by the suspect, the officer conducting the interrogation, and at least one witness, preferably another officer.

Interview Log
1. Identity of person interviewed
2. Identity of officers conducting interview
3. Location of interview
4. Date of interview
5. Time of arrest, if applicable
6. Location of arrest
7. Identity of officers making arrest
8. Time interview began
9. Time officers informed subject or suspect of his rights, and if more than one officer, name of officer advising subject or suspect
10. Time subject or suspect waived his rights
11. Time interview concluded
12. Time preparation of statement commenced
13. Identity of person preparing statement
14. Time statement completed
15. Time subject or suspect reviewed statement
16. Time subject or suspect signed written statement
17. A record of requests and complaints of subject and the action taken thereon, such as the time a subject requests permission to call an attorney, the time he made a call to his attorney, the time subject complained of illness, the time and action taken on this complaint, the time subject requested food, the time and action taken on this request, and the details as to how this request was handled

FIGURE 10–10 **Contents of a Typical Interview Log.**
Source: From Documenting and reporting a confession with a signed statement: A guide for law enforcement, p. 21. Published by U.S. Department of Justice.

Probable Cause to Search?

Officer Wheetley stopped Harris for an expired license plate. On approaching Harris's vehicle, Wheetley noticed that Harris was "visibly nervous" and unable to stop shaking. He also observed an open beer can in a cup holder. Wheetley asked for permission to search Harris's vehicle. Harris refused. Wheetley then went back to his cruiser and retrieved Aldo, a trained narcotics detection dog, and walked him around Harris's vehicle on a "free air sniff." Aldo alerted to the driver's side door handle. Harris then searched the truck, finding various items used in the manufacture of methamphetamine but not the drug itself.

Harris moved to suppress the items, claiming that Aldo's "false positive" did not give Wheetley probable cause to search. In a hearing on the subject, Wheetley testified to Aldo's training record and training performance. On cross-examination, Harris's attorney focused not on Aldo's training, but on the dog's certification and performance in the field. Wheetley acknowledged that Aldo's certification had expired before he stopped Harris and also that he did not keep complete records on Aldo's field performance.

The trial court denied the motion, and an intermediate state court affirmed. The Florida Supreme Court, however, reversed, holding that "the fact that the dog has been trained and certified is simply not enough to establish probable cause." It held that the state must present "evidence of the dog's performance history," including records showing "how often the dog has alerted in the field without illegal contraband having been found." It further noted that without such records, Wheetley could never have probable cause to conclude Aldo was capable of reliably detecting contraband.

The U.S. Supreme Court took up the case and, in *Florida* v. *Harris* (568 U.S. ___ [2013]), decided that the state is not required to supply evidence of a drug dog's performance history in order to determine whether probable cause to search existed. The Court's rationale was as follows:

> In testing whether an officer has probable cause to conduct a search, all that is required is the kind of

Moodboard/Corbis

"fair probability" on which "reasonable and prudent [people] act." *Illinois* v. *Gates*, 462 U. S. 213, 235. To evaluate whether the State has met this practical and common-sensical standard, this Court has consistently looked to the totality of the circumstances and rejected rigid rules, bright-line tests, and mechanistic inquiries. *Ibid*. . . . The Florida Supreme Court flouted this established approach by creating a strict evidentiary checklist to assess a drug-detection dog's reliability. Requiring the State to introduce comprehensive documentation of the dog's prior hits and misses in the field, and holding that absent field records will preclude a finding of probable cause no matter how much other proof the State offers, is the antithesis of a totality-of-the-circumstances approach.

The Supreme Court's decision in this case raises certain questions:

1. What are the drawbacks and advantages of drug dogs?
2. To what extent should a drug dog's history of false positives and false negatives factor into questions concerning the admissibility of evidence?
3. Do you agree with the Supreme Court's decision?

LEARNING OUTCOMES 1

Discuss the influence of the Fourth Amendment on searches and seizures.

A Fourth Amendment violation occurs when a government actor infringes on a person's reasonable expectation of privacy during a search or seizure. Seizures can be of people or property. Probable cause is more than 50% certainty; reasonable suspicion is between 1% and 50% certainty. Administrative justification balances society's interest in protecting public safety against individuals' privacy concerns. Search and arrest warrants must be issued by a neutral and detached magistrate and require a showing of probable cause and particularity. Searches that can be conducted without a warrant include searches incident to arrest, searches based on exigent circumstances, automobile searches, plain-view searches, and consent searches. Stop-and-frisk stems from the U.S. Supreme Court's decision in *Terry* v. *Ohio*, which permits police to briefly detain someone to determine whether criminal activity is afoot. Special-needs searches include inventories and checkpoints.

1. When does the Fourth Amendment apply to the activities of law enforcement officers?

2. What rules governing search and seizure are most relevant in the policing context?

3. What is the difference between a "frisk" and a "search" of a person?

4. Under what conditions is a warrantless vehicle inventory permitted?

5. What constitutes "reasonable suspicion"? How is the concept of reasonable suspicion relevant to police work?

Fourth Amendment The amendment to the U.S. Constitution that governs search and seizure.

search An activity performed in order to find evidence to be used in a criminal prosecution.

government action In the context of search and seizure law, one of two elements that must be considered when defining a Fourth Amendment search. (The other element is a reasonable expectation of privacy.) Government actions consist of measures to effect a search undertaken by someone employed by or working on behalf of the government.

reasonable expectation of privacy In the context of search and seizure law, one of two elements that must be considered when defining a Fourth Amendment search. (The other element is government action.) A reasonable expectation of privacy means that people who speak or act in private can reasonably expect that what they say or do will not be seen or heard by someone else.

seizure The confiscation of one's person (arrest) or property by a government agent.

reasonableness The elements of a situation that serve to justify a search or seizure.

justification The focus of a court's examination of the reasonableness of a search or seizure.

probable cause A set of facts and circumstances that would induce a reasonably intelligent and prudent person to believe that another particular person has committed a specific crime. Probable cause is the only justification for search and seizure mentioned in the Fourth Amendment.

reasonable suspicion A belief, based on a consideration of the facts at hand and on reasonable inferences drawn from those facts, that would induce an ordinarily prudent and cautious person under the same circumstances to conclude that criminal activity is taking place or that criminal activity has recently occurred. Reasonable suspicion is the standard for less intrusive stop-and-frisk searches; it is less than probable cause but more than a hunch.

administrative justification The standard for an administrative search based on the fact that government entities occasionally conduct searches in circumstances other than criminal investigations, such as a sobriety checkpoint set up for the purpose of apprehending drunk drivers. Sometimes called *special-needs* or *regulatory searches*, such searches attempt to achieve a balance between protecting individuals' privacy interests and protecting public safety.

search incident to arrest A warrantless search made at the time of or shortly following an arrest, which is conducted out of a concern for the safety of the arresting officer and others.

arm-span rule A doctrine established by the U.S. Supreme Court that limits a search incident to (i.e., immediately following) arrest to the area "within [the] immediate control" of the person arrested—that is, the area from within which he or she might have obtained either a weapon or something that could have been used as evidence against him or her.

protective sweep A permissible cursory visual inspection of places in which a person might be hiding. A protective sweep may be conducted by police up to the point of an arrest but must be supported by reasonable suspicion.

exigent circumstances A situation that makes a warrantless search constitutionally permissible, such as hot pursuit, the likelihood of a suspect escaping or presenting a danger to others, and evanescent evidence.

hot-pursuit exception One exception to the Fourth Amendment's warrant requirement, recognized by the U.S. Supreme Court in *Warden* v. *Hayden* (1967). The hot-pursuit doctrine provides that police officers may enter the premises where they suspect a crime has been committed or a perpetrator is hiding without a warrant when delay would likely endanger their lives or the lives of others and possibly lead to the escape of the alleged perpetrator.

evanescent evidence Evidence that is likely to disappear quickly.

plain-view doctrine The rule that the police may seize evidence without a warrant if they have lawful access to the object and it is immediately apparent (i.e., they have probable cause) that the object is subject to seizure.

stop-and-frisk The detaining of a person by a law enforcement officer for the purpose of investigation, accompanied by a superficial examination by the officer of the person's body surface or clothing to discover weapons, contraband, or other objects relating to criminal activity.

person inventory The search of an arrestee and his or her personal items, including containers found in his or her possession, as part of a routine inventory that is incident to the booking and jailing procedure. Often called *arrest inventory*.

vehicle inventory A warrantless inventory of a vehicle that is permissible on administrative or regulatory grounds. Vehicle inventories must follow a lawful impoundment, must be of a routine nature, must follow standard operating procedures, and must not be a pretext that attempts to conceal an investigatory search.

checkpoint A location at which a warrantless, suspicionless search is constitutionally permissible in furtherance of an overriding national or public-safety interest. National border entry points and sobriety checkpoints are examples.

Discuss the constitutional rules governing confessions and interrogations.

The due process voluntariness approach to confessions and interrogations holds that all confessions must be voluntary. The Sixth Amendment applies to confessions and interrogations when officers deliberately elicit incriminating information from an accused person after the initiation of criminal proceedings. The *Miranda* approach to confessions and interrogations requires that an attorney be provided to an accused person who is in custody and is being interrogated. *Miranda* warnings must be read carefully; critical information should not be omitted. Miranda rights can be waived, and the warnings can be dispensed with—for a short time—if there is an imminent threat to public safety that would be worsened if the warnings were read.

1. What rules regarding confessions and interrogations should police officers be aware of?

2. Which U.S. Supreme Court decisions are most relevant in the area of confessions and interrogations?

3. What rights are established by the Fifth Amendment to the U.S. Constitution? How do they apply to police work?

4. What rights of criminal defendants were established by the U.S. Supreme Court in the 1966 case of *Miranda* v. *Arizona*? Why did the U.S. Congress seek to override the *Miranda* decision?

Fifth Amendment An amendment to the U.S. Constitution that establishes due process rights, including the right to remain silent in the face of criminal accusations.

due process voluntariness approach A means for determining the admissibility of a suspect's self-incriminating statement based on whether it was made voluntarily. Involuntariness is held to occur when, under the totality of circumstances that preceded the confessions, the defendant is deprived of his or her "power of resistance."

Miranda rights The set of rights that a person accused or suspected of having committed a specific offense has during interrogation and of which he or she must be informed prior to questioning, as stated by the U.S. Supreme Court in *Miranda* v. *Arizona* (1966) and related cases.

functional equivalent of a question Any words or actions on the part of the police (other than those normally attendant to arrest and custody) that the police should know are reasonably likely to elicit an incriminating response from the suspect.

18 U.S.C. Section 3501 The U.S. Code designation assigned to the Crime Control Act of 1968, which, among other things, attempted to invalidate the *Miranda* decision.

References

1 *Riley* v. *California*, 573 U.S. ___ (2014).

2 Of course, other questions then arise, including whether the private citizen had the right to be in the place where the evidence was thought to be, how he or she gained access to that place, and so on. While the private seizure of evidence might not lead to its inadmissibility at court, it might provide grounds for a civil suit against the citizen or even for his or her arrest (in case of burglary or theft).

3 *Katz* v. *United States*, 389 U.S. 347 (1967).

4 Ibid., p. 353.

5 Ibid.

6 *California* v. *Greenwood*, 486 U.S. 35 (1988).

7 *Katz* v. *United States*, p. 351.

8 Ibid.

9 *United States* v. *Jacobsen*, 466 U.S. 109 (1984).

10 *Terry* v. *Ohio*, 392 U.S. 1 (1968); *United States* v. *Mendenhall*, 446 U.S. 544 (1980).

11 *Florida* v. *Bostick*, 501 U.S. 429 (1991).

12 *Beck* v. *Ohio*, 379 U.S. 89 (1964), p. 91.

13 *Brinegar* v. *United States*, 338 U.S. 160 (1949), p. 175.

14 *Terry* v. *Ohio*, 392 U.S. 1 (1968).

15 Ibid., p. 22.

16 Ibid., p. 13.

17 *United States* v. *Sokolow*, 490 U.S. 1 (1989), p. 7.

18 *Payton* v. *New York*, 445 U.S. 573 (1980).

19 *Steagald* v. *United States*, 451 U.S. 204 (1981).

20 *Johnson* v. *United States*, 333 U.S. 10 (1948), pp. 13–14.

21 *Coolidge* v. *New Hampshire*, 403 U.S. 443 (1971).

22 *United States* v. *United States District Court*, 407 U.S. 297 (1972).

23 *Payton* v. *New York*, 445 U.S. 573 (1980), pp. 602–3.

24 *Chimel* v. *California*, 395 U.S. 752 (1969), p. 763.

25 *Sibron* v. *New York*, 392 U.S. 40 (1968).

26 See *Rawlings* v. *Kentucky*, 448 U.S. 98 (1980).

27 *Preston* v. *United States*, 376 U.S. 364 (1964).

28 Ibid., p. 367.

29 See also *Chambers* v. *Maroney*, 399 U.S. 42 (1970).

30 *Chimel* v. *California*, 395 U.S. 752 (1969).

31 Ibid., p. 759.

32 Ibid., p. 768.

33 *Maryland* v. *Buie*, 494 U.S. 325 (1990).

34 *Arizona* v. *Gant*, 556 U.S. 332 (2009).

35 *Riley* v. *California*, 573 U.S. ___ (2014).

36 *Warden* v. *Hayden*, 387 U.S. 294 (1967).

37 Ibid., p. 298.

38 Ibid., pp. 298–99.

39 Ibid., p. 299.

40 *State* v. *Wren*, 115 Idaho 618 (1989), p. 625.

41 *United States* v. *George*, 883 F.2d 1407 (9th Cir. 1989).

42 *United States* v. *Santana*, 427 U.S. 38 (1976).

43 See, e.g., *Welsh* v. *Wisconsin*, 466 U.S. 740 (1984).

44 *Warden* v. *Hayden*, 387 U.S. 294 (1967), p. 299.

45 *Minnesota* v. *Olson*, 495 U.S. 91 (1990).

46 *Breithaupt* v. *Abram*, 352 U.S. 432 (1957).

47 See, e.g., *Kentucky* v. *King*, 563 U.S. ___ (2011).

48 *Missouri* v. *McNeely*, 569 U.S. ___ (2013).

49 *Kentucky* v. *King*, 563 U.S. ___ (2011).

50 *Carroll* v. *United States*, 267 U.S. 132 (1925).

51 *Husty* v. *United States*, 282 U.S. 694 (1931).

52 Ibid., p. 701.

53 *Coolidge* v. *New Hampshire*, 403 U.S. 443 (1971).

54 *United States* v. *Ross*, 456 U.S. 798 (1982), p. 800.

55 Ibid., p. 824.

56 *Coolidge* v. *New Hampshire*, 403 U.S. 443 (1971).

57 Ibid.

58 *Arizona* v. *Hicks*, 480 U.S. 321 (1987).

59 *Horton* v. *California*, 496 U.S. 128 (1990).

60 *Schneckloth* v. *Bustamonte*, 412 U.S. 218 (1973).

61 Ibid.

62 *Ohio* v. *Robinette*, 519 U.S. 33 (1996).

63 Ibid., pp. 39–40.

64 *United States* v. *Mendenhall*, 446 U.S. 544 (1980).

65 *Florida* v. *Jimeno*, 500 U.S. 248 (1991).

66 *State* v. *Brochu*, 237 A.2d 418 (Me. 1967).

67 *Terry* v. *Ohio*, 392 U.S. 1 (1968).

68 Ibid.

69 *United States* v. *Mendenhall*, 446 U.S. 544 (1980), p. 554, emphasis added.

70 *Sibron* v. *New York*, 392 U.S. 40 (1968).

71 *Pennsylvania* v. *Mimms*, 434 U.S. 106 (1977).

72 *Illinois* v. *Lafayette*, 462 U.S. 640 (1983).

73 *South Dakota* v. *Opperman*, 428 U.S. 364 (1976).

74 *Carroll* v. *United States*, 267 U.S. 132 (1925).

75 Ibid., p. 154. See also *United States* v. *Montoya de Hernandez*, 473 U.S. 531 (1985), p. 538.

76 *United States* v. *Martinez-Fuerte*, 428 U.S. 543 (1976).

77 *Michigan Dept. of State Police* v. *Sitz*, 496 U.S. 444 (1990).

78 *City of Indianapolis* v. *Edmond*, 531 U.S. 32 (2000).

79 Ibid., p. 32.

80 Ibid., p. 44.

81 *Illinois* v. *Lidster*, 540 U.S. 419 (2004).

82 *Miranda* v. *Arizona*, 384 U.S. 436 (1966).

83 *United States* v. *Patane*, 542 U.S. 630 (2004)

84 *Berkemer* v. *McCarty*, 468 U.S. 420 (1984), p. 442.

85 *Rhode Island* v. *Innis*, 446 U.S. 291 (1980), p. 300.

86 Ibid., p. 302, n. 8.

87 *United States* v. *Dickerson*, 166 F.3d 667 (4th Cir. 1999), p. 671.

88 *Dickerson* v. *United States*, 530 U.S. 428 (2000).

89 Ibid., p. 431.

90 Ibid., p. 443.

91 See, e.g., *California* v. *Prysock*, 453 U.S. 355 (1981), p. 359, and *Duckworth* v. *Eagan*, 492 U.S. 192 (1989), p. 198.

92 See, e.g., *Miranda* v. *Arizona*, 384 U.S. 436 (1966), p. 475; *Colorado* v. *Connelly*, 479 U.S. 157 (1986); *Fare* v. *Michael C.*, 442 U.S. 707 (1979), p. 725; *North Carolina* v. *Butler*, 441 U.S. 369 (1979).

93 *New York* v. *Quarles*, 467 U.S. 649 (1984).

94 *California* v. *Prysock*, 453 U.S. 355 (1981).

95 Ibid., p. 359.

96 Ibid.

97 *Duckworth* v. *Eagan*, 492 U.S. 192 (1989), p. 198.

98 Ibid., p. 203.

99 *Colorado* v. *Spring*, 479 U.S. 564 (1987).

100 Ibid., p. 577.

101 *Florida* v. *Powell*, 559 U.S. ___ (2010).

102 *Miranda*, p. 475.

103 Ibid.

104 Ibid., p. 476.

105 *Colorado* v. *Connelly*, 479 U.S. 157 (1986).

106 *Fare* v. *Michael C.*, 442 U.S. 707 (1979), p. 725.

107 *Berghuis* v. *Thompkins*, 560 U.S. 370 (2010).

108 *Fare* v. *Michael C.*, p. 733

109 *Michigan* v. *Mosley*, 423 U.S. 96 (1975).

110 Ibid., p. 106.

111 *Bobby* v. *Dixon*, 565 U.S. ___ (2011).

112 *Maryland* v. *Shatzer*, 559 U.S. 98 (2010).

113 *New York* v. *Quarles*, 467 U.S. 649 (1984).

114 Ibid., pp. 657–58.

115 Ibid., p. 656.

116 Ibid., p. 657.

117 Ibid., p. 664.

118 T. T. Burke, "Documenting and reporting a confession with a signed statement: A guide for law enforcement," *FBI Law Enforcement Bulletin*, February 2001, p. 17.

11

Civil Liability and Accountability

1 Identify the two main avenues for civil litigation against police officers.

2 Explain the different types of external accountability measures put in place to check police misconduct.

3 Discuss procedures for promoting accountability from within police agencies.

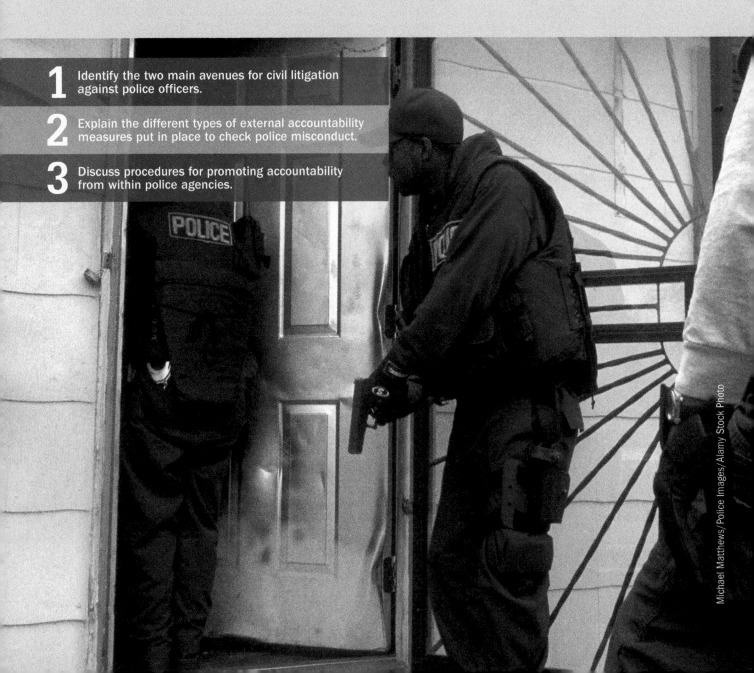

Michael Matthews/Police Images/Alamy Stock Photo

INTRO THE DOCTRINE OF QUALIFIED IMMUNITY

In a 2015 case, the U.S. Supreme Court held that the doctrine of qualified immunity shields police officers from civil liability so long as their conduct "does not violate clearly established statutory or constitutional rights of which a reasonable person would have known." A clearly established right is one that is "sufficiently clear that every reasonable official would have understood that what he is doing violates that right." Even so, in *Mullenix* v. *Luna*,[1] the Court tussled with the thorny issue of determining whether the doctrine of qualified immunity applied to a police officer's use of deadly force when a lower court had ruled that it did not. The case involved a man who fled from an arresting officer in a vehicle, reaching high speeds while phoning 911 to tell dispatchers that he was armed and would fire at pursuing officers if they did not end the chase. Another officer took up position ahead of where the chase was headed, and fired at the man's car as it approached an overpass in an attempt to disable it. His shots, however, killed the fleeing driver.

The relevant issue, the Court concluded, in determining whether that officer's actions were shielded under the

doctrine of qualified immunity "is whether existing precedent placed the conclusion that [the officer] acted unreasonably *in these circumstances*." (Italics added) The Court concluded that he had not acted unreasonably, and overturned the lower court's ruling which had found him liable for improper use of force. The thrust of this important case is that there can be no hard and fast rule in determining whether officers are protected by qualified immunity, but that each questionable instance of police behavior must be determined on its own merits.

▶ *Civil Liability*

One of the core principles of the democratic system of government is public accountability. The American system of government is designed to ensure that public officials ultimately answer to the people whom they serve. Making elected officials accountable is relatively easy; they can be voted out of office. This is less true for workers in civil service positions; they answer to the public through a complex chain of relationships. The police have not always been held closely accountable to the public. Times have changed, however, and the mechanisms for ensuring public accountability of police activity are the focus of this chapter.

While holding public officials accountable is certainly important, those officials enjoy many of the same legal protections that the rest of us do. Police officers who are sued, for example, can assert a number of defenses. Likewise, officers who are investigated by their departments for alleged misconduct enjoy a number of procedural protections. Bills of rights for police officers have emerged in an effort to preserve the due process rights of accused officers and to reduce the potential for wrongful firings, demotions, and transfers. This chapter examines efforts to balance the need for police accountability against the need to preserve due process protections for everyone, including the police.

Whenever a person's constitutional or other federal civil rights are violated, a lawsuit can be filed. Even if a person merely *believes* that his or her rights have been violated, litigation is still an option. Litigation is also an option for tort violations, or civil wrongs that do not rise to the level of a constitutional rights

violation. In either case, the worst that can happen for the plaintiff (the person bringing the lawsuit) is that the lawsuit will be dismissed and the plaintiff will be stuck with the attorney's bill.

What is the purpose of civil litigation? Aside from sometimes being the only remedy available to those who have been wronged, civil lawsuits are attractive because they sometimes result in monetary awards. Lawsuits in which people seek monetary compensation are called *damages suits*, and the money paid is called **damages**. In such suits, the plaintiff seeks payment for perceived or actual injuries. In addition to damages, plaintiffs can seek **injunctive relief**, which means that the plaintiff wants the court to bring the injurious or offensive action to a halt.

There are two main mechanisms for lawsuits against police officers (and their employing agencies, cities, and counties): Section 1983 liability and state tort liability. These are summarized in Figure 11–1 and discussed in further detail in the following sections.

- -

Section 1983 Liability

A portion of the U.S. Code, **42 U.S.C. Section 1983**, provides a remedy in federal court for the "deprivation of any rights . . . secured by the Constitution and laws" of the United States. Section 1983 states,

LEARNING OUTCOMES 1 · Identify the two main avenues for civil litigation against police officers.

Section 1983 Liability

Provides a remedy in federal court for the deprivation of any rights secured by the Constitution and laws.

Two requirements for a successful lawsuit
1. The defendant (the person being sued) must have acted under color of law.
2. A federal or constitutional rights violation must have occurred.

Defense:
Qualified immunity: officer has lapse in judgment or makes an honest mistake.

State Tort Liability

Alternative for aggrieved people who do not choose to sue under Section 1983. State tort claims tend to be reserved mostly for less serious claims.

Two types of state tort claims that matter in the law enforcement context
1. **Intentional tort:** defendant officer knowingly engaged in behavior.
2. **Negligence tort:** the mental state of the defendant officer is not at issue.

Defenses:
Public-duty doctrine: police protection is owed to general public, not individuals.
Contributory negligence: if plaintiff was also negligent, officer is not liable.
Comparative negligence: looks at who is to blame and assigns liability accordingly.
Assumption of risk: plaintiff voluntarily engaged in dangerous activity, so officer is not liable.
Sudden Peril: officer required to make split-second decision.

FIGURE 11–1 Law Enforcement Liability.

Every person who, under color of any statute, ordinance, regulation, custom, or usage, of any State or Territory or the District of Columbia, subjects, or causes to be subjected, any citizen of the United States or other persons within the jurisdiction thereof to the deprivation of any rights, privileges, or immunities secured by the Constitution and laws, shall be liable to the party injured in an action at law, suit in equity, or other proper proceeding for redress.

Color of Law

One of the requirements for a successful Section 1983 lawsuit is that the defendant, the person being sued, must have acted under color of law. The U.S. Supreme Court has said that someone acts under **color of law** when he or she acts in an official government capacity and with the appearance of legal power. This includes police officers, mayors, and a number of other government officials.[2] For example, a police officer who is on duty acts under color of law. Police officers also act under color of law when they (1) identify themselves as officers, (2) perform criminal investigations, (3) file official police documents, (4) make arrests, (5) invoke police powers inside or outside their jurisdiction, (6) settle personal vendettas with police power, or (7) display weapons or police equipment.[3]

By contrast, someone acting in a private capacity (e.g., an ordinary citizen) cannot be said to have acted under color of law.

Constitutional Violation

The second requirement for a successful Section 1983 lawsuit is that a federal or constitutional rights violation must have taken place. In the law enforcement context, the concern is almost exclusively over constitutional rights violations. In determining whether a **constitutional rights violation** has taken place, the plaintiff (the suing party) must establish that the conduct of the defendant (or defendants) violated a specific constitutional provision, such as the Fourth Amendment's prohibition against unreasonable searches and seizures (see Chapter 10); that is, "in any given Section 1983 suit, the plaintiff must still prove a violation of the underlying constitutional right."[4]

Recently, the courts have begun to require that constitutional rights violations alleged under Section 1983 be committed with a certain level of **culpability**; that is, plaintiffs generally have to prove that the defendant officer *intended* for the violation to occur. The practical result of this is that Section 1983 is now reserved for the most serious of constitutional rights violations. The level of culpability required for a constitutional rights violation depends on the type of unconstitutional conduct alleged by the plaintiff.[5]

Theories of Liability

The term **theory of liability** refers essentially to reasons offered as to why a particular person or entity should be held answerable under civil law for some action. A typical Section 1983 lawsuit will target an individual officer, that officer's supervisor, the city or municipality for which the officer works, or some combination of these. Besides suing the officer who may have been responsible for a constitutional rights violation, it is often attractive for plaintiffs to go after the "bigger fish" because that is where the money is. Cities and counties tend to have deeper pockets than the average police officer and are therefore more attractive targets for civil litigation. To date, cities and counties have been held liable only for failing to train officers[6] and for adopting unconstitutional policies and customs.[7] For the latter, the plaintiff must prove that the city or county adopted and implemented a policy or custom that led to the injury. Isolated incidents are not sufficient to hold a city or county liable.

Suing Federal Officials

Before 1971, it was not clear whether federal officials could be sued under Section 1983. In the 1971 case of *Bivens* v. *Six Unknown Named Agents*,[8] however, the U.S. Supreme Court held that federal law enforcement officers *can* be sued for Fourth Amendment violations. The decision has since been expanded to include liability for violations of constitutional rights embodied in other relevant amendments.[9]

Bivens claims are primarily limited to law enforcement officers, as many other federal officials enjoy absolute immunity. **Absolute immunity** means that the official cannot be sued under any circumstances. Federal officials who enjoy absolute immunity include judges[10] and prosecutors, among others.[11] By contrast, heads of federal agencies,[12] presidential aides,[13] and federal law enforcement officers *can* be sued. However, these and other federal officials enjoy qualified immunity, the same defense that applies to state officials in the Section 1983 context.

Defenses

The main defense to Section 1983 liability is **qualified immunity**. Qualified immunity is a judicially created defense. It emerged in response to two conflicting policy concerns: effective crime control and the protection of people's civil liberties. On the one hand, Section 1983 lawsuits are intended to deter police misconduct. But on the other hand, the U.S. Supreme Court has recognized that it is not fair to hold officials liable for lapses in judgment and honest mistakes.[14]

Similar to the Fourth Amendment's test for reasonableness, the courts have applied an **objective reasonableness** standard in order to determine whether qualified immunity should bar a successful lawsuit. In other words, a defendant police officer is said to have acted in an objectively reasonable fashion if he or she did not violate clearly established rights of which a reasonable person would have known. In some Section 1983 cases, police have benefited from qualified immunity even when they violated clearly established constitutional rights, as long as the mistake was a reasonable one.[15]

State Tort Liability

State tort claims are an alternative for aggrieved individuals who do not choose to sue under Section 1983. Moreover, **state tort liability** is an important avenue of redress because negligent acts or misconduct by the police that result in minor injuries are usually not serious enough to make Section 1983 litigation a viable option. State tort claims tend to be reserved mostly for less serious claims. There are exceptions, however, such as tort lawsuits for wrongful death, an admittedly serious act.

Types of Torts

There are two types of state tort claims that matter in the law enforcement context. First, **intentional torts** consist of actions that are highly likely to cause injury or damage. For a plaintiff to successfully sue for an intentional tort, he or she must also show that the defendant officer knowingly engaged in the behavior. To be liable for an intentional tort, an officer need not intend to harm; it need only be shown that the officer intended to engage in the behavior that *led* to the harm. Common forms of intentional torts that are applicable to policing include wrongful death, assault and battery, false arrest, and false imprisonment.

A second and more far-reaching tort claim involves negligence. In a **negligence tort**, the mental state of the defendant officer is not at issue. Plaintiffs need only demonstrate the presence of four elements to succeed with a negligence claim: (1) a legal duty between the officer and the plaintiff, (2) a breach of that duty, (3) proximate (direct) causation between the officer's actions and the alleged harm, and (4) actual damage or injury.

Defenses

Police officers who are sued for tort violations benefit from the so-called **public-duty doctrine**. It states that police protection (like any other government function) is owed to the general public, not to individuals. This means that if a police officer is not present to thwart a criminal act, the officer cannot be held liable for failure to protect. The reason for this barrier to liability is clear: It would be unreasonable to hold law enforcement officials liable every time they do not intervene in criminal activity.

There are situations, however, in which police officers owe a legal duty to an individual and, as such, can be held liable for failing to perform that legal duty. For example, if a police officer stops a motorist, confirms that he is drunk, but lets him or her go, a special relationship has been created; the officer should arrest the drunk driver or, at a minimum, ensure that he or she does not drive until he or she is sober. The officer could therefore be held liable under state tort law for negligent failure to protect.

However, even in situations in which a special relationship exists between a police officer and a private citizen, the officer may be able to assert one of several defenses to liability. The first such defense is known as **contributory negligence**. This defense holds that if an officer can show that the plaintiff was also negligent in, say, causing an accident, the officer should not be held liable. Contributory negligence can arise not only from the actions of a criminal defendant but also from those of third parties. If, during the course of a high-speed pursuit, a third motorist runs a red light and is struck by the officer, the officer may not be found liable because the motorist contributed to the crash by running a red light.

Unlike contributory negligence, the **comparative negligence** defense is not a total bar to state tort liability. Comparative negligence looks at who is to blame and assigns liability accordingly. If it is found that the police officer is 20% liable and the plaintiff is 80% liable, damages would be awarded in accordance with these percentages. The comparative negligence defense permits courts to determine fault and the extent to which each party contributed to an incident or injury.

The **assumption of risk** defense against state tort liability provides that if a plaintiff voluntarily engaged in a dangerous activity that led to his or her injury, then the police officer should not be held liable. If a suspect is injured during the course of a high-speed pursuit and sues the officer, the court may decide that the suspect assumed the risk of injury by fleeing from the police.

Finally, police defendants in state tort claims enjoy a defense referred to as **sudden peril**. This is basically an "emergency" defense for situations in which officers were required to make split-second decisions. This defense applies only in situations in which the injury or death is *clearly* attributed to the heat of the moment. If the officer asserting such a defense contributed in any way to the creation of the emergency situation, courts (and juries) may be inclined to find in favor of the plaintiff.

▶ Other External Accountability Measures

Lawsuits serve as a powerful check on police misconduct. The problem, however, is that litigation is not always a viable or desirable alternative. Other measures have been put in place to pick up where litigation leaves off. This section looks at what we call *external accountability measures*, those stemming from outside law enforcement agencies. A later section looks at internal measures that police agencies employ to deal with complaints of misconduct and impropriety.

There is some debate over whether police accountability should be internal or external. Some feel that the police themselves are most capable of reviewing allegations against them. Others feel that a balance between internal and external review is necessary. For example, one researcher observed that "the departmental administrative structure has by far the greatest potential for efficient, effective action to prevent, to investigate, to adjudicate, or to punish police misconduct"[16] but that external review allows outside scrutiny of the process and thereby lends credibility to internal review. Others feel that external review of police agencies is critical, arguing that true control occurs only when civilians have the primary responsibility for investigating misconduct.

A more comprehensive view recognizes that the issue of control must be examined as a partnership between the police *and* the community. From this perspective, external accountability mechanisms are essential. We will look at several such mechanisms: citizen oversight, citizen complaints, agency accreditation, the exclusionary rule, and criminal prosecution for serious misconduct.

Citizen Oversight

Not too long ago, the vast majority of police departments used only an internal process to handle disciplinary actions.[17] A survey of police agencies conducted during the 1980s revealed that only about 15% of them allowed "outsiders" into the review process. Today, however, a host of police agencies have established external (citizen) complaint review procedures.[18] The President's Task Force on 21st-Century Policing reiterated the importance and role of civilian review in modern policing:

LEARNING OUTCOMES 2 — Explain the different types of external accountability measures put in place to check police misconduct.

> Citizen review is not an advocate for the community or for the police. This impartiality allows oversight to bring stakeholders together to work collaboratively and proactively to help make policing more effective and responsive to the community. Civilian oversight alone is not sufficient to gain legitimacy; without it, however, it is difficult, if not impossible, for the police to maintain the public's trust.[19]

There is little consistency in the way external review is structured,[20] but three distinct approaches have been identified:[21] civilian review, civilian input, and civilian monitor (Figure 11–2).

Civilian Review

The **civilian review** model is one of the stronger models of citizen oversight. It occurs when a group of citizens investigates complaints against the police, adjudicates the complaints, and recommends punishment. This approach has been taken in cities like Washington, D.C.; Philadelphia; Rochester, New York; New York City; and Berkeley, California. The strongest argument against the civilian review model is that it vests

Civilian Monitor
Complaints are received by the police department, and the process, from beginning to end, is monitored by the external unit. Civilians *monitor* but do not *make* decisions.

Civilian Input
Reception and investigation of complaints is in the hands of civilians, but next steps are taken by the police department.

Citizen Oversight
A host of police agencies have established external (citizen) complaint review procedures.[i]
Citizen involvement in the complaint process will produce
(1) more objective and more thorough investigations;
(2) a higher rate of sustained complaints and more disciplinary actions against guilty officers;
(3) greater deterrence of police misconduct (through both general and specific deterrence); and
(4) higher levels of satisfaction on the part of both individual complainants and the general public.[ii]

Civilian Review
Group of citizens investigates complaints against the police, adjudicates the complaints, and recommends punishment.

[i]S. Walker and B. Wright, Citizen review of the police: A national survey of the 50 largest cities (Washington, DC: Police Executive Research Forum, 1995).

[ii]S. Walker and B. Wright, "Varieties of citizen review: The relationship of mission, structure, and procedures to police accountability," in Critical issues in policing: Contemporary readings, 3rd ed., ed. R. G. Dunham and G. P. Alpert (Prospect Heights, IL: Waveland, 1997).

FIGURE 11-2 Citizen Oversight and Police Accountability.

responsibility and authority for police discipline in the hands of individuals who have no expertise in police work and who likely do not have the capacity for investigating and understanding the issues involved in a disciplinary problem.[22] On the other hand, the civilian review model represents almost everything that critics of traditional internal review mechanisms desire.

Civilian Input

The **civilian input** model puts the reception and investigation of complaints in the hands of civilians, but the next steps are taken by the police department. In Kansas City, Missouri, the Office of Community Complaints (OCC) serves as the central clearing house for receiving complaints.[23] The OCC reviews all complaints and assigns them, as needed, to the police department's internal affairs unit for investigation. The internal affairs unit is staffed by sworn officers who investigate allegations of wrongdoing in the ranks. Once the investigation has been completed, the OCC reviews the results and makes recommendations to the chief. In Chicago, the Office of Professional Standards (OPS) is located in the police department but is staffed by nonsworn personnel. The OPS handles all citizen complaints involving excessive force, deadly force, and nondeadly force, while the department's internal affairs division is responsible for all other disciplinary issues.

Civilian Monitor

The **civilian monitor** model is similar to an ombudsman approach. With the civilian monitor model, complaints are received by the police department, and the process—from beginning to end—is monitored by the external unit. The key feature of this model is that the civilians *monitor* but do not *make* decisions. The monitoring consists of scrutinizing the internal process for inconsistencies or problems. For example, in San Jose, California, the Independent Police Auditor (IPA) receives and investigates complaints (as does the police department's internal affairs division). The IPA's mission consists of the following:

(a) Reviewing Police Department investigations of complaints against police officers to determine if the investigation was complete, thorough, objective, and fair.

(b) Making recommendations with regard to Police Department policies and procedures based on the IPA's review of investigations of complaints against police officers.

(c) Conducting public outreach to educate the community on the role of the IPA and to assist the community with the process and procedures for investigation of complaints against police officers.[24]

Other Citizen Oversight Models

The three models we just mentioned are not the only methods of providing citizen oversight. One team of researchers identified *four* classes of citizen review.[25] They overlap to some extent with the three just described. The first involves independent citizen review bodies in which nonsworn investigators conduct investigations and make recommendations to the police executive. Citizen review bodies are found, for example, in New Orleans and Cincinnati.[26] The second approach involves initial investigations by sworn police officers, followed by a review of the officers' reports by an individual or board that contains at least some nonsworn people. The individual or board then makes recommendations to the chief. Procedures of this type have been used in Kansas City, Missouri; Portland, Oregon; and Albuquerque, New Mexico.[27]

In the third approach, an internal affairs department investigates complaints and makes recommendations to the chief. Citizens who are not satisfied with the final disposition can appeal to a board containing at least some nonsworn individuals. The board reviews the case and may make different recommendations to the chief. In the fourth approach, auditors investigate citizen complaints. In both Seattle, Washington, and San Jose, California, for example, an auditor reviews the department's complaint procedure and recommends changes as necessary. Also, the auditor often contacts complainants to assess their satisfaction with the complaint process.[28]

It is also important to distinguish between the independent review of citizen complaints and citizen oversight.[29] Independent review occurs when a civilian review body investigates complaints filed against law enforcement officers and then forwards its recommendations to the chief or sheriff. Citizen oversight, in contrast, stresses community outreach, review of complaint policies by a civilian group, audits of complaint investigation procedures, information dissemination, and the like.

Citizen oversight represents an important step in promoting accountability, but its effectiveness in reducing or eliminating misconduct is unclear. This is because most of the mechanisms provide only for disciplinary recommendations; that is, most oversight groups can make only advisory recommendations to the chief police.[30] As two noted researchers observed, "The powers of citizen review procedures are far more limited than those of judges in the criminal process."[31] Nevertheless, certain cities vest citizens with the ability to make disciplinary decisions. Examples include the San Francisco Office of Citizen Complaints, the Milwaukee Fire and Police Commission, the Chicago Police Board, and the Detroit Police Commission.[32]

Citizen Complaints

In general, citizen oversight is concerned with investigations of police misconduct, including investigations of citizen complaints. **Citizen complaints** are documents filed by people who feel they have been wronged by one or more police officers in a department. An example of a citizen's complaint form is provided in Figure 11–3.

Citizen complaints are sometimes seen by administrators as "a barometer of police performance."[33] Complaints can indicate how officers are behaving on the street, which is useful because police officers are not always directly supervised by their superiors. Agencies should not have to *rely* on complaints to understand how they are doing, but complaints can often send important messages that would not otherwise be clear.

Many police agencies have centralized areas where all citizen complaints about police misbehavior or ill treatment of citizens must be reported. Complaints are confidentially received and permanently logged in chronological order of receipt. The complainant's information is also recorded, and an investigation is set into motion. Some agencies actively publicize their citizen complaint procedures. Visitors to the LAPD's website, for example, can find a link to a complaint form. Some agencies have even distributed citizen complaint forms to civic organizations and neighborhood groups. Still others require any police employee who is approached by a citizen with a complaint to report the complaint to the internal investigation registration desk within a set period of time after receiving the information.

Agency Accreditation

Accreditation refers to certification for having met all applicable requirements put in place by an accrediting body. Accreditation is a big issue in the academic world. Universities have to satisfy their accrediting bodies' requirements, or they risk losing their accreditation, which is akin to losing credibility. Accreditation has spilled over into law enforcement as well. It is a process intended to ensure that agencies remain accountable to the public and that they abide by the highest standards of conduct in the field.

The Commission on Accreditation for Law Enforcement Agencies (CALEA) was established in 1979 by the International Association of Chiefs of Police (IACP), the National Sheriffs' Association, the Police Executive Research Forum, and the National Organization of Black Law Enforcement Executives. Their goal was to evaluate and accredit police agencies that meet various standards.

The standards set forth by CALEA address nine major law enforcement subjects: (1) role, responsibilities, and relationships with other agencies; (2) organization, management, and administration; (3) personnel structure; (4) personnel process; (5) operations; (6) operational support; (7) traffic operations; (8) detainee and court-related activities; and (9) auxiliary and technical services.[34] These subjects are then broken into 38 content areas consisting of (as of this writing) 439 standards.[35]

A police agency seeking accreditation must pass through five phases: application, self-assessment, on-site assessment, commission review and decision, and maintenance of compliance and reaccreditation. The accreditation process is a voluntary one, so only agencies interested in being accredited apply. Once eligibility has been confirmed, both the agency and the commission sign an agreement that identifies what is expected of each party. Then the agency completes an agency profile questionnaire. The responses to the questionnaire provide important information to the accreditation manager and facilitate interaction between the agency and the commission. Next, the agency conducts a self-assessment in which it determines whether it complies with standards set forth by the commission. Proof of compliance is required. The on-site assessment consists of a visit by commission officials during which the agency's compliance with commission standards is determined. The assessors' final report is then forwarded to the commission for review. If, during the review period, the commission is satisfied that the agency meets all relevant standards, accreditation is granted. Accredited agencies then submit annual reports to the commission attesting to their continued compliance with relevant standards.

Accreditation may also provide additional benefits besides accountability and the maintenance of high standards. One is a reduction in insurance premiums.[36] This is not unlike a reduction in auto insurance premiums for drivers who take a

Abilene Police Department
Citizen Complaint/Commendations Form

File complaints or commendations about Police Department employees on this form. Return the completed form to the desk duty officer, 1st floor at the Police Department, 450 Pecan, or hand deliver to the City Manager's Office, 555 Walnut, Room 203, or by mail to P.O. Box 60 Abilene, Texas 79604.
Complaints will not be investigated until a Police Supervisor has contacted the Complaining Party.

Involved Officer/Employee(s) Information:

Name:	
Name:	

Person Making the Complaint/Commendation:

Name:		Phone:	
Address:		Phone:	

Information
Please provide as much information about the reason you were contacted by the officer/employee.
Specific information about the date, time and location will help in locating computer-based information if you do not know the officer/employee's name.

Date of Contact:		Approximate Time:		AM/PM
Location Contacted:				

Reason For The Complaint/Commendation: (attach additional pages if needed)

Witness Information:

Name:		Phone:	
Address:		Phone:	
Name:		Phone:	
Address:		Phone:	

Submitted by_____Date_____

FIGURE 11-3 Citizen's Complaint Form.
Source: Abilene (Texas) Police Department. Reprinted with permission.

safe-driving course. A person who has taken the course is presumably at less risk for getting in an accident or filing a claim. The same goes for police agencies. Those who maintain the highest standards are presumably the least likely to be sued. Evidence also suggests that accredited law enforcement agencies may be more likely to receive grant funds.[37]

Despite the apparent benefits associated with national accreditation, there has been a great deal of debate and controversy over the accreditation process.[38] Some state law enforcement associations have vocally opposed national accreditation standards, arguing that state-level accreditation is preferable.

This has resulted in an increase in state-level accreditation.[39] For example, the Washington Association of Sheriffs and Police Chiefs (WASPC) was directed by the state legislature to develop accreditation standards during the 1970s. The result was the WASPC Law Enforcement Accreditation Program.[40] Figure 11–4 depicts various benefits of state-level accreditation.

The Exclusionary Rule

Another important mechanism for ensuring the accountability of police agencies is the **exclusionary rule**, which mandates that

- Improved morale within the police agency
- Increased credibility with the agency's governing body
- Increased pride in the agency
- Systemized self-assessment
- Broadened perspectives
- Intensified administrative and operational effectiveness
- Confidence that recruitment, selection, and promotion processes are fair and equitable
- Strengthened understanding of agency policies and procedures by all police personnel
- Decreased susceptibility to litigation and costly civil court settlements
- Potential reduction in premiums for liability insurance
- Greater public confidence in the agency
- State and local acknowledgment of professional competence

FIGURE 11–4 **Benefits of Participating in the WASPC Accreditation Program.**
Source: Washington Association of Sheriffs and Police Chiefs, "Accreditation,"
http://www.waspc.org/accreditation www.waspc.org/stage.dll/?pid=1&scb=2
(accessed January 27, 2016)

evidence obtained in violation of the U.S. Constitution cannot be admitted in a criminal trial to prove guilt.[41] In the Supreme Court case of *Elkins* v. *United States*, Associate Justice Tom C. Clark provided eloquent reasoning for such a rule: "The criminal goes free, if he must, but it is the law that sets him free. Nothing can destroy a government more quickly than its failure to observe its own law, or worse, its disregard of the charter of its own existence."[42]

The so-called **fruit of the poisonous tree doctrine** has expanded the scope of the exclusionary rule to include evidence derived from materials that were unconstitutionally obtained. Suppose, for example, that a police officer illegally arrests someone. The fruit of the poisonous tree doctrine would require the exclusion of not only the evidence obtained in the search of the arrestee following that arrest but also, potentially, any other evidence (such as a confession)

obtained after that initial illegal act.[43] The question of what is considered "fruit," however, has become complicated over the years. This is partly due to the emergence of a number of exceptions to the fruit of the poisonous tree doctrine.

The exclusionary rule is intended to promote accountability and deter misconduct. Some would say, though, that the rule does not serve the same deterrent effect today that it perhaps once did. Its deterrent effect may have been diminished as the U.S. Supreme Court has become more conservative in its decisions. A variety of subsequently established exceptions to the rule (e.g., good faith and discussed below) helps to ensure that the criminal does not go free when reasonable mistakes are made. The deterrent effect is probably minimal, too, because the time elapsed between illegal police conduct and the decision to exclude evidence is usually rather lengthy.[44]

There is evidence, however, that many police organizations, fearful of losing criminal cases on technicalities, have instituted programs designed to teach trainees about constitutional guidelines. To that end, the exclusionary rule plays at least a minimal role in promoting accountability; when the police violate the Constitution, criminals go free. When criminals go free, the public demands answers. Thus, law enforcement officials recognize the importance of operating within established constitutional and legal boundaries.

Good-Faith Exception

As a general rule, when an honest mistake is made during the course of a search or seizure, any subsequently obtained evidence will be considered admissible. Two cases decided together were responsible for this good-faith exception: *United States* v. *Leon* and *Massachusetts* v. *Sheppard*.[45]

In *Leon*, police relied on a search warrant that was later declared invalid because it was not supported by probable cause. The Court upheld the search because the officers acted in good faith.

In *Sheppard*, officers had a difficult time finding a warrant form because it was the weekend, so they settled on a form previously used in another search for controlled substances. They made some changes to the form and presented it to a judge at his residence. The judge signed off on the warrant after making some changes of his own. But the references to controlled substances remained in the warrant, even though that was not what the officers set out to search for. A trial judge declared the warrant invalid, but the Supreme Court disagreed.

In both *Leon* and *Sheppard*, the Supreme Court concluded that evidence obtained in reasonable (good-faith) reliance on a defective warrant was admissible:

> [W]e cannot conclude that admitting evidence obtained pursuant to a warrant while at the same time declaring that the warrant was somehow defective will in any way reduce judicial officers' professional incentives to comply with the Fourth Amendment, encourage them to repeat their mistakes, or lead to the granting of all colorable warrant requests.[46]

Think About It...

The Exclusionary Rule Critics of the exclusionary rule claim that it creates public cynicism by letting otherwise guilty individuals escape prosecution. The question of whether the exclusionary rule is beneficial or harmful has been subjected to a fair amount of empirical research. Of particular interest is the incidence of cases where the rule resulted in the suppression of evidence and/or the extent to which search and seizure concerns dictate the decision to prosecute. *Do you support the argument that the exclusionary rule is a loophole? Why or why not? What other arguments can be raised for or against the exclusionary rule?*

B. Wylezich/Fotolia

The good-faith exception enunciated in *Leon* and *Sheppard* is not unqualified, however. If, for example, a warrant is "so lacking in indicia of probable cause as to render official belief in its existence entirely unreasonable, then evidence obtained following its service will not be admissible."[47] Similarly, if a warrant is "so facially deficient—i.e., in failing to particularize the place to be searched or things to be seized—that the executing officers cannot reasonably presume it to be valid, then the exception does not apply."[48]

The good-faith exception is not held in the highest regard by some. Critics believe that it gives police officers an incentive to "forum shop," or to find judges who will be quick to sign off on a warrant. Justice Brennan argued in opposition to the exception as follows:

> Creation of this new exception for good faith reliance upon a warrant implicitly tells magistrates that they need not take much care in reviewing warrant applications, since their mistakes will from now on have virtually no consequence: If their decision to issue a warrant is correct, the evidence will be admitted; if their decision was incorrect but [not "entirely unreasonable" and] the police rely in good faith on the warrant, the evidence will also be admitted. Inevitably, the care and attention devoted to such an inconsequential chore will dwindle.[49]

The good-faith exception has been extended to other situations besides searches and seizures based on defective warrants. For instance, if a police officer acts in reasonable reliance on a statute that is later found to be unconstitutional, then the good-faith exception will apply. In addition, if evidence is obtained following a search or seizure that is conducted in reasonable reliance on computer records that turn out to be inaccurate, then, again, the exception will apply. In *Arizona* v. *Evans*,[50] for example, a defendant was arrested during a traffic stop because the officer's computer showed an outstanding warrant that, unknown to the officer, had been quashed 17 days earlier. Evidence obtained from a search of the vehicle was admissible because, according to the Court, "there is no basis for believing that application of the exclusionary rule in these circumstances will have a significant effect on court employees responsible for informing the police that a warrant has been quashed."[51]

Criminal Prosecution

Various statutes at the state and federal levels provide criminal remedies for police misconduct. Some states make it a crime for police officers to trespass or to falsely arrest people. In fact, most criminal sanctions that apply to ordinary citizens also apply to police officers. Likewise, there are various statutes at the federal level that make it not only improper but also criminal for police officers to engage in certain types of conduct.

Federal Prosecution

At the federal level, the most common statute for holding police officers criminally liable is **18 U.S.C.A. Section 242**. Section 242 is to criminal liability what Section 1983 (discussed earlier) is to civil liability. It can be used to prosecute either a state or a federal law enforcement officer. Section 242 states,

> Whoever, under color of any law, statute, ordinance, regulation, or custom, willfully subjects any inhabitant of any State, Territory, or District to the deprivation of any rights, privileges, or immunities secured or protected by the Constitution or laws of the United States, or to different punishments, pains, or penalties, on account of such inhabitant being an alien, or by reason of his color, or race, than are prescribed for the punishment of citizens, shall be fined not more than $1,000 or imprisoned not more than one year, or both; and if death results shall be subject to imprisonment for any term of years or for life.

To be held liable under Section 242, a law enforcement officer must act with specific intent to deprive a person of important constitutional or other federal rights.[52] A finding of criminal liability under Section 242 also requires that a constitutional right be clearly established.[53] These restrictions have resulted in relatively few Section 242 cases. In fact, criminal liability under Section 242 is reserved for the most egregious forms of police misconduct.

Despite its relatively infrequent application, there have been a few cases in which Section 242 was invoked. For example, in *Miller* v. *United States* (1968),[54] a police officer was held criminally liable for allowing his canine unit to bite a suspect. In *Williams* v. *United States* (1951),[55] a defendant had been beaten, threatened, and physically punished for several hours, and the police officer was held criminally liable. Section 242 has also been applied in cases involving assault and battery of criminal defendants.[56]

Additional federal statutes make it a criminal act to unlawfully search and seize individuals (18 U.S.C.A. Section 2236), although applications of this statute are rare. For example, 18 U.S.C.A. Section 2235 makes it a crime to maliciously procure a warrant, and Section 2234 makes it a criminal offense to exceed the authority of a warrant. Regardless of which criminal statute applies, an important distinction between the various criminal statutes and 42 U.S.C. Section 1983 is that officers who are held *criminally* liable receive criminal convictions and can even go to prison; Section 1983, by contrast, is civil, meaning that it is used independently of the criminal process. A successful Section 1983 lawsuit will never result in the imprisonment of the defendant.

State Prosecution

The same laws that apply to ordinary citizens also apply to police officers. For example, if a police officer knowingly and intentionally kills someone and is not legally justified in doing so (i.e., it was not a justifiable killing that occurred in conjunction with the officer's official police duties), the officer can be held criminally liable for murder. Similarly, if a police officer trespasses on private property without appropriate justification, he or she can be held criminally liable. Criminal liability can extend to police officers for virtually any conceivable offense.

Three categories of offenses have been identified:[57] (1) violent and sex crimes, (2) drug crimes, and (3) other crimes. Examples of officers accused of violating state law include the so-called Miami River Cops, who were charged with murdering drug smugglers, and the police officer in Fort Myers, Florida, who was charged with sexual assault against a 19-year-old woman. Indeed, as of this writing, U.S. Border Patrol agents along the Arizona–Mexico border have become the targets of almost daily *criminal* complaints for a variety of actions.

Given the staggering amounts of money associated with the illegal drug trade, it is no wonder that some police officers cross the "thin blue line" and attempt to profit from illegal drugs. This appears to be the case with the infamous Rampart scandal in the LAPD. Officers in other cities have faced similar charges. In 1996, seven officers on the Chicago Police Department's Tactical Unit were charged with stealing and extorting drug money; seven officers in Atlanta were arrested in 1995 on drug charges; and a deputy in Tucson, Arizona, was arrested in 1999 for conspiracy to distribute drugs. The list, unfortunately, goes on.[58]

Police officers have also been held liable for such offenses as burglary, fabrication of evidence, perjury, and shoplifting. One report revealed that federal agents arrested three city police officers in Detroit who were planning a home invasion to steal $1 million in cash.[59]

This is not to suggest that police officers frequently engage in criminal activity—only that it does happen. No one is above the law, not even police officers. However, when officers break the law in order to protect the innocent or to prevent some greater harm, then they can claim a "law enforcement" or **public-duty defense**. Such a defense would, for example, be useful by an officer who finds the use of force necessary in effecting an arrest but is later accused of assault by the person arrested. The public-duty defense is meant to shield police officers from criminal liability when they act reasonably in such situations.

► *Accountability from the Inside*

The preceding section may give the impression that there is something wrong with internal accountability mechanisms, the organizational steps that police departments take to address wrongdoing. Nothing could be further from the truth. Internal affairs divisions and codes of ethics are effective methods for promoting the accountability of those charged with serving the public.

Internal Affairs

Many police agencies have developed innovative and highly regarded internal complaint review units, most commonly known as **internal affairs** divisions. Internal investigation units receive complaints that are filed in various manners: verbally or in writing, openly or anonymously, by civilians or sworn police officers, in person or by telephone, or by other means. Complaints must be investigated regardless of the manner of filing or the type of incident involved.

LEARNING OUTCOMES 3 — Discuss procedures for promoting accountability from within police agencies.

The internal affairs division in Oakland, California, for instance, is respected throughout the country.[60] According to one source, the "Internal Affairs Section of the Oakland Police Department works closely with the chief of police, who sets the tone for its rigorous investigations." Officers who have worked in internal affairs "help to pass on [the unit's] knowledge about citizens' complaints and educate the everyday cop about how internal affairs works. Ideally, these dynamics combine to make internal affairs respected, understood, and feared by the cops it polices."[61]

Functions and Procedures

The effectiveness of internal investigations of police misconduct depends on the accurate receipt and recording of all relevant information of improper personnel or organizational behavior, regardless of its source. Administrative efforts to minimize the potential for manipulating complaints have led to the designation of specifically identified individuals or offices as the point for registering employee misconduct complaints.

The following three types of complaints are critical to effective managerial control and must be fully investigated: (1) a citizen complaining about the police department or one of its employees, (2) a police employee complaining about another police employee, and (3) a police employee complaining about the police agency or its practices.[62]

Once they are recorded, complaints and reports must be managed in such a fashion as to ensure prompt, thorough, confidential investigations. Only the chief executive officer and police officials with a need to know are normally permitted access to information about the complainant, the complaint, or the investigation, at least during the initial investigative phase. Time limits for completing various aspects of the investigation and reporting to complainants are essential for the effective operation of internal affairs.

Another matter deserving careful consideration by the chief is the selection of staff investigators for internal affairs. Role conflicts are created when line police officers are assigned to investigate other line officers with whom they must work or when investigative officers are shifted back and forth between the internal affairs unit and operational units that are subject to investigations. In each of these instances, investigators may be tempted to be lenient with those officers accused of misconduct.

Although there is no universal agreement on this matter, internal investigations may be best served by police personnel who will never be reassigned to work under officers who have been the subject of their investigations. To prevent this situation from occurring, small police agencies sometimes use high-level staff commanders or investigators from other nearby police agencies or sheriff's departments. Larger organizations usually have the option of developing separate career paths for those who specialize in the investigation of other police officers. Such separate career routes have the advantage of permitting the use of rewards for vigorous, competent, and objective investigations. Together, all of these concerns have led to sophisticated procedures for tracking and investigating complaints against the police through internal affairs.

Officers' Rights during Investigations

A number of court cases have addressed the issue of police officers' rights during the course of internal investigations. For example, in *Garrity* v. *New Jersey* (1967),[63] the U.S. Supreme

Court ruled that information gained from the interrogation of a police officer could not be used in a criminal trial because it was not voluntary. In that case, a state deputy attorney general was asking police officers about ticket fixing. The officers were read their rights and then told that if they failed to answer the questions, they would be dismissed. Subsequent criminal convictions based on the officers' admissions were deemed unconstitutional because the admissions were not voluntary. Similarly, in *Gardner* v. *Broderick* (1967),[64] the Supreme Court ruled that police officers could not be fired for invoking their constitutional rights against self-incrimination. In *Gardner*, a police officer refused to answer questions from a grand jury on the grounds that the answers might incriminate him. The department fired the officer, but the Court held that this termination was unconstitutional. A number of other pertinent decisions have been handed down over the years, but most are beyond the scope of this introductory text.

Police Officers' Bill of Rights

To reduce the temptation for internal investigators to proceed against police employees in an insensitive fashion, some police agencies have formally adopted a statement of the rights of police officers who are accused of misconduct. Sometimes such conditions are contained in labor contracts; other times they are mandated by law. The typical **police officers' bill of rights** requires advanced notice to an officer who is being investigated, spells out procedures for resolving complaints that maintain due process protections, and limits the lengths to which an agency can go to secure information through interrogation and investigations.

Although the individual components of this list can be debated, fairness requires that officers deserve reasonable protection from inappropriate investigative practices. Procedures for ensuring that officers receive fair and appropriate treatment at the hands of specialized internal affairs investigators and their supervisors should be observed in the investigative process.

Several states have adopted bills of rights for police officers,[65] beginning with Florida in 1974. Supporters of such legislation argue that "the bill of rights merely ensures [that] the officer under investigation knows the subject of the investigation and is afforded rights and protections against certain interrogation techniques subject to abuse."[66] Critics claim that "the basic premises of such legislation only confound an already complex area of public police without substantially improving police labor–management relations."[67]

Codes of Ethics

Another mechanism for promoting accountability from within the law enforcement agency is a **code of ethics**, a statement of principles concerning the behavior of those who subscribe to the code. According to Joycelyn Pollock,[68] a leading police ethicist, these codes consist of several standard elements: "legality (enforcing and upholding the law), service (protecting and serving the public), honesty and integrity (telling the truth, being honest in action), loyalty (to other police officers), and the Golden Rule (treating people with respect or the way one would like to be treated)."[69]

The development of a code of ethics for law enforcement can be traced back to early movements to professionalize policing. During the 1930s, the IACP created a committee to make recommendations designed to promote professionalism. The committee agreed that one of the criteria for accomplishing this goal was the creation of a code of ethics. It was not until 1957, however, that the Law Enforcement Code of Ethics was unanimously approved by delegates attending the 64th IACP conference in Honolulu. Then, in 1989, IACP voted to replace the 1957 code with a newer version that reflects concern over a wider range of issues.

Among the issues covered in the 1989 code of ethics are (1) the responsibilities of police officers, (2) the performance of police duties, (3) discretion, (4) use of force, (5) confidentiality, (6) integrity, (7) cooperation with other agencies, (8) personal and professional responsibilities, and (9) private life. For example, with respect to an officer's private life, the code states, "Police officers will behave in a manner that does not bring discredit to their agencies or themselves." With respect to use of force, the code states, "A police officer will never employ unnecessary force or violence and will use only such force in the discharge of duty as is reasonable in all circumstances."[70]

Sentinel Event Reviews

A **sentinel event** is defined as a negative outcome that:

- signals underlying weaknesses in the system or process
- is likely the result of compound errors, [and]
- may provide, if properly analyzed and addressed, important keys to strengthening the system and preventing future adverse events or outcomes.[71]

Examples could include a "near miss," a wrongful conviction, the unintentional early release of a dangerous inmate, or an excess build-up of unresolved cold cases. As the National Institute of Justice puts it, ". . . anything that stakeholders can agree should not happen again could be considered a sentinel event."[72]

When things go wrong, our gut reaction is to blame someone or identify a specific error that needs "fixing." Sentinel events, however, are often the result of several factors, and rarely is a single individual responsible. Think about air disasters, for example. Rarely do plane crashes result from one person's actions or inaction. The vast majority of the time they are "system errors," or "organizational accidents." There may be several people involved, but to complicate matters, equipment could malfunction and even chance could enter the equation.

A sentinel event review, therefore, is a procedure designed to "take stock" of something that went wrong in order to prevent it in the future. It ". . . brings together all of the system's stakeholders (law enforcement, crime laboratory personnel, prosecutors, defense lawyers, judges, corrections officials, victim advocates, and others, depending on the event) to review the event and determine—through a deliberative, transparent, nonblaming process—how and why it happened and what can be done to prevent a similar outcome in the future."[73]

A Record-Keeping Mistake

Deputy Mark Anderson learned that Bennie Dean Herring, a man who was no stranger to law enforcement, drove to the Coffee County (Alabama) Sheriff's Department to retrieve an item from his impounded truck. Anderson asked the warrant clerk to check for any outstanding arrest warrants against Herring. When she found none, Anderson asked her to check with her counterpart in neighboring Dale County. Indeed, there was an outstanding arrest warrant for Herring in Dale County. Anderson and another deputy then followed Herring as he left the impound lot, stopped him, and arrested him. A search of Herring revealed methamphetamine in his pocket. The deputies also found a pistol in the vehicle.

The arrest in this case seemed like a slam dunk. However, unknown to the officers, the Dale County arrest warrant had been recalled several months earlier. Apparently, the computer database had not been updated. In other words, there really was no Dale County arrest warrant for Herring. With no arrest warrant and assuming that there was no other reason for the deputies to stop Herring, a question arose as to whether the contraband found during the arrest should have been

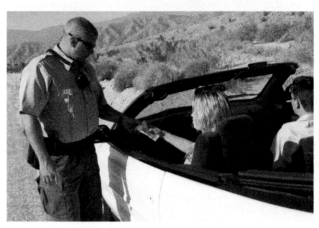

Moodboard/Alamy Stock Photo

admissible against Herring at trial. The case went all the way to the U.S. Supreme Court, which held that the deputies made an honest mistake and that the evidence against Herring should have been admissible in court.[74]

This case raises several questions:
1. Do you agree with the Supreme Court's decision in this case? Why or why not?
2. Is the exclusionary rule an adequate remedy for unconstitutional police conduct?
3. What exclusionary rule exception is most applicable in this case, and why?

Identify the two main avenues for civil litigation against police officers.

Police can be held liable for monetary and other damages under (1) 42 U.S.C. Section 1983 and (2) state tort law. For a Section 1983 lawsuit to succeed, the plaintiff must show that the defendant acted under color of law and violated an applicable constitutional provision. Defenses to Section 1983 liability include absolute and qualified immunity. Common state tort claims against police include intentional and negligent misconduct. There are several defenses to state tort liability, including the public-duty doctrine, contributory negligence, comparative negligence, assumption of risk, and sudden peril.

1. What are the two main avenues available to aggrieved parties seeking to sue for police civil liability?

2. What is a Section 1983 lawsuit? Who can be targeted by such suits?

3. What is meant by absolute immunity? Are law enforcement officers protected in the performance of their duties by the concept of absolute immunity? Why or why not?

4. What are some of the defenses against civil liability that law enforcement officers and their supervisors and departments might employ? How can civil liability promote accountability?

damages Monetary compensation awarded to the plaintiff in a successful civil lawsuit.

injunctive relief A court order to bring injurious or offensive action to a halt.

42 U.S.C. Section 1983 The federal statute that provides a remedy in federal court for the "deprivation of any rights . . . secured by the Constitution and laws" of the United States.

color of law The condition that exists when an individual acts in an official government capacity and with the appearance of legal power. Police officers, mayors, and a number of other government officials perform their duties under color of law.

constitutional rights violation Conduct that violates a specific constitutional provision.

culpability The state of deserving blame or being morally or legally responsible. Under the Section 1983 culpability requirement, plaintiffs generally must prove that the defendant officer *intended* for the violation to occur.

theory of liability Reasons offered as to why a particular person or other entity should be held answerable under law for some action.

Bivens* v. *Six Unknown Named Agents The 1971 U.S. Supreme Court ruling that held that federal law enforcement officers can be sued for Fourth Amendment violations. The decision has since been expanded to include liability for violations of constitutional rights embodied in other relevant amendments.

absolute immunity Protection from lawsuits enjoyed by federal officials when acting in their official capacities.

qualified immunity A liability defense that shields a police officer who has acted in an objectively reasonable fashion as long as he or she did not violate clearly established rights that a reasonable person would have known. Qualified immunity is an outgrowth of various U.S. Supreme Court decisions.

objective reasonableness A standard, used to determine whether qualified immunity applies, that looks at how a reasonable person would have acted under a given set of circumstances.

state tort liability An important avenue of redress for plaintiffs whose minor injuries, allegedly resulting from negligent acts or misconduct by the police, are not serious enough to make Section 1983 litigation a viable option.

intentional tort An action that is highly likely to cause injury or damage.

negligence tort A liability claim that must demonstrate that a legal duty existed between the officer and the plaintiff, that a breach of that duty occurred, that a proximate (direct) causation between the officer's actions and the alleged harm resulted, and that actual damage or injury occurred.

public-duty doctrine A doctrine stating that police protection (like any other government function) is owed to the general public, not to individuals. Police officers have used the public-duty doctrine as a liability defense.

contributory negligence A liability defense that holds that if an officer can show that the plaintiff or someone else was also negligent in an event, the officer should not be held liable. Contributory negligence can arise not only from the actions of a criminal suspect but also from the actions of third parties.

comparative negligence A partial defense against state tort liability that examines who is to blame and assigns liability accordingly.

assumption of risk A defense against state tort liability that provides that if a plaintiff voluntarily engaged in a dangerous activity that led to his or her injury, then the police officer should not be held liable.

sudden peril A defense against state tort liability that is used for cases in which police officers were required to make split-second decisions.

Explain the different types of external accountability measures put in place to check police misconduct.

External mechanisms for promoting police accountability in addition to civil liability include citizen oversight, citizen complaint procedures, agency accreditation, the exclusionary rule, and criminal prosecution.

Citizen oversight refers to the oversight of police actions and the investigation of complaints by nonsworn personnel. Citizen complaints promote accountability, but the fate of a complaint depends on who files it. Police agencies, like universities, seek accreditation to demonstrate that they meet critical professional standards. The exclusionary rule requires that evidence obtained in violation of the U.S.

Constitution be inadmissible in a criminal trial. The rule has been expanded with the fruit of the poisonous tree doctrine. There are several arguments for and against the exclusionary rule. Ultimately, however, it is rarely applied. Police officers, like ordinary citizens, can be held *criminally* liable for egregious misconduct.

1. What is meant by law enforcement agency accreditation? What is the accrediting agency? How does law enforcement accreditation promote police accountability?

2. What is the exclusionary rule? How does it promote police accountability?

3. What mechanisms are involved in civilian oversight of the police?

4. What is involved in the process of civilian review?

civilian review One of the stronger models of citizen oversight of a police agency in which a group of citizens investigates complaints against the police, adjudicates the complaints, and recommends punishment.

civilian input A model of civilian oversight of a police agency in which civilians receive and investigate complaints, but the next steps are taken by the police department.

civilian monitor A model of civilian oversight of a police agency that is similar to an ombudsman approach in which complaints are received by the police department and the process, from beginning to end, is monitored by civilians.

citizen complaint A document filed by someone who believes that he or she has been wronged by one or more police officers in a department.

accreditation Certification for having met all applicable requirements put in place by an accrediting body.

exclusionary rule A rule mandating that evidence obtained in violation of the U.S. Constitution cannot be admitted in a criminal trial. The exclusionary rule is an important mechanism for ensuring the accountability of police officials.

fruit of the poisonous tree doctrine An expansion of the scope of the exclusionary rule that requires the exclusion of any secondary evidence (such as a confession) that derives from evidence originally obtained in violation of the U.S. Constitution.

18 U.S.C.A. Section 242 The most common federal statute used to hold police officers criminally liable.

public-duty defense A legal defense that shields a police officer from criminal liability in situations in which he or she is legally performing an assigned or implied public duty and engages in a necessary and reasonable action that, for ordinary citizens, would be considered a crime.

LEARNING OUTCOMES 3

Discuss procedures for promoting accountability from within police agencies.

Accountability from inside police agencies is promoted via internal affairs divisions and professional codes of ethics. Internal affairs refers to either a division within a police agency or one or more officers who are tasked with investigating allegations of misconduct. The targets of internal affairs investigations enjoy a number of protections today. Sentinel event reviews help officials identify system breakdowns and prevent future problems. Codes of ethics encourage officers to abide by various professional standards.

1. How do police agencies promote accountability from within?

2. What is the role of the internal affairs division in police departments?

3. Why would officers want to work in the internal affairs division?

4. Can the sentinel event review process really be non-blaming? Why or why not?

5. Identify at least one law enforcement-related code of ethics. How seriously do police officers take codes of ethics?

internal affairs An investigative agency within a police department that is tasked with investigating allegations of misconduct or criminality by members of the department.

police officers' bill of rights A police agency's formal statement of the rights of officers who are accused of misconduct.

code of ethics A statement of principles concerning the behavior of those who subscribe to the code.

References

1 *Mullenix* v. *Luna*, 77 U. S. ____ (2015).

2 *Lugar* v. *Edmondson Oil Co.*, 457 U.S. 922 (1982), p. 937.

3 Michael S. Vaughn and Lisa F. Coomes, "Police civil liability under Section 1983: When do police officers act under color of law," *Journal of Criminal Justice*, vol. 23 (1995), pp. 395–415, quote on p. 409.

4 *Daniels* v. *Williams*, 474 U.S. 327 (1986), p. 330.

5 J. L. Worrall, "Culpability standards in Section 1983 litigation against criminal justice officials: When and why mental state matters," *Crime and Delinquency*, vol. 47 (2001), pp. 28–59.

6 See, e.g., *City of Canton* v. *Harris*, 489 U.S. 378 (1989).

7 See, e.g., *Monell* v. *Department of Social Services*, 436 U.S. 658 (1978).

8 *Bivens* v. *Six Unknown Named Agents*, 403 U.S. 388 (1971).

9 See, e.g., *Davis* v. *Passman*, 442 U.S. 228 (1979); *Sonntag* v. *Dooley*, 650 F.2d 904 (7th Cir. 1981); *Carlson* v. *Green*, 446 U.S. 14 (1980).

10 *Bradley* v. *Fisher*, 80 U.S. 335 (1871).

11 *Yaselli* v. *Goff*, 275 U.S. 503 (1927).

12 *Butz* v. *Economou*, 438 U.S. 478 (1978).

13 *Harlow* v. *Fitzgerald*, 457 U.S. 800 (1982).

14 See, e.g., *Harlow* v. *Fitzgerald*, 457 U.S. 800 (1982); *Wood* v. *Strickland*, 420 U.S. 308 (1975).

15 See, e.g., *Anderson* v. *Creighton*, 483 U.S. 635 (1987); *Malley* v. *Briggs*, 475 U.S. 335 (1988).

16 W. A. Kerstetter, "Who disciplines the police? Who should?," in *Police leadership in America*, ed. W. Geller, pp. 178, 188 (Chicago: American Bar Association, 1985).

17 P. West, "Investigation of complaints against the police: Summary report of a national survey," *American Journal of Police*, vol. 7 (1988), pp. 101–22.

18 S. Walker and B. Wright, *Citizen review of the police: A national survey of the 50 largest cities* (Washington, DC: Police Executive Research Forum, 1995).

19 President's Task Force on 21st Century Policing, *Final Report of the President's Task Force on 21st Century Policing* (Washington, DC: Office of Community Oriented Policing Services, 2015), p. 26.

20 A. J. Goldsmith, *Complaints against the police: The trend toward external review* (Oxford: Clarendon Press, 1991).

21 Kerstetter, "Who disciplines the police?"

22 A. E. Wagner and S. H. Decker, "Evaluating citizen complaints against the police," in *Critical issues in policing: Contemporary readings*, 3rd ed., eds. R. G. Dunham and G. P. Alpert, pp. 302–18 (Prospect Heights, IL: Waveland, 1997); Americans for Effective Law Enforcement, *Police civilian review boards*, AELE Defense Manual, Brief #82-3 (San Francisco: Americans for Effective Law Enforcement, 1982).

23 For more details, see http://kcmo.gov/police/office-of-community-complaints/ (accessed January 27, 2016).

24 City of San Jose, Office of the Independent Auditor, "Charter," www.sanjoseca.gov/ipa (accessed January 27, 2016).

25 S. Walker and V. W. Bumphus, *Civilian review of the police: A national survey of the 50 largest cities* (Omaha: University of Nebraska at Omaha, 1991).

26 S. Walker, *Citizen review resource manual* (Washington, DC: Police Executive Research Forum, 1995).

27 Ibid.

28 Ibid.

29 S. Walker, *Police accountability: The role of citizen oversight* (Belmont, CA: Wadsworth, 2001).

30 D. W. Perez, *Common sense about police review* (Philadelphia: Temple University Press, 1994).

31 S. Walker and B. Wright, "Varieties of citizen review: The relationship of mission, structure, and procedures to police accountability," in Dunham and Alpert, *Critical issues in policing*, p. 333.

32 Ibid.

33 A. E. Wagner and S. H. Decker, "Evaluating citizen complaints against the police," in Dunham and Alpert, *Critical issues in policing*, p. 310.

34 Commission on Accreditation for Law Enforcement Agencies, *Standards for law enforcement agencies*, 5th ed. (Fairfax, VA: Commission on Accreditation for Law Enforcement Agencies, 2006), www.calea.org (accessed January 27, 2016). © 2006. Reprinted with permission.

35 Ibid.

36 J. A. Conser and G. D. Russell, *Law enforcement in the United States* (Gaithersburg, MD: Aspen, 2000).

37 S. J. Hill, "The significance of police credentialing," *Police*, vol. 23 (March 1999), pp. 40–42.

38 W. E. Eastman, "National accreditation: A costly, unneeded make-work scheme," in *Police management today*, ed. J. Fyfe, pp. 49–54 (Washington, DC: International City Managers Association,1985); J. Pearson, "National accreditation: A valuable management tool," in Fyfe, *Police management today*, pp. 45–48.

39 J. W. Bizzack and V. Delacruz, "Demystifying police accreditation," *Law Enforcement News*, April 30, 1994, pp. 8, 11.

40 Washington Association of Sheriffs and Police Chiefs, *Accreditation program* (Olympia: Washington Association of Sheriffs and Police Chiefs, 1998).

41 *Weeks* v. *United States*, 232 U.S. 383 (1914); *Mapp* v. *Ohio*, 367 U.S. 643 (1961).

42 *Elkins* v. *United States*, 364 U.S. 206 (1960).

43 *Silverthorne Lumber Co.* v. *United States*, 251 U.S. 385 (1920).

44 M. Wilkey, "Why suppress evidence?," *Judicature*, vol. 62 (1978), p. 214.

45 *United States* v. *Leon*, 468 U.S. 897 (1984); *Massachusetts* v. *Sheppard*, 468 U.S. 981 (1984).

46 *United States* v. *Leon*, p. 917.

47 *United States* v. *Hove*, 848 F.2d 137 (9th Cir. 1988), p. 139.

48 *United States* v. *Leary*, 846 F.2d 592 (10th Cir. 1988), p. 607.

49 *United States* v. *Leon*, p. 956.

50 *Arizona* v. *Evans*, 514 U.S. 1 (1995).

51 Ibid., p. 15.

52 *Screws* v. *United States*, 325 U.S. 91 (1945).

53 *United States* v. *Lanier*, 520 U.S. 259 (1997).

54 *Miller* v. *United States*, 404 F.2d 611 (5th Cir. 1968).

55 *Williams* v. *United States*, 341 U.S. 97 (1951).

56 *Lynch* v. *United States*, 189 F.2d 476 (5th Cir. 1951).

57 M. L. Birzer, "Crimes committed by police officers," in *Police misconduct*, ed. M. J. Palmiotto, pp. 168–81 (Upper Saddle River, NJ: Prentice Hall, 2001).

58 Ibid.

59 M. W. Lyman, *The police: An introduction* (Upper Saddle River, NJ: Prentice Hall, 1999).

60 J. Douglas and J. Johnson, *Official deviance* (New York: Lippincott, 1977); D. Guyot, *Policing as though people matter* (Philadelphia: Temple University Press, 1991).

61 D. W. Perez and W. K. Muir, "Administrative review of alleged police brutality," in *And justice for all: Understanding and controlling police abuse of force*, eds. W. A. Geller and H. Toch, pp. 207–8 (Washington, DC: Police Executive Research Forum, 1995).

62 J. Angell, "The adequacy of the internal processing of citizen complaints by police departments" (master's thesis, Michigan State University, 1966).

63 *Garrity* v. *New Jersey*, 385 U.S. 483 (1967).

64 *Gardner* v. *Broderick*, 392 U.S. 273 (1967).

65 M. Chiuchiolo, "The law enforcement officer's bill of rights: Panacea or problem?," *Police Chief*, vol. 68 (1981), pp. 70–72.

66 H. Johnson, "A police officer's bill of rights: A needed protection for cops?," in *Controversial issues in policing*, ed. J. D. Sewell, p. 42 (Boston: Allyn and Bacon, 1999).

67 M. Scott, "A police officer's bill of rights: A needed protection for cops?," in Sewell, *Controversial issues in policing*, pp. 36–41.

68 J. M. Pollock, "Ethics in law enforcement," in Dunham and Alpert, *Critical issues in policing*, p. 366.

69 J. Pollock and R. Becker, "Ethical dilemmas in police work," in *Justice, crime, and ethics*, eds. M. Braswell, B. McCarthy, and B. McCarthy, pp. 83–103 (Cincinnati: Anderson, 1996).

70 L. K. Gaines, V. E. Kappeler, and J. B. Vaughn, *Policing in America*, 3rd ed., pp. 344–45 (Cincinnati: Anderson, 1999).

71 National Institute of Justice, *NIJ's sentinel events initiative*, http://nij.gov/topics/justice-system/pages/sentinel-events.aspx (accessed January 27, 2016).

72 National Institute of Justice, *Mending justice: Sentinel event reviews* (Washington, DC: National Institute of Justice, 2014), p. 4.

73 National Institute of Justice, *Testing a concept and beyond: Can the criminal justice system adopt a nonblaming practice?*, http://www.nij.gov/journals/276/Pages/sentinel-events.aspx (accessed January 27, 2016).

74 *Herring* v. *United States*, 555 U.S. 135 (2009).

12

Deviance, Ethics, and Professionalism

1 Discuss how various commissions established to examine police misconduct in the United States have uncovered deviance.

2 Identify several typologies of police deviance that scholars have proposed.

3 Discuss explanations for police deviance, its incidence, and methods of controlling it.

Sean Murphy/Stone/Getty Images

THE ABUSE OF POLICE POWER

In 2015, former Oklahoma City police lieutenant Daniel Holtzclaw was convicted of 18 counts of rape and sentenced to 263 years in prison.[1] The charges against Holtzclaw included four counts of first-degree felony rape and two counts of forcible oral sodomy. All of Holtzclaw's victims were black women with criminal records, and many of them were drug offenders. Holtzclaw was emboldened by the fact that he believed that the women would be too afraid to say anything about the assaults.

Holtzclaw's victims ranged in age from 17 to 58, and included a 57-year-old grandmother. Twelve of the victimized women said they were too afraid to report the attacks and thought that no one would believe that they had been sexually assaulted by a police officer. While it's clear that Holtzclaw's crimes reflect badly on the police profession, the situation was complicated by the fact that internal affairs officers apparently ignored a claim by a woman in 2013 that she had been groped and kidnapped by Holtzclaw in his police vehicle. The woman had been leaving the hospital where her daughter was receiving cancer treatments, when she was grabbed by the former officer and made to perform sex acts on him. She was eventually released—dropped off at the hospital that she had been leaving when Holtzclaw forced her into his vehicle. Although she reported the incident to hospital employees who called the police, she never heard from investigators.

Sue Ogrocki/Pool/Pi/ZUMA Press/Newscom

▶ Discovering Deviance

With the enormous power afforded to law enforcement officials comes the potential for abuse of that power. As in any job, when employees are given a large amount of autonomy, coupled with a significant degree of control over others, it is not surprising that some will step outside the bounds of acceptable conduct. Police training, supervision, professionalism, ethical standards, and legal constraints may deter some inappropriate behavior, but even the most effective controls do not work all the time or for all officers.

LEARNING OUTCOMES 1 Discuss how various commissions established to examine police misconduct in the United States have uncovered deviance.

When talk of police improprieties comes up, the term **corruption** inevitably surfaces. Corruption can be defined as dishonest or fraudulent conduct by public officials in a position of power: "Police officers act corruptly when, in exercising or failing to exercise their authority, they act with the primary intention of furthering private or departmental/divisional advantage."[2]

Corruption, though, is but one example of improper conduct. Perhaps a better term to apply to the material discussed in this chapter is **deviance**. *Deviance* is a broad term that applies to any behavior that is at odds with socially expected or accepted behavior. *Police deviance* thus refers to police behavior that is not regarded as appropriate by those in a position to make such determinations. Usually, this means training authorities, supervisors, the authors of professional standards, and the like, but it also means members of the wider society. Viewed in this way, police deviance can take a number of forms. It can range from the most flagrant physical abuses to seemingly innocuous behaviors that probably wouldn't catch the eye of any but the most ardent police critics. Varying degrees of deviance and corruption have characterized societies everywhere and are certainly not new. Criminal justice historian Samuel Walker describes police corruption during the eighteenth century:

> With few books and even less legal training available, many constables and justices of the peace simply did not know the law. Corruption was also a problem, as officials gave favored treatment to friends, relatives, and influential people. . . . [There were] also accounts of sheriffs and constables taking bribes to release prisoners or fix juries and assaulting citizens without any cause. In short, police corruption and brutality appeared at the very outset of American criminal justice history.[3]

Other historians have remarked that not only did early urban police protect the criminal element, but they practically encouraged crime:

> The police did not suppress vice; they licensed it. From New York . . . to San Francisco, and from Chicago . . . to New Orleans . . . they permitted gamblers, prostitutes, and saloon keepers to do business under certain well-understood conditions. These entrepreneurs were required to make regular payoffs [to the police].[4]

The Wickersham Commission

As patterns of misconduct were being revealed and policing entered the professional era, accounts of police deviance became even more common. This was partly due to the work of various crime commissions. The first of these to tackle the issue of improper police conduct was the 1929 Wickersham Commission (known officially as the *National Commission on Law Observance and Enforcement*) (see Figure 12–1).

One of the Wickersham report's authors, Walter Pollak, went on to argue successfully for the defense in 1932 in *Powell* v. *Alabama*,[5] in which the U.S. Supreme Court held that a defendant facing the death penalty is entitled to an attorney at trial. *Powell* arose from the famous Scottsboro case, in which eight African-American youths in Alabama were convicted of raping two white women and sentenced to die—without the assistance of counsel. This and some other successful cases that Pollak argued pointed to examples of questionable police conduct, shaky evidence, race discrimination, and other police misconduct.

The Knapp Commission

The formation of the **Knapp Commission** in 1970 marked another significant milestone in the investigation of police deviance. It was established in May of that year under the auspices of Mayor John V. Lindsay of New York in response to an article published by the *New York Times* that reported widespread corruption in the New York City Police Department (NYPD). Judge Whitman Knapp was appointed to chair the commission and investigate the extent to which the *New York Times* accurately portrayed the behaviors of the department.

The Knapp Commission's reference to grass- and meat-eating corruption (as noted in Figure 12–1) has since been expanded to include other types of police behaviors. Police expert Tom Barker, for example, expanded the commission's typology.[6] **White knights**, he argued, are the honest and upstanding officers who never step over the line between accepted and deviant conduct, no matter how great the pressure. **Straight shooters** are officers who, for the most part, are honest but will overlook some of the misconduct committed by their peers. Next are the **grass eaters** and **meat eaters** identified by the Knapp Commission. Finally, **rogues** are the most seriously deviant officers, according to Barker. In 2005, for example, a federal grand jury in Brooklyn indicted retired NYPD officers Stephen Caracappa and Louis Eppolito, saying that in the 1980s, the two had routinely passed confidential law enforcement information to members of organized crime and had worked as hit men for the mob, killing rival gangsters.[7] Even meat eaters view rouges, who engage in serious criminal activity, as extraordinarily corrupt.

▶ Typologies of Deviance

The Wickersham and Knapp crime commissions uncovered several varieties of police deviance. Since then, still other corrupt and deviant practices have come to light. This has prompted researchers to classify, or construct typologies of, police deviance. There are several such noteworthy efforts. We begin with one of the better-known typologies and then consider some others. The last part of this section looks at other forms of police deviance that do not fit neatly into any one category or set of categories.

> **LEARNING OUTCOMES 2** Identify several typologies of police deviance that scholars have proposed.

The Dark Side of Policing

Victor Kappeler, Richard Sluder, and Geoffrey Alpert's popular book *Forces of Deviance: Understanding the Dark Side of Policing*[8] identifies four types of police deviance: police crime, occupational deviance, police corruption, and abuse of authority (Figure 12–2). Each is discussed in this section. The order in which they appear is not intended to suggest that one is any more serious than the other.

Wickersham Commission

1929: first commission to tackle the issue of improper police conduct. Its report, *Lawlessness in Law Enforcement*, provided a blistering critique of police corruption around the country. Its authors found that the "third degree," or "the inflicting of pain, physical or mental, to extract confessions or statements," was "extensively practiced across the country."[i]

Knapp Commission

1970: Report identified two types of corrupt police officers: **grass eaters** and **meat eaters**. Grass eaters are the police officers who accept small gifts and engage in minor deviance, mostly in response to peer pressure. Meat eaters are the officers who actively seek out opportunities to exploit their positions, in a proactive and planned fashion, and who may be involved in large-scale and far-reaching corrupt activities. The difficulty facing police reformers is that while meat-eating corruption is much more serious, grass-eating corruption is far more commonplace.

[i]National Commission on Law Observance and Enforcement, *Report on lawlessness in law enforcement* (1931; repr., Montclair, NJ: Patterson Smith, 1968), p. 4.

FIGURE 12–1 Police Deviance and Corruption.

Police Crime

Officer uses official police powers to engage in criminal conduct.
Examples: entering private property with no legitimate reason, unjustifiable homicide.

Occupational Deviance

Using one's position for personal gain.
Examples: committing theft from the evidence locker to helping a friend get a speeding ticket removed from his or her driving record

Police Corruption

Misusing police authority to receive material reward or gain. Material reward or gain must be some tangible object, either cash, service, or goods that have cash value.
Example: skimming drugs from big busts

Abuse of Authority

Abuse of authority is basically the catchall category for other inappropriate conduct that does not necessarily amount to crime, deviance, or corruption.
Examples: excessive force, psychological abuse of citizens

FIGURE 12–2 The Dark Side of Policing.

Police Crime

In Chapter 11, we discussed different mechanisms for preserving the accountability of law enforcement officials. One of those is the criminal law. Generally, when police officers break the criminal law, they do so during the course of their legitimate duties and thus cannot be prosecuted as the rest of us can. Indeed, there are a number of so-called affirmative defenses that police officers can assert that immunize them from charges of criminal activity when they engage in activities that would be considered criminal for the rest of us. These include entering private property without permission, using physical force to complete an arrest, and even shooting a person. This is what Kappeler and his colleagues meant by **police crime**. They defined police crime as an "officer's use of the official powers of his or her job to engage in criminal conduct."[9] Researchers have uncovered several examples of police criminal behavior.[10]

Occupational Deviance

Occupational deviance refers to behavior that either does not conform to accepted standards of conduct or is not part of normal patrol work and is committed under the guise of police authority. Almost anyone can engage in occupational deviance. Consider embezzlement, an offense that nearly anyone can commit during the course of legitimate employment. Embezzlement is basically theft without a trespassory element. The occupational deviance Kappeler and his colleagues refer to, however, is behavior that is facilitated by virtue of serving as a police officer, and it can include much more than just deviance for personal gain. Occupational deviance is perhaps the most intractable problem for police administrators because it's common, it's difficult to detect, and it does not always rise to the level of a criminal offense.

Police Corruption

Remember that our definition of deviance *includes* corruption. Knowing that, it should come as no surprise that Kappeler and his colleagues liken police corruption to deviance. They defined **police corruption** as the misuse of police authority for personal gain.

More often, the term *police corruption* connotes serious and even criminal conduct committed by law enforcement officers. Thus, to minimize confusion, it is useful to put deviance in the *inappropriate but not necessarily flagrant* category. Corruption is a bit more serious, but if corruption is for personal gain, then simply accepting a free cup of coffee fits the term. Can we logically argue that an officer who accepts a free cup of coffee is the same as one who routinely skims drugs or cash from big busts? Probably not.

Abuse of Authority

Abuse of authority is basically the catchall category for other inappropriate conduct that does not necessarily amount to crime, deviance, or corruption. Kappeler and his colleagues identify three elements of **abuse of authority**:

- Officers may physically abuse a citizen through the use of excessive force.
- Officers may psychologically abuse a citizen through the use of verbal assault, harassment, or ridicule.
- Officers may violate a citizen's constitutional, federal, or state rights.[11]

Physical abuse and brutality are arguably the most serious forms of police misconduct, but they can also overlap with some of the other behaviors we have already discussed. Police crime, for example, can contain physical elements. If a police officer wrongfully (and intentionally) kills someone, then what we have is police crime and abuse of authority all wrapped up in a single case. Given the serious nature of physical force and, particularly, abuses of it, we return to this topic in Chapter 13.

Classifying Corruption

Some researchers have been content to use the term *corruption* to refer to all manner of police misconduct. For example, in his popular book *Conduct Unbecoming: The Social Construction of Police Deviance and Control*,[12] Maurice Punch identifies four categories of behavior that he considers to be corruption: **straightforward corruption**, **predatory corruption**, combative corruption, and the **perversion of justice**. The order in which they are presented in Figure 12–3 does not relate to their seriousness.

There have been many examples of police officers offering false testimony either to obtain a conviction or to satisfy vengeful motives. Officer Mark Fuhrman's perjured testimony during the famous O. J. Simpson trial is one example.[13] Then there are the findings of the **Mollen Commission**, which investigated allegations of police corruption in the NYPD during the 1990s. The commission drew this conclusion about the pervasiveness of police perjury:

> Officers reported a litany of manufactured tales. For example, when officers unlawfully stop and search a vehicle because they believe it contains drugs

or guns, officers will falsely claim in police reports and under oath that the car ran a red light (or committed some other traffic violation) and that they subsequently saw contraband in the car in plain view. To conceal an unlawful search of an individual who officers believe is carrying drugs or a gun, they will falsely assert that they saw a bulge in the person's pocket or saw drugs and money changing hands. To justify unlawfully entering an apartment where officers believe narcotics or cash can be found, they pretend to have information from an unidentified civilian informant or claim they saw the drugs in plain view after responding to the premises on a radio run. To arrest people they suspect are guilty of dealing drugs, they falsely assert that the defendants had drugs in their possession when, in fact, the drugs were found elsewhere where the officers had no lawful right to be.[14]

If the commission's observations seem inaccurate or troubling or even a little biased, then consider the findings from Myron Orfield's famous study of police perjury.[15] He interviewed prosecutors, judges, and defense attorneys and found that 52% believed that at least "half of the time" the prosecutor "knows or has reason to know" that police fabricate evidence at suppression hearings, where judges decide whether evidence should be excluded due to inappropriate police actions. More shocking still is the finding that more than 9 of the 10 prosecutors surveyed had knowledge of police perjury "at least some of the time." In fairness to police officers, Orfield's study also revealed that much of the perjured testimony given by police at suppression hearings was encouraged by prosecutors who would often say something like, "If this happens, we win. If this happens, we lose."[16]

Straightforward Corruption

According to Punch, straightforward corruption is simply any form of misconduct that provides a direct financial benefit to the officer. An officer who is in cahoots with organized crime figures and receives money for "looking the other way," for example, is said to engage in straightforward corruption.

Predatory Corruption

Refers to the actions of police officers who actively promote and engage in criminal and other wrongful activities. For example, instead of "looking the other way" and ignoring organized crime, the police *are* the organized criminals. Predatory corruption is arguably more serious than straightforward corruption.

Combative Corruption

Combative corruption refers to making arrests, gaining convictions, and ensuring lengthy sentences at whatever the cost and may be among the most common forms of police misconduct. Here are several examples of combative corruption:

- Flaking: Planting evidence on a suspect
- Padding: Adding evidence to strengthen a case against a suspect
- Using verbals, or words, to describe and incriminate a suspect
- Intimidating a witness
- Scoring on an informant: Shaking down an informant for money, drugs, and other items
- Burning: Revealing an informant's identity
- Paying an informant with illegally obtained drugs

Perversion of Justice

Consists of serious actions by a police officer, such as lying under oath (perjury), intimidating a witness, and performing other activities that resemble combative corruption. The difference between the two lies in the officer's motivations. Where combative corruption was concerned with "doing justice" (in the police officer's view), the perversion of justice refers to acting vengefully, of using one's position as a police officer to exact revenge on others. There is, of course, some overlap between these categories. The common thread running throughout each is behavior that is at odds with accepted standards.

FIGURE 12–3 ▶ Four Categories of Police Corruption.

Police Misconduct

Barker has argued not only that deviance should be couched in terms of corruption but also that any focus on corruption should be limited to those activities for which there is a monetary reward for the officers.[17] In Figure 12–4, we briefly consider eight examples of this form of corruption.

Corruption of Authority

Occurs when an officer agrees to accept free meals, discounts, and rewards by virtue of his or her position as a police officer. This type of corruption is perhaps the most innocuous and does not require any significant degree of organization. An officer who receives a free cup of a coffee or a free lunch from a restaurant owner fits into this category.

It is likely that the restaurant owner is attempting to curry favor with the police and possibly benefit from some added attention and/or surveillance of the restaurant that other business owners in the area would not necessarily receive.

Kickbacks

Illegal payments for services performed. An example of this form of corruption hails from Illinois. In January 2001, the public safety director of Cicero, Illinois, Emil Schullo, was indicted in a kickback scheme. He was accused of contracting out town investigative work to a private investigative firm in exchange for kickbacks amounting to 10 percent of the contracted billings. To Schullo's chagrin, the investigator was working with federal law enforcement officials and tape-recorded their conversations. Surprisingly, Schullo was the *ninth* Cicero official to be indicted for corruption. In 2003, Schullo was sentenced to more than nine years in prison.

Opportunistic Theft

A theft that occurs when an opportunity presents itself. Examples include theft from arrestees, crime victims, crime scenes, and unprotected places. This type of theft can be quite lucrative.

Shakedowns

Shakedowns consist of corrupt officers demanding money, goods, or other valuables from people in exchange for lenient treatment, protection, or some other illegitimate service. Basically, shakedowns are extortion. Shakedowns are less common today than they were in the past, so we have to look back in time for examples. During the 1960s, for instance, Seattle police officers were paid $200 each month in exchange for protecting a gay bathhouse called the Atlas Club.

Protecting Illegal Activities

The protection of illegal activities is not unlike a shakedown in the sense that police receive money for their services. Here, though, instead of seeking payment for protection, they seek payment for turning a blind eye to criminal activity. It is safe to say that the police protection of criminal activity is very much the exception these days. It was perhaps most frequent during the Prohibition era, when corrupt officers would routinely protect establishments that continued to serve liquor. Many of these so-called speakeasies could not have operated without police protection.

Fixes

Fixes occur when police officers fix a speeding ticket or other infraction or charge—that is, remove it from someone's record. Examples of ticket fixing are commonplace. For example, during the late 1980s, an NYPD officer, Robert Hanes, was fired for a ticket-fixing scheme in Queens traffic court. As recently as 2006, a police chief and city councilperson in Edwardsville, Kansas, were charged in a driving under the influence (DUI) ticket-fixing scheme.

In response to these sorts of problems, a number of states have implemented so-called **no-fix laws**—with varying degrees of success. Massachusetts has had one such law in place since 1962. It requires officers to account for every ticket they issue, even the voided ones, in an effort to prevent favoritism and unequal treatment.

Crimes

Crimes are among the most serious forms of misconduct. Opportunistic theft is, of course, a type of crime, but Barker was referring mostly to serious criminal activity, including burglary, robbery, rape, and murder. These actions are very much the exception, as the vast majority of police officers are law-abiding and professional, but there are numerous accounts of egregious criminal activity nevertheless.

Internal Payoffs

Refer to the "sale" of anything within a police department, from work assignments and time off to evidence and promotion. The sale of work assignments is not particularly serious, at least not in comparison to criminal activity and other egregious forms of misconduct. In some departments, for example, officers can sell their scheduled shifts to colleagues who are happy to earn pay for the time worked, plus a little extra. This kind of practice may raise some ethical concerns, but it certainly is not criminal. At the other extreme, though, offering money in exchange for promotion or, worse, offering to sell evidence, including contraband, is a serious action that can lead to dismissal and even criminal charges.

FIGURE 12-4 **Types of Police Misconduct Related to Money.**

Other Forms of Deviance

In addition to the deviance highlighted in Figure 12–4, there are other forms of deviance that either don't fit neatly into the categories we have already covered or overlap those categories. We wrap up our introduction to various forms of police deviance by exploring each of these problems: gratuities, police sexual misconduct, and temptations arising from the illicit drug trade.

Gratuities

Gratuities occur when officers accept something of value. Traditional examples of gratuities include a free cup of coffee, a free lunch, or a "police price" discount on a meal or other service. But gratuities can extend into other realms and include everything from free admission to sporting events to lavish gifts.

A person who simply gives a gift to a police officer may not expect anything in return, but there is always the possibility that it could *appear* otherwise. In other words, it just looks bad to accept free goods and services, whether the gift is an expression of someone's genuine thanks or is given with a more sinister motive in mind. The International Association of Chiefs of Police agrees; it considers gratuities to be unethical, but this does not stop officers from accepting them. In fact, the practice is actually quite common.

It is even a little risky to describe the acceptance of gratuities as a form of deviance. There are arguments for and against the practice. Stephen Coleman, a police ethics expert, has offered a series of arguments against the acceptance of gratuities:[18]

- The slippery slope to corruption: . . . It could be argued that although there seems to be a big difference between accepting a cup of coffee and accepting a six-figure bribe to look the other way while a murder is carried out, this is not really the case. For there is a logical slippery slope here, given that there is only a small difference between accepting a cup of coffee, and accepting a cup of coffee and a doughnut, and only a small difference between accepting a cup of coffee and a doughnut, and accepting a free meal. . . .

- The democratic ethos of policing: Given that, in a democracy, public services should be equally available to all, allowing a fee-for-service system for policing would be "anti-democratic."

- The public perception: A public perception that police are corrupt, whether or not true, will have a deleterious effect on police performance. To avoid this problem, police need to avoid even the appearance of corruptibility.[19]

There are, of course, two sides to every story. Coleman goes on to call attention to some reasons why police *should* accept freebies. One is that they are the building blocks of positive relationships. Second, some people draw on police services more than others. Why shouldn't they be allowed to tip those who serve them? It happens elsewhere in the service sector, some would say, so why not in public service?

For the most part, police departments, training academies, and law enforcement associations discourage the practice of accepting gratuities, mainly due to the slippery slope argument: Given the stigma attached to the acceptance of gratuities, an officer who accepts them might *feel* corrupt, thus greasing the slippery slope toward more serious misconduct. As Coleman puts it, "If officers feel that they are already compromised, they might find it easier to make more significant compromises later, because they feel that they have nothing to lose."[20] See Table 12–1 for a summary of the arguments for and against accepting gratuities.

Police Sexual Misconduct

As the story that opened this chapter shows, the position of authority that a police officer enjoys provides ample opportunity for stepping over the line. Recently, researchers have called attention to another type of police misconduct: police sexual misconduct, or **police sexual violence**.[21] If we use the term *sexual misconduct*, we can identify two forms. First, there is consensual on-the-job sex. One study from the 1970s found that 32% of 43 officers surveyed in a southern police department reported having sex with women while on duty.[22]

Other researchers have chosen to focus on what they call *police sexual harassment*. This seems to fit somewhere between consensual encounters and violent or nonconsensual ones. One study presented this officer's observation:

> You bet I get [sex] once in a while by some broad who I arrest. Lots of times you can just hint that if you are taken care of, you could forget about what they did. One of the department stores here doesn't like to prosecute. . . . If it's a decent looking woman, sometimes I'll offer to take her home and make my pitch. Some of the snooty, high class broads turn on real quick if they think their friends and the old man doesn't have to find out about their shoplifting.[23]

Both of these studies were conducted some years ago, but it is a safe bet that neither of these forms of sexual misconduct has vanished from the law enforcement landscape. This chapter's opening store offers proof! More disturbing still are nonconsensual, sometimes violent attacks by police officers. These are not only inappropriate but also potentially criminal.

Pete Kraska and Victor Kappeler, who authored perhaps the most comprehensive study of police sexual violence, defined the problem as "those situations in which a female citizen experiences a sexually degrading, humiliating, violating, damaging, or threatening act committed by a police officer through the use of force or police authority."[24] They went on to develop a "continuum of sexual violence." It begins with "unobtrusive behavior," such as watching victims, viewing private photographs or videos, and otherwise invading a citizen's privacy. Next, "obtrusive behavior" consists of custodial strip searches, cavity searches, deception to gain sexual favors, and similar actions. Finally, "criminal behavior" is just that: harassment, involuntary sexual contact, sexual assault, and even rape. While most sexual victimization by police may be of women, the sexual abuse of power by policewomen has yet to be explored.

How common is police sexual violence? Kraska and Kappeler examined news sources from January 1991 to June 1993

TABLE 12–1 | ARGUMENTS FOR AND AGAINST ACCEPTING GRATUITIES

Arguments in Support of Acceptance

Appreciation	It's natural and reasonable to show appreciation to those providing a public service. It's rude to refuse.
Not significant	Gratuities are not significant enough to buy or cultivate favors.
Officially offered	When offered officially by a company or corporation, no personal sense of obligation can develop.
Links with the community	It's part and parcel of fostering close links with the community, including businesspeople. In turn, it's a fundamental of "good policing."
Police culture	It's an entrenched part of police culture. Any attempt to end it will result in displeasure and cynicism.
Trust and discretion	Attempts to prohibit acceptance imply that officers cannot be trusted to exercise discretion and are incapable of making sensible moral judgments to guide their behavior.

Arguments against Acceptance

Sense of obligation	Even the smallest gift inevitably creates a sense of obligation if it becomes regularized.
"Slippery slope"	Gratuities lead to a "slippery slope" where the temptations become imperceptibly greater and refusal increasingly difficult.
Remove temptation	Not all officers can exercise proper judgment on what is reasonable to accept. It's more sensible for the organization to remove the temptation altogether.
Purchase preferential treatment	Businesses that offer gratuities are, in essence, seeking to purchase preferential treatment (for example, encourage greater police presence in the vicinity of their business).

Source: T. Newburn, *Understanding and Preventing Police Corruption: Lessons from the Literature* (London: Home Office, Policing and Reducing Crime Unit, 1999), p. 10. Reproduced under the terms of the Open Government License.

and identified 124 cases.[25] Most of the cases were actual court cases, not just news accounts. Ninety-one of the cases were from the federal courts. Nine of these involved "unobtrusive" behaviors, 67 involved "obtrusive" behavior, and 15 were criminal.[26] The vast majority of the court cases involved allegations of improper strip searches, but there were a few violations of privacy, sexual assaults, and rapes as well.

Drug War Temptations

Before the start of the "war on drugs" in the 1960s, police deviance was connected mostly with the protection of illegal gambling, prostitution, and other vice crimes. Officers were not faced with too many overt temptations to break the law. Since this country has sought to eradicate illicit drug use, however, those temptations have become quite pronounced.

Michigan State University police expert David Carter has identified two types of drug-related police corruption, both of which he says "have notably increased" in recent years.[27]

Type I drug corruption. This "occurs when an officer seeks to use his or her position simply for personal gain. This type of drug corruption includes the following: giving information to drug dealers about investigations, names of informants, planned raids, and so forth; accepting bribes from drug dealers in exchange for nonarrest, evidence tampering, or perjury; theft of drugs from the police property room for personal consumption; 'seizure' of drugs for personal use without arresting the person possessing the drugs; taking the profits of drug dealers' sales or their drugs for resale; extorting drug traffickers for money or property in exchange for nonarrest or nonseizure of drugs."[28]

Type II drug corruption. This "involves the officer's search for legitimate gains and may not even be universally perceived as being corrupt. 'Gain' may involve organizational benefit—perhaps a form of 'winning' or 'revenge.' Included are such actions as giving false statements to obtain arrest or search warrants against suspected or known drug dealers; perjury during hearings and trials of drug dealers; 'planting,' or creating evidence against known drug dealers; entrapment; and falsely spreading rumors that a dealer is a police informant in order to endanger that person."[29]

Victor Kappeler and his colleagues have come up with their own classification scheme for drug-related police corruption. It includes **use corruption**, **economic corruption**, **police violence**, and **subjugation of defendants' rights**. Use corruption refers to the personal use of illicit drugs. Two researchers found, for example, that 20% of the officers they surveyed reported using marijuana *on duty*.[30] Economic corruption is like Carter's Type I corruption cited above: Officers seek personal gain by stealing drugs, selling drugs, or extorting money from drug dealers. Police violence involves the use of improper physical force to extract confessions. Finally, the subjugation of defendants' rights refers to committing perjury or telling other lies or fabricating evidence in an attempt to secure drug convictions. The latter of these has also been called **noble-cause corruption**,[31] which has been defined as any corruption that occurs in connection with the goal of getting criminals off the streets and protecting the community.

Examples of Police Deviance

Police deviance, especially crime, is very much the exception, as we have said repeatedly. Even so, it would be impossible to detail all or even several of the more high-profile examples of police stepping over the line. What follows are two of the most high-profile examples of police corruption in history; few recent events have come close to the egregious misconduct in these cases.

The Miami Police Department

Corruption in the Miami Police Department has received widespread attention. In the 1980s, seven officers known as the Miami River Cops were indicted for several criminal acts. They began by stealing cash from motorists stopped for traffic violations, and they worked their way up to major thefts. Informants would alert the officers to the whereabouts of large drug caches, and they would steal the drugs instead of arresting the dealers. A jury deadlocked in their first criminal trial. After that, more officers were suspected of being involved, and ultimately 19 of them, all of whom were Hispanic, were convicted.

What made the River Cops scandal so notorious? It was audacity and seriousness of the acts these cops engaged in. They were charged with everything from theft to murder, but stealing from drug dealers was their bread and butter:

> [I]n September, 1984, K-9 Officer Rodolfo "Rudy" Arias, acting on a tip from a major drug trafficker named Luis Rodriguez, stopped and searched a vehicle. Inside, Arias found a small amount of cocaine and $16,000 in cash, which never made it to the MPD evidence lock-up. A month later, Arias and two other River Cops, Armando Lopez and Felix Beruvides, raided a poker game in Little Havana, where they seized $3,500 in cash. In April of 1985, Officers Coello and Garcia stopped motorist Menelao Estevez, who was carrying $11,000 in cash. The officers arrested Estevez for carrying an unregistered gun, and at booking Estevez was given a receipt for about half of the money.[32]

Allegations of misconduct at the Miami Police Department were by no means limited to the River Cops. The U.S. attorney for the Southern District of Florida noted in 1987 that "the Miami Police Department has an extraordinarily serious problem, equal or surpassing anything I've seen anywhere. Unfortunately, our probe is mushrooming and we could end up with the largest police corruption case in United States history."[33]

The Los Angeles Police Department

Nowhere has police corruption and deviance been more apparent than in the infamous scandal that unfolded a few years ago in the Los Angeles Police Department's (LAPD's) Rampart Division. It seems, given its size, that the LAPD has always been the focus of negative publicity because of some scandal or abuse committed by officers within the agency. The Rampart Division scandal, however, promptly became one of the most significant scandals in the department's history, if not the biggest scandal in the history of law enforcement.

The Rampart Division scandal revealed a series of problems that should interest police administrators who are intent on maintaining the integrity of their agencies. First, the scandal showed that it is difficult to ensure accountability in large police departments. Total supervision is difficult if not impossible in departments that are both large and spread across a substantial geographical area, as is definitely the case with the LAPD. Second, Rampart also revealed what can happen when administrators fail to take significant steps to tackle police corruption.

The events that set the Rampart Division scandal into motion began as early as 1997. On November 6 of that year, three suspects robbed a Los Angeles branch of Bank of America. The investigation into the robbery led to the arrest of West Los Angeles area officer David Mack. A second incident on February 26, 1998, involved the false imprisonment and beating of a handcuffed arrestee at the Rampart substation. The officer responsible for the beating of the suspect was a Rampart Division CRASH (Community Resources Against Street Hoodlums, the LAPD's elite street crime enforcement unit) officer by the name of Brian Hewitt. Two other CRASH officers admitted being involved in the beating.

On March 2, 1998, six pounds of cocaine were checked out from a property room at LAPD headquarters, supposedly to be used as evidence in a trial. When the cocaine was not returned to the property room, police officials initiated an internal investigation on March 27 to ascertain its whereabouts. On August 25, Rampart Division Officer Rafael A. Perez was arrested on suspicion of stealing the cocaine.

The investigations of all three incidents revealed that the suspect officers were associated with one another. They either worked as partners or were close friends. Hewitt and Perez were assigned to the Rampart Division, and Mack had previously been assigned to the division. This established a clear connection between the three officers. This information led then-Chief Bernard Parks to launch a special criminal task force in May 1998 to further investigate the incidents.

Ultimately, the CRASH unit officers involved in the beating at the Rampart substation were terminated, and Mack was convicted in federal court of bank robbery. Perez was prosecuted on drug charges, but his first trial resulted in a hung jury on December 23, 1998.

Nothing else of note occurred (or at least became publicized) until September 8, 1999, when, during jury selection for his second trial, Perez pled guilty to stealing eight pounds of cocaine from LAPD storage facilities. He then entered into a confidential plea agreement to receive a reduced sentence on the drug charges in exchange for identifying other Rampart Division police officers involved in illegal activities. This agreement marked the beginning of the public exposure of the Rampart Division scandal.

On September 15, 1999, the first public airing of the scandal, LAPD Chief Bernard Parks called a press conference during which he announced that Perez had implicated himself and another Rampart officer in the shooting of an unarmed man.

Parks went on to state that 12 officers had been either placed on leave or fired in connection with covering up the shooting. On September 16, 1999, Javier Francisco Ovando, the unarmed man who was shot and framed for assaulting the two officers, was freed from prison after serving three years of a lengthy term. At that point, the Federal Bureau of Investigation began an investigation into civil rights violations in the LAPD.

In an interview from jail on September 20, Perez called corruption in the LAPD a cancer. The next day, Chief Parks convened a board of inquiry (BOI) to investigate the scope of the Rampart Division scandal. Ultimately, more than 300 people were involved in the investigation, and special subcommittees were established to examine issues including personnel, work product, supervision and management, risk management, operations, corruption, integrity, and others.

On October 4, 1999, two LAPD officers linked to the Rampart corruption scandal were subpoenaed to testify before a grand jury focusing on two allegedly unjustified shootings by Rampart Division officers. In ensuing court actions, a judge overturned the convictions of four men and dismissed the case against a fifth. Subsequently, the Rampart Division scandal ballooned out of control.

On February 29, 2000, the BOI gave its 362-page report to Los Angeles Mayor Richard Riordan and members of the LAPD Police Commission (Parks's supervisors). The report cited numerous factors that were responsible for the scandal, including failures to check the backgrounds of new recruits, to monitor officer misconduct, and to supervise officers in the field. Simply put, accountability and control were compromised in the LAPD. The scandal was made possible because supervision suffered and the department's internal accountability mechanisms proved ineffective.

On September 19, 2000, federal officials essentially took over the LAPD when the Los Angeles City Council voted (10–2) to accept a consent decree that appointed a federal judge to act on behalf of the U.S. Justice Department to oversee reforms in the department for a period of five years. The consequences of not entering into the decree would have been a federal lawsuit against the LAPD. In 2013, a federal judge finally lifted the consent decree.

▶ *Explanations, Incidence, and Controls*

Criminological theory tells us why criminals offend. In much the same way, theories of police deviance explain what makes a law enforcement officer cross over to the dark side. There are far more theories of crime, however, than there are theories of police deviance. In addition to considering explanations of police deviance, it is also important to gauge the extent of the problem. The stories

LEARNING OUTCOMES 3 — Discuss explanations for police deviance, its incidence, and methods of controlling it.

Rotten Apple Theory

Police deviance caused by a few individuals who should not have become police officers and whose propensity toward corruption was not recognized during the recruitment and hiring phases.

Environmental Factors

Some officers become deviant as a result of either a corrupt political environment or the socialization process.

FIGURE 12–5 Explaining Police Deviance.

we have presented hardly capture the reality of police deviance. We described some of the more notorious cases, but what about the more mundane cases of police deviance—just how common are they? Finally, and perhaps most important, we need to consider what can be done to stop police deviance. It is not enough to wait around until something goes wrong. Administrators want to know what they can do to prevent police deviance before it becomes a problem.

Explaining Police Deviance

There are two main theories of police deviance. One explains deviance in terms of the isolated behavior of individual officers, while the other attributes deviance to the influence of environmental factors that could affect all police officers (Figure 12–5). These explanations roughly parallel classical and positivist theories of crime. Classical theories look at individual factors like personality; positivist theories look at environmental factors, including socialization and temptations in the environment.

The Rotten Apple Theory

The **rotten apple theory** attributes police deviance to a few individuals who should not have become police officers and whose propensity toward corruption was not recognized during the recruitment and hiring phases. The implication of this theoretical perspective is that police agencies must continue to refine and improve their hiring procedures. The hope is that adequate screening for candidates of the highest moral character may prevent deviance from taking root in the department.

Identifying "rotten apples"—that is, officer candidates with a propensity for deviance—is difficult. Skilled liars will not be screened out during hiring. Psychological exams can do only so much, usually identifying only the most unfit of applicants. In response to these problems, some researchers have studied citizen complaints against the police in an effort to determine which officers receive the most complaints—hoping to discern the most common characteristics of "problem" officers. The authors of one study found that 7% of the officers in one department were responsible for more than one-third of all the complaints. The officers were younger and had less experience, and the complaints against them were more likely to arise from their proactive (as opposed to reactive) contacts with citizens.[34] These findings suggest that it is important to monitor police–citizen encounters and to focus on less seasoned officers.

Environmental Factors

Positivist criminologists explain crime in terms of environmental factors like peer influence, family conditions, and neighborhood characteristics. Applying this line of thinking to police deviance, it may be that some officers become deviant as a result of either a corrupt political environment or the socialization process. If a city or its police department shows a pattern of problem behavior, then it is understandable that some officers will fall victim to it. Some of the examples discussed earlier revealed cultures of corruption within a department or city, making it pretty clear why police deviance spreads.

Cases of systemic corruption are rare, especially these days. This forces us to look at other environmental explanations of police deviance, namely, those stemming from the socialization process. It is easier to conceive of a few officers working together and reinforcing one another's behavior through graft and corruption than it is to conceive of a whole police department doing the same. In the discussion of police subculture in Chapter 5, we saw, for instance, that the code of silence pervades police work. The code certainly presents problems for administrators who are intent on rooting out corruption and

deviance. This, in turn, allows problems to persist because they are difficult to bring to light.

Some researchers have attributed police deviance to a mixture of constant and variable factors unique to police work. Examples of these factors appear in Table 12–2. Some would also say that the explanations of corruption that we have covered are too simple and that corruption is a nasty and complex self-reinforcing cycle.

How Common Is Police Deviance?

Noted police researcher Lawrence Sherman offered this enlightening commentary on the incidence of police corruption: "Most police departments have members who commit corrupt acts from time to time. Only some police departments, however, become corrupt police departments."[35] In other words, corruption was—and still is—relatively rare. The vast majority of law enforcement officers are law-abiding, upstanding professionals. Even so, it is important to consider just how common police deviance is. We also need to look beyond the high-profile cases and consider the whole gamut of police deviance, most of

---

TABLE 12–2 | FACTORS AFFECTING THE DEVELOPMENT OF POLICE DEVIANCE

Constant Factors

Discretion	The exercise of discretion is argued to have both legitimate and illegitimate bases.
Low managerial visibility	A police officer's actions are often low in visibility as far as line management is concerned.
Low public visibility	Much of what police officers do is not witnessed by members of the public.
Peer group secrecy	Police subculture is characterized by a high degree of internal solidarity and secrecy.
Managerial secrecy	Police managers have generally worked themselves up from the beat and share many of the values held by those they manage.
Status problems	Police officers are sometimes said to be poorly paid relative to their powers.
Association with lawbreakers, contact with temptation	Police officers inevitably come into contact with a wide variety of people who have an interest in police not doing what they have a duty to do. Such people may have access to considerable resources.

Variable Factors

Community structure	Refers to the degree of "anomie," the political "ethos," and the extent of culture conflict.
Organizational characteristics	Levels of bureaucracy, integrity of leadership, solidarity of work subcultures, moral career stages of police officers, and the perception of legitimate opportunities.
Legal opportunities for corruption	Moral: so-called victimless crimes associated with the policing of vice. Regulative: the exploitation of minor or trivial regulations, such as those associated with construction, traffic, and licensing.
Corruption controls	How the guardians are themselves "guarded."
Social organization of corruption	Two basic forms: arrangements and events.
Moral cynicism	Association with lawbreakers and contact with temptation are inevitable in police work, inclining officers toward moral cynicism.

Source: T. Newburn, *Understanding and preventing police corruption: Lessons from the literature* (London: Home Office, Policing and Reducing Crime Unit, 1999), p. 17. Reproduced under the terms of the Open Government License.

which is not as serious as the stories from New York, Los Angeles, and Miami would have us believe.

Unfortunately, just as it is difficult to estimate the true extent of crime (the so-called dark figure of crime), it is difficult to estimate the true prevalence of police deviance. Corrupt officers try to keep their activities private, just as criminals try to hide theirs. As a result, researchers have had to get creative. One researcher surveyed officers in a police department that he called South City. They were asked to estimate how frequently they thought officers engaged in five behaviors: sleeping on duty, using excessive force, having sex on duty, committing perjury, and drinking on duty. Sleeping on duty, brutality, and sex on duty were, surprisingly, considered the most common (40%, 39%, and 32%, respectively). In other words, officers estimated that nearly 4 in 10 officers slept on duty or used excessive force and that more than 3 in 10 had sex on duty.

Cases of officers selling drugs, stealing evidence, and committing crimes are relatively rare in comparison to less extreme examples of police deviance. Sleeping on the job, sexual misconduct, harassment, and similar behaviors are perhaps easier to commit without getting caught. In addition, they may be viewed as relatively minor when compared to some of the more serious examples of deviance and corruption cited earlier in this chapter. The studies just cited probably cannot be generalized to all law enforcement officials or police departments, but they provide some needed insight into the extent of the problem.

Controlling Police Deviance

Perhaps the best control for police deviance is to screen out applicants who are unfit for the job by conducting background investigations, polygraph evaluations, and psychological evaluations. Obviously, though, this approach has failed on more than one occasion. A remaining option is to constantly remind officers of how they should act when presented with ethical dilemmas. This is accomplished through the promotion of professional standards and through police codes of ethics (Figure 12–6).

If we move away from policing and focus on corruption throughout the public sector, we find a large body of literature about prevention.[36] One scholar advocates treating corruption as a disease.[37] First, the disease has to be identified (Stage One). Once the disease has been identified, so-called Stage Two and Stage Three responses can be crafted. Stage Two seeks to control the problem (e.g., audit systems or citizen oversight). Stage Three then seeks to subvert corruption (e.g., with undercover agents).

Professional Standards

As policing has matured over time, most of the rampant corruption we witnessed in the past has subsided. Continued reinforcement of professional standards, however, is critical. Joycelyn Pollock, one of the country's experts on police ethics, offers a number of suggestions in this regard.[38] She couches these in terms of some simple questions for officers to answer. The first is the so-called **first-page test**. The question is, "How would you feel if your action appeared on the front page of the newspaper?" The second question is, "How will you feel about your action when looking back on it?" Finally, "Would you consider your action fair if you were each of the other parties involved?" Or, put differently, "Did you treat others the way you would want to be treated?"[39] Pollock goes on to note,

> These questions are sometimes overlooked when making day-to-day decisions. Thoughtful policing involves being sensitized to the ethical nature of decision-making and, if being egotistic at times, at least recognizing such actions for what they are.[40]

Pollock also points out that police officers, as professionals, need to distinguish between good police work and what it means to be a good person. The two do not always go hand in hand. "Good" police officers are those who make many arrests, catch criminals, and so on. But Pollock notes that "being a 'good' officer may be contradictory to being a 'good' person, and the good people who become officers may be distressed to find that being a good person is not 'good enough.'"[41] So police officers must be constantly aware that being a good person is part of being a good officer. It is not all about making good busts at all costs. Indeed, one of the hallmarks of a profession is abiding by certain standards of conduct, and that means following the rules and upholding the law.

Codes of Ethics

Those police departments that do not train their officers how to act when presented with ethical dilemmas can at least adopt appropriate codes of ethics. The professional associations that many officers are affiliated with (such as the Fraternal Order of Police) have them.

In fact, most professions have ethical codes of one form or another. Doctors, nurses, and attorneys have them. Even the authors of this textbook have to abide by ethical codes either established through their place of employment or promulgated by the professional associations with which they are affiliated (such as the Academy of Criminal Justice Sciences).

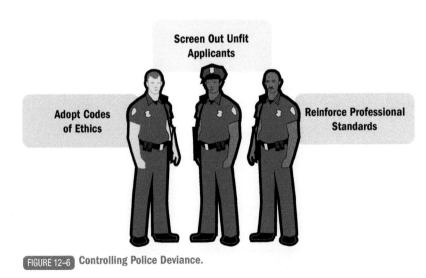

Screen Out Unfit Applicants

Adopt Codes of Ethics

Reinforce Professional Standards

FIGURE 12–6 **Controlling Police Deviance.**

Consent Decrees

During the 1990s, Congress gave the Civil Rights Division of the U.S. Justice Department authority to sue state and local governments in federal court in order to correct any "pattern or practice" of police misconduct. To avoid drawn-out courtroom battles, police departments that find themselves subjected to Justice Department misconduct investigations often enter into so-called consent decrees with the federal government. A **consent decree** is a voluntary agreement, approved by a federal court, between both parties that the police department in question will cease the improprieties of which it is suspected. The decree outlines specific policy and practice changes sought by the federal government.

A number of police departments have entered into consent decrees with the federal government in the wake of corruption scandals. Pittsburgh, Pennsylvania, was the first to do so. It was required to make a number of changes. One was the implementation of a computerized early-warning system to track officers' compliance. Another was to more carefully document the use of force, traffic stops, and the like. The decree also required reforms to the Bureau of Police citizen complaint procedure. Progress was monitored by a federal official who reported quarterly on Pittsburgh's progress.

Not only was Pittsburgh the first city to have its police department enter into a consent decree with the federal government, but it was also the first to have its progress subjected to research. The Vera Institute of Justice collected data from before and after the Pittsburgh consent decree was put in place.[42] The organization interviewed stakeholders in the community, conducted focus groups with officers, interviewed citizens, and analyzed official data. After analyzing the data, researchers concluded that "[t]here are strong signs a year after most of the decree has been lifted that federal intervention can encourage long-term improvements in police accountability."[43] To date, nearly 30 police departments have entered into consent decrees with the federal government, most recently Albuquerque.

Manslaughter and A Probationary Sentence

In 2016, former Conroe, Texas, police sergeant, Jason Blackwelder, was convicted of manslaughter for shooting 19-year-old Russell Rios in the back of the head. Blackwelder, who was off-duty, spotted Rios being pursued by WalMart security personnel as he pulled up at the store with his family. Blackwelder joined the chase, and said that when he caught up with Rios, the younger man put him into a choke-hold. Fearing for his life, the sergeant said he pulled a handgun from his waistband and fired at Rios. Expert witnesses for the prosecution argued at trial that if what Blackwelder said was true, then the bullet could not have entered the back of Rios head as it did. Defense witnesses testified otherwise. In the end, a Montgomery County jury handed down a guilty verdict, but recommended that Blackwelder be placed on probation instead of going to prison. The judge agreed, and sentenced him to five years of supervised probation. Phil Grant, a Montgomery County, Texas, prosecutor told reporters that he could not recall an officer being indicted for a shooting in the county in the last 30 years—and Blackwelder seems to be the first case of an actual conviction.

Jason Fochtman/AP Images.

This case raises a number of interesting questions:

1. Why haven't other officers been indicted for shootings in Montgomery County in the last 30 years? Is it because they all acted within the law? Might there be another reason?

2. Why did Blackwelder receive a probationary sentence? Given that he was convicted, then wouldn't you have expected his sentence to be greater?

3. Do you believe that Blackwelder fired in self-defense? Did the jury?

CHAPTER 12 Deviance, Ethics, and Professionalism

Discuss how various commissions established to examine police misconduct in the United States have uncovered deviance.

The Wickersham (1929) and Knapp Commissions were credited with uncovering police deviance. The Wickersham Commission, in its report *Lawlessness in Law Enforcement*, found that the "third degree," or "the inflicting of pain, physical or mental, to extract confessions or statements," was "extensively practiced across the country."

1. What did the Wickersham and Knapp Commissions investigate?

2. What did the commissions find? How did their findings differ, if at all?

3. What sources of information were especially important to members of both commissions?

4. What's the difference between a grass eater and a meat eater?

corruption Dishonest or fraudulent conduct by public officials in a position of power.

deviance Any behavior that is at odds with socially expected or accepted behavior.

Knapp Commission A commission to investigate police corruption that was appointed by New York City Mayor John V. Lindsay in 1970 in response to a *New York Times* article that reported widespread corruption in the NYPD.

white knight An honest and upstanding officer who never steps over the line between accepted and deviant conduct, no matter how great the pressure to do so.

straight shooter An honest police officer who will overlook some misconduct committed by peers.

grass eater A police officer who accepts small gifts and engages in minor acts of deviance but does not actively pursue opportunities for corruption.

meat eater A police officer who actively seeks out and plans opportunities to exploit his or her position for personal gain.

rogue A seriously deviant officer.

Identify several typologies of police deviance that scholars have proposed.

Scholars have proposed several typologies of police deviance. Some focus on forms of corruption, while others focus on types of deviance. Gratuities (i.e., gifts) are perhaps the most minor form of deviance. Some people don't regard them as deviance at all but rather as relationship builders. Police sexual misconduct includes everything from consensual sex on duty to rape. The ongoing "war on drugs" presents significant temptations to officers to step over the line.

1. Describe the typologies of police deviance discussed in this chapter and give examples of each.

2. List and describe some infamous instances of police deviance.

3. When and where did the Mollen Commission function? What was its purpose? What did it find?

4. What is meant by the term *noble-cause corruption*? How does it apply to police work?

5. What is meant by the term *perversion of justice*? How does it apply to police corruption?

police crime An officer's use of the official powers of his or her job to engage in criminal conduct.

occupational deviance Behavior performed under the guise of police authority that either does not conform to accepted standards of conduct or is not part of normal patrol work.

police corruption The misuse of police authority for personal or organizational gain.

abuse of authority A catchall category for various forms of inappropriate police conduct that do not necessarily amount to crime, deviance, or corruption.

straightforward corruption Any form of police misconduct that provides direct financial benefit to police officers.

predatory corruption A form of police corruption that consists of more than just passive participation (e.g., looking the other way while a fellow police officer commits a crime). In predatory corruption, officers actively promote and engage in criminal and other wrongful activities.

perversion of justice A kind of police corruption that consists of serious actions by a police officer, such as lying under oath (perjury), intimidating a witness, and performing other activities that resemble combative corruption.

Mollen Commission A commission appointed by New York City Mayor David N. Dinkins in 1992 to investigate allegations of police corruption in the NYPD.

gratuity Something of value that is freely given to police officers simply because they are police officers. Examples include a cup of coffee, a lunch, or a "police price" discount on a meal or other service.

police sexual violence A sexually degrading, humiliating, violating, damaging, or threatening act committed by a police officer against a (usually female) citizen through the use of force or police authority.

use corruption Drug-related police corruption that consists of an officer's personal use of illicit drugs.

economic corruption Drug-related police corruption in which an officer seeks personal gain by stealing drugs, selling drugs, or extorting money from drug dealers.

police violence In the context of drug investigations, the use of improper physical force to extract a confession or to obtain evidence.

subjugation of defendants' rights In the context of drug investigations, an officer's lying or committing perjury or fabricating evidence in the name of securing a drug conviction.

noble-cause corruption Any corruption that occurs in connection with the goal of getting criminals off the streets and protecting the community.

LEARNING OUTCOMES 3

Discuss explanations for police deviance, its incidence, and methods of controlling it.

Two theories of police deviance were offered in this chapter. The rotten apple theory argues that deviance is primarily the result of the corrupt activities of a few rogue officers. A second perspective, environmental theory, attributes deviance to peer pressure and other organizational factors. The true extent of police corruption remains elusive, rather like the dark figure of crime. Police deviance, however, can be controlled through rigorous hiring procedures, professional standards and training, and codes of ethics.

1. How common is police deviance?
2. How does the rotten apple theory explain police deviance?
3. How does environmental theory explain police deviance?
4. How can police deviance be controlled?

rotten apple theory A perspective that attributes police deviance primarily to a few individuals whose propensity toward corruption was not recognized during the recruitment and hiring phases.

first-page test A series of questions proposed by Joycelyn Pollock that police officers can ask themselves to reinforce professional ethical standards.

consent decree A legal settlement in which one entity agrees to take certain actions or rectify a particular problem without admitting to any illegality. Consent decrees are sometimes used in law enforcement following corruption scandals; a decree requires the police department to fix a particular problem and/or end a particular course of action.

References

1 Alfred Ng and Jason Silverstein, "Jury convicts ex-Oklahoma cop Daniel Holtzclaw of rape, sodomy charges; faces life in prison," *New York Daily News*, December 11, 2015, http://www.nydailynews.com/news/crime/jury-convicts-ex-oklahoma-rape-charges-article-1.2462256 (accessed May 20, 2016). Jason Silverstein, "Oklahoma City police ignored early sexual assault complaint about Officer Daniel Holtzclaw, lawsuit says" *New York Daily News*, March 8, 2016, http://www.nydailynews.com/news/national/cops-early-complaint-daniel-holtzclaw-lawsuit-article-1.2557135, (accessed May 20, 2016).

2 J. Kleinig, *The ethics of policing* (Cambridge: Cambridge University Press, 1996), p. 166.

3 S. Walker, *Popular justice: A history of American criminal justice*, 2nd ed. (New York: Oxford University Press, 1998), pp. 26–27.

4 R. M. Fogelson, *Big-city police* (Cambridge, MA: Harvard University Press, 1977), p. 32.

5 *Powell* v. *Alabama*, 287 U.S. 45 (1932).

6 T. Barker, *Police ethics: Crisis in law enforcement* (Springfield, IL: Charles Thomas, 1996).

7 Associated Press, "Ex-cops accused of doubling as mob hitmen," www.msnbc.msn.com/id/7434863/ns/us_news-crime_and_courts (accessed January 28, 2016).

8 Reprinted by permission of Waveland Press, Inc., from Victor E. Kappeler et al., "Breeding deviant conformity," in *Forces in deviance: Understanding the dark side of policing* (Long Grove, IL: Waveland Press, Inc., 1998). All rights reserved.

9 Reprinted by permission of Waveland Press, Inc., from Victor E. Kappeler et al., "Breeding deviant conformity," in *Forces in deviance: Understanding the dark side of policing* (Long Grove, IL: Waveland Press, Inc., 1998). All rights reserved.

10 For a fairly thorough account, see M. L. Birzer, "Crimes committed by police officers," in *Police misconduct: A reader for the 21st century*, ed. M. J. Palmiotto, pp. 168–81 (Upper Saddle River, NJ: Prentice Hall, 2001).

11 Reprinted by permission of Waveland Press, Inc., from Victor E. Kappeler et al., "Breeding deviant conformity," in *Forces in deviance: Understanding the dark side of policing* (Long Grove, IL: Waveland Press, Inc., 1998). All rights reserved.

12 Maurice Punch, *Conduct unbecoming: The social construction of police deviance and control* (London: T avistock, 1985).

13 "Mark Fuhrman's 10/2/96 plea agreement to felony perjury at O. J. Simpson's criminal trial," www.lectlaw.com/files/case63.htm (accessed January 28, 2016).

14 Cited in C. Slobogin, "Testifying: Police perjury and what to do about it," *University of Colorado Law Review*, vol. 67 (1996), pp. 1037–60, quote on pp. 1042–43.

15 M. W. Orfield, Jr., "Deterrence, perjury, and the heater factor: An exclusionary rule in the Chicago criminal courts," *University of Colorado Law Review*, vol. 107 (1992), p. 75.

16 Ibid.

17 Barker, *Police ethics*.

18 S. Coleman, "When police should say 'no!' to gratuities," *Police Ethics*, Winter–Spring 2004, pp. 33–44.

19 Ibid., pp. 34–37.

20 Ibid., p. 39.

21 See P. B. Kraska and V. E. Kappeler, "To serve and pursue: Exploring police sexual violence against women," *Justice Quarterly*, vol. 12 (1995), pp. 85–109.

22 T. Barker, "An empirical study of police deviance other than corruption," *Journal of Police Science and Administration*, vol. 3 (1978), pp. 264–72.

23 A. D. Sapp, "Sexual misconduct by police officers," in *Police deviance*, eds. T. Barker and D. Carter, pp. 83–95 (Cincinnati: Anderson, 1986), p. 88.

24 See Kraska and Kappeler, "To serve and pursue."

25 Ibid.

26 Ibid.

27 D. L. Carter, "Drug use and drug-related corruption of police officers," in *Policing perspectives: An anthology*, eds. L. K. Gaines and G. W. Cordner, pp. 311–23 (Los Angeles: Roxbury, 1999).

28 K. J. Peak, *Policing America: Methods, issues, challenges*, 5th ed. (Upper Saddle River, NJ: Prentice Hall, 2006), p. 307.

29 Ibid.

30 P. B. Kraska and V. E. Kappeler, "Police on-duty drug use: A theoretical and descriptive explanation," *American Journal of Police*, vol. 7 (1988), pp. 1–28.

31 J. Crank and M. Caldero, *Police ethics: The corruption of noble cause* (Cincinnati: Anderson, 1999).

32 K. M. Lersch, "Drug related police corruption: The Miami experience," in *Police misconduct: A reader for the 21st century*, ed. M. J. Palmiotto (Upper Saddle River, NJ: Prentice Hall, 2001), p. 139.

33 George Volsky, "Wide Miami inquiry into police is seen," *New York Times*, December 13, 1987, p. 29, col. 1.

34 K. Lersch and T. Mieczkowski, "Who are the problem-prone officers? An analysis of citizen complaints," *American Journal of Police*, vol. 15 (1996), pp. 23–44.

35 L. W. Sherman, *Controlling police corruption: The effects of reform policies* (Washington, DC: U.S. Department of Justice, 1978), p. 32.

36 See, e.g., R. Klitgaard, "Subverting corruption," *Finance and development*, June 2000, www.imf.org/external/pubs/ft/fandd/2000/06/klitgaar.htm (accessed January 28, 2016).

37 Ibid.

38 J. M. Pollock, "Ethics and law enforcement," in *Critical issues in policing: Contemporary readings*, 4th ed., eds. R. G. Dunham and G. P. Alpert, pp. 356–73 (Prospect Heights, IL: Waveland, 2001).

39 Ibid., p. 369.

40 Ibid.

41 Ibid., p. 370.

42 R. C. Davis, N. J. Henderson, and C. W. Ortiz, *Can federal intervention bring lasting improvement in local policing? The Pittsburgh consent decree* (New York: Vera Institute of Justice, 2005).

43 Ibid., p. 4.

13

The Use of Force

1 Identify the various levels of force, explain how they are controlled by policy, and describe their applications in police work.

2 Describe the legal standards for the use of deadly force, and the different patterns of deadly force including suicide by cop.

3 Describe legal standards governing nondeadly force, including less lethal weapons.

4 List three types of excessive force.

Scott Houston/Alamy Stock Photo

Intro **A HIGHER STANDARD OF POLICING**

In 2016, the Washington, D.C.-based Police Executive Research Forum released a report entitled *Use of Force: Taking Policing to a Higher Standard*.[1] The report contained 30 guiding principles intended to increase both officer safety as well as the safety of community members. By implementing the report's principles, PERF said, officers could learn how to "'slow down' some incidents and avoid escalating others to the point where officers or members of the public are endangered." The report's first principle? That "the sanctity of human life should be at the heart of everything an agency does."

Richard Cavalleri/Shutterstock

▶ *Use of Force*

Police **use of force** is defined as the use of physical restraint by a police officer when dealing with a member of the public.[2] Law enforcement officers are authorized to use the amount of force that is reasonable and necessary given the circumstances. Most officers are trained in the use of force and typically encounter numerous situations during their careers when the use of force is appropriate—for example, when making some arrests, restraining unruly combatants, or controlling a disruptive demonstration. Force may involve hitting; holding or restraining; pushing; choking; threatening with or using a baton, a flashlight, or chemical or pepper spray; restraining with a police dog; using a Taser or a similar energy weapon; or threatening with or using a gun.

A more complex issue is the use of *excessive* force. The International Association of Chiefs of Police defines **excessive force** as "the application of an amount and/or frequency of force greater than that required to compel compliance from a willing or unwilling subject."[3] When excessive force is employed, the activities of the police often come under public scrutiny and receive attention from the media and legislators. A police officer's use of excessive force can also result in lawsuits by members of the public who feel that they have been treated unfairly. Whether the use of excessive force is aberrant behavior on the part of an individual officer or is the practice of an entire law enforcement agency, both the law and public opinion generally condemn it.

Kenneth Adams, an expert in the use of force by police, notes that there is an important difference between the terms *use of excessive force*, such as shoving or pushing when simply grabbing a suspect would be adequate, and the *excessive use of force*, which refers to the phenomenon of force being used unacceptably, often on a department-wide basis. The distinction "deals with relative comparisons among police agencies, and there are no established criteria for judgment."[4] The *use of excessive force* and the *excessive use of force* may also be distinguished from the *illegal use of force*, which refers to situations in which the use of force by police violates a law or statute.[5]

Excessive force can be symptomatic of **problem police officers**. Problem officers are those who exhibit problem behavior, as indicated by a large number of citizen complaints, frequent involvement in use-of-force incidents, and other evidence.[6] The **Christopher Commission**, which studied the structure and operation of the Los Angeles Police Department (LAPD) in the wake of the Rodney King beating, found a number of "repeat offenders" on the force.[7] According to the commission, approximately 1,800 LAPD officers were alleged to have used excessive force or improper tactics between 1986 and 1990. Of these officers, more than 1,400 had only one or two allegations against them. Another 183 officers had 4 or more allegations, 44 had 6 or more, 16 had 8 or more, and 1 officer had 16 such allegations. The commission also found that, generally speaking, the 44 officers with six complaints or more had received positive performance evaluations that failed to record "sustained" complaints or to discuss their significance.

Use of force and *use of excessive force* are not one and the same. Most of this chapter is concerned with the legitimate use of force. We save the discussion of improper force for the end of the chapter. What, then, are the types of force? When can force be used? How often do officers use force? What distinguishes deadly force from nondeadly force? What are the rules governing an officer's use of force? We answer these and related questions in the next few sections.

LEARNING OUTCOMES 1 Identify the various levels of force, explain how they are controlled by policy, and describe their applications in police work.

Levels of Force

Seven levels of use of force have been identified in police work (Figure 13–1). Our concern in this chapter is primarily with the last two types of force noted in Figure 13–1 (impact techniques and deadly force). These are the most likely to result in the injury or death of a suspect. Moreover, of all of the levels of

Deadly force. This is force that is capable of killing the suspect. An example is the use of a gun.[i]

Impact techniques. Impact techniques may involve physical contact or the use of chemical spray or stunning weapons.

Pain compliance. These tactics seek the suspect's compliance by causing pain. They should not cause lasting physical injury.

Firm grips. These are physical grips on the body directing a suspect when and where to move. They are not intended to cause pain.

Command voice. An officer's command voice is more vibrant than his or her speaking voice, and the officer's request takes the form of an order: "Sir, I asked you for your vehicle papers once. Now I'm *telling* you to give them to me *now*."

Verbalization. Officers are taught to speak persuasively. If verbalization doesn't work, officers move on to more forcible options.

Mere presence. It is believed that the simple presence of an officer, the embodiment of the authority of the state, will deter dangerous and criminal behavior.

[i]Republished with permission from Anderson Publishing. From Understanding Police Culture by John P Crank, p. 78, 1998; permission conveyed through Copyright Clearance Center, Inc.

FIGURE 13–1 **Levels of Force.**

force, they attract the most attention. All too often, it seems, bystanders record what they perceive to be police brutality. Sometimes such recordings *do* reveal brutality. Other times, though, untrained bystanders may fail to understand that what an officer did to apprehend a resistant suspect followed the police agency's policy to the letter.

Use-of-Force Policy

Justifiable force is not applied arbitrarily. Police officers are trained to use only the necessary level of force to gain control over a situation or to subdue an unruly suspect. Sometimes they are taught a **force continuum**, or use-of-force continuum. Other times their policy manuals contain elaborate descriptions of proper and improper force. Some agencies combine both approaches. Figure 13–2 contains some force-related terminology that will help you work through this section.

An example of a use-of-force continuum, this one from the Federal Law Enforcement Training Center, appears in Figure 13– 3. The left side looks at the suspect's action. The right side looks at the appropriate response the officer should use. So, for example, if the suspect is compliant, an officer should use only "cooperative controls." These include verbal commands. At the other end of the continuum, if the officer perceives that the suspect is assaultive and likely to inflict serious injury or death, deadly force is justified.

Some agencies have abandoned use of force continuum, usually for one of two reasons. First, the force continuum does not have a formal legal basis. Those who subscribe to this perspective argue that agencies should fall back on legal guidelines, especially those carved out by the U.S. Supreme Court. One of those guidelines stems from the landmark nondeadly force case of *Graham* v. *Connor*, which we discuss later in this chapter's Nondeadly Force section. A second problem with the force continuum is ambiguity with respect to where certain weapons should be located on it. A baton, for example, can be used to both gently nudge someone and deal a fatal blow. Where should a baton fall on the continuum?

In an important study, police experts Geoffrey Alpert and Roger Dunham found that the **force factor**—the level of force used by the police relative to the suspect's level of resistance—is a key element to consider in attempting to reduce injuries to both the police and suspects.[8] The force factor is calculated by measuring both the suspect's level of resistance and the officer's level of force on an equivalent scale and by then subtracting the level of resistance from the level of police force used. Results from the study indicate that, on average, the level of force that officers use is closely related to the type of training that their departments emphasize.

Suspect resistance

No resistance. Suspect was cooperative and followed all verbal instructions given by the officer.

Slight resistance. Suspect resisted the officer's actions, and the officer had to use strong directive language or minimal force (skills) to encourage suspect to cooperate and follow directions.

Moderate or high resistance. Suspect impeded officer's movement or resisted cuffing or placement in a car. This level of resistance required the officer to use arm/wrist locks, distraction techniques, or fighting skills to gain compliance and control.

Violent or explosive resistance. In this, the most extreme, level of resistance, the suspect struggled or fought violently and required the officer to (1) use fighting skills to disengage; (2) use a chemical agent, baton, or firearm; or (3) continue

fighting to gain control. In some cases in this resistance category, the officer may have decided that he or she needed to use weapons or other special tactics to gain control instead of engaging the suspect directly.

Officer force

No force. Officer used typical verbal commands.

Slight force. Officer had to use strong directive language or minimal physical force to encourage the suspect to cooperate and follow directions.

Forcibly subdued suspect with hands. Officer used an arm/wrist lock, take down, block, punch, or kick, or he or she struck or wrestled the suspect.

Forcibly subdued suspect using methods other than hands. Officer used chemical agent, baton, gun, or other special tactics or weapons.

FIGURE 13–2 **Force-Related Terminology.**
Source: G. P. Alpert and R. G. Dunham, "The Force Factor: Measuring Police Use of Force relative to suspect Resistance," in *Use of Force by Police: Overview of National and Local Data* (Washington, DC: Bureau of Justice Statistics, 1999), p. 55. Full report available at http://bjs.ojp.usdoj.gov/index.cfm?ty=pbdetail&iid=809 (accessed January 29, 2016).

Applications of Force

The National Institute of Justice estimates that nearly 40 million people nationwide have face-to-face contact with the police over a typical 12-month period. Of those, approximately 575,000 are subjected to the use of force or the threat of force.[9] On the whole, then, police use force quite rarely.

Studies show that police use weaponless tactics in approximately 80% of use-of-force incidents and that half of all use-of-force incidents involve merely grabbing or holding the suspect.[10] For example, a study of more than 7,000 police arrests in Phoenix revealed that no weapon was displayed, much less used, in about 95% of the arrests.[11] In addition, female officers are less likely to use physical force and firearms and are more likely to use chemical weapons (mostly pepper spray) than are their male counterparts.

Who is most likely to experience police force? Perhaps not surprisingly, males, African-Americans, and younger people are most likely to experience force:

Males were more likely than females to have force used or threatened against them during their most recent contact with police . . . Blacks were more likely than whites or Hispanics to experience use or threat of . . .

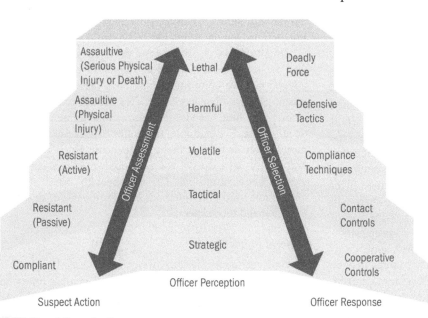

FIGURE 13–3 **Use-of-Force Continuum.**
Source: Federal Law Enforcement Training Center, Department of Homeland Security.

Individuals between the ages of 16 and 29 were more likely than those age 30 or older to experience contact that resulted in force or the threat of force.[12]

The nature of the contact is also associated with whether force is used. People whose contact was initiated by the police were much more likely to see force used. Indeed, about 80% of the contacts involving use of force were initiated by the police. This, too, is not surprising because police-initiated contacts are those where officers generally witness a criminal act or a person they suspect of having committed a crime. Sometimes these suspects flee, and force is required to stop them.

▶ Deadly Force

Generally speaking, **deadly force** is force that is likely to cause death or significant bodily harm. *Black's Law Dictionary* adopts a more general definition, namely, "force that may result in the death of the person against whom the force is applied."[13] According to data collected by the FBI, the number of justifiable homicides by police averages nearly 400 per year.[14]

The use of deadly force by law enforcement officers, especially when it is *not* considered justifiable, is one area of potential civil liability that has received considerable attention in recent years. Historically, the "fleeing-felon rule" applied to most U.S. jurisdictions. It held that officers could use deadly force to prevent the escape of a suspected felon, even when that person represented no immediate threat to the officer or to the public. This, as we will see, has changed.

> **LEARNING OUTCOMES 2** Describe the legal standards for the use of deadly force, and the different patterns of deadly force including suicide by cop.

Legal Standards

The 1985 U.S. Supreme Court case of **Tennessee v. Garner**[15] specified the conditions under which deadly force can be used to apprehend a suspected felon. Edward Garner, a 15-year-old suspected burglar, was shot to death by Memphis police after he refused their order to halt and attempted to climb over a chain-link fence. In an action initiated by Garner's father, who claimed that his son's constitutional rights had been violated, the Court held that the use of deadly force by the police to prevent the escape of a fleeing felon could be justified only where the suspect could reasonably be thought to represent a significant threat of serious injury or death to the public or to the officer and where deadly force is necessary to effect the arrest. In reaching its decision, the Court declared that "[t]he use of deadly force to prevent the escape of *all* felony suspects, whatever the circumstances, is constitutionally unreasonable."

More specifically, the Court ruled that deadly force may be used when two criteria are present: (1) It is necessary to prevent the suspect's escape, and (2) the officer has probable cause to believe that the suspect poses a serious threat of death or serious physical injury to others. Given the nature of the *Garner* case,

one would think the Court would have handed down a unanimous decision, but three justices dissented, noting that the statute struck down by the majority "assist[s] the police in apprehending suspected perpetrators of serious crimes and provide[s] notice that a lawful police order to stop and submit to arrest may not be ignored with impunity."[16] In any case, to further grasp the reach of *Garner*, it is important to consider the notion of what kind of offender poses a "serious threat." Courts will generally consider present and/or past dangerousness.

Present Dangerousness

According to Victor Kappeler of Eastern Kentucky University, "[A] dangerous suspect is, generally, an armed suspect who can inflict serious physical harm."[17] Fingernail clippers, for example, cannot be considered a deadly weapon.

In one illustrative case, one of the federal district courts concluded that the police used deadly force inappropriately in killing a woman (Hegarty) when

> Hegarty repeatedly asked the officers to leave, but she neither threatened them nor did she fire any shots while the officers were present. In fact, the officers decided to enter Hegarty's home forcibly only after it appeared that she had put down her rifle. Hegarty did not threaten injury to herself at any time, nor were there other individuals in danger.[18]

Past Dangerousness

A suspect can also pose a serious threat based on his or her past conduct or based on the nature of the crime in question. Less serious offenses, in general, do not enhance the police authority to use deadly force.

It should be emphasized that only a handful of courts have permitted deadly force based solely on past dangerousness, and the U.S. Supreme Court has never sanctioned such action. In fact, a federal circuit court of appeals has held that the use of deadly force to apprehend a suspect charged with a serious crime is unconstitutional.[19] For example, if a suspect committed robbery but was then confronted by the police and, following their orders, raised his hands, he could not then be shot.

Finally, if police are going to defend deadly force based on past dangerousness, then the serious offense that the suspect is alleged to have committed must have been committed in the recent past. In other words, officers should avoid deadly force if too much time has elapsed between the crime and the use of deadly force. For example, if a police officer used deadly force based solely on the fact that a suspect committed homicide several months ago, the officer's actions would probably be considered unconstitutional. This is especially true if the officer could have used other methods besides the use of deadly force to apprehend the suspect.

Federal Policy

In 1995, following investigations into the actions of federal agents at the deadly siege of the Branch Davidian compound at Waco, Texas, and the tragic deaths associated with a 1992 assault by the Federal Bureau of Investigation (FBI) on antigovernment separatists in Ruby Ridge, Idaho, the federal

Federal Policy The federal deadly force policy, as adopted by the FBI, contains the following elements:

Defense of life. Agents may use deadly force only when necessary—that is, only when they have probable cause to believe that the subject poses an imminent danger of death or serious physical injury to the agent or to others.

Fleeing subject. Deadly force may be used to prevent the escape of a fleeing subject if there is probable cause to believe that the subject has committed a felony involving the infliction or threatened infliction of serious physical injury or death and that the subject's escape would pose an imminent danger of death or serious physical injury to the agents or to others.

Verbal warnings. If feasible, and if doing so would not increase the danger to the agent or to others, a verbal warning to submit to the authority of the agent should be given prior to the use of deadly force.

Warning shots. Agents may not fire warning shots.

Vehicles. Agents may not fire weapons solely to disable moving vehicles. Weapons may be fired at the driver or other occupant of a moving motor vehicle only when the agent has probable cause to believe that the subject poses an imminent danger of death or serious physical injury to the agent or to others and when the use of deadly force does not create a danger to the public that outweighs the likely benefits of its use.

FIGURE 13-4 **Deadly Force.**
Source: From FBI Training on the New Federal Deadly Force Policy by John C. Hall, Federal Bureau of Investigation.

government announced that it was adopting an "imminent danger" standard for the use of deadly force by federal agents. The federal imminent danger standard restricts the use of deadly force to situations in which the lives of agents or others are in danger. When the new standard was announced, federal agencies were criticized for not adopting it sooner. The federal policy, as adopted by the FBI, is highlighted in Figure 13–4.

Think About It...

Tennessee v. Garner *Tennessee* v. *Garner* was important because it set the standard for police deadly force; no longer could an officer shoot an unarmed fleeing felon. Many law enforcement agencies were forced to revise their deadly force policies, but other agencies already had restrictive deadly force
policies in place prior to *Garner*, suggesting that the decision may have only had a modest effect. *Do you think the* Garner *decision made a difference in how often officers shoot their weapons? Why or why not? Read the* Garner *decision and summarize the Supreme Court's logic for its rule. Three justices dissented. Read the case and summarize their perspective.*

1qaz7ty/Shutterstock

Patterns of Deadly Force

Studies of killings by the police have often focused on claims of discrimination—that is, that African-American and minority suspects are more likely to be shot than Caucasians. But research has not provided solid support for such claims. While individuals shot by police are more likely to be minorities, an early study by criminologist James Fyfe found that police officers will generally respond with deadly force when mortally threatened and that minorities are considerably more likely to use weapons in assaults on officers than are whites.[20] Complicating the picture further, Fyfe's study showed that minority officers are involved in the shootings of suspects more often than other officers, a finding that may be due to the assignment of minority officers to poor inner-city areas. However, a later study by Fyfe, which analyzed police shootings in Memphis, Tennessee, found that African-American property offenders were twice as likely as Caucasians to be shot by police.[21] Recent studies have also found that male, nonwhite, younger offenders are disproportionately represented in use of force statistics.[22]

Although relatively few police officers ever fire their weapons at suspects during the course of their careers, those who do may become embroiled in social, legal, and personal complications. The personal side of police shootings is well summarized in the title of an article that appeared in *Police Magazine*. The article, "I've Killed That Man Ten Thousand Times," demonstrates how police officers who have to use their weapons may be haunted by years of depression and despair.[23] According to author Anne Cohen, all departments did to help officers who had shot someone was to "give him enough bullets to reload his gun." The stress and trauma that police officers suffer from having shot someone are now being realized, and many departments have developed mechanisms for dealing with them.[24] Shootings are often accompanied by legal complications, too. Even in cases where officers are justified in their actions, surviving family members may bring suit and repeatedly drag officers into court, sometimes for years.

Suicide by Cop

Police officers have particular difficulty dealing with instances of **suicide by cop**, in which individuals who are determined to die engage in behavior that causes responding officers to resort to deadly force. In one case, John T. Garczynski, Jr., a father of two preteen boys, died in a hail of 26 police bullets fired by officers who had surrounded his vehicle in a Boca Raton, Florida, condominium parking lot.[25] Garczynski, a Florida Power and Light Company employee, appeared to have been despondent over financial problems and the breakup of his marriage. The night before his death, Garczynski met his wife at a bowling alley and handed her a packet containing a suicide note, a typed obituary, and a eulogy to be read at his funeral. After he left, Garczynski's wife called police, and officers used the help of a cell phone company to locate Garczynski. As deputies surrounded Garczynski's 2003 Ford Explorer, he attempted to start the vehicle. One of the officers yelled "Freeze" and then "Let me see your hands." It was at that point, deputies said, that Garczynski pointed a gun at them, and they fired.

Rebecca Stincelli, author of the book *Suicide by Cop: Victims from Both Sides of the Badge*,[26] says that an incident like the one involving Garczynski can be devastating for police officers. "In the past, people have used rope, a gun, gas, jumped off a building. A police officer is just another method," says Stincelli. "They say it's nothing personal. [But] they are wrong. It's very personal" for the officers involved.[27] The FBI notes that "suicide-by-cop incidents are painful and damaging experiences for the surviving families, the communities, and all law enforcement professionals."[28]

A study of fatal shootings by Los Angeles police officers found that an astonishingly large number—more than 10%—could be classified as suicide by cop.[29] Recently, researchers have identified three main categories of suicide by cop: direct confrontations, in which suicidal subjects instigate attacks on police officers for the purpose of dying; disturbed interventions, in which potentially suicidal subjects take advantage of police intervention in their suicide attempt in order to die; and criminal interventions, in which criminal suspects prefer death to capture and arrest.[30]

Several steps for managing suicide-by-cop scenarios have been suggested:

- Contain the area, while remaining aware that too close a containment may allow the precipitator [the suicidal person] to provoke a deadly confrontation.

- If time and circumstances allow, make a clear demand for compliance—a demand that will usually be ignored.

- Ask the person what he or she wants (specifically, ask if they are trying to die).

- If family, friends, or acquaintances of the subject are present, ask if they are aware of the subject's mental health history, chemical dependency, or any criminal record.

- Remain a good listener, while avoiding making promises or committing to anything.

- Use a less-lethal weapon only as a diversionary tactic before making a planned attempt to apprehend but never as a stand-alone tactic, as the use of such devices without an immediate attempt to apprehend may in fact escalate the situation.[31]

It may seem silly to ask the apparently suicidal individual about his or her intentions, but failure to do so can result in needless death:

> While the individual shot by police may have committed a suicidal act, he may not have been suicidal. In fact, the offender's physical survival probably did not enter his thought processes at the moment he made his fateful decision. Instead, this person was momentarily indifferent to the consequences of his threatening behavior. Rather than suicide by cop, he committed "death by indifference."[32]

▶ *Nondeadly Force*

We defined *deadly force* as force that is likely to cause death or significant bodily harm. **Nondeadly force** is basically the opposite: force that is *unlikely* to cause death or significant bodily harm. We cannot safely say that nondeadly force will always prevent injury or preserve loss of life because sometimes—rarely—people die as a result of injuries suffered from nondeadly force. This is more true of so-called less lethal weapons, which we will introduce shortly, than physical force, although people sometimes die or suffer long-term injury from physical force, too.

Legal Standards

In the 1989 case of **Graham v. Connor**,[33] the U.S. Supreme Court declared that claims of excessive nondeadly force must be judged under the Fourth Amendment's reasonableness clause:

LEARNING OUTCOMES 3 Describe legal standards governing nondeadly force, including less lethal weapons.

> [A]ll claims that law enforcement officers have used excessive force—deadly or not—in the course of an arrest, investigatory stop, or other "seizure" of a free citizen should be analyzed under the Fourth Amendment and its "reasonableness" standard.[34]

The Court also said that whether deadly force has been used appropriately should be judged from the perspective of a reasonable officer on the scene and not with the benefit of

The Severity of the Crime

Whether the Suspect Is Resisting or Attempting to Flee the Scene

Whether the Suspect Poses a Threat

FIGURE 13–5 Legal Standards for the Use of Nonlethal Weapons.

20/20 hindsight. The justices wrote, "The calculus of reasonableness must embody allowance for the fact that police officers are often forced to make split-second judgments—in circumstances that are tense, uncertain, and rapidly evolving—about the amount of force that is necessary in a particular situation."[35]

In helping to decide what a reasonable police officer would do, courts need to consider three factors: the severity of the crime, whether the suspect poses a threat, and whether the suspect is resisting or attempting to flee the scene (Figure 13–5). Generally, if the crime in question is a serious one and the suspect is dangerous or resists arrest, the suspect will have difficulty prevailing with a claim of excessive force.

Less Lethal Weapons

Less lethal weapons offer what may be a problem-specific solution to potential incidents of suicide by cop as well as a generic solution to at least some charges of use of excessive force. Less

lethal weapons are designed to disable, capture, or immobilize rather than kill.

Efforts to provide law enforcement officers with less lethal weapons like stun guns, Tasers, rubber bullets, beanbag projectiles, and pepper spray began in 1987.[36] Now the use of these weapons is commonplace in policing. As Table 13–1 shows, 81% of agencies employed conducted energy weapons. Even more employed pepper spray and batons. Note how, in general, the larger the agency, the more likely it is to employ less lethal technologies.

More exotic types of less lethal weapons are also available today. They include snare nets fired from shotguns, disabling sticky foam that can be sprayed from a distance, microwave beams that heat the tissue of people exposed to them until they desist or lose consciousness, and high-tech guns that fire bolts of electromagnetic energy at a target, causing painful sensory overload and violent muscle spasms. The National Institute of Justice says, "The goal is to give line officers effective and safe alternatives to lethal force."[37]

As their name implies, however, less lethal weapons are not always safe and may sometimes cause death. On October 21, 2004, for example, 21-year-old Emerson College student Victoria Snelgrove died hours after being hit in the eye with a plastic pepper spray–filled projectile. Police officers had fired the projectile at a rowdy crowd celebrating after the Red Sox won the American League Championship. Witnesses said that officers fired into the crowd after a reveler near Fenway Park threw a bottle at a mounted Boston police officer.[38] The following sections look at three families of less lethal weapons (see also Figure 13–6). There are others besides those we discuss here, but these are some of the most widely used.

TABLE 13–1 | SELECTED LESS-LETHAL WEAPONS BY AGENCY SIZE

Population Served	Number	Pepper Spray	Batons	Conducted Energy Weapons*
All sizes	12,326	94%	87%	81%
1,000,000 or more	16	100	100	100
500,000–999,999	36	100	100	83
250,000–499,999	53	96	98	93
100,000–249,999	224	98	96	90
50,000–99,999	446	98	95	87
25,000–49,999	878	98	93	85
10,000–24,999	1,986	96	91	83
2,500–9,999	3,873	93	87	85
2,499 or fewer	4,815	91	83	75

*Includes Tasers and stun guns.

Source: B.A. Reaves, *Local Police Departments, 2013: Equipment and Technology* (Washington, DC: Bureau of Justice Statistics, 2015), p. 2.

Conducted Energy Devices

Example: TASER. The typical CED shocks a person with 50,000 volts, causing involuntary contractions of the skeletal muscles and leading to instant immobilization. Although the device has been used inappropriately in a few noteworthy cases, the CED is arguably one of the most effective tools in the law enforcement arsenal.

Impact Munitions

Examples: foam rubber bullets, wooden dowels, beanbags, and other projectiles that are usually fired from 12-gauge shotguns or 37/40-millimeter gas grenade launchers. Impact munitions are designed to stun or otherwise temporarily incapacitate a suspect or dangerous individual so that law enforcement officers can subdue and arrest that person with less danger of injury or death to themselves and others.

Pepper Spray

Pepper spray or oleoresin capsicum (OC), is a so-called lachrymatory (inflammatory) agent that causes irritation to the eyes and skin. Pepper spray, like tear gas, causes the eyes to close tightly and tear up, and it may even cause temporary blindness. It also causes the mucous membranes of the nose, throat, and sinuses to burn and swell, making breathing difficult. OC spray is very effective when used to subdue a resistant suspect. Note that pepper spray is not the same as tear gas.

FIGURE 13-6 **Less Lethal Weapons.**
Source: National Institute of Justice, Impact Munitions Use: *Types, Targets, and Effects* (Washington, DC: National Institute of Justice, 2004).

Conducted Energy Devices

The most popular **conducted energy device (CED)** is the familiar Taser. One of the most common Taser models is the so-called X26C. The X26C uses a replaceable cartridge containing compressed gas that deploys two small probes that remain attached to the device at a maximum length of 35 feet. Electrical pulses travel through the wires and into the body of the target, affecting the functions of the nervous system.

Some Tasers have two modes: "probe" and "touch stun." In the "probe" mode, a cartridge projects and attaches to a suspect's clothing or penetrates the skin with barbs. Between the barbs and the pistol-like Taser unit are two small wires. An electrical charge is then sent down the wires, disabling the suspect. The "touch stun" mode requires the officer to touch the suspect with the unit (similar to a stun gun); wires are not used. For obvious reasons, the "probe" mode is safer for the officer.

There are some concerns over the use and safety of CED. A recent Police Executive Research Forum study called attention to the need for national guidelines governing their use, particularly the use of Tasers, and the organization offered more than 50 recommendations for proper and safe operation of the devices.[39] Their recommendations included the following:

1. CEDs should only be used against suspects who are actively resisting or exhibiting active aggression or to prevent individuals from harming themselves or others. CEDs should not be used against passive suspects.

2. No more than one officer at a time should activate a CED against a person.

3. When activating a CED, law enforcement officers should use it for one standard cycle (five seconds) and stop to evaluate the situation. If subsequent cycles are necessary, agency policy should restrict the number and duration of those cycles to the minimum activations necessary to place the subject in custody.

4. Training protocols should emphasize that multiple activations and continuous cycling of a CED appear to increase the risk of death or serious injury and should be avoided where practical.

5. Officers should be trained to recognize the limitations of CED activation and should be prepared to transition to other force options as needed.[40]

The need for such guidelines is critical because despite their supposedly nonlethal nature, CEDs *have* been implicated in some deaths. Medical examiners have attributed some Taser-related deaths (and other deaths in police custody) to a condition known as **excited delirium**, an overdose of adrenaline that can occur in heated confrontations with the police.

Impact Munitions

Earlier in this chapter, we mentioned a force continuum. There is also a **weapons continuum**. Traditional less lethal technologies require that officers be in close proximity to suspects. Whether employing a baton, a can of pepper spray, or a Taser in "touch stun" mode to get the job done, an officer has to be a few feet from the suspect. Lethal weapons, especially guns, by contrast, do not require close proximity. These devices can be put on a continuum that moves the threat of injury to the officer from low to high. Guns generally present a low risk to officers, whereas batons present a fairly high risk. In response to this problem, less lethal technologies have been developed that can be used from a distance. Such devices are most commonly called **impact munitions**. For example, the 12-gauge launching cap produced by Combined Tactical Systems can fire a large rubber projectile from a distance of 75 to 100 meters. Beanbags can also be fired from these types of devices.

Law enforcement officers need to be careful to use impact munitions from proper distances. When employed from too great a distance, less lethal weapons can be ineffective. On the other hand, when fired from less than 30 or so feet, these devices can cause serious injury, including broken bones. Death can even occur if the devices are not used as intended. A National Institute of Justice study of 373 incidents involving impact munitions found that 8 individuals died as a result of injuries sustained from the weapons.[41] Most of the deaths were caused by broken ribs that pierced the heart or lungs. At least one suspect died as a result of being hit in the neck with a beanbag round.

Pepper Spray (Oleoresin Capsicum)

Pepper spray, or oleoresin capsicum, is a so-called lachrymatory (inflammatory) agent that causes irritation to the eyes and skin. There are two forms of tear gas: chlorobenzylidenemalononitrile gas and chloroacetophenone gas. These gases are irritants and are used more often than pepper spray to control unruly crowds rather than to gain compliance from an individual.

The active ingredient in pepper spray is capsaicin, a derivative of the fruit from plants in the *Capsicum* genus, which includes certain peppers, notably the cayenne pepper—hence the term *pepper spray*. The spray is usually packaged in small pressurized canisters that are carried on the person and can be dispensed quickly to subdue a suspect or for self-defense. The spray is most effective when sprayed in the eyes. Pepper spray, unlike some of the other less lethal technologies, can be acquired legally by non–law enforcement personnel but not in all states. Most states that permit its sale have laws that penalize improper use of the spray.

Pepper spray is aptly called a less lethal weapon because some people *have* died as a result of its use.[42] A study of pepper spray's effectiveness was conducted by researchers at the University of North Carolina.[43] They examined injuries to officers and suspects and complaints of excessive force before and after police departments adopted the use of pepper spray. The researchers found an overall decline in officer injuries, but the decline apparently preceded the introduction of pepper spray, and the effect varied across police departments. The researchers found fewer suspect injuries due to the introduction of pepper spray. Finally, complaints of excessive force declined markedly after pepper spray came into use.

Another study looked at in-custody deaths following the use of pepper spray. Researchers at the University of Texas Southwestern Medical Center identified 63 such cases and concluded, for the most part, that pepper spray was not the culprit.[44] The researchers went on to conclude that pepper spray did not cause *or* contribute to death in 61 of the 63 identified cases. The two remaining deaths were of asthmatics whose conditions were exacerbated by pepper spray.

Researchers at the University of California, San Diego, measured the effects of both pepper spray and a placebo spray on police recruits who were then placed in either a sitting position or in the "hogtie" (feet and hands bound behind the back) position.[45] The study found that pepper spray alone does not cause respiratory problems in either position. It should be noted, however, that the study participants were healthy police recruits and that they were allowed to wear goggles to minimize the harmful effects of the pepper spray. Even so, it is safe to say that pepper spray is likely the safest less lethal weapon, especially when compared to some of the other weapons we have discussed in this chapter.

▶ Excessive Force and Abuse of Authority

Recall that excessive force is not the same as use of force. Excessive force is *inappropriate* force. To clarify even further, consider the distinction between ends and means. In our democratic system of government, we are very concerned with process. Applied to policing, *process* refers to the means or procedures police use to perform their jobs. We are nervous about the prospect of giving police unlimited authority. On the other hand, we don't like to ignore the ends either—in other words, crime control. We want police to control crime *and* preserve our liberty. But when the ends become more of a concern than the means, inappropriate or excessive force is a likely result.

Excessive force is not the only form of inappropriate police conduct. It is also possible to abuse one's authority. We saw some examples of this in the preceding chapter. We also looked at the consequences of violating people's legal rights in Chapters 11 and 12. It is important here, however, to point out that in addition to excessive force, abuse of authority is also inappropriate. Abuse of authority, which was defined in the previous chapter, can be thought of as something of an umbrella under which excessive force falls. An officer can abuse his or her authority without resorting to physical force. In either case, the end result is a person who is improperly and unjustly made to suffer in one way or another.

Types of Excessive Force

Excessive force and abuse of authority take at least three distinct forms (Figure 13–7). Neither is quite the same as, say, accepting a gratuity or

LEARNING OUTCOMES 4 List three types of excessive force.

FIGURE 13–7 Examples of Excessive Force.

receiving a kickback (see Chapter 12). Each leads to a measure of discomfort, if not pain or even death, on the part of a criminal suspect—or even an innocent person. Physical brutality, verbal and psychological abuse, and other so-called rights violations are discussed in this section. Think of these as appearing on a continuum that moves from most to least serious.

Physical Brutality

Perhaps the most notorious example of police brutality ever was the infamous 1991 Rodney King incident. King was stopped for speeding and for fleeing from police. He did not cooperate once he was stopped, and officers applied force to subdue him, but a bystander's video recording of the incident revealed something else. King was hit and kicked more than 50 times as 27 officers from various agencies stood by. In addition, the beating continued even after King appeared to be under control. King received 11 fractures to his skull, a broken ankle, and several other serious injuries. So serious was the incident that an independent commission, the Christopher Commission (named for Warren Christopher, former deputy attorney general and deputy secretary of state for the United States), was appointed to investigate it—along with other alleged problems in the LAPD. Three officers who were criminally charged in the incident were acquitted in 1992, inciting one of the largest riots in Los Angeles history.

In 2008, LAPD officers were once again criticized by the press for their handling of another incident, an immigration rally. Two officers were reassigned after the incident, but this has not stopped people from trying to connect the dots—from Rodney King to the Rampart Division scandal to the crackdown at the 2000 Democratic National Convention, which took place at Los Angeles's Staples Center. Critics argue that the LAPD is plagued by a warrior culture that, like an ocean liner, is difficult to turn around.

Sadly, recent incidents suggest that brutality continues to exist, though not necessarily on an agency-wide basis—or even because of a group of "bad apples." Certain unjustifiable policing shootings can amount to brutality. For example, in 2015, Michael Slager, a white North Charleston, South Carolina, police officer was charged with murder for shooting Walter Scott, an African-American, from behind as he fled (unarmed) from a traffic stop. The two had been involved in a physical altercation, with Slager having discharged his Taser. Scott was not subdued and reportedly fled to escape the Taser. In any case, he was not threatening Slager at the time he was shot. Other cases in which officers are indicted or otherwise criminally charged for inappropriate shootings continue to occur from time to time.

Verbal and Psychological Abuse

The old idiom "sticks and stones may break my bones, but words will never hurt me" couldn't be further from the truth. We know from some high-profile school shootings that words definitely hurt. Any child of a dysfunctional family, even one where physical abuse was never a problem, knows that communication problems and insults can take their toll. There is no reason why police officers should be excused when they engage in verbal abuse. When the things they say and do exclusive of the application of physical force go beyond standards of acceptability, they can be considered abusive. Such actions include everything from insulting suspects to denying them basic necessities during the course of an aggressive interrogation.

There is a fine line between psychological pressure and abuse. Consider police interrogation. Assume that a detective lies to a suspect by saying that an accomplice has implicated him. Is this abuse or just good detective work? On the one hand, it is not a verbal assault, ridicule, harassment, or even a threat of harm. It is, however, something that could instill fear. What if, to take it one step further, the detective *indirectly* threatened the suspect, perhaps by claiming that a jury would surely find him guilty? This type of deception is increasingly common, especially in the wake of the U.S. Supreme Court's famous *Miranda* decision (see Chapter 10). *Miranda* has, for better or for worse, made it more difficult for police to secure confessions. As such, they have had to resort to creative means of doing so, including deception. Richard Leo, a researcher who has documented this trend, summarized one exchange between a detective and a suspect that illustrates the point:

> Detective: If you take this to a jury trial, they're going to hit you hard. They're going to slam you real hard. He's trying to lie to us, he must think we're stupid. Ladies and gentlemen of the jury, we have the evidence that shows he broke the window. He says "no, I didn't do it." Now do you want to be lenient with this guy?
>
> The suspect interjects: No, I'm not going to go for this one.
>
> Detective: Fine, we'll take it to a jury trial, but they're going to say he's guilty, he's guilty. You had a chance to tell the truth. They'll say: he had a chance. The sergeants talked to him and gave him an opportunity to explain how it happened, to give his side of the story, and what did he do? He lied. That's what he's going to say. He's going to say you lied. You had a chance to tell the truth but you lied. That's exactly what he's going to say.[46]

We are not suggesting that this exchange amounts to abuse, but at what point does deception go too far? This is not an easy question to answer. Gone are the days where psychological pressures were combined with physical force in a mix commonly called the **third degree**, but words alone can go pretty far toward directly harming an individual.

Other Rights Violations

If an officer physically and unnecessarily abuses a suspect during an arrest, there is a clear rights violation that might enable the suspect to claim a violation of the Fourth Amendment right to be free from unreasonable seizures. Likewise, a detective who coerces a suspect into confessing or who violates the suspect's *Miranda* rights also commits a rights violation. Specifically, the detective violates the suspect's Fifth Amendment right to be free from compelled self-incrimination. There are other rights, however, that can also be violated without physical abuse and in the absence of verbal or psychological abuse. David Carter calls this **legal abuse**:

> This form of abuse occurs with greater frequency than the other categories. Legal abuse is defined as any violation of a person's constitutional, federally protected, or state-protected rights. Although the individual may not suffer any apparent psychological damage in the strictest sense, an abuse of authority has nonetheless occurred. In all cases of physical abuse and in many cases of verbal abuse, there will also be a legal question. However, legal abuse can—and does—occur frequently without the other forms.[47]

What if, for example, a police officer pushes a suspect up against a brick wall before conducting a pat-down search, and the suspect bumps his head, causing it to bleed? The injury is by no means serious, and we would probably be remiss to call it brutality. A bystander may not even take notice. But what if the force is unnecessary? If it is not abuse and it is not psychological pressure, what can the suspect do? If the seizure in this case is not justified, what remedies are available? There are not too many (see Chapter 11), but this doesn't make the incident any more acceptable than a full-on physical assault.

The Michael Brown Shooting

Michael Brown, an unarmed black teenager, was shot and killed by a white Ferguson, Missouri, police officer, Darren Wilson, on August 9, 2014.[48] (See also "the Ferguson effect," the opening story in Chapter 6). Just before noon that day, Brown and a friend, Dorian Johnson, left a nearby convenience store. Surveillance video showed Brown stealing some cigarillos. Minutes later, Officer Wilson pulled his cruiser alongside the two young men. Upon noticing that Brown fit the description of the suspect in the convenience store theft, he asked Brown and Johnson to move to the sidewalk. An altercation ensued, then two shots were fired from inside the vehicle. Officer Wilson claimed that the shots were fired when he and Brown struggled over his service weapon. One bullet grazed Brown's thumb. Brown then ran east and Wilson gave chase. Brown stopped, turned around, and reportedly moved toward Wilson. Officer Wilson then shot Brown several times, fatally wounding him.

As with many police–citizen altercations where force is used, the details surrounding the Michael Brown shooting are cloudy. Some witnesses reported seeing Brown reach through Wilson's car window and punch him. Others said Brown never laid a

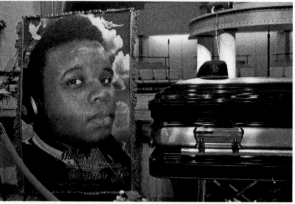

Robert Cohen/St. Louis Post-Dispatch/MCT/ Tribune Content Agency LLC/Alamy Stock Photo

hand on Wilson. Likewise, some witnesses reported that Brown never moved toward Wilson before he was shot. Others said he did. Officer Wilson testified that Brown charged at him. In the end, a grand jury decided *not* to indict Wilson. The announcement set off a wave of street protests, and rioting ensued. Since then, all police shootings, especially of minority suspects by white officers, have received intense criticism and scrutiny.

The case of Michael Brown raises some interesting questions:

1. The officer involved in the Michael Brown shooting was not indicted by the grand jury that heard the case. Why?
2. Do you think that the officer who shot Brown had other options available to him? What would they have been?
3. If other options were available, why didn't he use them?

CHAPTER 13　The Use of Force

Identify the various levels of force, explain how they are controlled by policy, and describe their applications in police work.

Levels of force range from an officer's mere presence all the way up to deadly force. Use-of-force policies usually refer to a force continuum that describes the appropriate levels of force to use in response to the level of resistance or force used by the suspect.

1. What are the kinds of police use of force that this chapter discusses?

2. Which is the type of force most commonly used by police officers?

3. What is meant by the term *force continuum*? Provide examples of levels of force that might be identified by a force continuum.

4. What is meant by the term *force factor*? How does it relate to a suspect's level of resistance?

use of force　The use of physical restraint by a police officer when dealing with a member of the public.

excessive force　The application of an amount and/or frequency of force greater than that required to compel compliance from a willing or unwilling subject.

problem police officer　An officer who exhibits problem behavior, as indicated by a large number of citizen complaints, frequent involvement in use-of-force incidents, and other evidence.

Christopher Commission　The commission that studied the structure and operation of the LAPD in the wake of the Rodney King beating incident.

force continuum　The spectrum of force available to a police officer, from the absence of physical force to the use of a deadly weapon.

force factor　The level of force used by a police officer relative to the suspect's level of resistance.

Describe the legal standards for the use of deadly force, and the different patterns of deadly force including suicide by cop.

Deadly force is force that is likely to cause death or significant bodily harm. Strict legal standards govern the use of deadly force. In general, it is unconstitutional for an officer to shoot an unarmed fleeing felon. Such shootings are permissible only if the officer has probable cause to believe that the suspect poses a serious risk of danger to others. Roughly 3,600 suspects are shot at by police officers each year. Of these, about 600 die from injuries they receive. Suicide by cop refers to situations in which individuals who are determined to end their lives engage in behavior that causes responding officers to resort to deadly force.

1. What is the meaning of deadly force within the law enforcement context?

2. What legal standards govern the use of deadly force by police officers?

3. What is meant by *suicide by cop*? How can suicide-by-cop situations be avoided?

4. What is the significance of the U.S. Supreme Court case of *Tennessee* v. *Garner* for law enforcement officers? What standards did it set?

deadly force　Force that is likely to cause death or significant bodily harm.

Tennessee* v. *Garner　The 1985 U.S. Supreme Court case that specified the conditions under which deadly force could be used to apprehend suspected felons.

suicide by cop　An incident in which an individual who is determined to die engages in behavior meant to provoke responding officers to resort to deadly force.

Describe legal standards governing nondeadly force, including less lethal weapons.

Nondeadly force is the opposite of deadly force; it is force that is unlikely to cause death or significant bodily harm. Claims of excessive force are judged under the Fourth Amendment's reasonableness clause. Nondeadly force would be excessive if a "reasonable person" would feel that it was unreasonable to employ such force in a given situation. Less lethal weapons, including CEDs, impact munitions, and pepper spray, have been developed as alternatives to (but not replacements for) deadly force.

1. What legal standards govern the use of nondeadly force by police officers?

2. What kinds of less lethal technologies are available to law enforcement agencies today?

3. How might today's less lethal weapons be effectively employed in place of deadly force?

4. What is the significance of the 1989 U.S. Supreme Court case of *Graham* v. *Connor* for considerations involving the use of nondeadly force by police officers?

nondeadly force　Force that is unlikely to cause death or significant bodily harm.

Graham* v. *Connor　The 1989 U.S. Supreme Court case in which the Court declared that claims of excessive nondeadly force must be judged under the Fourth Amendment's reasonableness clause.

less lethal weapon A weapon that is designed to disable, capture, or immobilize rather than kill.

conducted energy device (CED) A device that uses electrical shock to incapacitate a suspect. Examples are the Taser and the Sticky Shocker. Also called *electromuscular disruption technology*.

excited delirium A condition in which a suspect experiences an overdose of adrenaline during a heated confrontation with the police.

weapons continuum The array of nonlethal and lethal weaponry available to police officers, the selection of which depends on the situation.

impact munitions Munitions designed to stun or otherwise temporarily incapacitate a suspect or a dangerous individual so that law enforcement officers can subdue and arrest that person with less risk of injury or death to themselves and to others.

pepper spray A so-called lachrymatory (inflammatory) agent that causes irritation to the eyes and skin. Also called *oleoresin capsicum*.

LEARNING OUTCOMES 4

List three types of excessive force.

Excessive force falls into three general categories: (1) physical abuse, (2) verbal and psychological abuse, and (3) other rights violations. The latter includes constitutional rights violations that result from police actions besides abuse. An example would be a shove or a push.

1. Identify three types of excessive force and provide examples of each.
2. What is meant by the term *the third degree*?

3. Do you believe that excessive force is a serious problem in policing today? Explain.
4. What can police administrators do to ensure that officers under their command refrain from using excessive force?

third degree A formerly common coercive interrogation technique that combined psychological pressures with physical force.

legal abuse Any violation of a person's constitutionally, federally, or state-protected rights.

References

1 Police Executive Research Forum, *Use of force: Taking policing to a higher standard* (Washington, DC: PERF, 2015).

2 Some of the material in this section is adapted or derived from National Institute of Justice, *Use of force by police: Overview of national and local data* (Washington, DC: National Institute of Justice, 1999).

3 International Association of Chiefs of Police, *Police use of force in America, 2001* (Alexandria, VA: International Association of Chiefs of Police, 2001), p. 1.

4 K. Adams, "Measuring the prevalence of police use of force," in *Police violence: Understanding and controlling police abuse of force*, eds. William A. Geller and Hans Toch, pp. 52–93 (New Haven, CT: Yale University Press, 2005).

5 International Association of Chiefs of Police, *Police use of force in America, 2001*, p. 1.

6 S. Walker, G. P. Alpert, and D. J. Kenney, *Responding to the problem police officer: A national study of early warning systems* (Washington, DC: National Institute of Justice, 2000).

7 Some of the wording in this paragraph is adapted from Human Rights Watch, "The Christopher Commission report," www.hrw.org/reports98/police/uspo73.htm (accessed January 29, 2016).

8 G. P. Alpert and R. G. Dunham, *The force factor: Measuring police use of force relative to suspect resistance—A final report* (Washington, DC: National Institute of Justice, 2001).

9 C. Eith and M. R. Durose, *Contacts between police and the public, 2008* (Washington, DC: Bureau of Justice Statistics, 2011).

10 J. H. Garner and C. D. Maxwell, "Measuring the amount of force used by and against the police in six jurisdictions," in National Institute of Justice, *Use of force by police*, p. 41. Full report available at www.ncjrs.gov/pdffiles1/nij/176330-2.pdf (accessed January 29, 2016).

11 Ibid., p. 30.

12 Eith and Durose, *Contacts between police and the public*, 2008, p. 12.

13 *Black's law dictionary*, 6th ed. (St. Paul, MN: West, 1990), p. 398.

14 Federal Bureau of Investigation, *Crime in the United States, 2013: Expanded homicide data*, https://www.fbi.gov/about-us/cjis/ucr/crime-in-the-u.s/2013/crime-in-the-u.s.-2013/offenses-known-to-law-enforcement/expanded-homicide/expanded_homicide_data_table_14_justifiable_homicide_by_weapon_law_enforcement_2009-2013.xls (accessed February 1, 2016).

15 *Tennessee* v. *Garner*, 471 U.S. 1 (1985).

16 Ibid., p. 28.

17 V. E. Kappeler, *Critical issues in police civil liability*, 3rd ed. (Prospect Heights, IL: Waveland, 2001), p. 72.

18 *Hegarty* v. *Somerset County*, 848 F. Supp. 257 (1994), p. 257.

19 *Hemphill* v. *Schott*, 141 F.3d 412 (1998).

20 J. Fyfe, *Shots fired: An examination of New York City Police firearms discharges* (Ann Arbor, MI: University Microfilms, 1978).

21 J. Fyfe, "Blind justice? Police shootings in Memphis," paper presented at the annual meeting of the Academy of Criminal Justice Sciences, Philadelphia, March 1981.

22 W. Terrill and S. D. Mastrofski, "Situational and officer-based determinants of police coercion," *Justice Quarterly*, vol. 19 (2002), pp. 215–48.

23 A. Cohen, "I've killed that man ten thousand times," *Police Magazine*, July 1980.

24 For more information, see Joe Auten, "When police shoot," *North Carolina Criminal Justice Today*, vol. 4, no. 4 (Summer 1986), pp. 9–14.

25 Details for this story come from S. Slater, "Suicidal man killed by police fusillade," *Palm Beach Post*, March 11, 2005, p. 1A.

26 R. Stincelli, *Suicide by cop: Victims from both sides of the badge* (Folsom, CA: Interviews and Interrogations Institute, 2004).

27 Slater, "Suicidal man killed by police fusillade."

28 A. J. Pinizzotto, E. F. Davis, and C. E. Miller III, "Suicide by cop: Defining a devastating dilemma," *FBI Law Enforcement Bulletin*, vol. 74, no. 2 (February 2005), p. 15.

29 "Ten percent of police shootings found to be 'suicide by cop,'" *Criminal Justice Newsletter*, September 1, 1998, pp. 1–2.

30 R. J. Homant and D. B. Kennedy, "Suicide by police: A proposed typology of law enforcement officer–assisted suicide," *Policing: An International Journal of Police Strategies and Management*, vol. 23, no. 3 (2000), pp. 339–55.

31 A. L. Honig, "Police-assisted suicide: Identification, intervention, and investigation," *Police Chief*, October 2001, pp. 89–93, quote on p. 93.

32 G. T. Williams, "Death by indifference," *Law and Order*, December 2003, pp. 66–69, quote on p. 67.

33 *Graham* v. *Connor*, 490 U.S. 386, 396–97 (1989).

34 Ibid., p. 490.

35 Ibid.

36 D. W. Hayeslip and A. Preszler, *NIJ initiative on less-than-lethal weapons*, NIJ Research in Brief (Washington, DC: National Institute of Justice, 1993).

37 Ibid.

38 T. Farragher and D. Abel, "Postgame police projectile kills an Emerson student," *Boston Globe*, October 22, 2004, www.boston.com/news/local/massachusetts/articles/2004/10/22/postgame_police_projectile_kills_an_emerson_student (accessed January 29, 2016).

39 J. M. Cronin and J. A. Ederheimer, *Conducted energy devices: Development of standards for consistency and guidance* (Washington, DC: Police Executive Research Forum, 2006), https://www.bja.gov/Publications/CED_Standards.pdf (accessed January 29, 2016).

40 Ibid., p. 23.

41 National Institute of Justice, *Impact munitions use: Types, targets, and effects* (Washington, DC: National Institute of Justice, 2004), p. 3.

42 For some research in this area, see R. J. Kaminski, S. M. Edwards, and J. W. Johnson, "Assessing the incapacitative effects of pepper spray during resistive encounters with police," *Policing: An International Journal of Police Strategies and Management*, vol. 22 (1999), pp. 7–29, and R. J. Kaminski, S. M. Edwards, and J. W. Johnson, "The deterrent effects of oleoresin capsicum on assaults against police: Testing the velcro-effect hypothesis," *Police Quarterly*, vol. 1 (1998), pp. 1–20.

43 National Institute of Justice, *The effectiveness and safety of pepper spray: Research for practice* (Washington, DC: National Institute of Justice, 2003), www.ncjrs.gov/pdffiles1/nij/195739.pdf (accessed January 29, 2016).

44 Ibid., p. 10.

45 Ibid., p. 11.

46 R. A. Leo, "*Miranda*'s revenge: Police interrogation as a confidence game," *Law and Society Review*, vol. 30 (1996), pp. 259–88, quote on p. 278.

47 Cited in R. Roberg, K. Novak, and G. Cordner, *Police and society*, 3rd ed. (Los Angeles: Roxbury, 2005), p. 333. See also Carter, "Theoretical dimensions in the abuse of authority by police officers," in *Police Deviance*, 3rd ed., eds. Thomas Barker and David L. Carter (Cincinnati: Anderson, 1994), p. 273.

48 *New York Times*, "What Happened in Ferguson?," http://www.nytimes.com/interactive/2014/08/13/us/ferguson-missouri-town-under-siege-after-police-shooting.html?_r=0 (accessed January 29, 2016).

Glossary

18 U.S.C. Section 3501 The U.S. Code designation assigned to the Crime Control Act of 1968, which, among other things, attempted to invalidate the *Miranda* decision.

18 U.S.C.A. Section 242 The most common federal statute used to hold police officers criminally liable.

42 U.S.C. Section 1983 The federal statute that provides a remedy in federal court for the "deprivation of any rights . . . secured by the Constitution and laws" of the United States.

absolute immunity Protection from lawsuits enjoyed by federal officials when acting in their official capacities.

abuse of authority A catchall category for various forms of inappropriate police conduct that do not necessarily amount to crime, deviance, or corruption.

accepted lie A lie that is necessary in furthering the police mission.

accreditation Certification for having met all applicable requirements put in place by an accrediting body.

administrative justification The standard for an administrative search based on the fact that government entities occasionally conduct searches in circumstances other than criminal investigations, such as a sobriety checkpoint set up for the purpose of apprehending drunk drivers. Sometimes called *special-needs* or *regulatory searches*, such searches attempt to achieve a balance between protecting individuals' privacy interests and protecting public safety.

affirmative action The practice of taking proactive steps to boost the presence of historically marginalized groups (typically minorities and women) in the ranks of an organization by giving preference to members of those groups.

affront According to John Van Maanen, the first of three steps police officers use in identifying an "asshole." It occurs when an officer's authority is questioned.

Americans with Disabilities Act (ADA) U.S. legislation passed in 1990 that forbids discrimination against the disabled.

anthropometry A technique developed by Alphonse Bertillon in 1882 for identifying people based on their body measurements. Also called *Bertillon measurements*.

arm-span rule A doctrine established by the U.S. Supreme Court that limits a search incident to (i.e., immediately following) arrest to the area "within [the] immediate control" of the person arrested—that is, the area from within which he or she might have obtained either a weapon or something that could have been used as evidence against him or her.

assumption of risk A defense against state tort liability that provides that if a plaintiff voluntarily engaged in a dangerous activity that led to his or her injury, then the police officer should not be held liable.

August Vollmer (1876–1955) An early and especially effective advocate of police reform whose collaboration with the University of California established the study of criminal justice as an academic discipline.

Bivens v. Six Unknown Named Agents The 1971 U.S. Supreme Court ruling that held that federal law enforcement officers can be sued for Fourth Amendment violations. The decision has since been expanded to include liability for violations of constitutional rights embodied in other relevant amendments.

bobby The popular British name given to a member of Sir Robert Peel's Metropolitan Police Force.

booking The process of fingerprinting, processing, and photographing a suspect, after which he or she is typically placed in a holding cell. The suspect may also be required to submit to testing (such as for alcohol) or be required to participate in a lineup.

boundaryless policing Any of various technology-based intelligence efforts designed to combat crime and terrorism.

Bow Street Runners An early English police unit formed under the leadership of Henry Fielding, magistrate of the Bow Street region of London. Also referred to as *thief takers*.

broken windows model A model of policing based on the notion that physical decay in a community (e.g., litter and abandoned buildings) can breed disorder and lead to crime by signaling that laws are not being enforced. Such decay is thought to push law-abiding citizens to withdraw from the streets, which signals that lawbreakers can operate freely. The model suggests that by encouraging the repair of run-down buildings and by controlling disorderly behavior in public spaces, police agencies can create an environment in which serious crime cannot easily flourish.

Bureau of Alcohol, Tobacco, Firearms, and Explosives (ATF) A tax-collection, enforcement, and regulatory arm of the U.S. Department of Justice.

bureaucracy The administrative structure of a large or complex organization, typically employing task-specialized bureaus or departments.

burnout The progressive loss of idealism, energy, purpose, and concern that results from the conditions of work.

CalGang A sophisticated software database of known gang members that field officers in California can access quickly. GangNet is a modified version of the software that is used nationwide.

centralized policing model The less prevalent model of state police organization, in which the tasks of major criminal investigations are combined with the patrol of state highways.

chain of command The supervisory channel within a law enforcement organization.

checkpoint A location at which a warrantless, suspicion-less search is constitutionally permissible in furtherance of an overriding national or public-safety interest. National border entry points and sobriety checkpoints are examples.

Christopher Commission The commission that studied the structure and operation of the Los Angeles Police Department in the wake of the Rodney King beating incident.

citizen complaint A document filed by someone who believes that he or she has been wronged by one or more police officers in a department.

citizen patrol A preventive patrol program staffed by citizen volunteers.

citizen police academy A training experience that offers citizens an opportunity to learn about the policing profession and even to experience some of the same situations that uniformed officers experience.

civil disobedience Law-breaking used as a political tactic to prove a point or to protest against something.

civil law The branch of modern law that governs relationships between parties.

civil service A system in which employees are hired, retained, advanced, disciplined, and discharged on the basis of merit (i.e., their abilities and qualifications).

civil service commission A federal, state, or local agency charged with ensuring that employees in civil service positions receive specific protections.

civilian input A model of civilian oversight of a police agency in which civilians receive and investigate complaints, but the next steps are taken by the police department.

civilian monitor A model of civilian oversight of a police agency that is similar to an ombudsman approach in which complaints are received by the police department and the process, from beginning to end, is monitored by civilians.

civilian review One of the stronger models of citizen oversight of a police agency in which a group of citizens investigates complaints against the police, adjudicates the complaints, and recommends punishment.

civilianization "A law enforcement agency's hiring of non-sworn personnel to replace or augment its corps of sworn officers" in an effort to reduce costs and improve service.

clarification According to John Van Maanen, the second of three steps police officers use in identifying an "ass-hole." It occurs when the officer attempts to ascertain what kind of person he or she is dealing with.

code of ethics A statement of principles concerning the behavior of those who subscribe to the code.

college system A police academy training model intended to enhance the professional aspects of police training curricula by exposing trainees to problem solving, sensitivity to marginalized groups, and other valuable topics in addition to required technical knowledge.

color of law The condition that exists when an individual acts in an official government capacity and with the appearance of legal power. Police officers, mayors, and a number of other government officials perform their duties under color of law.

community era By most accounts, the contemporary era of U.S. law enforcement, which stresses service and an almost customer-friendly approach to police work.

community justice A relatively new and innovative set of ideas about how the goals of the criminal justice system can be achieved. It favors original, nontraditional approaches to crime control that draw heavily on input and cooperation from the community.

community policing A collaborative effort between the police and the community that identifies problems of crime and disorder and involves all elements of the community in the search for solutions to these problems.

comparative negligence A partial defense against state tort liability that examines who is to blame and assigns liability accordingly.

Compstat A goal-oriented police management process that relies heavily on computer technology and accountability of top-level administrators.

computer-aided drafting (CAD) A technology, adapted to meet the needs of police officers and criminal investigators, that facilitates the drafting of crime scenes on a computer so that they can be viewed three-dimensionally.

conducted energy device (CED) A device that uses electrical shock to incapacitate a suspect. Examples are the Taser and the Sticky Shocker. Also called *electromuscular disruption technology*.

consent decree A legal settlement in which one entity agrees to take certain actions or rectify a particular problem without admitting to any illegality. Consent decrees are sometimes used in law enforcement following corruption scandals; a decree requires the police department to fix a particular problem and/or end a particular course of action.

constitutional rights violation Conduct that violates a specific constitutional provision.

contingency theory A management theory that recognizes that there are often different types of tasks within a single organization, including repetitive tasks that call for standardization and control and nonrepetitive tasks that call for flexibility and participatory management.

contributory negligence A liability defense that holds that if an officer can show that the plaintiff or someone else was also negligent in an event, the officer should not be held liable. Contributory negligence can arise not only from the actions of a criminal suspect but also from the actions of third parties.

corruption Dishonest or fraudulent conduct by public officials in a position of power.

council-manager form The most common form of city government in cities of more than 12,000 people. It consists of an elected city council (usually between 5 and 12 people) responsible for all policy decisions for the city. Mayors under this form of municipal government generally perform ceremonial duties and serve as the voice—and often the leader—of the city council.

crime peak A time of day when a particular crime increases in frequency.

criminal intelligence A synergistic product intended to provide meaningful and trustworthy direction to law enforcement decision makers about complex criminality, criminal enterprises, criminal extremists, and terrorists. Also, a process that evaluates information collected from diverse sources, integrates the relevant information into a cohesive package, and produces a conclusion or estimate about a criminal phenomenon by using the scientific approach to problem solving.

criminalistics The use of technology in the service of criminal investigation; the application of scientific techniques to the detection and evaluation of criminal evidence.

critical incident An emergency situation that evokes immediate police response and that takes priority over all other police work.

culpability The state of deserving blame or being morally or legally responsible. Under the Section 1983 culpability requirement, plaintiffs generally must prove that the defendant officer *intended* for the violation to occur.

culture A set of shared values, norms, and behaviors that form a way of life.

Customs and Border Protection (CBP) The U.S. law enforcement agency, established after the terrorist

attacks on September 11, 2001, that combined the entire U.S. Border Patrol with portions of the U.S. Customs Service, U.S. Immigration, and the Animal and Plant Health Inspection Service. CBP was given the mission of controlling and protecting America's borders and ports of entry, including international airports and international shipping ports.

dactylography An early name for fingerprinting.

damages Monetary compensation awarded to the plaintiff in a successful civil lawsuit.

deadly force Force that is likely to cause death or significant bodily harm.

decentralized policing model A model of policing in which central governments exercise relatively few police powers and in which the majority of police services are provided by separate local and regional agencies.

democracy A form of government that vests supreme authority in the people, usually through their freely elected representatives.

deterrence theory A perspective that holds that crime will be less likely to occur when the potential for getting caught outweighs any likely benefits from breaking the law.

deviance Any behavior that is at odds with socially expected or accepted behavior.

deviant lie A lie that expressly violates the rules and legal requirements.

directed patrol A form of patrol that involves concentrating the police presence in areas where certain crimes are a significant problem.

distress A harmful form of stress that can threaten an individual's functioning or overload his or her capacity to cope with environmental stimuli.

dominion John Crank's substitute for the term territoriality, which refers to an officer's sense of personal ownership over the area for which he or she is responsible.

double marginality A situation in which black officers treat black suspects harshly to gain the respect of their white counterparts and to avoid giving the impression that they are biased toward members of their own race.

dramaturgical discipline Achieving a balance between merely reporting facts and putting a "spin" on those facts to create a desired impression.

dramaturgy In the law enforcement context, the act of putting on a display of high-mindedness.

Drug Enforcement Administration (DEA) The U.S. law enforcement agency tasked with enforcing controlled-substance laws and regulations.

dual federalism An interpretation of the U.S. Constitution that suggests a system in which the only powers vested in the federal government are those explicitly listed in the document, with the remaining powers being left to the states.

due process of law A right guaranteed by the Fifth, Sixth, and Fourteenth Amendments and generally understood, in legal contexts, to mean the due course of legal proceedings according to the rules and forms established for the protection of individual rights. In criminal proceedings, due process of law is generally understood to include the following basic elements: a law creating and defining the offense, an impartial tribunal having jurisdictional authority over the case, accusation in proper form, notice and opportunity to defend, trial according to established procedure, and discharge from all restraints or obligations unless convicted.

due process voluntariness approach A means for determining the admissibility of a suspect's self-incriminating statement based on whether it was made voluntarily. Involuntariness is held to occur when, under the totality of circumstances that preceded the confessions, the defendant is deprived of his or her "power of resistance."

economic corruption Drug-related police corruption in which an officer seeks personal gain by stealing drugs, selling drugs, or extorting money from drug dealers.

equal employment opportunity Fair employment practices mandated by Title VII of the Civil Rights Act of 1964.

Equal Employment Opportunity Commission (EEOC) The federal agency that is empowered by Title VII of the Civil Rights Act of 1964 to "intervene on behalf of affected individuals," to "file suit against businesses or governmental entities in cases of discrimination," to intervene in cases of alleged sexual harassment, and to investigate cases of employer retaliation.

eustress A positive form of stress that does not threaten or harm the individual but is pleasurable, challenging, or exciting.

evanescent evidence Evidence that is likely to disappear quickly.

evidence-based policing The use of the best available research on the outcomes of police work to implement guidelines and evaluate agencies, units, and officers.

excessive force The application of an amount and/or frequency of force greater than that required to compel compliance from a willing or unwilling subject.

excited delirium A condition in which a suspect experiences an overdose of adrenaline during a heated confrontation with the police.

exclusionary rule A rule mandating that evidence obtained in violation of the U.S. Constitution cannot be admitted in a criminal trial. The exclusionary rule is an important mechanism for ensuring the accountability of police officials.

exigent circumstances A situation that makes a warrantless search constitutionally permissible, such as hot pursuit, the likelihood of a suspect escaping or presenting a danger to others, and evanescent evidence.

Federal Bureau of Investigation (FBI) The investigative arm of the U.S. Department of Justice.

federalism A political doctrine holding that power is divided (often constitutionally) between a central governing body (e.g., the federal government) and various constituent units (the states).

field training officer (FTO) A veteran police officer tasked with providing on-the-job training and performance critique during a rookie police officer's initial assignment following graduation from the academy.

Fifth Amendment An amendment to the U.S. Constitution that establishes due process rights, including the right to remain silent in the face of criminal accusations.

firearms training system (FATS) A full-size, fully interactive training device, not unlike flight and driving simulators, that exposes police trainees to realistic shooting scenarios. The realism is enhanced by fully encasing the trainees in a particular surrounding rather than simply putting them in front of a television screen.

first-page test A series of questions proposed by Joycelyn Pollock that police officers can ask themselves to reinforce professional ethical standards.

focused patrol A form of patrol that focuses police efforts on certain problems, locations, or times.

foot patrol The oldest method of police patrol, which entails officers walking through neighborhoods. Foot patrol tends to enhance rapport between citizens and officers, but it clearly limits an officer's ability to give chase if the need arises.

force continuum The spectrum of force available to a police officer, from the absence of physical force to the use of a deadly weapon.

force factor The level of force used by a police officer relative to the suspect's level of resistance.

forensic evidence Physical evidence whose usefulness in a court of law may not be immediately apparent to an untrained observer but can be demonstrated through the application of accepted scientific techniques.

Fourth Amendment The amendment to the U.S. Constitution that governs search and seizure.

frankpledge system The ultimate outgrowth of the night watch system of social control, dating to the twelfth century, in which ten households were grouped into a tithing, and each adult male member of the tithing was held responsible for the conduct of the others.

Frederick W. Taylor (1856–1915) A classical organizational theorist who posited that worker productivity could be increased through careful attention to how work was allocated and who performed what functions.

fruit of the poisonous tree doctrine An expansion of the scope of the exclusionary rule that requires the exclusion of any secondary evidence (such as a confession) that derives from evidence originally obtained in violation of the U.S. Constitution.

functional equivalent of a question Any words or actions on the part of the police (other than those normally attendant to arrest and custody) that the police should know are reasonably likely to elicit an incriminating response from the suspect.

fusion center An intelligence-gathering unit, often constituted as a collaborative effort that serves various agencies.

geographic profiling Using crime-mapping technology to identify the likely whereabouts or residences of repeat or serial offenders.

government action In the context of search and seizure law, one of two elements that must be considered when defining a Fourth Amendment search. (The other element is a reasonable expectation of privacy.) Government actions consist of measures to effect a search undertaken by someone employed by or working on behalf of the government.

Graham v. Connor The 1989 U.S. Supreme Court case in which the Court declared that claims of excessive nondeadly force must be judged under the Fourth Amendment's reasonableness clause.

grass eater A police officer who accepts small gifts and engages in minor acts of deviance but does not actively pursue opportunities for corruption.

gratuity Something of value that is freely given to police officers simply because they are police officers. Examples include a cup of coffee, a lunch, or a "police price" discount on a meal or other service.

Henry Fielding (1707–1754) An English magistrate who founded what some have called London's first police force, the Bow Street Runners.

Homeland Security Act of 2002 U.S. legislation enacted after the terrorist attacks of September 11, 2001, that created the cabinet-level Department of Homeland Security.

Homicide Investigation and Tracking System (HITS) A geographic profiling system that ties various databases together (gang files, sex offender registries, parole records, and department of motor vehicle records) to facilitate simultaneous database searches.

hostile work environment A form of sexual harassment involving situations in which unwelcome sexual contact and comments have the effect of "unreasonably interfering with an individual's work performance or creating an intimidating environment."

hot-pursuit exception One exception to the Fourth Amendment's warrant requirement, recognized by the U.S. Supreme Court in *Warden* v. *Hayden* (1967). The hot-pursuit doctrine provides that police officers may enter the premises where they suspect a crime has been committed or a perpetrator is hiding without a warrant when delay would likely endanger their lives or the lives of others and possibly lead to the escape of the alleged perpetrator.

hot spot A concentrated area of significant criminal activity, such as a street corner known for its prostitution traffic.

hot time A period during the day when crime is particularly problematic, such as after dark on a Friday night.

Illinois Crime Survey A series of influential reports, published in 1929, on homicide, juvenile justice, and justice operations in Chicago that criticized the corrupt political influence on the justice system.

Immigration and Customs Enforcement (ICE) The largest investigative component of the federal Department of Homeland Security. ICE focuses specifically on illegal immigration.

impact munitions Munitions designed to stun or otherwise temporarily incapacitate a suspect or a dangerous individual so that law enforcement officers can subdue and arrest that person with less risk of injury or death to themselves and to others.

impression management A media relations concept that involves controlling the presentation of information to achieve a desired public perception.

injunctive relief A court order to bring injurious or offensive action to a halt.

institution An organizational structure through which values and norms are transmitted over time and from one location to another within a society.

institutional value A sense of agreement within a particular culture about how to accomplish a valued objective.

intelligence Information that has been analyzed and integrated into a useful perspective.

intelligence-led policing The collection and analysis of information to produce an intelligence end product designed to inform police decision making at both the tactical and the strategic level. Also called *intelligence-driven policing*.

intentional tort An action that is highly likely to cause injury or damage.

internal affairs An investigative agency within a police department that is tasked with investigating allegations of misconduct or criminality by members of the department.

International Association of Chiefs of Police (IACP) Founded in 1893, the best-known association for law enforcement professionals.

International Police Association (IPA) Founded in 1950, the largest police professional association in the world.

International Union of Police Associations (IUPA) An international police association, founded in 1954 and chartered by the AFL-CIO, that represents all rank-and-file officers and functions more as a lobbying group than as a professional association.

Joint Terrorism Task Force (JTTF) An FBI-sponsored group composed of federal, state, and local law enforcement personnel who are brought together to focus on a specific threat.

justification The focus of a court's examination of the reasonableness of a search or seizure.

Knapp Commission A commission to investigate police corruption that was appointed by New York City Mayor John V. Lindsay in 1970 in response to a *New York Times* article that reported widespread corruption in the New York City Police Department.

Lawrence W. Sherman A noted police researcher, and contemporary proponent of evidence-based policing.

legal abuse Any violation of a person's constitutionally, federally, or state-protected rights.

less lethal weapon A weapon that is designed to disable, capture, or immobilize rather than kill.

local agency One of the three levels of law enforcement activity in the United States—the other two being state and federal—that encompasses organizations like municipal police departments, sheriff's departments, and other lesser-known agencies (including campus police, transit police, and specialized agencies at public schools, airports, state capitols, medical facilities, state parks, certain prosecutors' offices, and others). Together, the personnel in these local agencies far outnumber all state and federal law enforcement officials combined.

Max Weber (1864–1920) A classical organizational theorist, widely acknowledged as the father of bureaucracy, who identified five principles that he suggested are characteristic of an effective bureaucratic organization.

mayor-council form A form of municipal government that can be categorized in two ways. The strong-mayor variation gives the mayor almost limitless authority over city operations, including the hiring and dismissal of key officials. In the weak-mayor variation, which is more common in small towns, the mayor serves largely at the behest of the city council.

meat eater A police officer who actively seeks out and plans opportunities to exploit his or her position for personal gain.

Metropolitan Police Act The legislation adopted by the British Parliament in 1829 that established the world's first large-scale organized police force in London.

Miranda rights The set of rights that a person accused or suspected of having committed a specific offense has during interrogation and of which he or she must be informed prior to questioning, as stated by the U.S. Supreme Court in *Miranda* v. *Arizona* (1966) and related cases.

Mollen Commission A commission appointed by New York City Mayor David N. Dinkins in 1992 to investigate allegations of police corruption in the New York City Police Department.

money laundering The process by which criminals or criminal organizations seek to disguise the illicit nature of their proceeds by introducing them into the stream of legitimate commerce and finance.

municipal police department One of the types of local law enforcement agencies in the United States. Specifically, the law enforcement agency that serves a municipality.

National Black Police Association The parent association, founded in 1972, for local and regional associations of African-American police professionals.

National Criminal Intelligence Sharing Plan (NCISP) A formal intelligence-sharing initiative that addresses the security and intelligence needs recognized after the tragic events of September 11, 2001. It describes a nationwide communications capability that will link together all levels of law enforcement personnel, including officers on the streets, intelligence analysts, unit commanders, and police executives, for the purpose of sharing critical data.

negligence tort A liability claim that must demonstrate that a legal duty existed between the officer and the plaintiff, that a breach of that duty occurred, that a proximate (direct) causation between the officer's actions and the alleged harm resulted, and that actual damage or injury occurred.

noble-cause corruption Any corruption that occurs in connection with the goal of getting criminals off the streets and protecting the community.

nondeadly force Force that is unlikely to cause death or significant bodily harm.

nonsworn personnel Support staff members of a law enforcement agency who are not empowered to make arrests.

norm A rule or expectation for behavior that characterizes a particular social group.

objective reasonableness A standard, used to determine whether qualified immunity applies, that looks at how a reasonable person would have acted under a given set of circumstances.

occupational deviance Behavior performed under the guise of police authority that either does not conform to accepted standards of conduct or is not part of normal patrol work.

Office of Community Oriented Policing Services (COPS Office) An agency within the U.S. Department of Justice tasked with administering and supervising federal funds allocated to improve community policing capabilities.

organization A group in which individuals work together to accomplish specified tasks or goals.

Orlando Winfield "O. W." Wilson (1900–1972) A Progressive Era reformer, professor of police administration, and protégé of August Vollmer whose writings and teachings continue to influence contemporary U.S. law enforcement.

paradox of policing A phenomenon in which a police officer's fear of being injured or killed is stronger than is justified by actual rates of injury or death within the profession.

parish Under the frankpledge system, a group of ten tithings. Also referred to as a *hundred*.

participatory management A form of leadership that allows subordinates to participate in decision making and planning, especially with regard to the manner in which their own units are operated.

particularistic perspective The view that individual officers differ from one another in various ways, including values, role orientation, and preferred styles of policing.

patronage system A system of hiring in which decisions are based more on an individual's political support for an officeholder than on his or her abilities and qualifications. Patronage was common in police agencies during the political era.

pepper spray A so-called lachrymatory (inflammatory) agent that causes irritation to the eyes and skin. Also called *oleoresin capsicum*.

person inventory The search of an arrestee and his or her personal items, including containers found in his or her possession, as part of a routine inventory that is incident to the booking and jailing procedure. Often called *arrest inventory*.

perversion of justice A kind of police corruption that consists of serious actions by a police officer, such as lying under oath (perjury), intimidating a witness, and performing other activities that resemble combative corruption.

pin map An early crime-mapping technique that used colored pins to track criminal events on a map of the police department's jurisdictional area.

plain-view doctrine The rule that the police may seize evidence without a warrant if they have lawful access to the object and it is immediately apparent (i.e., they have probable cause) that the object is subject to seizure.

plebe system A police academy model that closely parallels a military-style boot camp and that aims to produce well-groomed and disciplined officers.

police commission An agency maintained in some large cities that acts like a corporate board of directors, setting policy and overseeing the police department's operations.

police corruption The misuse of police authority for personal or organizational gain.

police crime An officer's use of the official powers of his or her job to engage in criminal conduct.

police officers' bill of rights A police agency's formal statement of the rights of officers who are accused of misconduct.

police sexual violence A sexually degrading, humiliating, violating, damaging, or threatening act committed by a police officer against a (usually female) citizen through the use of force or police authority.

police subculture The shared values and norms and the established patterns of behavior that tend to characterize policing; also called *police culture*.

police training officer (PTO) program A police training method that focuses on developing an officer's learning capacity, leadership, and problem-solving skills.

police violence In the context of drug investigations, the use of improper physical force to extract a confession or to obtain evidence.

political era The period of American policing during the late nineteenth and early twentieth centuries during which police forces served more to regulate crime pursuant to the wishes of corrupt politicians (who used patronage to give police jobs to handpicked loyalists) than to control crime in the interests of the public good.

posttraumatic stress disorder (PTSD) A condition that sets in following a traumatic event with which the sufferer cannot cope. It has been described as an event outside the usual human experience—one that is experienced in a markedly distressing way, with intense fear, terror, bewilderment, and a sense of helplessness.

predatory corruption A form of police corruption that consists of more than just passive participation (e.g., looking the other way while a fellow police officer commits a crime). In predatory corruption, officers actively promote and engage in criminal and other wrongful activities.

predictive policing The use of analytical techniques to identify likely targets for criminals and prevent crime.

pretext stop A traffic stop based on more than one motive. For example, an officer stops a vehicle for a legitimate reason but is also suspicious about the driver.

preventive patrol The practice of canvassing neighborhoods in an effort to discourage people from committing crime.

private policing The acquisition and use of security products and services, as well as the application of specialized knowledge in areas like crime control, investigation, and risk management, by nonsworn personnel.

private security The industry that provides for-profit security products and services, which include three broad categories: the provision of guards, equipment, and investigative or consulting services.

probable cause A set of facts and circumstances that would induce a reasonably intelligent and prudent person to believe that another particular person has committed a specific crime. Probable cause is the only justification for search and seizure mentioned in the Fourth Amendment.

problem police officer An officer who exhibits problem behavior, as indicated by a large number of citizen complaints, frequent involvement in use-of-force incidents, and other evidence.

problem-oriented policing A method of policing that is geared toward identifying and solving problems within a community that are particularly troublesome and then crafting creative solutions to them. Also called *problem-solving policing*.

protective sweep A permissible cursory visual inspection of places in which a person might be hiding. A protective sweep may be conducted by police up to the point of an arrest but must be supported by reasonable suspicion.

public information officer A police department's spokesperson. The media must go through the public information officer to gather information about the department.

public-duty defense A legal defense that shields a police officer from criminal liability in situations in which he or she is legally performing an assigned or implied public duty and engages in a necessary and reasonable action that, for ordinary citizens, would be considered a crime.

public-duty doctrine A doctrine stating that police protection (like any other government function) is owed to the general public, not to individuals. Police officers have used the public-duty doctrine as a liability defense.

qualified immunity A liability defense that shields a police officer who has acted in an objectively reasonable fashion as long as he or she did not violate clearly established rights that a reasonable person would have known. Qualified immunity is an outgrowth of various U.S. Supreme Court decisions.

quality circle A group of qualified employees from all ranks who work together, often around one table, to solve organizational problems.

quality-of-life offense A minor law violation that demoralizes residents and businesspeople by creating disorder. Sometimes called *petty crime*.

quasi-military An organizational structure that follows the military model to some extent, but with subtle differences.

quid pro quo **harassment** A form of sexual harassment that generally involves a demand for sexual favors in exchange for some perk or benefit, such as a promotion or a favorable job assignment.

racial profiling The use of discretionary authority by law enforcement officers in encounters with minority motorists, typically within the context of a traffic stop, that results in the disparate treatment of minorities.

racial quota A requirement for hiring and promoting a specified number of minorities.

reasonable expectation of privacy In the context of search and seizure law, one of two elements that must be considered when defining a Fourth Amendment search. (The other element is government action.) A reasonable expectation of privacy means that people who speak or act in private can reasonably expect that what they say or do will not be seen or heard by someone else.

reasonable suspicion A belief, based on a consideration of the facts at hand and on reasonable inferences drawn from those facts, that would induce an ordinarily prudent and cautious person under the same circumstances to conclude that criminal activity is taking place or that criminal activity has recently occurred. Reasonable suspicion is the standard for less intrusive stop-and-frisk searches; it is less than probable cause but more than a hunch.

reasonableness The elements of a situation that serve to justify a search or seizure.

reform era The period of American policing during the early to mid-twentieth century, during which efforts were made to professionalize police forces and to eliminate the influence of corrupt politicians.

remedy According to John Van Maanen, the last of three steps police officers use in identifying an "asshole." It consists of the officer's response to an affront.

response time The time it takes for police officers to respond to a call for service.

reverse discrimination Discrimination against nonminorities that occurs when the hiring and promotion of minorities are based more on race than on any other criterion.

rogue A seriously deviant officer.

rotten apple theory A perspective that attributes police deviance primarily to a few individuals whose propensity toward corruption was not recognized during the recruitment and hiring phases.

saturation patrol A form of patrol that involves concentrating the police presence in a certain area in an effort to catch criminals and to deter would-be offenders.

search incident to arrest A warrantless search made at the time of or shortly following an arrest, which is conducted out of a concern for the safety of the arresting officer and others.

search An activity performed in order to find evidence to be used in a criminal prosecution.

seizure The confiscation of one's person (arrest) or property by a government agent.

sexual harassment Unwelcome sexual advances, requests for sexual favors, and other verbal or physical conduct of a sexual nature.

sheriff's department One of the types of local law enforcement agencies in the United States. Specifically, the law enforcement agency that serves a county or parish.

sheriff The modern-day term for the Old English *shire-reeve*. In the United States today, the senior law enforcement official in a county.

shire Under the frankpledge system, a collection of several parishes.

shire-reeve The Old English term for *sheriff*. Literally, "the keeper of the shire."

Sir Robert Peel (1788–1850) A former British home secretary whose criticisms of the state of policing in London led to the passage of the Metropolitan Police Act and the establishment of the world's first large-scale organized police force in that city in 1829.

sixth sense A healthy sense of suspicion; the experience-based ability to intuit when something is amiss.

slave patrol A crude form of private policing, often carried out by citizen volunteers. Slave patrols were created in the eighteenth century to apprehend runaway slaves and to ensure that slaves did not rise up against their owners.

smart policing A systemwide and strategic view of police operations that includes consideration of causal factors of crime, system impact of police actions, partnerships with community organizations to support crime-prevention activities, and more effective policing that stresses integration of analytics, evidence-based practices, and emerging technology tools into ongoing police operations.

solidarity The tendency among police officers to stick together and associate with one another.

span of control The number of subordinates supervised by one person.

split-second syndrome A condition confronting police officers that involves three central features of policing—the urgency of police–citizen encounters, the involuntariness of such encounters, and a public setting—all of which combine to place officers in the position of having to make quick on-the-spot decisions.

state tort liability An important avenue of redress for plaintiffs whose minor injuries, allegedly resulting from negligent acts or misconduct by the police, are not serious enough to make Section 1983 litigation a viable option.

stop and frisk The detaining of a person by a law enforcement officer for the purpose of investigation, accompanied by a superficial examination by the officer of the person's body surface or clothing to discover weapons, contraband, or other objects relating to criminal activity.

straight shooter An honest police officer who will overlook some misconduct committed by peers.

straightforward corruption Any form of police misconduct that provides direct financial benefit to police officers.

strategic intelligence A type of intelligence that provides information to decision makers about the changing nature of threats, enabling them to develop response strategies and reallocate resources for effective threat prevention.

street environment One of two settings identified by John Crank (the other is the traffic stop) in which police officers perform daily tasks that involve interaction with ordinary citizens and with other criminal justice professionals.

stress Anything that places a positive or negative adjustive demand on an organism.

subculture Cultural patterns that distinguish some segment of a society's population.

subjugation of defendants' rights In the context of drug investigations, an officer's lying or committing perjury or fabricating evidence in the name of securing a drug conviction.

sudden peril A defense against state tort liability that is used for cases in which police officers were required to make split-second decisions.

suicide by cop An incident in which an individual who is determined to die engages in behavior meant to provoke responding officers to resort to deadly force.

sworn personnel Members of a law enforcement agency who are empowered to make arrests.

systems perspective A view of organizational style, rooted in biology, that posits that organizations are living organisms that strive for a state of equilibrium, or balance, and that affect or are affected by their environment.

tactical intelligence A type of intelligence that includes gaining or developing information related to threats of terrorism or crime and using this information to apprehend offenders, harden targets, and use strategies that will eliminate or mitigate the threat.

Taking Command Initiative A project undertaken by the International Association of Chiefs of Police to assess the current state of homeland security efforts in the United States and to develop and implement the actions needed to protect American communities from the specter of both crime and terrorism.

Tammany Hall The corrupt Democratic Party political "machine" that operated in New York City in the late nineteenth and early twentieth centuries and that used patronage to control city operations.

technical training model A police academy training model that emphasizes the technical aspects of police work and provides little or no training in such nontechnical areas as stress management, interaction with difficult people, problem solving, and sensitivity to marginalized groups.

Tennessee v. Garner The 1985 U.S. Supreme Court case that specified the conditions under which deadly force could be used to apprehend suspected felons.

territorial imperative The sense of obligation, even protectiveness, that develops in officers who routinely patrol the same area.

Texas Rangers A militia originally formed by Stephen F. Austin in 1823 to protect the territory of Texas against Native American raids, criminals, and intruders. Today, the Rangers serve as part of the Texas Department of Public Safety.

theory of liability Reasons offered as to why a particular person or other entity should be held answerable under law for some action.

thief taker An alternative name for Henry Fielding's Bow Street Runners.

third degree A formerly common coercive interrogation technique that combined psychological pressures with physical force.

third-party policing A recently coined term that describes police efforts to persuade or coerce nonoffending persons to take actions that are outside the scope of their routine activities and that are designed to indirectly minimize disorder caused by other persons or to reduce the possibility that crime may occur.

tithing Under the frankpledge system, a group of ten households.

tolerated lie A lie that is used to defend a questionable discretionary decision.

trace evidence Minute, nearly invisible evidence of a crime that would escape all but the most skilled investigators.

U.S. Marshals Service (USMS) The oldest American law enforcement agency. Its mission includes judicial security and fugitive investigation and apprehension.

universalistic perspective The view that all police officers are similar and that they exhibit some of the same characteristics and behavior patterns.

use corruption Drug-related police corruption that consists of an officer's personal use of illicit drugs.

use of force The use of physical restraint by a police officer when dealing with a member of the public.

value A standard of goodness, desirability, behavior, beauty, or interaction that serves as a guideline for living within a particular culture.

vehicle inventory A warrantless inventory of a vehicle that is permissible on administrative or regulatory grounds. Vehicle inventories must follow a lawful impoundment, must be of a routine nature, must follow standard operating procedures, and must not be a pretext that attempts to conceal an investigatory search.

Violent Crime Control and Law Enforcement Act of 1994 The U.S. legislation that established the Office of Community Oriented Policing Services (the COPS Office) in the U.S. Justice Department.

watchman An early officer on foot patrol who, during the hours of darkness, watched for fires and criminal activities. Upon detecting such events, the watchman's role was to sound the "hue and cry" to evoke a defensive response from the citizenry. This style of policing dates back to the early to mid-eighteenth century in England.

weapons continuum The array of nonlethal and lethal weaponry available to police officers, the selection of which depends on the situation.

white knight An honest and upstanding officer who never steps over the line between accepted and deviant conduct, no matter how great the pressure to do so.

Wickersham Commission A commission appointed by President Herbert Hoover in 1929 to investigate the operations and problems of the criminal justice system. Formally known as the National Commission on Law Observance and Enforcement.

William M. "Boss" Tweed (1823–1878) A corrupt American politician who became notorious as the powerful leader of New York City's Tammany Hall.

Name Index

Leinen, S., 64
Leo, R. A., 230
Leonard, V. A., 58
Lersch, K. M., 102, 211, 212
Levin, Bud, 159
Levitt, S., 115
Levkov, J. S., 121
Lieberman, J. D., 150
Lifsher, M., 59
Lindbergh, Charles, 10
Lindsay, B., 137
Lindsay, John V., 205
Loftin, C., 115
Lopez, Armando, 211
Los Angeles Police Department, 23, 47, 48,
    59, 61, 64,211, 221
Lovell, J. S., 25, 26
Lovrich, N. P., 20, 133, 134
Lowy, J., 118
Lundman, R. J., 102
Lyman, J. L., 3
Lyman, M. W., 196

M

Macdonald, J. M., 102
Mack, David, 211
Maguire, E. R., 37, 66, 134
Mahoney, T., 68
Manning, Peter K., 85, 95, 102, 132
Maple, Jack, 150
Marenin, O., 20
Martin, John S., Jr., 119
Martin, S. E., 98, 103
Marvell, Thomas B., 115
Marx, G. T., 16, 123
Mastrofski, S. D., 101, 103, 104, 134,
    151, 225
Maxfield, Michael G., 80
Maxwell, C. D., 223
Mayne, Richard, 3
Mazerolle, Lorraine, 112, 139, 140
McCampbell, M. S., 61
McCarthy, B., 197
McCrary, Justin, 37
McDowall, D., 115
McGaughey, S., 19
McGillis, D., 137
McHenry, C., 67, 71
McInnis, B., 149
McKinney (TX) Police Department, 48
McLaren, R. C., 8
McLaury, Frank, 10
McLaury, Tom, 10
McPherson, Marlys, 137
McVeigh, Timothy, 111
Meredith, C., 137
Meyer, J., 20
Mieczkowski, T., 212
Miller, C. E. III., 226
Miller, M., 100

Miller, W., 5
Milton, C., 64
Monkkonen, E. H., 7
Moody, Carlisle E., 115
Moore, M. H., 6, 134, 135, 150
Morash, Merry, 66
More, H. W., 58
Morehouse, B., 154
Morris, C., 5
Muir, W. K., 196
Muir, William Ker, Jr., 96–97
Murphy, D. W., 20
Murphy, P. V., 101
Murrah, Alfred P., 159
Murray, Alex, 156
Murray, G., 53

N

Namazzi, N., 20
Nardulli, P. F., 101
National Black Police Association,
    26–27, 27
National Center for Women
    and Policing, 68
Newburn, T., *210, 213*
New York State Division of Criminal Justice
    Services, 61
Niederhoffer, E., 102
Nislow, J., 59, 118
Nolan, Daniel, 121
Novak, K. J., *99*, 101, 102, 137, 231

O

O'Connor, Sandra Day, 181
Office of Community-Oriented Policing
    Services, 62, *155*
Orfield, Myron W., Jr., 207
Ortiz, C. W., 215
Osborn, Albert S., 121
Osborne, Erma, 116
Owens, E., 115
Owings, C., 64

P

Palmiotto, Michael J., 138, 211
Paquette, C., 137
Park, Bernard, 23, 211, 212
Parkhurst, Charles H., 7
Parks, Roger B., 134
Parsons, D., 64, 65
Pate, Anthony M., 135, 137
Pate, Tony, 101, 115
Peak, Ken J., 58, 59, 60, 61, 62, 97, 122,
    148, 210
Pederson, D., 152
Peel, Robert, 3, 121

Perez, D. W., 192, 196
Perez, Rafael A., 211
Perez-Penajan, Richard, 76
Perry, W. L., 149
Petersilia, J., 121
Peterson, Marilyn B., 152, 153, 154
Phillips, C. D., 101
Pinizzotto, A. J., 226
Piquero, A. R., 64, 101
Pitts, S., 62
Pogrebin, M. R., 79
Police Executive Research Forum
    (PERF), 62, 133, *133*, 137, 150, 157
Police Foundation, 64
Pollak, Walter, 205
Pollock, Joycelyn M., 197, 214
Poole, E. D., 79
Preiss, J., 20
President's Commission on Law
    Enforcement and Administration
    of Justice, 64
Price, C. C., 149
Punch, Maurice, 207
Pynes, J. E., 61

R

Radzinowicz, L., 3
Ragonese, P., 83
Rainey, H. G., 48
Randolph, L. H., 4
Rashbaum, W. K., 116
Ratcliffe, Jerry H., 137
Raymond, J., 152
Reaves, Brian A., 47, 65, 148, 149, *227*
Reisig, Michael D., 20, 131, 134
Reisig, Mike, 131
Reiss, A. J., 101, 102, 103
Reno, Janet, 24
Rettammel, R. J., 19
Reuland, M., 137
Reynolds, K. M., 135
Richardson, R., 19
Rickman, Steve, 157
Riksheim, E. C., 101
Riordan, Richard, 212
Ritti, R., 101
Robbins, S. P., 48
Roberg, R., 50, *99*, 101, 102, 103, 231
Roberts, D. J., 150
Rodriguez, Luis, 211
Roehl, J., 133
Rogan, D. P., 135
Rohr,, C. A., 120
Rojek, J., 117
Rokeach, M., 100
Roosevelt, Theodore, 7, 10
Rosenbaum, D. P., 134, 137
Rosenfeld, R., 117
Roth, J. A., 133, 134
Rouse, A., 134

Subject Index

Page numbers that are *italicized* indicate figures, bold indicates bold appearance in the text, *t* indicates tables.